The Complete Spanish

ALEXEI SUETIN

Translated by Malcolm Gesthuysen

B. T. Batsford Ltd, *London*

First published 1991

ISBN 0 7134 6929 3

A CIP catalogue record for this book is available from the British Library

Typeset by Lasertext, Manchester
and printed in Great Britain by
Dotesios Ltd, Trowbridge, Wilts
for the publishers,
B. T. Batsford Ltd, 4 Fitzhardinge Street,
London W1H 0AH

A BATSFORD CHESS BOOK
Adviser: R. D. Keene GM, OBE
Technical Editor: Andrew Kinsman

Contents

Foreword

In this book, I have by no means tried to provide an encyclopaedia of opening variations, but have attempted to concentrate upon those systems which are topical, incorporating all the latest information. Of course, this restriction places a limit on the extremely wide range of ideas and variations found in this ancient but eternally youthful opening. In this instance I have had to be guided by practical considerations; the aim was to create a manual for the active chessplayer, and this is what I am offering to the reader.

In processing the flow of information from recent years, one is forced to the conclusion that the Closed Systems and the Open Defence still attract the greatest interest. But the Marshall Attack and the Archangel Variation also enjoy considerable popularity. Of course, the reader must pass his own judgement on these matters.

In the first four chapters we shall discuss the many alternatives to 3 … a6. There was a time (during the 1930s and 1940s) when the older defences had almost become extinct. However, in recent years many of these old systems have recovered their popularity, and now it is possible to assert that each of them has a respectable place in a modern opening repertoire.

Chapters 5 to 8 deal with important early deviations which avoid the Open Variation (dealt with in Chapter 9) and the various Closed set-ups. Chapters 10 to 17 cover the backbone of the Spanish Opening, including the highly topical and seemingly ever-fashionable Marshall Attack (Chapter 12), and the theoretically critical Zaitsev Variation, the battleground for so many great Kasparov v Karpov tussles, which is dealt with in Chapter 16. However, such is the richness and variety of plans and ideas in the Spanish that there are variations to suit all tastes and styles.

1 Classical System

1	**e4**	**e5**
2	**♘f3**	**♘c6**
3	**♗b5**	**♗c5** *(1)*

This system was mentioned in a book entitled *Classical Defences* as long ago as 1490. Analyses of this line can be found in the works of Ponziani (18th century) and Jaenisch (19th century). Despite its long history, it still appears regularly and, moreover, is continually being enriched with new ideas.

Black aims to create pressure with his pieces against White's centre. Formerly it was considered that White had the better chances, but nowadays it is not possible to be so categorical.

1
W

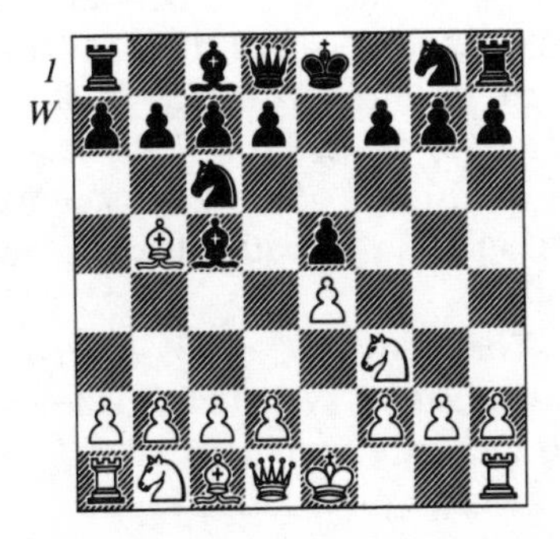

The main continuations are:

A 4 c3
B 4 0–0

Let us first consider some rarer continuations:

(a) **4 b4!?** ♗xb4 5 ♗b2 d6 6 0–0 ♗d7 7 d4 with sharp play where Black has little to fear (Petran–Lajos, Hungary 1971).

(b) **4 ♘xe5** ♕g5 (also interesting is 4 … ♘d4) 5 ♘g4 h5 6 ♗xc6 dc 7 d4 ♗xg4 8 ♗xg5 ♗xd1 and Black has no difficulties.

Also, neither 4 ♗xc6 dc 5 ♘xe5 ♗xf2+! 6 ♔xf2 ♕d4+, nor 4 ♘c3 ♘d4 5 ♘xe5 ♕g5! etc, is very promising for White.

A

4 c3

Now Black's main choice is between:

A1 4 … ♘f6
A2 4 … ♘ge7
A3 4 … f5

A1

4 … ♘f6 *(2)*

Let us consider for a moment some other continuations, which do not enjoy popularity:

(a) **4 … ♕f6** 5 d4! ed 6 e5 ♕g6 7 cd ♗b4+ (in White's favour is 7 … ♘xd4 8 ♘xd4 ♕b6 9 e6 — also good is 9 ♕g4 — 9 … ♗xd4 10 ed+ ♗xd7 11 ♗xd7+ ♔xd7 12 ♗e3 c5 13 ♘d2; Vasiliev–Kuznetsov, USSR 1962) 8 ♘c3 d5 9 0–0 ♘e7 10 ♕b3 ♗xc3 11 bc with a better game for White (Blackburne and Pillsbury–Schiffers and Steinitz, Nürnberg 1896).

(b) **4 … ♕e7** 5 d4 ed 6 0–0 dc 7 ♘xc3 a6 8 ♘d5 ♕d8 9 ♗a4 and White has the advantage (Keres).

Unattractive for Black are both 4 … ♗b6 5 d4 ed 6 cd ♘ce7 7 ♘c3 c6 8 ♗d3 d5 9 e5, and 4 … d6? 5 d4 ed 6 cd ♗b4+ 7 ♔f1 d5 8 ♕a4! etc.

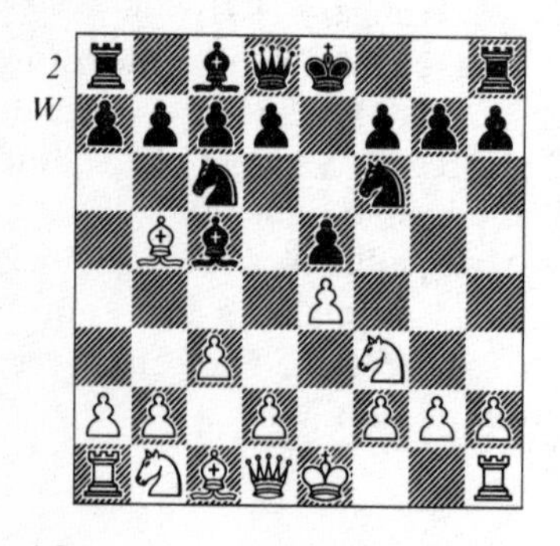

After 4 … ♘f6 White has a choice of:

A11 5 0–0
A12 5 d4

A11

5 0–0 0–0

5 … ♘xe4?! 6 ♕e2 (after 6 d4 ed 7 cd ♗e7 — 7 … ♗b6?! — 8 d5 ♘d6 9 ♗a4 ♘a5 10 ♗f4 0–0 play is unclear) 6 … f5 (6 … d5 7 d3) 7 d3 ♘f6 8 d4 ♗e7 9 de ♘e4 10 ♘bd2 is to White's advantage (Evans–Weinberger, USA 1963).

6 d4 ♗b6 *(3)*

Bad is 6 … ed? 7 e5 ♘e4 8 cd ♗b6 9 d5 ♘e7 10 ♗d3 f5 11 ♘bd2 ♘c5 12 d6! etc. (Smyslov–Randviir, Pärnu 1947).

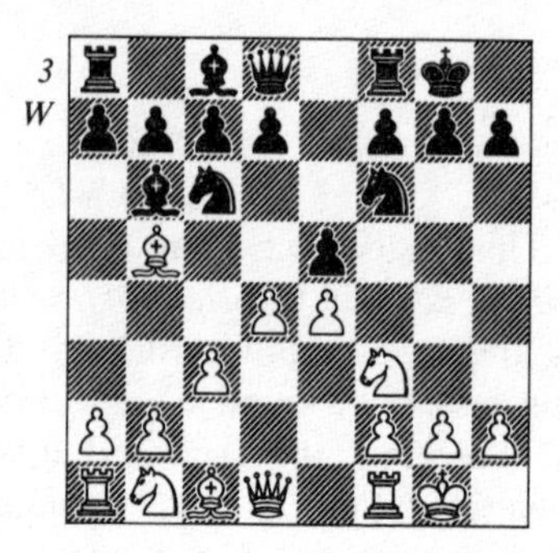

A critical position, in which White has several possible plans:

A111 7 ♗g5
A112 7 ♖e1
A113 7 de
A114 7 ♗xc6

In the game Ehlvest–Short, Belgrade 1989, there occurred 7 ♕d3!? d5?! 8 ♗xc6 bc 9 ♘xe5 ♘xe4 10 ♘d2 ♗f5 11 ♕f3 ♕f6 12 ♘xc6 ♖ae8 13 ♘xe4 ♖xe4 14 ♘b4 ♕e6 15 ♘d3 c6 16 ♗d2 ♖e8 17 ♖ae1 f6 18 ♕d1 ♕f7 19 ♖xe4 ♗xe4 20 ♘f4 g5 21 ♘h5 ♗g6 22 ♘g3 h5 23 ♕f3 with advantage to White.

The move 7 ♕d3 deserves investigation. Note that 7 a4 leads to the main variations after 7 … a5 8 ♗g5 or 8 ♖e1.

A111

7 ♗g5

And now:

A1111 7 ... h6

A1112 7 ... d6

A1111

7 ... h6

8 ♗h4 d6

Not good is 8 ... g5? 9 ♘xg5! ♘xe4 (9 ... hg 10 ♗xg5 leads to a fatal pin) 10 ♘f3 ♘g5 11 ♘xe5 ♘xe5 12 ♗xg5 ♕xg5 13 f4 ♕f5 14 fe ♕xe5 15 ♕d3 c6 16 ♗a4 ♖e8 17 ♘d2 ♕e3+ 18 ♕xe3 ♖xe3 19 ♘c4 with a marked positional advantage to White (Ivkov–Aaron, Tel Aviv OL 1964).

9 a4

Other continuations briefly:

(a) **9 ♕d3** ♗d7 (or 9 ... ♕e7 10 ♘bd2 ♗g4?! 11 ♖fe1 ♖ad8 12 a4 a5 13 ♘c4 ed 14 ♗xc6 bc 15 ♘xd4 ♗d7 16 e5 with advantage to White; Petrushin–Dolekhadyan, Pleven 1985) 10 ♘bd2 a6 (or 10 ... ♕e7 11 a4 a6 12 ♗xf6 ♕xf6 13 de ♘xe5 14 ♘xe5 ♗xb5 15 ab de 16 ba ♖xa6 17 ♖xa6 ba 18 ♘c4 with pressure for White; Stein–van Scheltinga, 1965) 11 ♗c4 ♕e7 12 ♖fe1 ♔h8 13 ♗b3! followed by ♘c4 and White has the better chances (Ehlvest–Salov, USSR 1988).

(b) **9 ♗xc6** bc 10 de de 11 ♘bd2 ♗g4 12 ♘c4 g5 13 ♗g3 ♘xe4 14 ♕xd8 ♖fxd8 15 ♘fxe5 ♗e6 16 ♖fe1 ♘xg3 17 hg ♗c5 18 b3 a5 19 a4 and White stands better (Schwarz).

9 ... a5

After 9 ... a6(?) 10 ♗xc6 bc 11 a5! ♗a7 12 de de 13 ♕xd8 ♖xd8 14 ♘xe5 g5 15 ♗g3 ♗b7 16 ♘c4 White has a marked advantage (Sokolov–Lounek, Pula 1964).

10 ♖e1 *(4)*

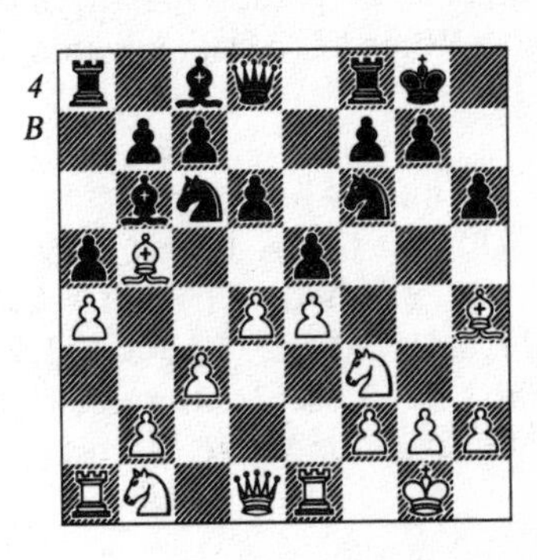

4
B

Now the following variations may arise:

(a) **10 ... ♕e7** 11 ♘a3 (in the event of 11 ♗xc6 bc 12 ♘bd2 g5 13 ♗g3 ♘h5 14 ♘xe5 ♘xg3 15 ♘ec4 ♘xe4 15 ♘xe4 ♗e6 17 ♕f3 f5! Black gets excellent play; Vasyukov–Meleghegyi, Tbilisi 1965) 11 ... ed 12 ♗xc6 bc 13 ♘xd4 g5 14 ♗g3 ♗g4 15 ♕c2 ♖ae8 16 ♘c4 with a positional advantage to White (Unzicker–Borodin, Vienna 1968).

(b) **10 ... ♗g4** 11 ♗xc6 bc 12 de de 13 ♘bd2!? (Suetin) 13 ... g5 14 ♗g3 ♘d7 15 ♘c4 f6 16 ♕e2 ♕e7 17 ♖fd1 ♖fd8 18 h3 ♗e6 with roughly equal chances (Salov–Winants, Brussels 1988).

(c) **10 ... ed** 11 ♗xc6! (also not bad is 11 ♘xd4! ♘xd4 12 cd g5 13 ♗g3 d5 14 ed ♘xd5 15 ♘c3 c6 16 ♗c4 ♗e6 17 ♘e4 with slightly better chances for White; Gligoric–Zuidema, Belgrade 1964) 11 ... bc 12 ♘xd4 ♖e8 (or 12 ... g5 13 ♗g3 ♗g4 14 f3 ♗d7 15 ♘a3!) 13 ♘d2 g5 14 ♗g3 ♗xd4 15 cd ♖b8 16 f3 (Spassky–Zuidema, Belgrade 1964). In both cases White has a clear advantage.

A1112

7 ... d6
8 a4

Also not bad is 8 ♗xc6 bc 9 de de 10 ♕a4 ♕d6 11 ♘bd2 ♗e6 12 ♖ad1 ♘d7 13 ♘b3 ♗xb3 14 ♕xb3 ♘c5 15 ♕c2 with somewhat better play for White (Keres).

8 ... a5

And now:

(a) **9 ♘a3** ed 10 ♗xc6 bc 11 ♘xd4 h6 12 ♘xc6 ♕e8 13 ♗xf6 gf 14 ♘d4 ♕xe4 15 ♖e1 ♕g4 16 ♕xg4 ♗xg4 17 ♘c6 with better chances for White (Osnos–Buchman, Leningrad 1968).

(b) **9 de** ♘xe5 10 ♘xe5 de 11 ♕f3 h6! 12 ♖d1 hg 13 ♖xd8 ♖xd8 14 h3 g4! with good counterplay for Black (Karaklajic–Vasyukov, Bela Crkva 1989).

A112

7 ♖e1

After this, play often transposes to the plan with 7 ♗g5 considered above. For example: 7 ... d6 8 ♗g5 h6 9 ♗h4 ♕e7 10 a4 etc. Here we shall consider the independent continuations.

7 ... d6 *(5)*

After 7 ... ed?! 8 e5 ♘e8 (interesting is 8 ... ♘g4 and if 9 h3 then 9 ... ♘xf2 10 ♔xf2 f6! with plenty of counterplay for Black) 9 cd d5 10 h3 ♘e7 11 b3 c6 12 ♗d3 f5 13 ♘c3 ♘c7 14 ♘a4 ♘e6 15 ♘xb6 ab 16 a4 White stands better (Robatsch–Zuidema, Amsterdam 1966).

5
W

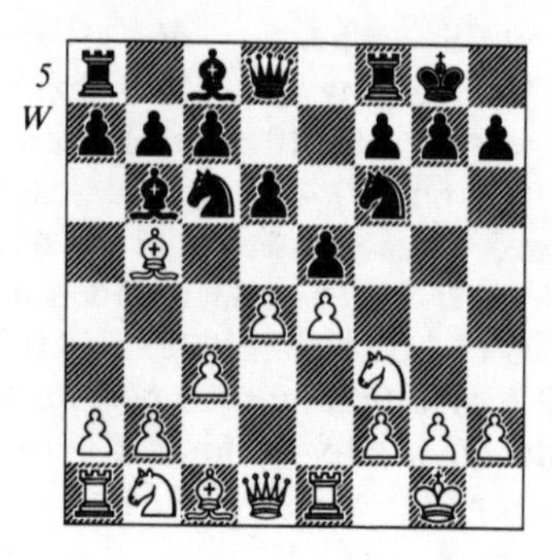

Now the following variations may arise:

(a) **8 a4** a5 (worse is 8 ... a6(?) 9 ♗xc6 bc 10 de ♘g4 — or 10 ... de 11 ♕xd8 ♖xd8 12 ♗g5 — 11 ♖e2 de 12 ♘bd2 ♕e7 13 a5 ♗a7 14 ♘c4 with lasting pressure for White) 9 ♗g5 ♕e7 (9 ... h6!?) 10 ♘a3 h6 11 ♗xf6! ♕xf6 12 ♘c4 ♗g4 13 ♗xc6 ♗xf3 14 ♕xf3 bc 15 de de 16 ♕xf6 gf 17 ♖ad1 and the ending is in White's favour (Keres).

(b) **8 h3** ♗d7 9 a4 a6 10 ♗xc6 ♗xc6 11 ♗g5 h6 12 ♗h4 ♖e8 13 d5 ♗d7 14 ♘bd2 ♔h7 15 ♘c4 ♗a7 16 ♕d2 ♖g8 17 g4 g5 18 ♗g3 ♕e7 with roughly equal play (Ljubojevic–Salov, Brussels 1988).

A113

7 de ♘xe4 *(6)*
8 ♕d5

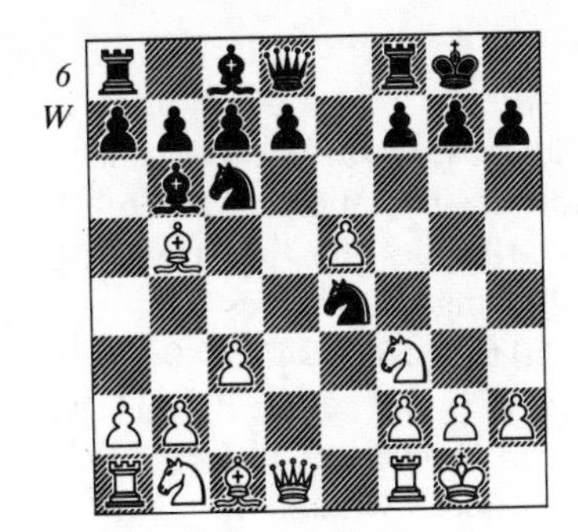

Other continuations do not pose serious problems for Black: 8 ♘bd2 d5 9 ♕e2 ♘xd2 10 ♗xd2 ♗g4!; or 8 ♗d3 d5 9 ed ♘xd6 10 ♗g5 f6 11 ♗f4 ♗f5 with comfortable equality.

8 … ♘c5

9 ♗g5

In the event of 9 ♗f4 or 9 ♗e3, there follows 9 … ♘e7 10 ♕d1 ♘e6 and Black consolidates his position. Black also has no difficulties after 9 ♘a3 a6 10 ♗e2 ♘e7 11 ♕d1 ♘e6, or 9 b4 ♘e7 10 ♕d1 ♘e4 11 ♗d3 d5 etc.

9 … ♘e7 *(7)*

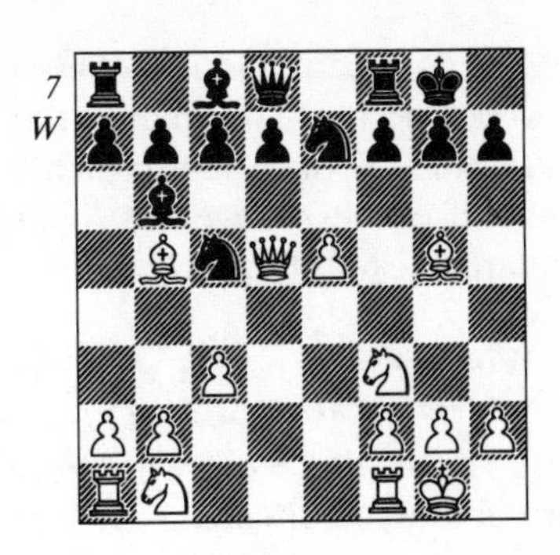

An alternative is 9 … ♕e8. For example: 10 ♘a3 (after 10 ♖e1 ♕e6 11 ♕xe6 ♘xe6 12 ♗h4 f6 13 ef gf 14 ♘bd2 d5 15 c4 ♘ed4!, or 10 ♘bd2 d6 11 ed ♗e6 12 ♗xc6 bc 13 ♕d4? f6; Gipslis–Spassky, Riga 1959, Black has excellent play) 10 … a6 11 ♗c4 ♘e7 12 ♕d2 ♗a7 with a minimal advantage to White (Zuidema–Gebauer, Zürich 1962).

10 ♕d1

After 10 ♕c4 a6! (but not 10 … h6? 11 ♕h4! ♖e8 12 ♗xh6!) 11 ♕h4 ♘g6 12 ♗xd8 (12 ♕h5 ♕e8 13 ♗c4 ♘xe5; or 12 ♕g3 ♘e4, favour Black) 12 … ♘xh4 13 ♗xh4 ab 14 ♘a3 ♘d3 15 ♘xb5 ♘xb2 Black has at least equal chances (Gipslis–Suetin, USSR Ch. 1963).

10 … ♘e4

11 ♗h4 d5

12 ♘bd2 c6

13 ♗d3 ♗f5

Worse is 13 … f5 14 ef ♘xf6 15 ♕c2 g6 16 ♖ae1 ♗f5 17 ♘e5! ♗xd3 18 ♕xd3 ♘f5 19 ♗g5 ♕c7 20 ♖e2 with advantage to White (Tal–Quinones, Amsterdam 1964).

14 ♕c2 ♘xd2

Now the following variations may arise: 15 ♗xf5 ♘xf3+! (in the event of 15 … ♘xf1 16 ♗xh7+ ♔h8 17 ♖xf1 ♕d7 18 ♖e1 ♕e6 19 ♗d3 ♖ae8 20 ♗g5 White has good attacking chances; Polugayevsky–Boleslavsky, Moscow 1963) 16 gf ♔h8 17 ♖ae1 ♕c7 18 ♗h3 ♖ae8 19 f4 f5! 20 e5 ♘g6 21 ♗g3 with equal chances (Geller–Spassky, Moscow 1962).

A114

7 ♗xc6

This is a continuation offering few prospects. As in many other variations of the Spanish, White should not exchange his light-squared bishop too early.

7 ... dc

Worse is 7 ... bc 8 ♘xe5 ♘xe4 9 ♖e1 ♘d6 10 ♗f4 f6 11 ♘d3 ♘f7 12 ♘d2 d6 13 ♕f3 with pressure for White (Schmid–Scheipl, Bad Kissingen 1954).

8 ♘xe5

White also achieves nothing after 8 ♗g5 ♗g4 9 ♘bd2 (or 9 h3 ♗xf3 10 ♕xf3 ed 11 e5 ♕d5!) 9 ... ed 10 e5 h6 11 ♗h4 g5 12 ef gh (analysis by Schmid).

8 ... ♘xe4
9 ♖e1

And now:

(a) **9 ... ♘d6** 10 ♗f4 a5 11 c4 f6 12 c5 fe 13 ♗xe5 ♘c4 14 cb ♘xb6 with equal chances (O'Kelly–Karaklajic, Bognor Regis 1960).

(b) **9 ... ♘f6** 10 a4 a5 11 ♗g5 c5 12 ♘d2! h6 13 ♗xf6 ♕xf6 14 ♘e4 and Black has serious difficulties (Schmid–O'Kelly, corr. 1954).

A12

5 d4 *(8)*

8
B

5 ... ed *(9)*

After 5 ... ♗b6 White may transpose to variations considered above, by means of 6 0–0 0–0. Besides this, he also has the following possibilities:

(a) **6 ♗xc6** bc 7 ♘xe5 0–0 8 0–0 ♘xe4 9 ♖e1 ♘d6 10 ♗f4 with better chances for White (Teschner–Alexander, Hastings 1953/4).

(b) **6 ♕e2** ed 7 e5 0–0 8 cd ♖e8 9 ♗e3 ♘d5 10 ♘c3 ♘xe3 11 fe and White's position is preferable (Tal–van Geet, Wijk aan Zee 1968).

(c) **6 ♘xe5** ♘xe5 7 de ♘xe4 8 ♕g4 ♗xf2+ 9 ♔d1 (9 ♔e2 ♕h4 10 ♕xg7 ♖f8 11 ♘d2 ♗c5 12 ♘f3 ♕f2! 13 ♔d1 ♗e7 14 ♖e1 ♕b6 with unclear play — Belyavsky–Ivanchuk, Linares 1989) 9 ... ♕h4 10 ♕xg7 ♖f8 11 b4 ♕h5 12 ♔c2 ♕g6 13 ♕xg6 fg 14 ♘d2 ♘xd2 15 ♗xd2 and White stands a little better (Euwe).

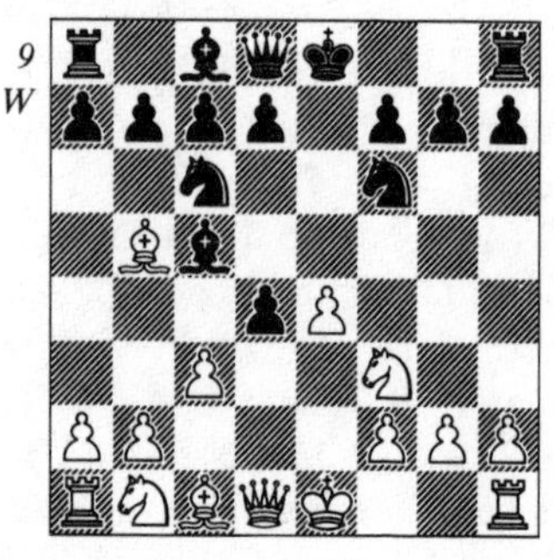
9
W

6 e5

Other variations:

(a) **6 cd** ♗b4+ 7 ♘c3 ♘xe4 8 0–0 ♗xc3 9 bc 0–0 10 d5 ♘xc3 11 ♕d3 ♘xb5 12 ♕xb5 ♘e7 13 d6 cd 14 Ba3 Ng6 15 Bxd6 Re8.

(b) **6 0–0** Nxe4 7 cd Bb6 8 Qc2 Nd6! 9 Re1+ Ne7 10 Bd3 h6 11 Qe2 Kf8.

In the first case Black has a secure position. In the second, it is not easy for White to demonstrate any compensation for the loss of a pawn.

6 ... Ne4

Worse is 6 ... Nd5? 7 0–0 0–0 8 cd Bb6 9 Bc4 Nce7 10 Bg5 Qe8 11 Qb3 c6 12 Nbd2 h6 13 Bxe7 Nxe7 14 Ne4 with advantage to White (Smyslov–Barcza, Varna OL 1962).

7 0–0

Also worthy of consideration are:

(a) **7 cd** Bb4+ 8 Kf1 a6 9 Bd3 d5 10 ed Nf6 11 dc Qxc7 12 Nc3.

(b) **7 Qe2!?** d5 8 ed 0–0 9 dc Qd5 10 Bc4 Qf5 11 Bd3 Re8 12 Ng5.

In both cases White has somewhat better chances.

7 ... d5 *(10)*

8 Nxd4

After 8 ed 0–0 9 dc Qf6 10 Bxc6 bc 11 cd Bb6 12 Re1 Bf5

10
W

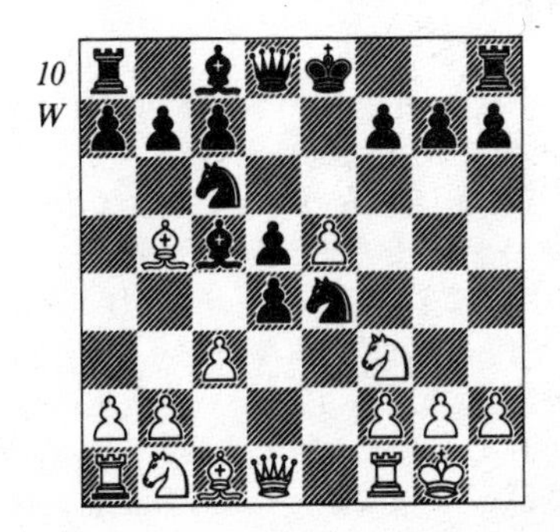

13 Nc3 Rfe8 14 Nxe4 Bxe4 15 Bg5 Qd6 16 Bd8 Bxc7 17 Bxc7 Qxc7 White has an extra pawn, but it is hard to make use of it (Euwe).

8 ... 0–0

9 Bxc6

Also not bad is 9 f3 Ng5 10 Be3 Ne6 11 f4 f6 12 Kh1 Bxd4 13 cd fe 14 de with advantage to White (Nezhmetdinov–Veltinov, USSR 1963).

9 ... bc

10 Be3 Qe8

11 f3 Nd6

12 Bf2 *(11)*

11
B

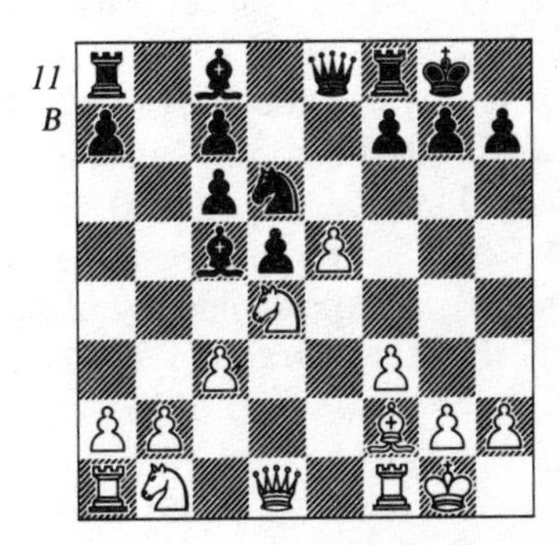

In this position White has the better prospects, as is shown by the following variations:

(a) **12 ... Qxe5** 13 Nxc6 Bxf2+ 14 Rxf2 Qe8 15 Nb4 Bb7 16 Na3 with a positional advantage to White (Gligoric–Keller, Zürich 1959).

(b) **12 ... Nc4** 13 b4! Bb6 14 Re1 a5 15 Nbd2 Na3 16 N2b3 Qd7 17 ba Bxd4 18 Bxd4 Nc4 19 Bc5 Re8 20 Bb4 Nxe5 21 Qd4 Nc4 22 Qh4! with a marked advantage for White (Larsson–Nicander, corr. 1961).

A2

4 … ♘ge7 *(12)*

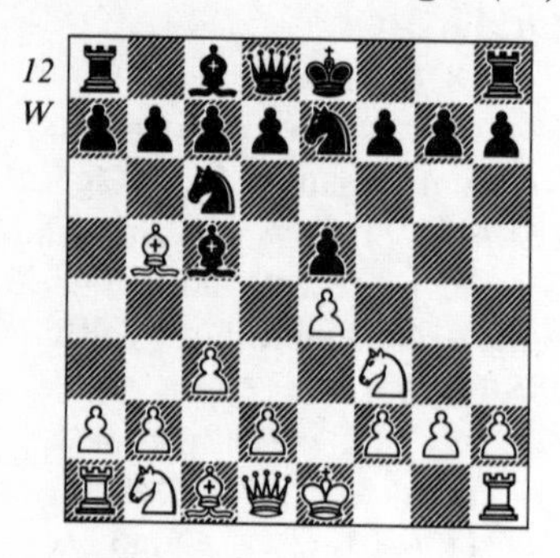

5 0–0

After 5 d4 ed 6 cd ♗b4+ 7 ♗d2 ♗xd2+ 8 ♕xd2 a6 (also not bad is 8 … d5 9 ed ♘xd5) 9 ♗a4 d5 10 ed ♕xd5 11 ♘c3 ♕e6+ 12 ♔f1 ♕c4+ 13 ♔g1 0–0 14 d5 ♘a7 15 ♖e1 ♘f5 16 h3 ♘b5 chances are approximately equal (Tal–Fischer, Curaçao 1961).

5 … ♗b6
6 d4 ed
7 cd d5
8 ed ♘xd5
9 ♖e1

9 ♘e5 ♕f6!

9 … ♗e6 *(13)*

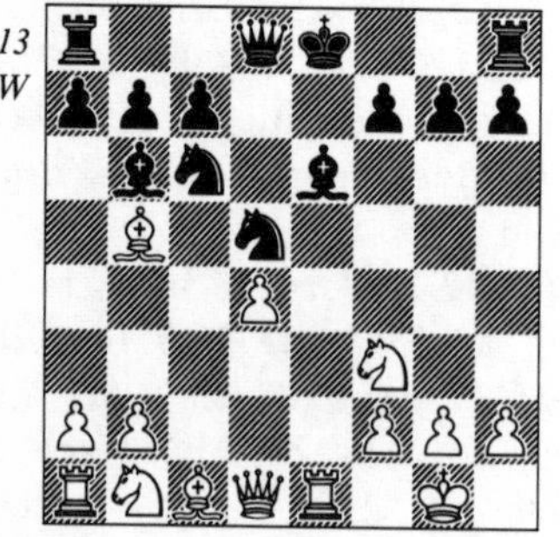

Now the following variations are possible:

(a) **10 a4** a6 11 ♗xc6+ bc 12 ♗g5 ♕d6 13 ♘bd2 0–0 14 ♘c4 ♕b4 15 ♖c1 and White has the better chances (Keres).

(b) **10 ♗g5** ♕c8 (after 10 … ♕d6 11 ♘bd2 h6 12 ♘e4! ♕b4 13 ♗xc6 bc 14 ♕c1! hg 15 ♕xc6 ♔e7 16 a3 ♕xb2 17 ♘eg5 ♘f4 18 ♕e4! White has a strong attack) 11 ♘e5 0–0 12 ♘xc6 bc 13 ♗xc6 and White's advantage in this position is minimal (Hondi–Tabor, Hungary 1970).

Other moves that have been played here are 10 ♘g5, 10 ♘e5 and 10 ♘c3, but White has not obtained any advantage.

A3

4 … f5!?

This immediate counterattack against White's pawn foundations in the centre leads to sharp play and has been comparatively little studied until now. White has two main continuations:

A31 5 d4
A32 5 ef

A31

5 d4

Let us mention some of the less testing continuations:

(a) **5 ♗xc6** dc 6 ♘xe5 ♗d6 7 ♕g5+ g6 8 ♘xg6 ♘f6 9 ♕h4 ♖g8 10 e5 ♖xg6 11 ef ♗e6 12 0–0 (or 12 f7+ ♔xf7 13 ♕xh7+ ♖g7 14 ♕h5+ ♔g8) 12 … ♕d7 13 d4 0–0–0 14 ♗h6 ♖dg8 15 ♗xg7 ♖8xg7 16 fg ♕xg7 and Black gets excellent counterplay in both cases.

(b) **5 0–0** fe 6 ♗xc6 dc 7 ♘xe5 ♘f6 6 d4 ed 9 ♘xd3 ♗e7.

(c) **5 ♘xe5** ♘xe5 6 d4 ♕e7 7 0–0 fe and here too Black gets a good game in all variations.

5 … fe *(14)*

After 5 … ed(?) 6 e5 (also good is 6 cd ♗b4+ 7 ♘c3 fe 8 ♗g5) 6 … dc 7 ♘xc3 ♘ge7 8 0–0 d5 9 ed ♕xd6 10 ♕a4 ♗d7 11 ♖d1 ♕e6 12 ♗c4 ♘d8 13 ♕b3 ♕b6 14 ♕c2 (Milic–Kuprejanov, Yugoslavia 1962).

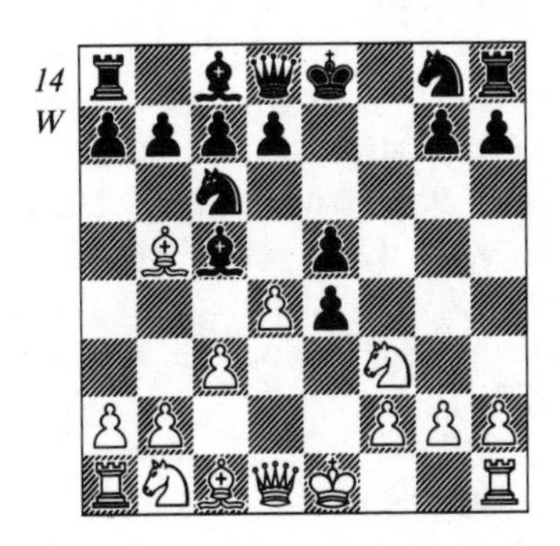
14
W

Here there are three lines:

A311 6 dc
A312 6 ♘fd2
A313 6 ♗xc6

A311

6 dc

The following continuations have also been tried:

(a) **6 ♘g5** ♗b6! 7 d5 e3! 8 ♘e4 (8 dc bc 9 ♗xe3 ♗xe3 10 ♘e4 ♕h4!) 8 … ♘f6 9 dc bc 10 ♗d3 ♘xe4 11 ♕h5+ ♔f8 12 ♗xe4 ef+ 13 ♔e2 ♕f6 and Black has a strong attack for the sacrificed piece (Keres).

(b) **6 ♘xe5** ♘xe5 7 ♕h5+ ♘f7 8 ♗c4 ♕e7 9 dc ♘f6 10 ♕xf7+ (10 ♗xf7+ ♔f8! 11 ♕g5 ♔xf7 12 0–0 b6 with approximate equality — Suetin) 10 … ♕xf7 11 ♗xf7+ ♔xf7 12 ♗f4 ♘d5 13 ♗g3 b6 14 ♘a3! ♗a6 15 0–0–0 ♗d3 16 f3 bc 17 fe ♗xe4 18 ♗xc7 ♖he8 19 ♗d6 ♖ac8 20 ♘c4 ♘b6 21 ♘e3! and White has slightly better chances in the ending (Kavalek–Hase, Lucerne OL 1982).

6 … ef
7 ♕xf3 ♘f6

In the game Gligoric–Spassky, Amsterdam 1964, there occurred 7 … ♕e7 8 ♕h5+ g6 9 ♕e2 d6 10 0–0 ♘f6 11 ♗g5 0–0. After 12 cd cd 13 ♘d2 White would have had the slightly better game.

8 0–0

After 8 ♗g5 0–0 9 ♘d2 ♕e8! the chances are equal.

8 … 0–0

And now:

(a) **9 ♗g5** ♕e8 10 ♘bd2 d6 11 cd cd 12 ♘e4 ♘xe4 13 ♕xe4 ♗e6 14 ♖ad1 d5 15 ♕b4 ♕g6 16 ♖fe1 ♖f5 17 ♗c1 ♖af8 with equal chances (Matulovic–Nicevski, Skopje 1967).

(b) **9 ♘d2** ♕e7 (or 9 … d5 10 cd cd 11 ♗xc6 bc 12 ♕xc6 ♗f5) 10 ♘e4 ♘xe4 11 ♕xe4 d6 12 cd cd 13 ♗e3 ♗f5 14 ♕d5+ ♗e6 15 ♕d2 h6 with a minimal advantage to White (Solovev–Ivanov, Moscow 1950).

A312

6 ♘fd2 ♗b6 *(15)*

Other continuations are worse:

(a) **6 … ♗e7?** 7 d5 ♘b8 8 ♕h5+ g6 9 ♕xe5 ♘f6 10 ♘xe4 0–0 11 ♗h6 ♖e8 12 0–0.

(b) **6 … e3?!** 7 fe ♗b6 8 ♗xc6 dc 9 ♕h5+ g6 10 ♕xe5+ ♕e7 11 ♕xh8 ♕xe3+ 12 ♔f1 ♕f4+ 13 ♔e2 ♗g4+ 14 ♘f3 (Keres).

In both cases White has the advantage.

15
W

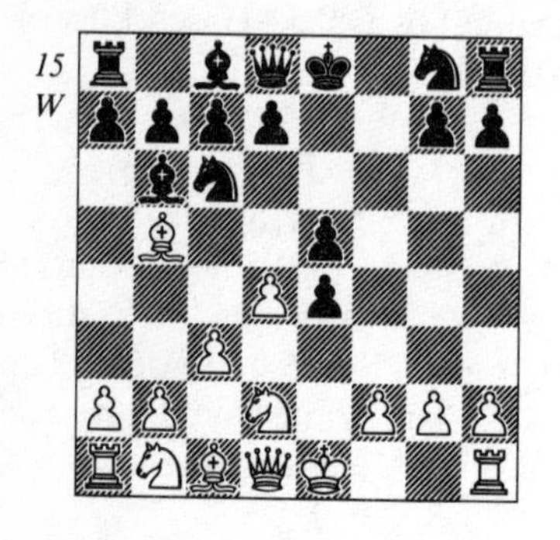

After 6 … ♗b6 the following variations may arise:

7 d5 ♘f6!? (7 … ♘ce7 8 ♘xe4 favours White) 8 dc (in the event of 8 0–0 ♘e7 9 ♕e2 c6 10 d6 ♘f5 11 ♘e4 ♘xe4! 12 ♕xe4 ♕f6 13 ♗g5 ♘xd6! Black has an excellent game; Colle–Vidmar, Bled 1931) 8 … bc 9 ♗e2 d5 10 ♘b3 0–0 11 0–0 c5 12 a4 a5 13 ♗e3 ♕e7 14 ♘a3 ♗e6 15 ♗g5 c6 16 c4 h6 17 ♗h4 ♔h8 with chances for both sides (Nezhmetdinov–Miagmasuren, Ulan Bator 1965).

A313

6 ♗xc6 dc

6 … ef 7 ♗xf3 ed 8 0–0 favours White.

7 ♘fd2

The alternative is 7 ♘xe5, with the following variations:

(a) **7 … ♕d5** 8 ♕h5+!? (the game Arnason–Rantanen, Helsinki 1986, went 8 ♗f4 ♗d6 9 c4! ♕e6 10 ♕h5+ g6 11 ♕e2 with a somewhat better game for White) 8 … g6 9 ♕e2 ♗d6 10 0–0 ♗f5 11 ♘c4 (Hübner–Hess, Lugano 1989). By playing 11 … ♘f6 12 ♘xd6 cd 13 ♗h6 ♘g4 14 ♗g5 0–0, and then ♖ae8, Black can equalise.

(b) **7 … ♗d6** 8 ♕h5+ g6 9 ♕e2 (9 ♘xg6 ♘f6 10 ♕h6 ♖g8 11 ♘h4 ♗f8 12 ♕e3 ♕e7 is good for Black) 9 … ♕h4 10 ♘d2 ♗f5 11 g4! ♗xe5 12 gf ♗f6 13 fg hg 14 ♕xe4+ with advantage to White (Davies–Speelman, Hastings 1987/8).

7 … ♗d6

Also possible is 7 … ♕g5 8 dc ♘f6 (but not 8 … ♕xg2? 9 ♕h5+ ♔d8 10 ♖f1 ♗h3 11 ♕xe5 ♘f6 12 ♕g3!) 9 ♕e2 (9 ♖g1 ♕h4 10 ♘f1 ♗g4 11 ♕a4 ♖d8 12 ♗e3 ♖d1+ 13 ♕xd1 ♗xd1 14 ♔xd1 ♘g4 with equal chances; Lobron–Wedberg, Dortmund 1983) 9 … ♕xg2 10 ♕f1 ♕g4 11 ♘c4 ♕h5 12 ♗e3 ♗e6 13 ♘bd2 0–0–0 14 ♕g2 with advantage to White (de Firmian–Rogers, USA 1986).

8 de e3!?
9 fe ♗c5
10 ♕h5+ g6
11 ♕f3 *(16)*

16
B

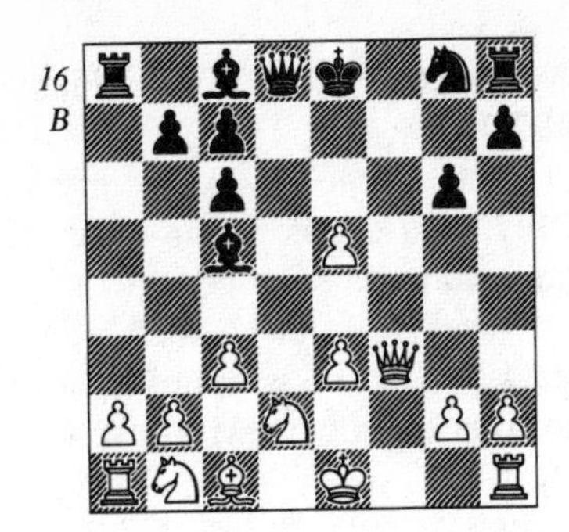

In this position the following variations may arise:

(a) **11 … ♕h4+!** 12 g3 (12 ♕f2 ♕xf2+ 13 ♔xf2 ♘h6 14 ♘f3 0–0 15 ♖e1 ♗f5 is good for Black) 12 … ♕h3 13 ♘e4 ♗g4 14 ♕f1 ♗e7 15 ♕xh3 ♗xh3 16 ♘f2 ♗e6 17 e4 0–0–0 with excellent play for Black (Keres).

(b) **11 … ♕d5** 12 ♕xd5 cd 13 e4 ♗e6 14 ♘b3 ♗b6 15 ♘d4 ♗xd4 16 cd de 17 ♘c3.

(c) **11 … ♗e6** 12 ♘e4 ♗d5 13 c4 ♗b4+ 14 ♗d2 ♗xd2+ 15 ♘bxd2 (Lange).

(d) **11 … ♗f5** 12 ♘b3 ♗b6 13 ♘d4 ♘h6 14 0–0.

In all these cases White has the advantage.

A32

5	**ef**	**e4**
6	**d4**	

6 ♕e2(?) ♕e7! 7 ♘g1 ♘f6 is good for Black.

6	**…**	**ef** *(17)*

17
W

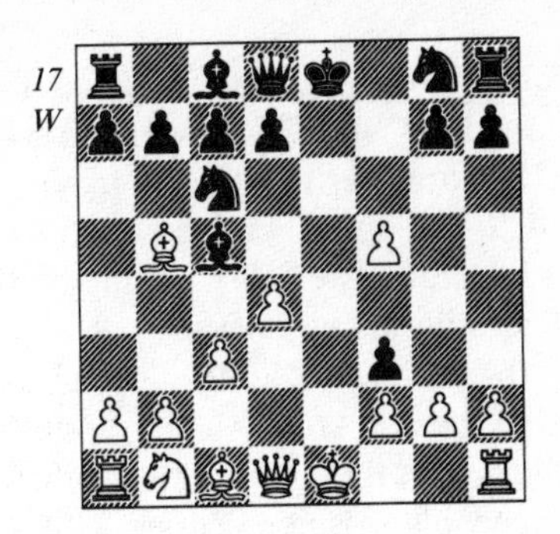

The alternative is 6 … ♗b6, with the following variations:

(a) **7 ♘e5!** ♘xe5 (in White's favour is 7 … ♘f6 8 g4! 0–0 9 g5) 8 de ♕h4 9 0–0 c6 10 ♗e2! d5 11 ed ♘f6 12 ♘a3! ♗xf5 13 ♘c4 with better chances for White (Fine).

(b) **7 ♘g5!?** ♘f6 8 0–0 d5 9 a4 a5 11 f3 with an initiative for White.

(c) **7 ♗g5** ♘f6 8 ♘h4 0–0 9 ♘d2 d5 10 ♘f1 ♘e7 11 ♘e3 c5 12 0–0 cd 13 cd ♘c6 with good play for Black (Mechkarov).

7	**dc**	**♕e7+**
8	**♗e3**	**fg**
9	**♖g1**	**♘f6** *(18)*

18
W

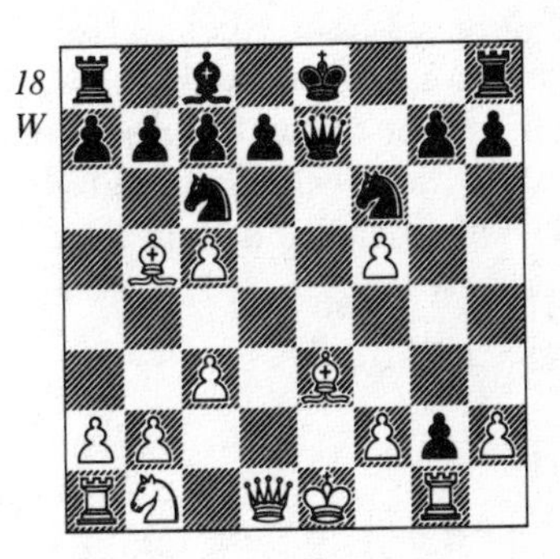

In this critical position the following lines are possible:

(a) **10 ♖xg2** 0–0 11 ♘d2!? (also possible is 11 ♕e2!? d5 12 cd cd 13 ♗d3 ♗d7 14 ♘d2 ♖ac8 15 0–0–0 with somewhat better play for White — Keres) 11 ... d5 12 cd cd 13 ♕c2 ♘e5 (Unzicker–Campora, Bern 1987). By playing 14 0–0–0 ♘fg4 15 ♕b3 ♔h8 16 ♗d4 ♗f5 17 ♖dg1 White can maintain his initiative.

(b) **10 ♘d2** b6 11 ♖xg2 ♗b7 12 ♖g3 bc 13 ♕e2 0–0 14 0–0–0 ♔h8 15 ♖dg1 ♖f7 with double-edged play (Luike–Zilber, USSR 1957).

(c) **10 ♕f3?!** 0–0! 11 ♘d2 d6 12 cd (12 0–0–0!?) 12 ... cd 13 0–0–0 ♘e5 14 ♕xg2 ♗xf5 with excellent play for Black (Vasyukov–Arsenev, Moscow 1962).

B

4 0–0

This is White's other important continuation in the Classical System. Quite often in practice this amounts to a simple transposition of moves, as after 4 ... ♘f6 5 c3 0–0 6 d4 ♗b6 there arise the variations considered above. In this section we shall consider only those plans which are original. The main choice here is between:

B1 4 ... ♘f6
B2 4 ... ♘d4

B1

4 ... ♘f6

Rarer continuations are:

(a) **4 ... ♕f6** 5 c3 (possible are 5 ♘c3 ♘ge7 6 ♘d5; or 5 d3 h6 6 ♗e3 ♗b6 7 c4 ♘d4 8 ♘xd4 ed 9 ♗d2 c6 10 f4) 5 ... ♘ge7 6 b4 ♗b6 7 ♘a3 g5?! 8 d4! with advantage to White (Karpov–Mariotti, Portoroz/Ljubljana 1975).

(b) **4 ... ♘ge7** 5 ♘xe5?! (after 5 c3 ♗b6 6 d4 play transposes to variations already considered) 5 ... ♘xe5 6 d4 c6 7 ♗e2 ♗d6 8 de ♗xe5 9 c4 d5 with full equality for Black (Browne–Mariotti, Venice 1971).

(c) **4 ... d6** 5 c3 ♗d7 6 d4 ♗b6 7 ♘a3 ♘ge7 8 ♘c4 0–0 9 a4 ed 10 cd ♗g4 11 ♘xb6 ab 12 ♖a3 with slight but lasting pressure for White (Keres).

5 ♘xe5 *(19)*

A passive continuation is 5 d3 d6 (or 5 ... ♘d4) 6 c3 0–0 7 ♘bd2 ♕e7 with good play for Black. 5 c3 0–0 6 d4 leads to variations already familiar.

After 5 ♘xe5 the following variations may arise:

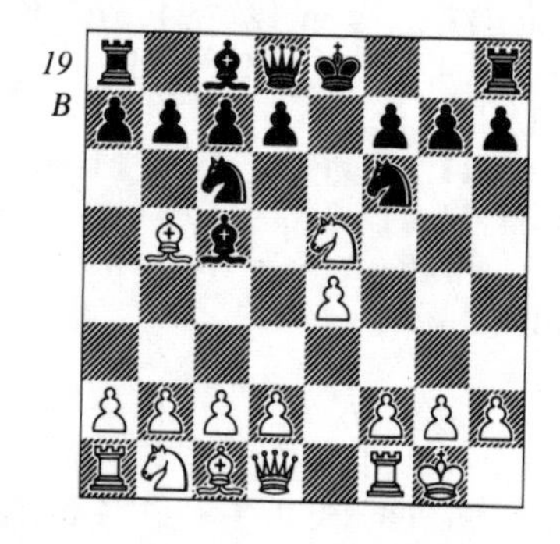
19
B

(a) **5 ... ♘xe4** 6 ♕e2 (after 6 ♘xf7?! ♔xf7 — 6 ... ♕h4 7 d4! — 7 ♕h5+ g6 8 ♕d5+ ♔g7 9 ♗xc6 ♖e8! 10 ♗a4 c6 11 ♕d1 ♕f6 Black has the advantage) 6 ... ♘xe5 7 ♕xe4 ♕e7 8 d4 ♘c6 (8 ... ♘g6 9 ♗xd7+! ♗xd7 10 ♕xb7 favours White) 9 ♗xc6 (after 9 ♕xe7+ ♗xe7 10 c3 a6 11 ♗d3 0–0 12 ♗f4 d6 13 ♘d2 ♗d7 14 ♖fe1 ♖fe8 15 ♘c4 ♗f6 Black stands better; Makarov–Gulko, Moscow 1967, also in Black's favour is 9 ♕g4?! h5! 10 ♕d1 — 10 ♕xg7 ♗xd4 11 ♕g3 — 10 ... ♘xd4 11 b4 ♗b6 12 c4 0–0 13 c5 ♘xb5 14 a4 ♕f6 15 ♖a2 ♘d6; Timoshchenko–Gulko, Baku 1976) 9 ... dc 10 ♖e1 ♕xe4 11 ♖xe4+ ♗e7 12 ♗f4 ♗f5 13 ♖e2 ♔d7 14 ♗xc7 ♗xc2! with equality (Keres).

(b) **5 ... ♘xe5** 6 d4 c6 (lines favouring White are 6 ... a6 7 ♗e2 ♘xe4 8 dc ♘xc5 9 b4 ♘e6 10 f4 ♘c6 11 f5!, 6 ... ♗e7 7 de ♘xe4 8 ♕g4 ♘g5 9 ♗xg5, and also 6 ... ♗d6?! 7 de ♗xe5 8 f4) 7 de ♘xe4 8 ♗d3 d5 9 ed ♘f6 10 ♗g5 (also good is 10 ♖e1+ ♗e6 11 ♗g5! ♕xd6 12 ♘d2, or 10 ♗f4 ♗xd6 11 ♗xd6 ♕xd6 12 ♘c3) 10 ... ♕xd6! 11 ♘c3 ♗e6 12 ♗xf6 gf 13 ♘e4 with a considerable advantage to White (Shamkovich–Aronin, Moscow 1962).

(c) **5 ... 0–0** 6 ♘d3 ♘xe4 7 ♘xc5 ♘xc5 8 d4 ♘e4 9 d5 ♘e7 10 ♖e1 ♘f6 11 d6! cd 12 ♘c3! with a clear advantage to White (Dückstein–Miagmasuren, Tel Aviv OL 1964).

B2

4 ... ♘d4 *(20)*

A simplifying manoeuvre, which has long been considered by theory a reliable way of getting equality. But here too certain problems remain for Black.

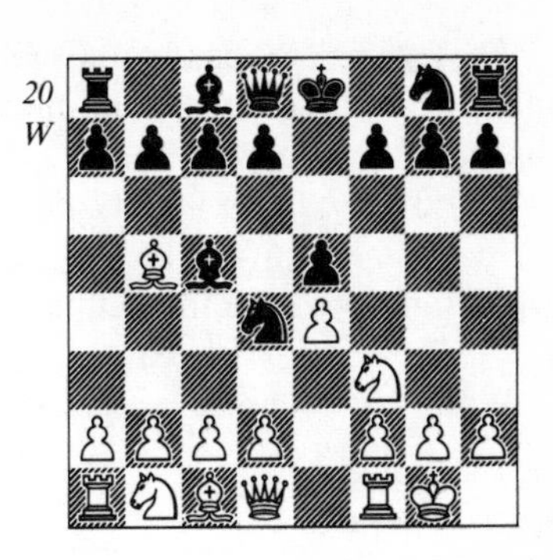

20
W

5 ♘xd4

Other possibilities:

(a) **5 b4!?** ♗xb4 (5 ... ♗b6 6 ♘xd4 ♗xd4 7 c3 ♗b6 8 d4 promises White a certain initiative; White also has the better chances after 5 ... ♘xb5 6 bc d6 7 a4!, or 5 ... ♘xf3+ 6 ♕xf3 ♗xb4 7 ♗b2 ♕f6 8 ♕g3 ♗d6 9 f4 ♗f8 10 ♘c3) 6 ♘xd4 ed 7 ♗b2 ♕g5 (also possible is 7 ... ♗c5 8 c3 ♕f6 9 ♕h5 ♗b6 10 cd ♘e7) 8 ♗d3 ♗c5 9 c3 d5! 10 cd de 11 ♗b5+ c6 12 dc!? ♗h3 13 g3 cb 14 ♖e1 ♘f6 15 ♗xf6 ♕xf6 16 ♘c3 with roughly equal play (Ghinda–Hector, Budapest 1986).

(b) **5 ♘xe5?!** ♘xb5 6 ♘xf7 ♔xf7 7 ♕h5+ g6 8 ♕xc5 c6 9 d4 d6 and it is hard for White to demonstrate any compensation for the loss of a piece.

(c) **5 ♗a4** ♘xf3+ ♕xf3 ♘f6 with a good game for Black.

5 ... ♗xd4

After 5 ... ed the opening transposes to Bird's Defence.

6 c3 ♗b6
7 d4

The game Velickovic–Osterman, Yugoslavia 1988, continued instead 7 ♘a3 c6 8 ♗a4 d6 9 d4 ed 10 cd ♘e7 11 d5 0–0 12 dc bc 13 ♗g5 f6 14 ♗f4 ♗a6 15 ♖e1 with slight pressure for White.

7 ... c6

White has a choice between:

B21 8 ♗a4
B22 8 ♗c4

B21

8 ♗a4 d6

In White's favour is 8 ... ed 9 cd d5 10 ed! ♕xd5 11 ♘c3 ♕xd4 12 ♖e1+ ♗e6 13 ♕f3 ♘e7 14 ♗g5 h6 15 ♗xe7 ♔xe7 16 ♖ad1 (Klavin–Zhuravlev, Riga 1968).

9 ♘a3

The following possibilities have also been tried:

(a) **9 de** de 10 ♕h5 ♕f6 11 ♘d2 ♗c7 (Pietzsch–Starck, East Germany 1963).

(b) **9 ♕d3** ♘f6 10 ♗g5 h6 11 ♗h4 0–0 12 ♘d2 ♕e7 13 ♗c2 g5 14 ♗g3 ♘h5 15 ♘c4 ♘f4 (Nedeljkovic–Vukovic, Yugoslavia 1957).

(c) **9 ♗e3** ♘f6 10 de de 11 ♕xd8+ ♗xd8.

(d) **9 f4** ed! 10 cd d5 11 e5 ♘h6.

(e) **9 d5** ♘e7 10 ♘d2 0–0 11 ♘c4 ♗c7 12 ♘e3 a5 13 c4 ♗b6 14 ♔h1 cd 15 ♘xd5 ♘xd5 16 ♕xd5 ♗e6 17 ♕d3 ♖c8 (Harandi–L. Bronstein, Buenos Aires OL 1978).

In each case Black has no difficulties.

9 ... ♘f6 *(21)*

If 9 ... ♗c7 or 9 ... ♕e7 then 10 d5! is strong, increasing the pressure in the centre.

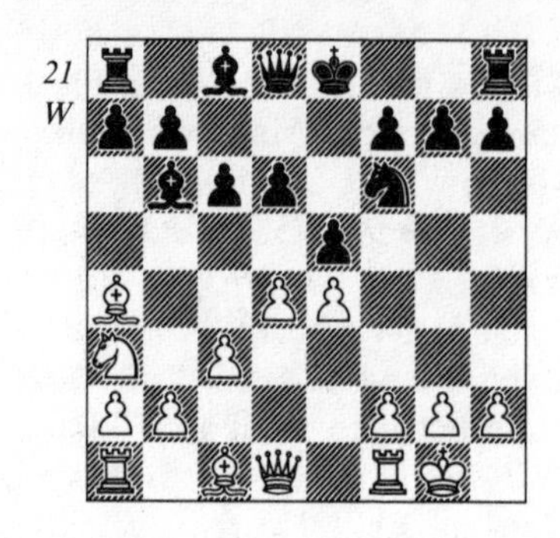

21
W

After 9 ... ♘f6 the following variations arise:

(a) **10 ♗c2** ♗e6 11 ♗g5 h6 12 ♗xf6 ♕xf6 13 d5 ♗d7 14 ♘c4 ♗c7 15 ♕d3 cd 16 ed (Yudovich–Redeleit, corr. 1964).

(b) **10 ♗g5** h6 11 ♗xf6 ♕xf6 12 d5 ♗d7 13 ♘c4 ♗c7 14 ♕d3 0–0 15 ♗b3 cd 16 ♕xd5 ♗c6 17 ♕d3 (Vasyukov–Hennings, Moscow 1964).

(c) **10 ♘c4!?** ♘xe4 11 de d5 12 ♘xb6 ab.

In each case White's chances are somewhat better.

B22

8 ♗c4 d6 *(22)*

And now:

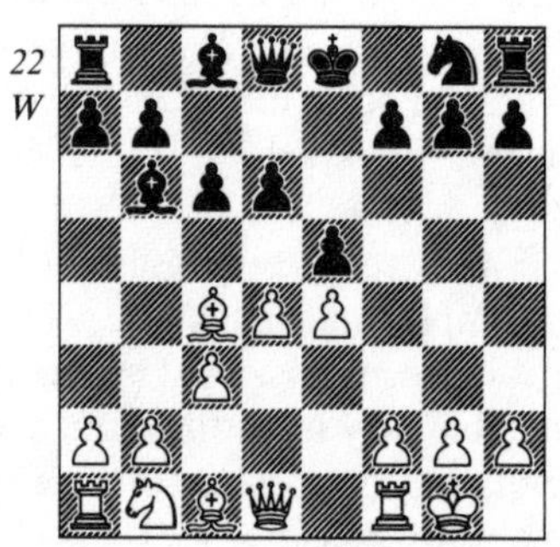

22
W

(a) **9 ♔h1** ♘f6 10 ♕d3 0–0 11 ♗g5 h6 12 ♗h4 ♕e7.

(b) **9 ♕b3** ♕e7 10 ♗e3 ♘f6 11 de de 12 ♗xb6 ab.

(c) **9 a4** ♘f6 10 de de 11 ♕xd8+ ♗xd8 12 ♖e1 0–0 13 ♘d2 ♗c7 14 h3 ♖d8 (Nezhmetdinov–Filip, Bucharest 1954).

(d) **9 ♕b3** ♕e7 10 ♗e3 ♘f6 11 de de 12 ♗xb6 ab 13 ♕xb6 ♘xe4 14 ♖e1 ♘d6 15 ♗f1 0–0 16 a4 f6 17 ♘d2 ♗e6 18 ♘e4 ♘xe4 19 ♖xe4 ♗d5 (Eber–L. Bronstein, Rio de Janeiro 1979).

(e) **9 ♗e3** ♘f6 10 de de 11 ♕xd8+ ♗xd8 12 f3 ♗b6 13 ♔f2 ♔e7 14 ♘d2 ♖d8 15 ♖ad1 ♗e6 16 ♗e2 ♗xe3+ 17 ♔xe3 ♘e8 (Kau–Zaitsev, USSR Ch. 1962).

In all cases Black has no particular difficulties, which testifies to the fact that the manoeuvre 8 ♗c4 is harmless.

2 Steinitz and Berlin Defences

In this chapter we deal with 1 e4 e5 2 ♘f3 ♘c6 3 ♗b5:

A 3 ... d6
B 3 ... ♘f6

A

3 ... d6 *(23)*

This move characterises the system which bears the name of Steinitz, although it was examined by Ruy Lopez as long ago as 1561. Note that this defence had a respectable place in the opening repertoires of Lasker and Capablanca. After that time, from the 1930s onwards, interest in this system fell noticeably. As a rule, players nowadays do not aim so much for symmetry and equality (which are characteristic of such a formation) as for active counterplay. But this defence has not fallen completely into disuse and has maintained a rather solid reputation. Nowadays it is closely linked in practice with the Berlin Defence.

4 d4

Definitely the most forceful reaction. After other continuations Black has no difficulties.

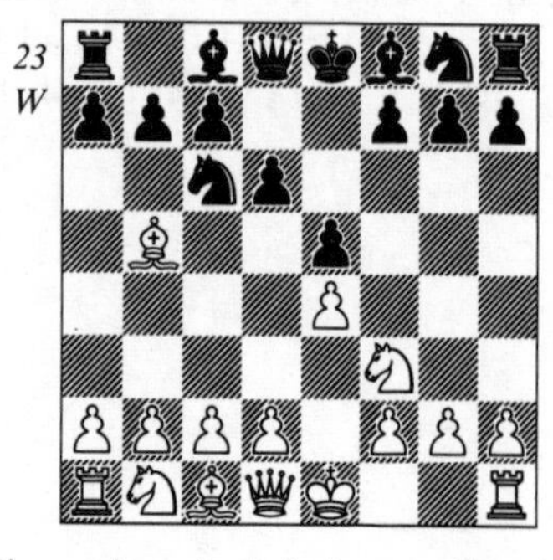
23
W

Thus after 4 c3 it is possible for Black to play not only the quiet 4 ... ♗d7 but also the active 4 ... f5.

4 ... ♗d7

In recent years the immediate 4 ... ed has frequently been played, after which, besides 5 ♘xd4 — which will be considered later — White can play 5 ♕xd4. After this a possible line is 5 ... ♗d7 6 ♗xc6 ♗xc6 7 ♘c3 ♘f6 8 ♗g5 ♗e7 9 0–0–0 0–0 10 ♖he1 ♖e8 11 ♔b1 with a freer game for White.

The extravagant 4 ... ♗g4?! is in White's favour: 5 d5 (also quite good is 5 de) 5 ... a6 6 ♗a4 b5 7 dc ba 8 c4 and then ♘c3 (Réti–Spielmann, Berlin 1919).

5 ♘c3

The most flexible move. After 5 d5 ♘b8 6 ♗d3 ♗e7 7 ♘c3 ♘f6 8 0–0 0–0 Black's defence is solid.

After 5 ♘c3 Black's main possibilities are:

A1 5 … ed
A2 5 … ♘f6

A1

5 … ed
6 ♘xd4 *(24)*

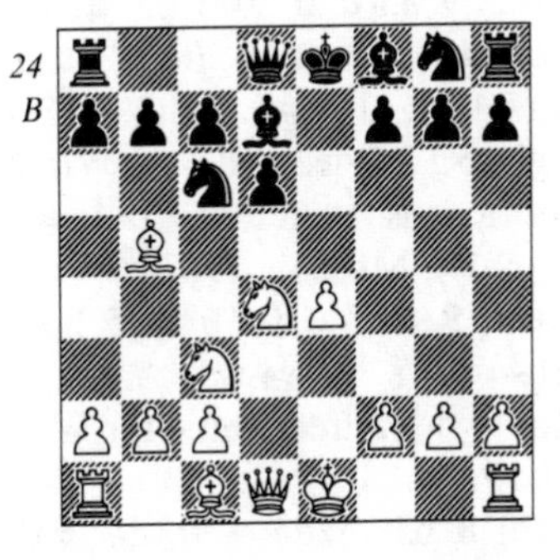

This is a critical position in this variation. Black has a choice between:

A11 6 … ♘f6
A12 6 … g6

A11

6 … ♘f6
7 ♗xc6

7 0–0 ♗e7 8 ♗xc6 leads to variation A2.

7 … ♗xc6

In the event of 7 … bc White may continue 8 ♕d3, with the intention of castling long.

8 ♕d3 g6

Or 8 … ♗d7 9 ♗g5 ♗e7 10 0–0–0 0–0 11 f4 with an initiative for White.

9 ♗g5

Worse is 9 ♘xc6 bc 10 ♕a6 ♕d7 11 ♕b7 ♖c8 12 ♕xa7 ♗g7 with counterplay for Black (Nimzowitsch–Capablanca, St. Petersburg 1914).

9 … ♗g7
10 0-0-0!

An active plan introduced into practice by Alekhine. After 10 … ♕d7 11 h3 0–0 12 ♖he1 ♖fe8 13 ♕f3 ♘h5 14 g4 White is clearly better (Alekhine–Brinkmann, Kecskemét 1927).

A12

6 … g6 *(25)*

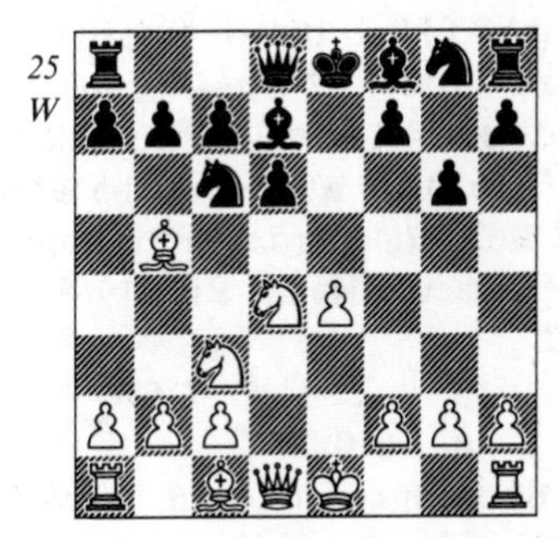

An old continuation, which in recent decades has been the subject of greater investigation.

7 ♗e3

Also not bad is 7 0–0 ♗g7 8 ♗xc6 bc 9 ♖e1 (9 f4!?) 9 … ♘e7 10 ♗f4 c5 11 ♘f3 0–0 12 e5! with pressure for White (Keres).

7 … ♗g7
8 ♕d2 ♘f6 *(26)*

Or 8 … ♘ge7 9 f3 a6 10 ♗e2 0–0 11 h4! followed by 0–0–0 and a kingside attack.

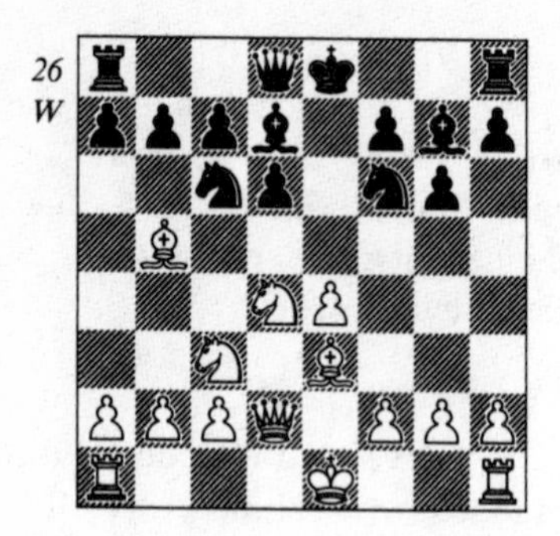
26
W

Here the following variations arise:

(a) **9 ♗xc6** bc 10 ♗h6 ♗xh6 11 ♕xh6 ♘g4 12 ♕d2 and White's chances are clearly better (Kholmov–Kimmelfeld, Moscow 1970).

(b) **9 f3** 0–0 10 0–0–0 ♘xd4 11 ♗xd4 ♘xe4! 12 ♘xe4! ♗xb5 13 ♕c3 ♗xd4 14 ♕xd4 f5 15 ♕d5+ ♖f7 16 ♘xd6 ♕xd6 17 ♕xb5 ♕b6 18 ♕e2 with approximate equality (Miklyaev–Nisman, Riga 1968).

A2

5 … ♘f6
6 0–0

By means of 6 ♗xc6! ♗xc6 7 ♕d3 White may bring about a position considered in variation A11. The move 6 de is not completely harmless; after 6 … ♘xe5 (worse is 6 … de 7 ♗g5 ♗b4 8 0–0 ♗xc3 9 bc h6 10 ♗h4 ♕e7 11 ♕d3 a6 12 ♗a4 ♖d8 13 ♕e3 with advantage to White; Lasker–Forgacs, St. Petersburg 1909) 7 ♗xd7+ ♕xd7 Black has good chances to equalise.

6 … ♗e7 *(27)*

Sometimes 6 … ed 7 ♘xd4 ♗e7 is played here. In many cases this leads to one of the main variations by transposition. But other lines are possible. For example:

(a) **8 ♗xc6** bc, and now:

(a1) **9 ♕f3** 0–0 10 ♖e1 c5 (10 … ♖b8 and 10 … ♖e8 have also been played) 11 ♘f5 ♗xf5 12 ♕xf5 ♘d7 13 ♘d5 ♘b6 with a minimal advantage to White (Polugayevsky–A. Zaitsev, USSR Ch. play-off 1969).

(a2) **9 b3** 0–0 10 ♗b2 ♖e8 11 ♖e1 ♗f8 12 ♕d3 g6 13 ♖ad1 ♗g7 14 ♗c1 ♘g4 15 h3 ♘e5 16 ♕g3 c5 17 ♘de2 and here White's position is preferable (Klovan–Klovsky, Moscow 1967).

(a3) **9 ♕d3** 0–0 10 ♗g5 h6 11 ♗h4 ♘h7 12 ♗xe7 ♕xe7 13 ♖ae1 with a freer game for White (Schwarz).

(b) **8 b3** ♘xd4 9 ♕xd4 ♗xb5 10 ♘xb5 ♘d7 11 ♗a3 a6 12 ♘c3 ♗f6 13 ♕d2 0–0 14 ♖ad1 ♖e8 15 ♖fe1 ♘b6 16 ♗b2 ♕d7 17 a4 ♕c6 18 a5 ♘d7 with equality (Tal–Larsen, match 1965).

(c) **8 ♗f4** 0–0 9 ♗xc6 bc 10 e5 ♘e8 11 ♕f3 d5 12 ♖ad1 g6 13 ♗h6 ♘g7 14 ♖fe1 ♖b8 15 b3

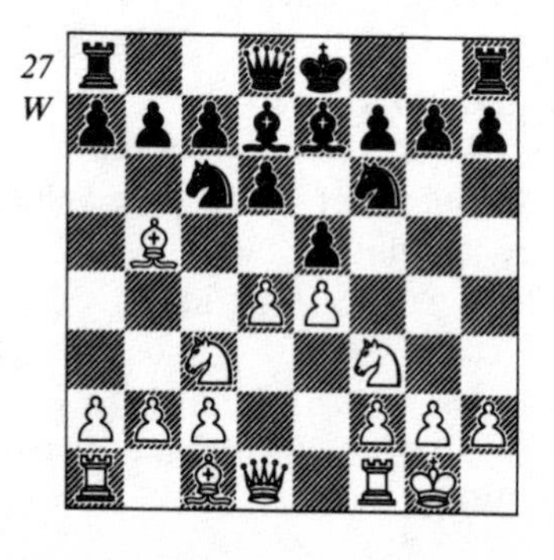
27
W

and White has a spatial advantage (Geller–Shamkovich, Riga 1968).

(d) **8 ♗g5** 0–0 9 ♗xc6 bc 10 ♕d3 h6 11 ♗h4 ♘h5 12 ♗xe7 ♕xe7 with equal play.

After 6 ... ♗e7 White has a choice between:

A21 7 ♗xc6
A22 7 ♖e1

A21

7 ♗xc6

Let us first consider the following variations:

(a) **7 ♗g5** 0–0 8 de (in the event of 8 ♗xc6 ♗xc6 9 de de 10 ♕xd8 ♗xd8 11 ♘xe5 ♗xe4 12 ♗xf6 ♗xf6 13 ♘d7 ♗xc3 14 ♘xf8 ♗xb2 15 ♖ab1 ♗a3 Black has excellent compensation for the exchange — Keres) 8 ... ♘xe5 (8 ... de 9 ♖e1!) 9 ♗xd7 ♘fxd7 10 ♗xe7 ♘xf3+ 11 ♕xf3 ♕xe7 12 ♘d5 ♕d8 13 ♖ad1 ♖e8 14 ♖fe1 ♘b6 15 ♕c3! with a minimal advantage to White (Schlechter–Lasker, match 1910).

(b) **7 de** ♘xe5 8 ♗xd7+ ♘exd7 9 ♘d4 0–0 10 ♘f5 ♖e8 11 ♕f3 ♗f8 12 ♕g3 ♔h8 with a minimal advantage to White.

7 ... ♗xc6 *(28)*

And now:

(a) **8 ♖e1** ed 9 ♘xd4 ♗d7 10 b3 (also not bad is 10 ♗g5 h6 11 ♗h4 0–0 12 ♕d3 c6 13 ♖ad1) 10 ... 0–0 11 ♗b2 c6 12 ♕d3 ♕c7 13 ♖ad1 ♖fe8 14 ♘de2 ♖ad8 15 ♘f4 ♗f8 16 ♕g3 with better play for White (Pillsbury–Steinitz, Vienna 1898).

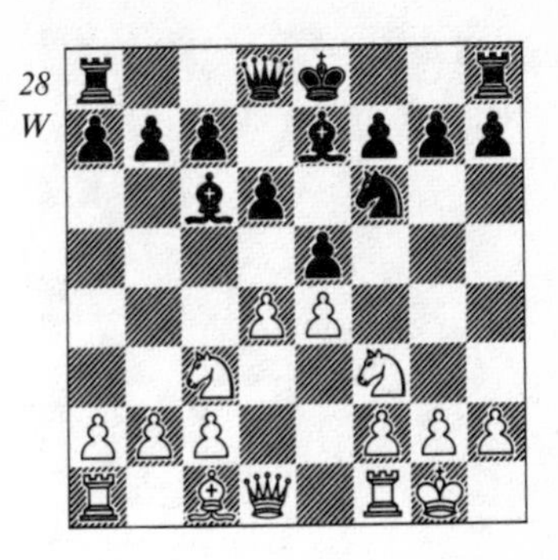
28
W

(b) **8 ♕d3** ed (bad is 8 ... ♘xe4? 9 ♘xe4 d5 10 ♘g3 e4 11 ♕e3 ef 12 ♖fe1!, and after 8 ... ♘d7 9 d5 ♘c5 10 ♕c4 ♗d7 11 b4 White stands better) 9 ♘xd4 ♗d7 (in White's favour is 9 ... 0–0 10 ♘f5 ♗d7 11 ♘g3 ♖e8 12 b3 ♗f8 13 ♗b2 g6 14 ♘d5 ♗g7 15 c4 — Suetin) 10 ♗g5 0–0 11 ♖ae1 h6 12 ♗h4 ♘h7 13 ♗xe7 ♕xe7 14 ♘d5 ♕d8 15 c4! with pressure for White (Lasker–Capablanca, World Ch. match 1921).

A22

7 ♖e1 ed

If Black attempts to hold on to the centre, he loses: 7 ... 0–0? 8 ♗xc6 ♗xc6 9 de de 10 ♕xd8 ♖axd8 (or 10 ... ♖fxd8 11 ♘xe5 ♗xe4 12 ♘xe4 ♘xe4 13 ♘d3 f5 14 f3 ♗c5+ 15 ♔f1!) 11 ♘xe5 ♗xe4 12 ♘xe4 ♘xe4 13 ♘d3 f5 14 f3 ♗c5+ 15 ♘xc5 ♘xc5 16 ♗g5 ♖d5 17 ♗e7.

8 ♘xd4 0–0 *(29)*

And now:

9 ♗xc6 bc (after 9 ... ♗xc6 10 ♘xc6 bc 11 ♘e2 ♕d7 12 ♘g3 ♖fe8 13 b3 and ♗b2 White has a clear positional advantage) 10 ♗g5

29
W
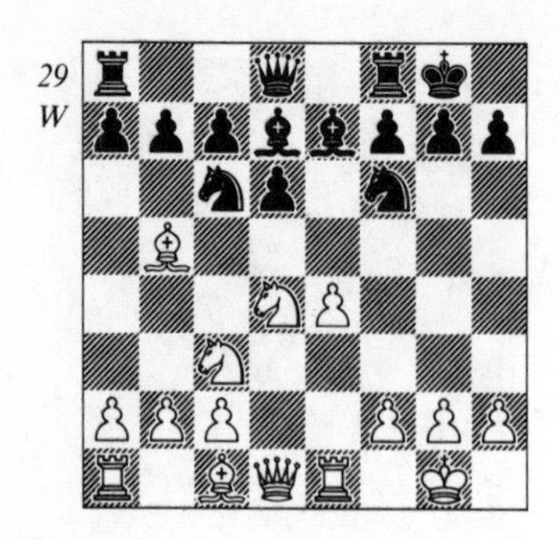

(also not bad is 10 ♗f4; on 10 b3 there follow 10 ... d5!; after 10 ♕f3 ♖e8 11 e5 de 12 ♘xc6 ♗xc6 13 ♕xc6 ♗b4 14 ♗g5 ♕d6 Black has good chances of equality) 10 ... h6 11 ♗h4 ♖e8 12 ♕d3 (interesting is 12 e5!? ♘h7 13 ♗g3 a5 14 ♕d3 ♗f8 15 ♖ad1) 12 ... ♘h7 13 ♗xe7 ♖xe7 14 ♖e3 ♕b8 15 b3 ♕b6 and Black is not worse (Capablanca–Lasker, World Ch. match 1921).

B

3 ... ♘f6 *(30)*

30
W
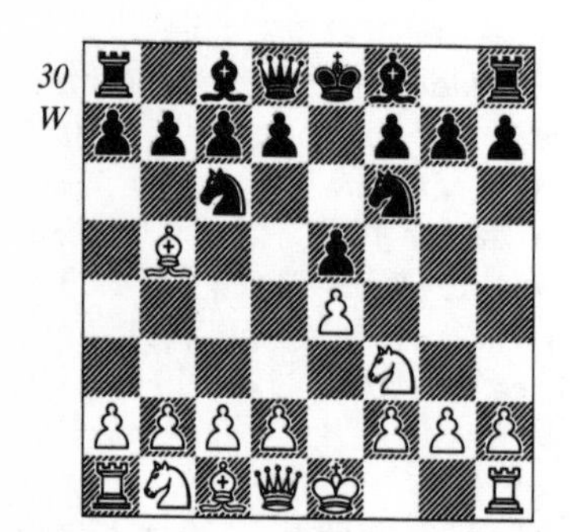

Let us now consider the Berlin Defence, one of the most reliable defences in the Spanish Opening. Classical simplicity is combined here with noticeably increased activity and a greater variety of plans for Black in comparison with the Steinitz Defence (with which in many variations it is closely connected).

4 0–0

The main continuation. Continuations like 4 d3, 4 ♕e2 and 4 ♗xc6 offer relatively few prospects and are quite passive.

On the other hand, lively play is reached after 4 d4 ed (unattractive is 4 ... ♘xd4? 5 ♘xd4 ed 6 e5 c6 7 ♕xd4 ♘d5 8 ♗c4 ♘c7 9 ♗f4 with a powerfully centralized position for White; in the event of 4 ... ♘xe4 White plays 5 0–0, transposing to the main line, or 5 de) 5 0–0 (after 5 e5 ♘e4 6 0–0 ♗e7 7 ♘xd4 0–0 8 ♘f5 d5 the game is level; 5 ♘xd4?! ♘e4 6 0–0 ♕f6!) 5 ... a6 6 ♗a4 (6 ♗xc6 dc is not dangerous for Black) 6 ... ♗e7, when there arises one of the variations with an early d2–d4 (see Chapter 8). Also not bad is 5 ... ♗e7.

4 ... ♘xe4

After 4 ... d6 5 d4, or 4 ... ♗e7 5 ♘c3 d6 6 d4, play leads to the Steinitz Defence, and 4 ... ♗c5 leads to the Classical System. In practice this occurs frequently.

5 d4

The most testing continuation. Let us consider other continuations, which are rarer nowadays:

(a) **5 ♖e1** ♘d6 (bad is 5 ... d5? 6 ♘xe5 ♗e7 7 ♘xf7!; a dangerous line is 5 ... ♘f6? 6 ♘xe5 ♗e7 7 d4 0–0 8 ♘c3!) 6 ♘xe5 ♗e7 (worse is 6 … ♘xe5 7 ♖xe5+ ♗e7 8 ♗d3 0–0 9 ♕f3!) 7 ♗d3 (7 ♘c3?! ♘xb5 8 ♘d5 0–0 9 ♘xc6 dc 10 ♘xe7+ ♔h8 is not dangerous for Black) 7 … 0–0 8 ♘c3 ♗f6 (also possible is 8 … ♘xe5 9 ♖xe5 ♗f6 10 ♖e3 g6 11 b3 ♘e8) 9 ♘g4 ♗d4 10 ♘e2 ♗b6 11 ♘f4 ♘e8 12 ♘d5 d6 13 ♘ge3 ♘f6 14 ♘xb6 ab 15 ♗f1 d5 with equal chances; Stein–Smyslov, Moscow 1961.

(b) **5 ♕e2** ♘d6 6 ♗xc6 dc 7 ♘xe5 ♗e7 8 ♖e1 ♗e6 9 d4 ♘f5 and Black has no difficulties.

After 5 d4 Black's main choice is between:

B1 5 … ♗e7
B2 5 … ♘d6

Also possible is 5 … a6, when White hardly has anything better than 6 ♗a4, transposing to the Open Defence: 6 ♗a4 b5 7 ♗b3 d5. It is risky to transpose to the Riga Variation: 5 … ed?! 6 ♖e1 d5 (or 6 … f5 7 ♘xd4 ♗c5? 8 ♖xe4+!), where White, besides 7 ♘xd4, may play 7 ♕xd4 ♕d7 8 ♗xc6 ♕xc6 9 c4! with an attack against Black's foundations in the centre (Fine).

B1

5 … ♗e7 *(31)*
6 ♕e2

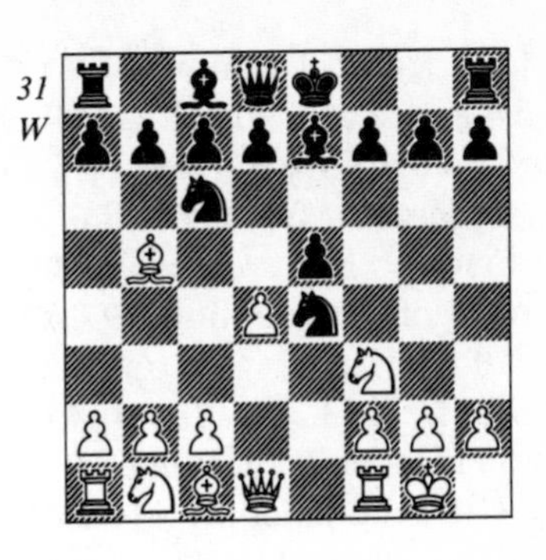
31
W

Besides this well-tried continuation, the following variations are possible:

(a) **6 de** 0–0 7 ♕d5 (interesting is 7 ♗e3!? a6 8 ♗c4 d6 9 ♗d5 ♗f5 10 ♘d4 ♘xd4 11 ♕xd4 de 12 ♕xe5 ♘d6 13 ♘c3 with pressure for White; Romanishin–Knezevic, Leningrad 1977; and also 7 ♕e2) 7 … ♘c5 8 ♗e3 ♘e6 9 ♘c3 a6!? (9 … f6) 10 ♗c4 (10 ♗a4?! b5 11 ♗b3 — Sax–Rivas Pastor, Thessaloniki OL 1988 — where Black can equalise by playing 11 … ♖b8 12 ♖ad1 ♘a5) 10 … d6 11 ed ♕xd6 12 ♖ad1 ♕xd5 13 ♘xd5 ♗d8 14 ♖fe1 with a lasting initiative for White (Tringov–Filip, Havana OL 1966).

(b) **6 ♖e1** ♘d6 7 ♗xc6 dc 8 de ♘f5 9 ♕xd8+ ♗xd8 10 ♘c3 0–0 11 h3 ♖e8 12 ♗f4 with a minimal advantage to White (Damjanovic–Neikirch, Polanica Zdroj 1966).

(c) **6 ♕e1?!** ♘d6 7 ♗xc6 bc 8 de ♘b7 9 b3 0–0 10 ♕c3 c5! with equality (Zaitsev–Yudovich, Moscow 1972).

(d) **6 d5** ♘d6! 7 ♘c3 ♘xb5 8 ♘xb5 a6 9 ♘c3 ♘b8 10 ♘xe5 d6 and then 0–0 with equality.

6 … ♘d6

Besides this main variation, the following should also be taken into consideration:

(a) **6 ... d5?!** (Trifunovic) 7 ♘xe5 ♗d7 8 ♗xc6 (8 ♘xd7 ♘xd4! 9 ♘e5+ c6 10 ♗xc6 ♘xc6 11 ♘f3 0–0 promises White nothing — Trifunovic) 8 ... ♗xc6 9 ♖e1 (worthy of consideration is 9 ♘xc6 bc 10 ♖e1 f6 11 ♘d2 ♘xd2 12 ♗xd2 ♖b8 13 a3 ♔f8 14 ♗b4! with advantage to White) 9 ... ♗d7 10 ♘d2 (after 10 ♗f4 c6 11 ♘xd7 — 11 ♘d2 — 11 ... ♕xd7 12 ♘d2 f5 13 ♘xe4 fe 14 ♕h5+ g6 15 ♕h6 ♗f6 16 c3 ♗g7 Black gets a good game; Shamkovich–Trifunovic, Sarajevo 1963) 10 ... ♘d6 11 ♘xd7 ♕xd7 12 ♘f3 f6 13 ♗f4 ♔f7 14 ♕d3 with pressure for White (Balashov–Dzyuban, Moscow 1982).

(b) **6 ... f5** 7 de 0–0 8 ♘c3 ♘xc3 9 ♕c4+ ♔h8 10 ♕xc3 and it is difficult for Black to complete the development of his queenside.

7 ♗xc6

B11 7 ... bc
B12 7 ... dc

B11

7	**...**	**bc**
8	**de**	**♘b7** *(32)*

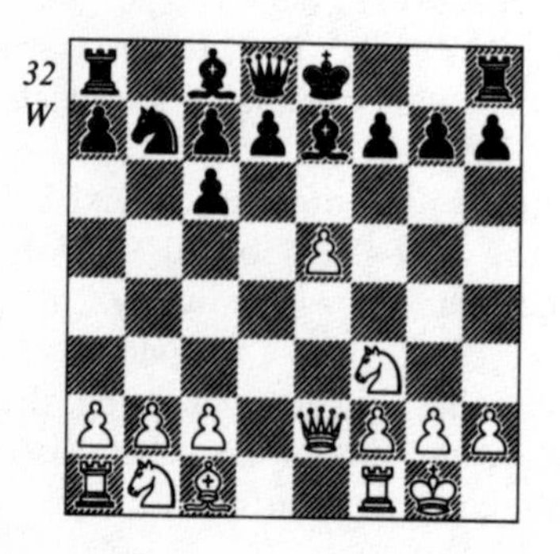

32 W

For a long time this move was considered almost obligatory. Nowadays one sometimes encounters 8 ... ♘f5. For example: 9 ♕e4 g6 10 ♖d1 0–0 11 ♘c3 ♕e8 12 ♘d4 ♘xd4 13 ♕xd4 f6 14 ♗h6 ♖f7 with complicated play in which White stands a little better (Korsunsky–Vladimirov, USSR 1979).

9 ♘c3

An ancient and reliable continuation, which, however, has quite a few 'competitors'.

(a) **9 c4** 0–0 (9 ... d5!?) 10 ♘c3 f6 11 ♗e3 ♕e8! 12 ♖fe1 fe 13 ♘xe5 d6 14 ♘d3 ♗f6 with approximate equality (Yudovich).

(b) **9 b3** 0–0 10 ♗b2 a5 11 a4 d5 12 ed cd 13 ♘bd2 ♖e8 14 ♖fe1 ♗d7 15 ♘c4 d5 with equal play (Geller–Gipslis, Moscow 1967).

(c) **9 ♕c4!?** 0–0 10 ♘c3 ♘c5 11 ♖d1 d5 12 ed cd 13 ♗e3 d5 14 ♗xc5 dc 15 ♖xd8 ♖xd8 16 ♗xf8 ♔xf8 17 ♘e5 and White's position is preferable (Sinprayoon–Lim, New Zealand 1977).

(d) **9 ♘d4!?** 0–0 10 ♖d1 ♗c5! with chances for both sides.

9 ... 0–0

And now:

B111 10 ♖e1
B112 10 ♘d4

B111

10 ♖e1 *(33)*

Note that after 10 ♖d1?! d5 11 ed cd Black has no particular difficulties.

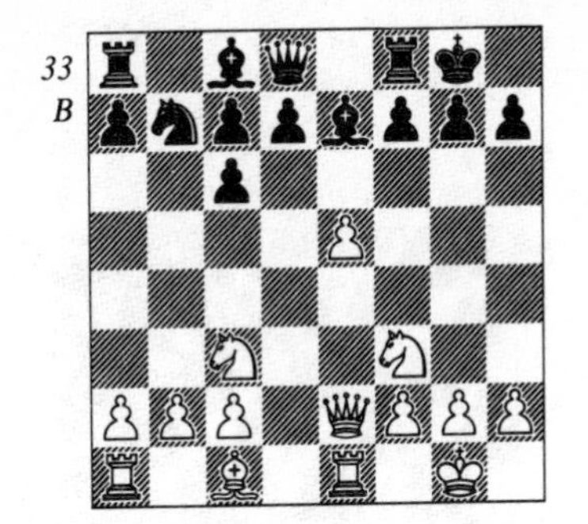

33
B

A critical position, where Black has a choice between:

B1111 10 … d5!?
B1112 10 … ♘c5

B1111

10 … d5!?

Until recently this continuation was neglected by theory, but now opinions on it vary. In passing, let us consider the following variations:

(a) **10 … f6** 11 ♗f4 fe 12 ♗xe5 ♗c5 13 ♗d4 ♗xd4 14 ♕c4+ with a clear positional advantage for White.

(b) **10 … ♖e8** 11 ♕c4! ♘c5 12 ♘g5 ♗xg5 13 ♗xg5 ♕xg5 14 ♕xc5 ♖e6 (Schlechter–Lasker, Paris 1900). Now, with 15 ♕d4 White maintained his pressure in the centre.

11 ed ♗xd6

In the game Balashov–Smyslov, Leningrad 1977, there followed: 12 ♗g5 ♕d7 13 ♘e4 c5 14 ♖ad1 ♕c6 15 ♕c2 f6 16 ♗f4 ♗g4 17 ♗xd6 cd 18 ♕f4 ♗xf3 19 ♕xf3 ♖ac8 20 ♖d5 ♖ce8 21 ♕d1 ♕a4 with equal chances.

B1112

10 … ♘c5

A well-studied continuation, in which, however, Black has a few problems on the way to obtaining full equality.

11 ♘d4

Other possibilities:

(a) **11 ♗e3** ♘e6 12 ♖ad1 d5 (also interesting is 12 … ♖b8 or 12 … ♗b4) 13 ed cd 14 ♘d4 (in the 2nd game Karpov–Korchnoi, World Ch. 1981, Black played 14 … ♗d7 15 ♘f5 d5 16 ♘xe7+ ♕xe7 17 ♕d2; with 17 … ♕f6 he could have obtained equal chances) 15 ♗xd4 ♖e8 16 ♕f3 d5 17 ♘a4 ♗f8 18 ♗c5! ♖xe1 19 ♖xe1 ♗g4 (19 … ♕a5 20 b4!) 20 ♕g4 ♕a5 21 c3 ♗c5 22 ♘xc5 ♕xc5 23 ♕d7 ♖f8 24 h4! with advantage to White (Tal–Portisch, Brussels 1988).

(b) **11 ♗f4** ♘e6 12 ♗g3 ♖b8 13 h3 f5 14 ef ♗xf6 15 ♘e5 ♗xe5 16 ♕xe5 d6 17 ♕e4 ♗d7 18 ♖ad1 with a minimal advantage to White (Geller–Bastian, Baden-Baden 1985).

11 … ♘e6
12 ♗e3 ♘xd4
13 ♗xd4 c5
14 ♗e3 d5
15 ed ♗xd6 *(34)*

An important stage in the transition to the middlegame.

(a) **16 ♘e4** ♗b7 17 ♘xd6 cd 18 ♖ad1 ♕f6 19 c4 ♖fe8 20 ♕g4 ♖e6! and Black's defence holds (Keres).

(b) **16 ♕h5** ♗b7 17 ♖ad1 ♖c8

34
W

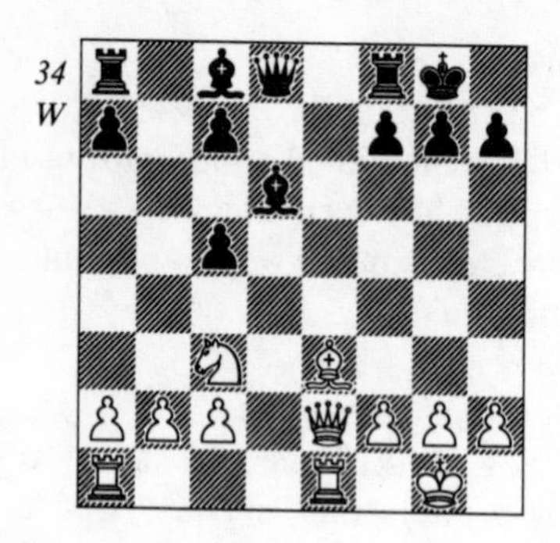

18 ♘b5 (18 f3!?) 18 … ♕f6 19 ♘xd6 cd with approximate equality (Tarrasch–Lasker, match 1908).

(c) **16 ♖ad1** ♗b7!; or 16 … ♕f6 17 ♕h5 ♖b8 18 ♗c1 ♕f5 with equality (Capablanca–Réti, Vienna 1914).

B112

10	**♘d4**	**♗c5**

After 10 … ♘c5 11 ♖d1 ♕e8 12 ♘f5 f6 13 ♗h6! ♘e6 14 ♕g4 White has a very strong attack.

11	**♖d1**	

White achieves nothing after 11 ♗e3 ♕e8 12 f4 d5!, or 11 ♘f5?! d5.

11	**…**	**♕e8**

Other possibilities:

(a) **11 … ♖e8** 12 ♕h5 ♕e7 13 ♗f4 ♗xd4 14 ♖xd4 d5 15 ♘e2 ♘c5 16 ♖dd1 (Yudovich–Masseev, corr. 1964). By playing 16 … a5 17 ♘d4 ♗d7 Black would have had a strong defence.

(b) **11 … ♗xd4** 12 ♖xd4 d5 13 ed cd 14 b4! ♖e8 15 ♗e3 ♗e6 16 ♕f3 d5 17 ♗f4! and Black has serious difficulties (Keres–Unzicker, match 1956).

12	**♗f4**	**♗xd4**
13	**♖xd4**	**♘c5**
14	**♗g3** *(35)*	

35
B

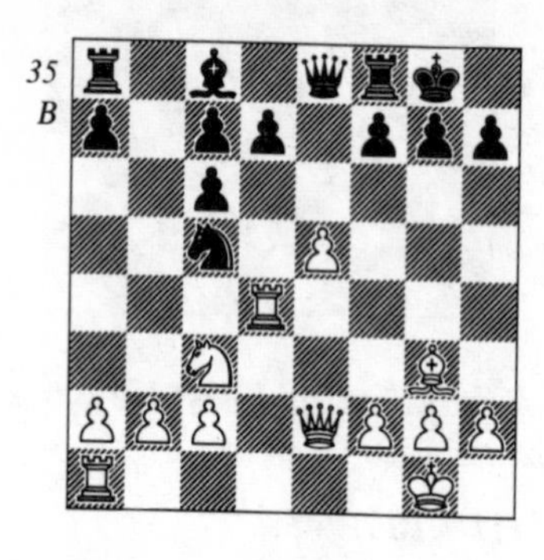

After 14 … d5 15 ed ♕xe2 16 ♘xe2 ♗a6 17 ♘c3 Black does not have compensation for the pawn.

B12

7	**…**	**dc**
8	**de**	**♘f5**
9	**♖d1**	**♗d7** *(36)*

36
W

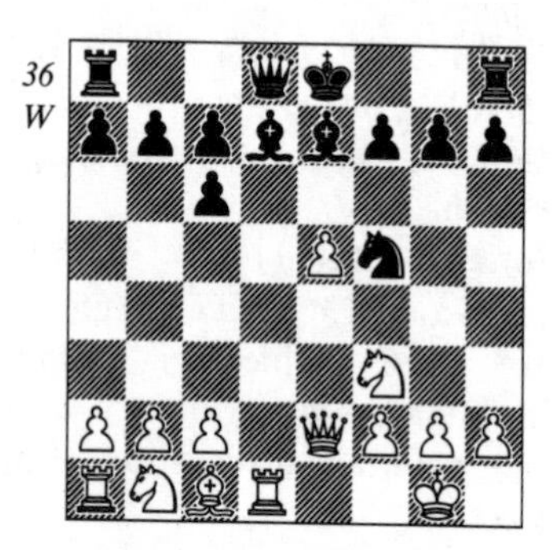

And now:

(a) **10 ♘c3** 0–0 11 ♘e4 ♕c8 12 h3 c5?! 13 ♗g5 ♗e6 14 ♗xe7 ♘xe7 15 ♘xc5 with an extra pawn for White (Geller–Bronstein, Moscow 1967).

(b) **10 e6!?** fe 11 ♘e5 ♗d6 12

♕h5+ g6 13 ♘xg6 ♘g7 14 ♕h6 ♘f5 15 ♕h3 ♖g8 16 ♕xh7 ♖g7 17 ♕h5 ♕f6 18 ♘e5+ ♔e7 19 ♘g4 ♕g6 20 ♕xg6 ♖xg6 21 h3 e5 with sharp play and chances for both sides (Ivkov–Trifunovic, Sarajevo 1963).

(c) **10 g4?!** ♘h6! 11 g5 ♘f5 12 e6 fe 13 ♘e5 ♗d6 14 ♕h5+ g6 15 ♘xg6 ♘g7 16 ♕h6 ♘f5 17 ♕h3 ♖g8 18 ♕xh7 ♖g7 19 ♕h5 ♔f7 with unclear play (Showalter).

B2

5 ... ♘d6 *(37)*

This is now the most common continuation. Black aims to simplify the position and move into the endgame.

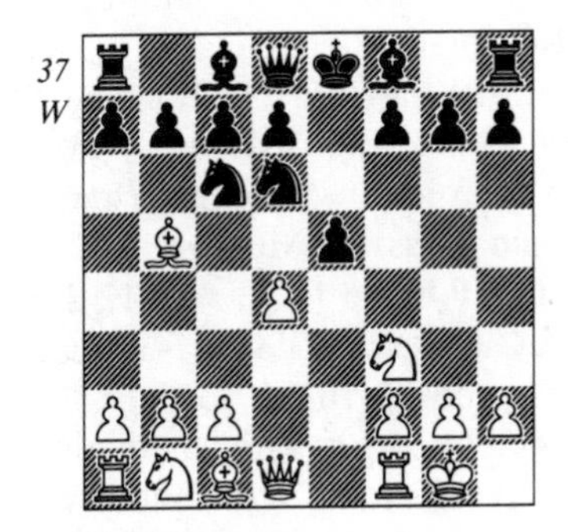

6 ♗xc6

Of course this is the most solid and logical way to continue. We shall examine other variations:

(a) **6 de!?** ♘xb5 7 a4 ♘bd4 (or 7 ... d6 8 e6!? fe — 8 ... ♗xe6 9 ab ♘e5 10 ♘d4 ♗d7 11 ♕f3 ♕c8 12 ♘c3 ♗e7 13 ♘d5 — 9 ab ♘e7 10 ♘c3 — 10 ♘g5! with unclear play) 8 ♘xd4 ♘xd4 9 ♕xd4 d5 10 b4 ♗f5 11 ♖e1 ♗e7 12 ♖e2 c6 13 ♗a3 ♕b6 14 ♕f4 ♗e6 15 ♘d2 g5 16 ♕f3 with sharp play and chances for both sides (Suetin–Bannik, Vladimir 1960).

(b) **6 ♗g5** ♗e7 7 ♗xe7 ♕xe7 8 ♗xc6 dc 9 de ♘f5 10 ♘c3 ♗e6 11 ♕d2 ♖d8 12 ♕f4 0–0 13 ♘e4 h6 14 h4 (Fischer–Fuller, USA 1963). With 14 ... c5 Black was able to obtain full equality.

6 ... dc

In White's favour is 6 ... bc 7 de ♘b7 8 ♗g5! ♗e7 9 ♗xe7 ♕xe7 10 ♘c3 0–0 11 ♖e1 etc., with pressure in the centre.

7 de ♘f5

The move 7 ... ♘e4!?, recommended by Petrosian and Suetin in the 1960s, is being adopted more frequently. For example: 8 ♕e2 ♗f5 9 ♗e3, and now:

(a) **9 ... ♗g6!?** 10 ♘d4 ♗c5 11 ♖d1 ♕e7 12 f3 ♘g5 13 ♘c3 0–0–0 with counterplay for Black (Petrosian and Suetin, 1966).

(b) **9 ... ♕e7** 10 ♖e1 (or 10 ♖d1 h6!? — 10 ... ♗g4 — 11 ♘a3 g5 12 ♘d4 ♗g6 13 ♕f3 ♕e5 14 ♘c6 ♕b2! with approximate equality; Kindermann–Westerinen, Thessaloniki OL 1988) 10 ... ♗g6 11 ♘d2 ♘xd2 12 ♕xd2 with better chances for White (Tseshkovsky–Malanyuk, Alma-Ata 1989).

8 ♕xd8+ ♔xd8 *(38)*

9 ♘c3

Other plans:

(a) **9 b3** ♔e8 (9 ... h6 10 ♗b2 ♗e6 11 c4!? — also good is 11 ♘bd2 a5 12 h3 e5 13 a4 ♔e8?! 14 ♖ad1 ♖d8 15 c4!; Sax–Torre, Biel

38
W

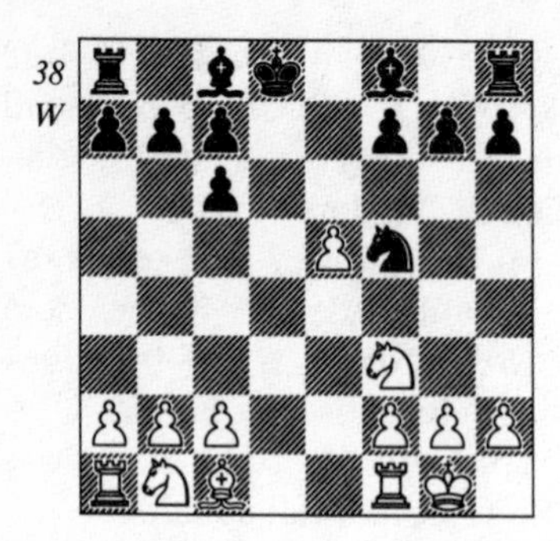

1985 — 11 ... a5 12 ♘c3 ♗b4(?) — 12 ... ♔c8 13 ♘e2 ♗c5 — 13 ♘e2 ♗c5 14 h3 g5 15 ♘c3 ♔c8 16 ♘e4 with a better game for White; Benjamin–Torre, Thessaloniki OL 1988) 10 ♗b2 ♗e7 11 ♘bd2 a5 12 a4 ♗e6 13 ♘e4 and Black must fight for equality (Hort–Minev, Varna 1969).

(b) **9 ♗g5+** ♔e8 10 ♘c3 h6 11 ♗f4 ♗e6 12 ♖ad1 ♖d8 13 ♘e4 c5 with equality (Harmonist–Tarrasch, Breslau 1889).

(c) **9 ♖d1+** ♔e8 10 ♘c3 ♗e7 11 ♗f4 ♗e6 12 ♘g5 ♗xg5 13 ♗xg5 h6 14 ♗f4 ♔e7 15 ♘e4 ♖hd8 16 f3 ♘d4 with a good game for Black (Magamedov–Karaklajic, Bela Crkva 1989).

(d) **9 h3** ♔e8 10 ♘c3 h6 11 ♘e2 ♘e7 12 ♘g3 ♗e6 13 ♘d4 ♗c4 14 ♖d1 c5 15 ♘b3 b6 16 f4 h5 17 ♘e4 h4 with a good game for Black (Yudasin–Yakovich, USSR 1985).

(e) **9 c4!?** ♗e6 10 b3 h6 11 ♘c3 ♔c8 12 h3 a5 13 g4 ♘e7 14 ♘d4 with better chances for White (Watson–Sturua, Frunze 1982).

After 9 ♘c3 Black's main choice is between:

B21 9 ... ♔e8
B22 9 ... h6

B21

9 ... ♔e8

We shall also indicate some other variations:

(a) **9 ... ♗e7** 10 ♗g5! h5 11 ♖ad1+ ♔e8 12 ♘e2 ♗e6 13 ♘f4 with advantage to White (Schmid–Toran, Munich OL 1958).

(b) **9 ... ♗e6** 10 ♘g5 ♔e8 11 ♘xe6 fe 12 ♘e4 and here Black is in difficulty (Gufeld–Shamkovich, Kislovodsk 1968).

10 ♘e2 *(39)*

The following variations are also possible:

(a) **10 ♘e4** h6! 11 ♖e1 ♗e6 12 g4 ♘e7 13 h3 ♖d8 14 ♘g3 c5 15 ♘h5 ♘d5 with equal chances (Stein–Spassky, Moscow 1967).

(b) **10 b3** h6 11 h3 ♗e6 12 ♗b2 ♗b4 13 ♘e2 ♖d8 14 ♘f4 ♗d5 15 ♘xd5 cd 16 g4! ♘e7 17 ♔g2 ♘g6 18 ♔g3 with a minimal advantage to White (Ljubojevic–Kavalek, Reggio Emilia 1985/86).

39
B

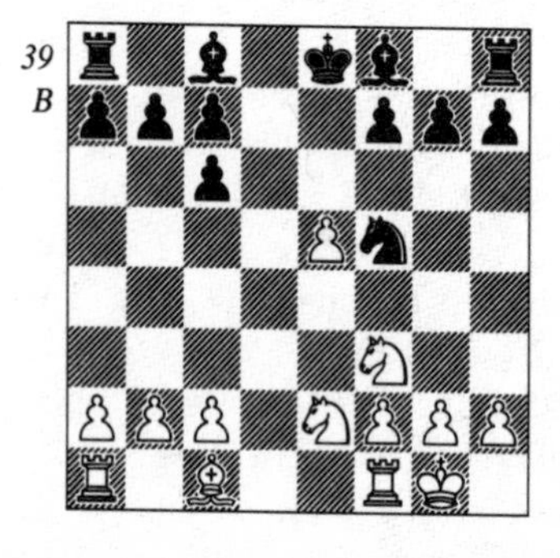

From the diagram position the following variations may arise:

(a) **10 … ♗e6** 11 ♘f4 (after 11 b3 ♗c5 12 ♗b2 h6 13 ♘f4 ♗d5 14 ♘xd5 cd 15 g4 ♘e7 16 ♔g2 a5 17 ♘e1 h5 the chances are level; Serper–Dautov, USSR 1986) 11 … ♗d5 12 ♘xd5 cd 13 g4 ♘e7 14 ♗f4 ♘g6 15 ♗g3 c6 16 ♖fe1 ♗c5 17 c3 ♘f8 18 b4 ♗b6 19 ♔g2 ♘e6 20 ♘h4 and Black has to fight for equality (Fischer–Bisguier, USA 1963).

(b) **10 … ♘e7** (a little-studied continuation is 10 … h5!?) 11 ♗g5 ♗e7 12 ♖fd1 ♘h6 with approximate equality; Khalifman–Faibisovich, Leningrad 1985; also worthy of consideration is 10 … ♗c5 11 ♖d1 a5 12 a4 ♘e7 13 ♘ed4 ♗xd4 14 ♘xd4 h6 and it is hard for White to demonstrate any advantage; Shamkovich–Bykhovsky, Moscow 1963) 11 h3 ♘g6 12 ♘ed4 ♗e7 13 ♖e1 ♘h4 14 ♘xh4 ♗xh4 15 g4 ♗e7 16 ♘f5 ♗xf5 17 gf f6 and Black maintains the equilibrium (Kuzmin–Keres, USSR Ch. 1973).

B22

9 … h6

10 ♘e2

Let us consider other variations:

(a) **10 b3** ♗e6 11 ♘e2 ♗d5 12 ♘d2 a5 13 c4 ♗e6 14 ♘f4 a4 15 ♗b2 ♗b4 16 ♘f3 ♔c8 and Black's defence is very strong (Tal–Romanishin, Leningrad 1977).

(b) **10 ♗f4** ♗e6 11 h3 ♗e7 12 g4 (Pfleger–Troianescu, Polanica Zdroj 1971).

(c) **10 ♗d2** ♗e6 11 ♘e2 c5 12 ♗c3 (Tarrasch–Lasker, Hastings 1895).

(d) **10 h3** ♗e6 11 g4 ♘e7 12 ♘d4 ♗d7 13 ♗f4 c5 14 ♘de2 ♔c8 15 ♖ad1 g5 16 ♗g3 ♘g6 17 f4 (Geller–Romanishin, USSR Ch. 1977).

In all cases White has the freer game, but Black's foundations are firm.

10 … ♔e8

Unattractive for Black is 10 … g5?! 11 h3 ♗g7 12 ♖d1+ ♗d7 13 g4 ♘e7 14 ♘g3 ♘g6 15 ♘h5! with better play for White.

11 ♘f4

And now:

(a) **11 … ♘e7** 12 h3 ♘d5 13 c3 ♘xf4 14 ♗xf4 with a level game (Gipslis–Spassky, Moscow 1967).

(b) **11 … ♗e6** 12 b3 ♗c5 13 ♗b2 a5 14 ♖ad1 with slight pressure for White (Timoshenko–Psakhis, Tallinn 1989).

3 Schliemann Defence

1	**e4**	**e5**
2	**♘f3**	**♘c6**
3	**♗b5**	**f5** *(40)*

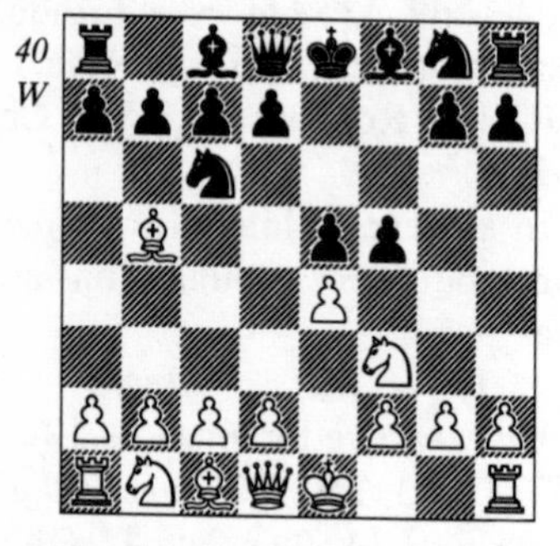

40
W

This sharp gambit continuation was introduced into practice in the middle of the 19th century by the Russian theorist, Jaenisch, but is named the Schliemann Defence in English-speaking countries after a German who published a series of articles on it in the 1860s. Since the 1950s, interest in this system has been reawakened and it has been enriched by various novelties.

White has the following main possibilities:

A 4 ♘c3
B 4 d3
C 4 de

A

4 ♘c3

A move first played by Dyckhoff. This continuation, in which White strives for active play for his pieces and heads for complications, poses substantial problems for Black and is met in practice more frequently than other lines.

Before considering this system we shall take a look at a few less important variations: White gets nothing from either 4 ef e4 5 ♕e2 ♕e7 6 ♗xc6 dc 7 ♘d4 ♕e5 8 ♘f3 ♕xf5 9 ♘c3 ♘f6 10 d3 ♗b4; or 4 ♗xc6 dc 5 ♘xe5 ♕d4 6 ♘f3 ♕xe4+; Black also has no problems after 4 ♕e2 fe 5 ♕xe4 ♘f6 6 ♕e2 ♗d6! 7 ♗xc6 dc 8 ♘xe5 0–0 9 d4 ♕e8 etc.

After 4 ♘c3 Black has a choice of:

A1 4 … fe
A2 4 … ♘d4
A3 4 … ♘f6

A dubious continuation is 4 … ♗b4?! 5 ef ♘f6 6 0–0 0–0 7 d4 ♘xd4 8 ♘xd4 ed 9 ♕xd4 ♗xc3 10 ♕xc3 d5 11 ♗d3 b6 12 b4!

with advantage to White (Suetin–Zinn, Berlin 1965).

A1

4 ... fe
5 ♘xe4

Now there is another branch in the analysis:

A11 5 ... d5
A12 5 ... ♘f6

Other variations are met more rarely:

(a) **5 ... ♗e7** 6 d4 ed 7 0–0 d5 8 ♘g3 ♗g4 9 h3 ♗xf3 10 ♕xf3 ♕d7 11 ♘f5 with pressure for White.

(b) **5 ... a6** 6 ♗xc6 bc 7 d4 d5 8 ♘xe5 (also quite good is 8 ♘g3) 8 ... de 9 ♕h5 g6 10 ♘xg6 ♘f6 11 ♕e5+ ♔f7 12 ♘xh8+ ♔g8 13 ♗g5 ♗g7 14 ♗xf6 ♕xf6 15 ♕e8+ with advantage to White (Gurgenidze–Lein, USSR Ch. 1961).

A11

5 ... d5 *(41)*

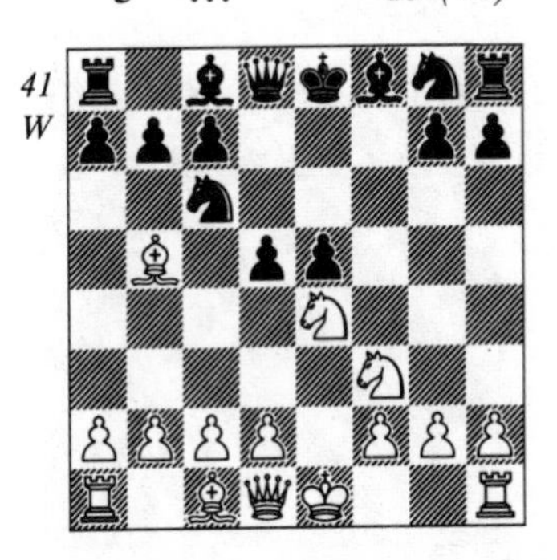

A critical position, in which White has a choice between the gambit line 6 ♘xe5 and the quiet 6 ♘g3.

A111 6 ♘xe5
A112 6 ♘g3

A111

6 ♘xe5 de
7 ♘xc6 ♕d5

Other moves are frequently tried:

(a) **7 ... bc** 8 ♗xc6+ ♗d7 9 ♕h5+ ♔e7 10 ♕e5+ ♗e6 11 ♗xa8 (also good is 11 d4 ♘f6 12 d5 ♘xd5 13 ♗g5+ ♘f6 14 ♖d1 ♕c8 15 f4 ef 16 0–0; on the other hand, after 11 f4?! ef 12 0–0 ♖b8 13 d4 ♕d6! 14 ♗g5+ ♘f6 15 ♖xf3 — 15 ♗xf3 ♔d7 — 15 ... ♕xc6 16 ♗xf6+ ♔d7 17 d5 ♕xd5 18 ♖d3 ♕xd3 19 cd ♗d6 20 ♕e4 gf 21 ♖e1 ♖be8 Black has excellent play; Bushuev–Nosov, USSR 1962) 11 ... ♕xa8 12 ♕xc7+ ♔e8 13 0–0 ♗e7 14 d3 with better chances for White (Evans–Dückstein, Lugano OL 1968).

(b) **7 ... ♕g5** 8 ♕e2 ♘f6 (8 ... ♕xg2? 9 ♕h5+!) 9 f4, and now:

(b1) **9 ... ♕h4**+ 10 g3 ♕h3 11 ♘e5+! c6 12 ♗c4 ♗c5 13 d3 ♘g4 14 ♘f7 ♗f2+ 15 ♔d1 e3 16 ♕f3 ♕xh2 17 ♕e4+ ♔f8 18 ♗xe3 ♗g4+ 19 ♔d2 ♖e8 20 ♘e5 with better prospects for White (Kavalek–Ljubojevic, Amsterdam 1975).

(b2) **9 ... ♕xf4** 10 ♘e5+ (after 10 ♘xa7+ ♗d7 11 ♗xd7+ ♔xd7! 12 ♕b5+ ♔e6 13 ♕c4+ ♔d7 it is hard for White to strengthen his attack; Schmittdiel–Inkiov, Gausdal 1989) 10 ...

c6 11 d4 ♕h4+ 12 g3 ♕h3 13 ♗c4 ♗e6 14 ♗g5 ♗d6 15 0–0–0 0–0–0 16 ♕f1 with roughly equal chances. For example: 16 … ♖he8 17 ♕xh3 ♗xh3 18 ♘f7 ♖d7 19 ♘xd6+ ♖xd6 20 ♗f4 ♖d7 21 ♖he1 ♘d5 22 ♗e5 ♗g4 23 ♖d2 e3!? 24 ♖d3 ♘b6 25 ♗b3 e2 26 ♗e3 a5 27 a4 c5!, as in Popovic–Inkiov, Palma de Mallorca 1989.

8 c4 ♕d6 *(42)*

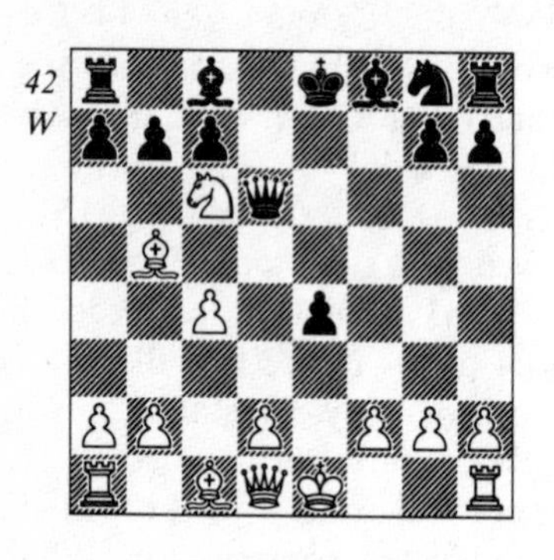

9 ♘xa7+

In this very sharp and complicated situation White has the following alternatives:

(a) **9 ♕h5+** g6 10 ♕e5+ (but not 10 ♘e5? c6 11 ♘xg6 ♕xg6 12 ♕e5+ ♘e7 13 ♗xc6+ bc 14 ♕xh8 ♕xg2) 10 … ♕xe5 11 ♘xe5+ c6 12 ♗a4 ♗g7 13 d4 ed 14 0–0! ♗xe5 15 ♖e1 ♗e6 16 ♖xe5 ♔f7 17 ♗b3 ♘f6 18 ♗g5 with a minimal advantage to White (Szalanczy–Polaizer, Balatonbereny 1981).

(b) **9 c5?!** ♕xc5 10 ♕a4 ♘f6! 11 d4 ed (also good is 11 … ♕b6 or 11 … ♕d6) 12 0–0 ♗d6! 13 ♘e5+ c6 14 ♘xc6 0–0 with excellent play for Black.

9 … ♗d7

In the event of 9 … c6 (9 … ♔d8 10 ♘xc8 ♔xc8 11 d4!) 10 ♘xc8 ♖xc8 11 ♗a4 White has a considerable advantage.

10 ♗xd7+ ♕xd7

11 ♕h5+

After 11 ♘b5 ♘f6 12 0–0 ♗c5! 13 d4 ed 14 ♖e1+ ♔f7 15 ♗e3 (15 ♗f4 ♖he8 16 ♖e3!?) 15 … ♖he8 Black has excellent compensation for the pawn (Gufeld–Seredenko, USSR 1962).

11 … g6

11 … ♔d8 12 ♕a5 ♔e8 13 0–0 ♘f6 14 d4 ed 15 ♗e3 gives White the better game (Keres).

12 ♕e5+ ♔f7

13 ♘b5

Less clear is 13 ♕xh8 ♘f6 14 ♘b5 ♖d8 15 0–0 ♗c5 16 ♕xd8 ♕xd8 17 b4 ♗xb4 18 ♗b2 c6 19 ♘c3 ♗c5 and Black has quite good counterchances.

13 … c6 *(43)*

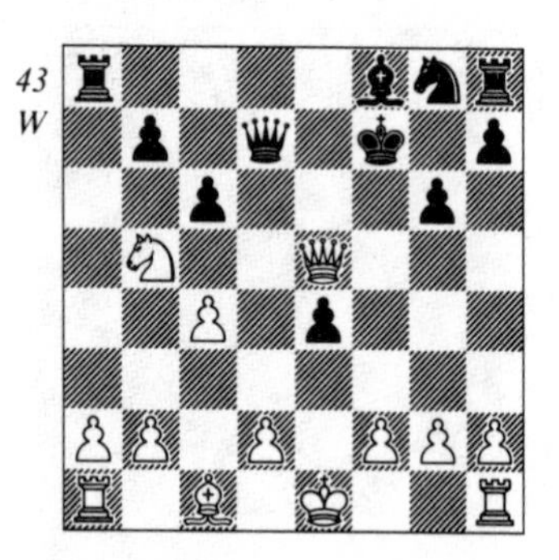

And now:

(a) **14 ♕d4** ♕e7 (other tries: 14 … ♕f5 15 ♘d6+ ♗xd6 16 ♕xd6;

14 ... ♕g4 15 0–0!; 14 ... ♘f6 15 ♕xd7+ ♘xd7 16 ♘c3 ♘c5 17 0–0 ♗g7 18 f3!; finally, 14 ... ♕xd4 15 ♘xd4 ♗g7 16 ♘e2! — White stands clearly better) 15 ♕xh8 (also good is 15 ♘c3 ♘f6 16 0–0 ♖d8 17 ♕e3! — Keres) 15 ... ♘f6 16 b3 ♖d8 17 ♗b2 ♗g7 18 ♗a3! with better chances for White (Chandler).

(b) **14 ♕xh8** ♘f6 15 ♘c3 ♖e8 16 b3 (after 16 0–0 ♗d6 — also good is 16 ... ♕d3 — 17 ♕xe8+ ♕xe8 18 d4 ed 19 ♗d2 ♕e5 20 g3 ♕e6 chances are equal; Katuryan–Fridmans, USSR 1983) 16 ... ♗c5 17 ♕xe8+ ♔xe8 18 0–0 ♕d3 19 ♗b2 ♕xd2 20 ♘a4 ♗d4 with chances for both sides (Kavalek–Möhring, Mariánské Lázne 1962).

(c) Note also that **14 ♘c3?!** ♖e8 15 ♕a5 ♘f6 16 h3 ♗d6 17 c5 ♕f5! (Zinn) is not dangerous for Black, and neither is **14 b3** ♘f6 15 ♗b2 ♗g7 16 ♘c3 ♘g4 etc.

A112

6 ♘g3 *(44)*

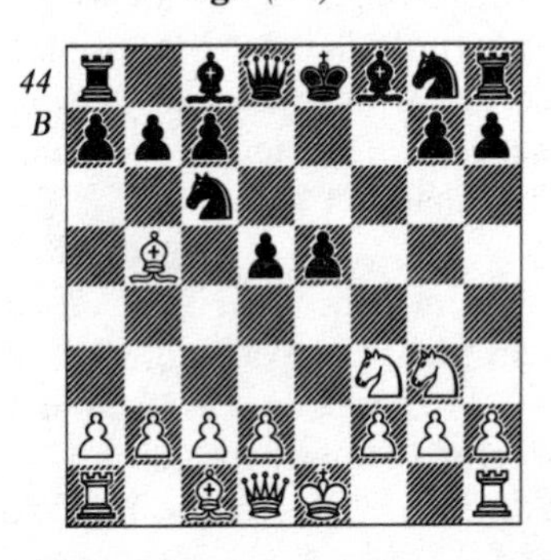
44
B

A quieter plan. White attempts to create piece pressure against Black's strengthened centre.

6 ... ♗g4

The following variations are also of interest:

(a) **6 ... e4** 7 ♘d4 ♕f6!? 8 ♕h5+ ♔e7 9 ♘hf5+ ♔e6 10 ♕e8+ ♘ce7 with sharp play (Keres).

(b) **6 ... ♕f6** 8 d4 e4 8 ♘e5! ♗d6 9 ♘xc6 ♗d7 10 ♕h5+ g6 11 ♕xd5 bc 12 ♕xe4+ ♔f8 13 ♗e2 ♖e8 14 ♕d3 ♕h4 15 ♗d2 ♘f6 16 0–0–0 with a clear advantage to White (Vasyukov–Bonch-Osmolovsky, Moscow 1960).

Note that 6 ... ♗d6? is bad in view of 7 ♘xe5!

7 h3

Other possibilities:

(a) **7 d4** e4 8 h3 ♗d7 9 ♗xc6 ♗xc6! 10 ♘e5 ♘f6 with a comfortable position for Black.

(b) **7 d3** ♘f6 8 h3 ♗xf3 9 ♕xf3 ♗c5 10 ♗e3 ♗xe3 11 fe 0–0 12 ♗xc6 bc 13 0–0 g6 14 ♕e2 ♕e7 15 c3 c5 with good play for Black (Andersson–Göransson, corr. 1965).

(c) **7 0–0!?** ♘f6 8 c4! ♗c5 9 ♗xc6+ bc 10 ♕a4 0–0 11 ♘xe5 ♕d6 12 ♘d3! ♗d4 13 c5! ♗xc5 14 ♘xc5 ♕xc5 15 d3 ♖ab8 16 ♗e3 ♕b5 17 ♕xb5 ♖xb5 18 ♖fc1 ♖xb2 19 ♖xc6 with a clear advantage to White (Geller–Inkiov, Moscow 1986).

7 ... ♗xf3
8 ♕xf3 ♘f6 *(45)*

In this critical position White has a wide choice of continuations, although he can scarcely reckon on obtaining any tangible advantage.

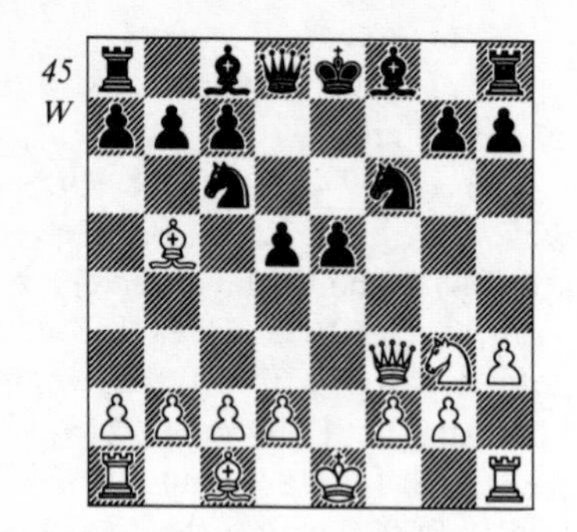

45
W

(a) **9 d3** ♗d6 10 ♘h5 0–0 11 ♘xf6+ ♕xf6 12 ♕xf6 gf (Tseitlin–Kupreichik, Minsk 1969).

(b) **9 ♘h5** e4 10 ♘xf6+ ♕xf6 11 ♕h5+ ♕f7 12 ♕xf7+ ♔f7 13 ♗xc6 bc 14 f3 ef 15 0–0 ♗c5+ 16 ♔h1 f2 17 c3.

(c) **9 0–0** ♗d6 10 ♘h5 e4 11 ♕f5 0–0! 12 ♘xf6+ ♕xf6 13 ♕xd5+ ♔h8.

(d) **9 c4!?** ♕f7 10 ♗xc6 bc 11 0–0 ♗d6 12 d3 ♖b8 13 b3 ♖e8 14 ♗e3 a5.

(e) **9 ♕c3** ♕d6 10 ♗xc6+ ♕xc6 11 ♕xc6+ bc 12 d3 ♗d6 13 ♗d2 0–0 14 0–0 ♘d7.

In all of these variations Black obtains equality.

A12

5 … ♘f6 *(46)*

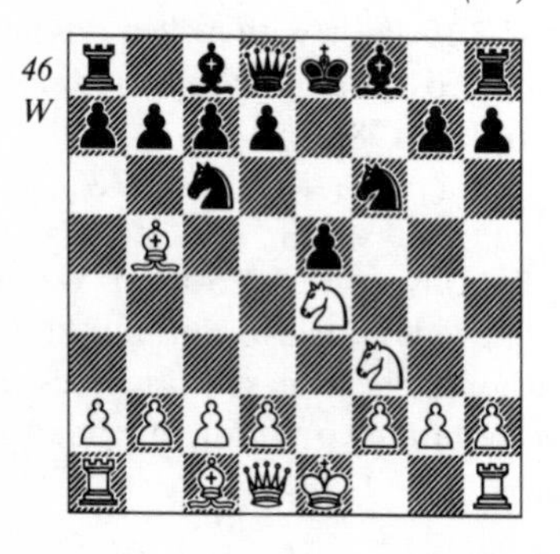

46
W

For a long time this continuation was not popular. But now the situation is very different, as there has been intense development of the theory of this line. White's main choices are:

A121 6 ♕e2
A122 6 ♘xf6+

A121

6 ♕e2

There has been little study of 6 d3. For example: 6 … d5 7 ♘g3 ♗d6 8 c4! a6 9 ♗xc6+ bc 10 c5 ♗xc5 11 ♘xe5 0–0 12 0–0 (Kristiansen–Mortensen, Copenhagen 1985).

6 … d5

Or 6 … ♕e7 7 0–0 d5 8 ♘xf6+ (also good is 8 ♘g3 ♗g4 9 ♕xe5 ♗xf3 10 ♕c3!) 8 … gf 9 d4 e4 10 ♘h4 f5 11 c4!? with an initiative for White.

7 ♘xf6+ gf
8 d4 ♗g7
9 de

Interesting is 9 c4!? a6 10 ♗a4 ♗g4 11 de 0–0 12 cd ♘xe5! 13 ♗e3 c5! with roughly equal chances (Mortensen–Wedberg, Copenhagen 1983).

9 … 0–0 *(47)*

Recently the move 9 … fe?! has been tried. For example: 10 ♘xe5 0–0 11 ♗xc6 bc 12 ♘xc6 ♕d7 (worthy of consideration is 12 … ♕d6!? 13 ♘e7+ ♔h8 14 ♘xc8 ♕b4 15 ♔f1 ♖ac8 with unclear play) 13 ♘e7+ ♔h8 14 0–0 ♗b7 15 ♗g5 ♕d6 16 ♕g4 ♗a6 17 ♖fe1 ♕b6 18 ♕h4 with advantage to White (Mikhalchishin–Annageldyev, USSR 1988).

47
W

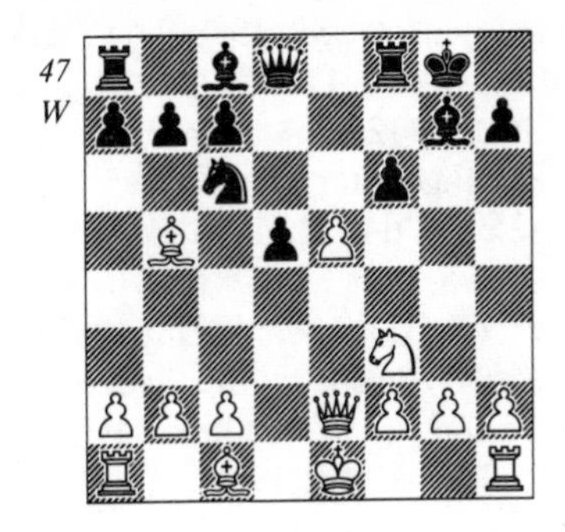

10 ♗xc6

Let us consider other variations:

(a) **10 ef?!** ♕xf6 11 ♕d1 ♖e8+ (or 11 ... ♘d4 12 ♕xd4 ♕e7+ 13 ♘e5 ♗xe5 14 ♕xd5+ ♔h8 15 ♗e2 with equal chances; Klovan–Arbakov, USSR 1984) 12 ♗e2 ♗g4 13 0–0 (13 ♕d5+!? ♔h8 14 ♗e3) 13 ... ♖e2! 14 ♕xe2 ♘d4 15 ♕d3 ♗f3 16 gf ♘xf3 17 ♔g2 ♖f8 and Black has dangerous threats (Izrafilov–Grudski, Minsk 1987).

(b) **10 e6** ♘e5 11 0–0 (or 11 ♗f4 c6 12 ♗d3 ♘xd3 13 ♕xd3 ♗e6 with full equality for Black; Psakhis–Grosar, Ljubljana 1987) 11 ... ♗e6 12 ♘d4 ♗d7 13 f4 c6 14 ♗a4 ♕b6! 15 c3 ♖ae8 16 ♗c2 ♘g4 17 ♕d3 f5 18 h3 c5!? and Black has the better prospects (Klundt–Schell, Dortmund 1985).

10	**...**	**bc**
11	**e6**	**♖e8**
12	**0–0**	**♗xe6** *(48)*

The following variations are also possible:

(a) **12 ... ♖xe6** 13 ♕d3 c5 (or 13 ... ♖e4 14 ♗e3 a5 15 ♖fe1 ♕d6 16 ♘d2 ♖b4 17 ♘b3 with pressure for White; Kuzmin–Arbakov, USSR 1985) 14 ♖d1 c6 15 c4! with advantage to White.

(b) **12 ... c5** 13 ♕b5 ♗f8 14 ♗e3 d4 15 ♖fd1 ♗d6 16 ♗xd4!? cd 17 ♘xd4 ♗e6 18 ♘xe6 ♖xe6 19 ♕d5 ♕e8 20 ♖e1 ♗e5 21 f4 ♖d8 22 ♕b3 ♖b8 23 ♕g3 ♕g6 with equal chances (Nenashev–Arbakov, Moscow 1986).

48
W

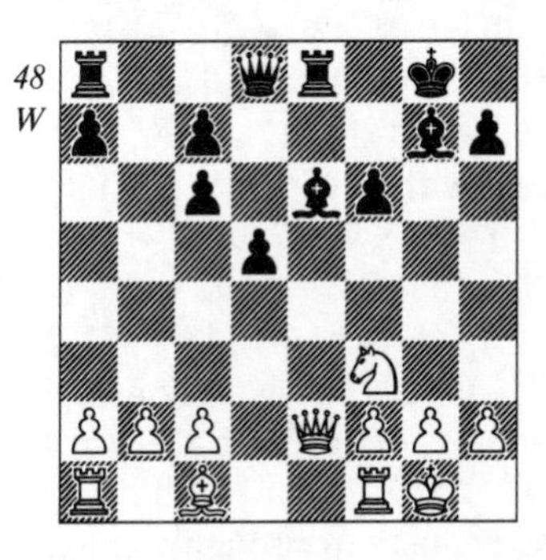

13 ♘d4

In the game Sax–Schell, Hungary 1984, there followed: 13 ♕d3?! c5 14 ♘h4 ♕d7 15 ♗f4 ♖ab8 16 b3 ♖b4 17 ♕g3 ♖e4 18 ♖ad1 with slightly better play for White.

13 ... ♕d7

13 ... ♕d6!? 14 ♕f3 leads to equality (Ochoa–Chiburdanidze, Bilbao 1987).

14	**♘xe6**	**♕xe6**
15	**♕xe6**	**♖xe6**
16	**♗e3**	**♗f8**
17	**♖fd1**	

With somewhat the better play for White.

A122

6 ♘xf6+ ♕xf6

After 6 … gf 7 d4 d6 (7 … e4 8 ♘g5!) 8 0–0 (interesting is 8 d5!?) 8 … ♗d7 9 ♖e1 ♕e7 10 de de 11 ♗xc6 ♗xc6 12 ♘xe5! fe 13 ♕h5+ ♕f7 14 ♕xe5+! ♔d7 15 ♕d4+ White has a dangerous attack.

7 ♕e2

An alternative is 7 0–0. For example: 7 … ♘d4 8 ♘xd4 ed 9 ♖e1+ (9 b3!?) 9 … ♗e7 10 ♕e2 c6 11 ♗d3 d6 (worse is 11 … d5? 12 b3 0–0 13 ♕xe7 ♕xf2+ 14 ♔h1 ♗h3 15 ♖g1! ♖ae8 16 ♕xf8+ ♖xf8 17 ♗a3 ♖e8 18 ♖af1 with advantage to White) 12 b3 0–0! 13 ♕xe7 ♕xf2+ 14 ♔h1 ♗h3 15 ♕e4!? ♗xg2+ 16 ♕xg2 ♕xe1+ 17 ♕g1 ♕f2 18 ♕xf2 ♖xf2 19 ♗b2 c5 (Saksis–Auzinsh, corr. 1983/4). After 20 ♔g1! ♖af8 21 ♖e1 ♖xd2 22 ♗c1 ♖df2 23 ♖e7 the chances are roughly equal.

8 ♗xc6

And now:

(a) **8 … bc** 9 ♕xe5 (or 9 ♘xe5 0–0 10 0–0 ♗d6 11 d4 c5 12 ♗e3 b6 13 f4 cd 14 ♗xd4 ♗b7 15 ♕g4 ♖ae8 16 ♖ad1 ♕h6 17 ♖de1 with a minimal advantage for White; Kuporosov–Yandemirov, USSR 1986) 9 … ♕f7 (or 9 … d6 10 ♕xf6 ♗xf6 11 d3 ♗f5 12 0–0 ♔d7 13 ♖b1 ♖hb8 14 b3 with better play for White; A. Rodriguez–Antunes, Holguin 1989) 10 d3 d6 11 ♕f4 with somewhat better play for White.

(b) **8 … dc** 9 ♘xe5 (after 9 ♕xe5 ♗g4 10 ♕xf6 ♗xf6 11 c3 c5! Black is clearly better; Petelin–Khagiyan, USSR 1988) 9 … ♗f5 10 d3 0–0–0 11 0–0 ♖he8 12 f4 ♗d6 13 ♕f2 ♔b8 (White has the advantage after 13 … ♗xe5 14 fe ♖xe5 15 d4! ♖a5 16 ♗d2!) 14 ♗e3 a6 15 ♗d4 ♕f8 16 ♘c4 ♗c8 17 a3! g6 18 b4 ♕h6 19 ♗c5 ♗e6 20 ♗xd6 cd 21 ♘a5! with advantage to White (Glek–Arbakov, USSR 1985).

A2

4 … ♘d4 *(49)*

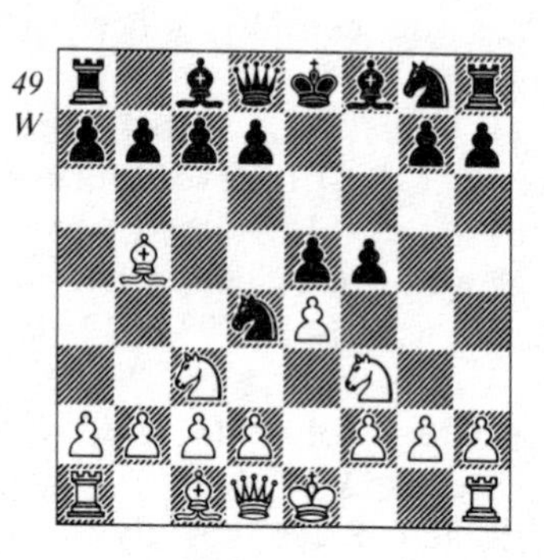
49
W

This knight thrust was recommended by Alekhine, but it only began to be properly investigated in the 1950s. Practice has shown that White has the better chances. The choice here is rather wide:

A21 5 ♗a4
A22 5 ♗c4
A23 5 ef
A24 5 ♘xe5

A21

5 ♗a4

Let us consider the following variations:

(a) **5 ♘xd4** ed 6 ♘d5!? (worse is 6 ♘e2 c6! 7 ♗d3 fe 8 ♗xe4 d5 9 ♗f3 d3! 10 cd ♗d6 11 d4 ♘h6 12 0–0 0–0 13 ♘g3 ♕h4 with advantage to Black; Karaklajic–Matulovic, Yugoslavia 1958) 6 ... c6 7 ef ♕g5 (after 7 ... cd 8 ♕h5 ♔e7 9 0–0 ♘f6 10 ♖e1 ♔d6 11 ♕f3!? a6 12 ♗f1 ♔c7 13 b3 ♗d6 14 ♗b2 ♖e8 15 ♗d4 b6 chances are equal; Kostakiev–Kolev, Bulgaria 1986) 8 ♘c7+ ♔d8 9 ♘xa8 ♕xg2 10 ♖f1 cb 11 d3 ♘f6 12 c3 ♗c5 13 ♗f4 (13 ♔d2!?) 13 ... ♘d5 and Black has a dangerous attack.

(b) **5 0–0** c6 6 ♗a4 ♘f6!? 7 ♘xe5 ♗c5 8 b4!? ♗b6 9 ♘c4 ♗c7 10 e5 0–0 11 ♗b3 ♘g4 12 f4 gives White a certain initiative (Kupreichik–Bellon, Barcelona 1984).

5 ... ♘f6 *(50)*

After 5 ... c6 6 ♘xe5 (6 0–0 b5!; or 6 d3 d6 7 ♘xd4 ed 8 ♘e2 ♕a5+, and Black has no difficulties) 6 ... ♕f6 7 ♘d3 fe 8 ♘xe4 ♕g6 9 ♘g3 d5 10 ♘f4 White's position is preferable.

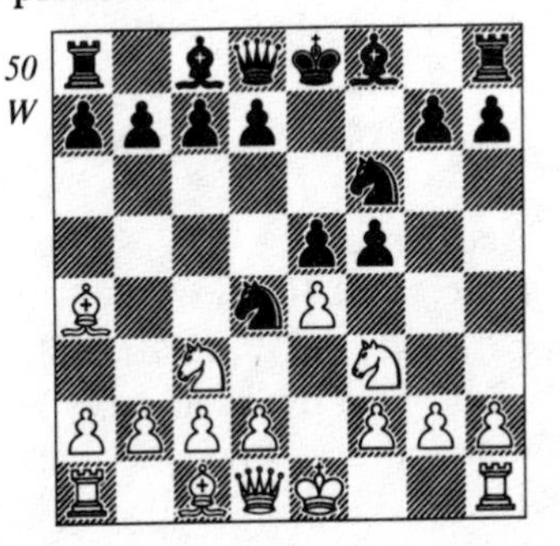
50
W

6 0–0

Other possibilities:

(a) **6 ef** ♗c5 7 0–0 0–0 8 ♘xd4 (8 ♘xe5 d5 9 ♘f3!?) 8 ... ed 9 ♘e2 d5 10 d3 ♗xf5 11 ♗f4 ♗d6 12 ♗xd6 ♕xd6 13 ♘xd4 ♘g4 14 g3 ♕h6 15 h4 ♗c8 16 ♕e2 ♕f6 17 c3 c5 18 ♘c2 with advantage to White (Chandler–Inkiov, Nis 1983).

(b) **6 ♘xe5** fe 7 0–0 ♗c5 8 d3! ed 9 ♕xd3 and White stands better (Suetin).

6 ... ♗c5
7 ♘xe5 0–0 *(51)*

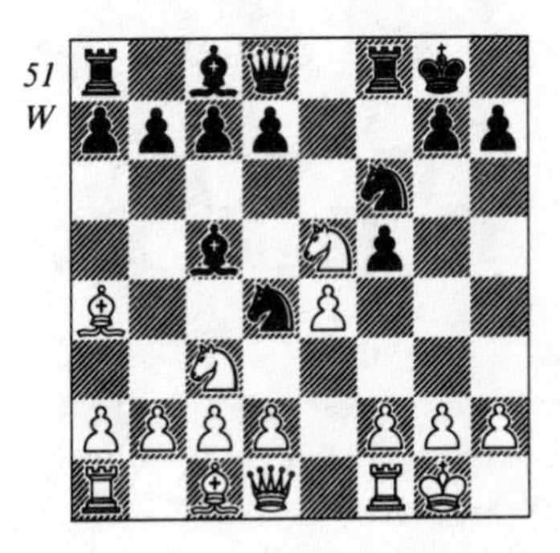
51
W

And now:

(a) **8 ef** d5 9 ♘e2 (after 9 ♘f3 ♗xf5! 10 ♘xd4 ♗xd4 11 d3 c6, or 9 d3 ♗xf5 10 ♗g5 c6 Black has a satisfactory position) 9 ... ♕e7 10 ♘xd4 ♕xe5 11 ♘f3 ♕xf5 12 d4 ♗d6 13 c3 and White has the better chances (Zurakhov–Zaitsev, Leningrad 1963).

(b) **8 ♘d3** fe! 9 ♘xc5 d5 10 d3 ♘g4 11 ♘5xe4 de 12 ♘xe4 ♕h4 13 h3 ♘e5 14 f4 ♗g4 15 ♕d2 ♗xf3 and Black has good chances to equalise (Mechkarov).

A22

5 ♗c4 c6 *(52)*

In White's favour is 6 … d6 6 0–0 (also not bad is 6 d3 or 6 ef ♗xf5 7 ♘xd4 ed 8 ♕f3! with better chances for White) 6 … ♘f6 7 ef ♗xf5 8 ♘xd4 ed 9 ♖e1+ ♗e7 10 ♘e2 c5 11 ♘f4 d5 12 ♘xd5! ♘xd5 13 ♕f3 with a clear advantage to White (Euwe).

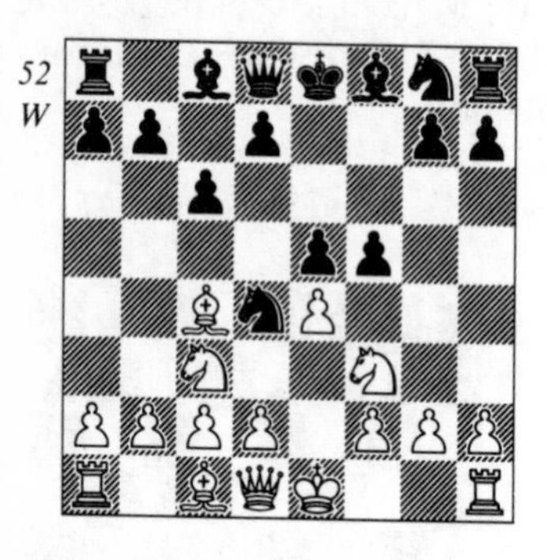
52
W

6 0–0

After 6 ♘xe5 ♕e7 7 ♕h5+ g6 8 ♘xg6 ♘f6 9 ♘xe7+ ♘xh5 10 ♘xc8 ♘xc2+ 11 ♔d1 ♘xa1 12 ef d5 13 ♗e2 ♘f4 Black has a good game (Mechkarov).

6 … d6

After 6 … ♘xf3+ 7 ♕xf3 ♕f6 8 d4 ed 9 e5 ♕h4 10 ♘e2 ♗c5 11 b4! White has a marked advantage (Bogolyubov–Réti, Stockholm 1919).

7 ef ♘xf5
8 ♖e1

In the game Novopashin–Babenyshev, Kiev 1962, there occurred 8 … ♗e7 9 ♗b3 ♘f6 10 d3 ♕b6 11 h3 ♗d7 (11 … ♖f8!?) 12 g4 ♘d4 13 ♘xd4 ed 14 ♗f4 d5 15 ♘a4 ♕d8 16 ♘c5 with a positional advantage to White.

A23

5 ef *(53)*

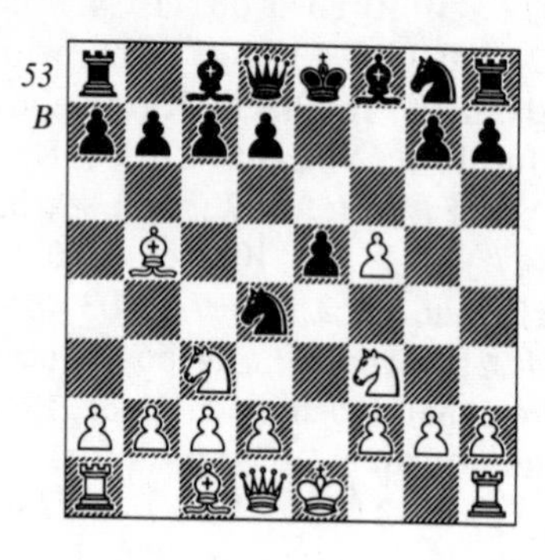
53
B

5 … ♘xb5

Other possibilities:

(a) **5 … c6** 6 ♗d3!? ♘xf3+ 7 ♕xf3 ♘f6 8 ♕e2 ♕e7 9 b3 d5 10 b3 ♗d7 11 ♗b2 0–0–0 12 0–0–0 ♖e8 13 ♕f2 ♔b8 14 g4! with better chances for White (Wedberg–de la Villa Garcia, Lugano 1988).

(b) **5 … ♘f6** 6 0–0 ♗c5 7 ♘xd4 ed 8 ♖e1+ ♗e7 9 ♘e2 a6 10 ♗d3 c5 11 b4 0–0 12 bc ♗xc5 13 ♘f4! and Black is in serious trouble (Matanovic–Janosevic, Sarajevo 1958).

6 ♘xb5 d6
7 d4 e4
8 ♘g5 ♗xf5
9 d5 *(54)*

And now:

(a) **9 … c6!** 10 ♘c3 ♘f6 11 0–0 ♗e7 12 ♖e1 0–0 13 dc d5! 14 cb ♖b8 and Black has excellent compensation for the pawn (Keres).

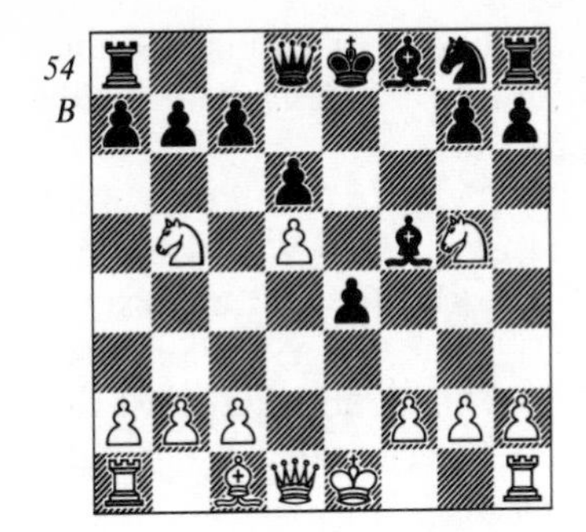
54
B

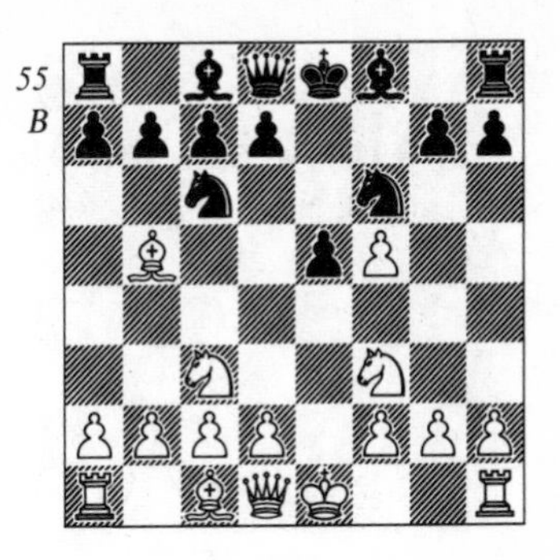
55
B

(b) **9 … c5** 10 ♘c3 ♘f6 11 f3 ♕e7 12 fe ♘xe4 13 ♘gxe4 ♗xe4 14 0–0.

(c) **9 … ♘f6** 10 ♘d4 ♗g4 11 ♕d2.

In both cases Black has excellent counter-chances for the sacrificed pawn (Keres).

A24

5 ♘xe5 ♕f6
6 ♘f3

And now:

(a) **6 … fe** 7 ♘xd4! ♕xd4 8 0–0 c6 9 ♗a4 ♘f6 (9 … d5 10 d3!) 10 d3 ed 11 ♖e1+ ♔f7 12 ♗e3 with advantage to White.

(b) **6 … ♘xb5** 7 ♘xb5 fe 8 ♕e2 ♕e7 9 ♘d4 d6 10 0–0 ♘f6 11 d3 a6 12 ♘c3 ♗g4 13 f3 ef 14 ♕f2 0–0–0 15 ♘xf3 ♔b8 16 ♗g5 h6 17 ♖ae1 ♕f7 with equal play (Bolobovich–Nikitin, Moscow 1963).

A3

4 … ♘f6
5 ef *(55)*
5 … ♗c5

Other possibilities:

(a) **5 … ♘d4** 6 0–0 c6 7 ♗e2 d6 8 ♖e1 ♘xf5 9 d4 with better chances for White (Matanovic–Tolush, Leningrad 1957).

(b) **5 … e4?!** 6 ♘h4 (also good is 6 ♘g5 d5 7 d3 ♗xf5 8 de de 9 ♕e2 ♗b4 10 ♗d2 ♕e7 11 ♕c4! with pressure for White) 6 … d5 7 d4 and White's prospects are noticeably superior.

6 0–0

Other moves:

(a) **6 ♘xe5** 0–0 7 ♘f3 d5 8 d4 and then ♗g5 with a positional advantage to White (Marovic).

(b) **6 d3** 0–0 7 ♗g5 ♘d4 8 ♗c4+ ♔h8 9 0–0 c6.

(c) **6 ♕e2** ♕e7 7 ♗xc6 dc 8 ♕xe5 ♕xe5 9 ♘xe5 ♗xf5 10 d3 0–0 11 0–0 ♖ae8 12 ♘c4 ♗g4 (Bertok–Fuderer, Yugoslavia 1951).

In the last two variations Black has splendid counterplay.

6 … 0–0 *(56)*

And now:

7 ♘xe5 ♘xe5 (after 7 … ♘d4?! 8 ♘f3 c6 9 ♗d3!? — also good is 9 ♘xd4 ♗xd4 10 ♗a4 d5 11 ♘e2 — 9 … d5 10 b4! ♘xf3+ 11 ♕xf3 ♗xb4 12 ♗b2 White has a clear advantage — analysis by

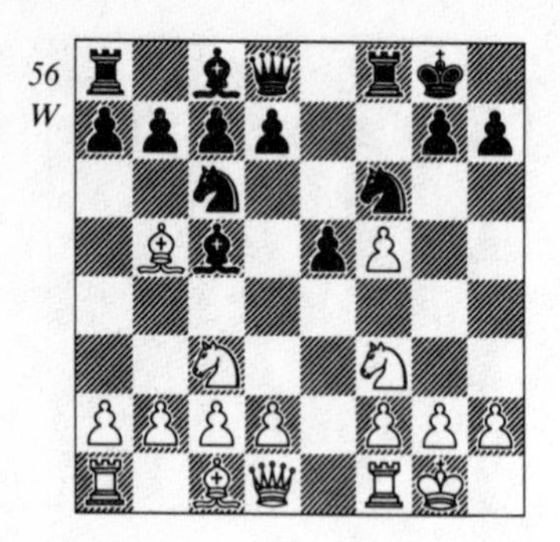
56
W

Boleslavsky and Suetin) 8 d4 ♗xd4 9 ♕xd4 d6 10 ♗f4 (10 f4!?) 10 … ♗xf5 11 ♗xe5 de 12 ♕xe5 ♗xc2 13 ♗c4+! ♔h8 14 ♘b5 with an initiative for White (Stein–Nadezhdin, USSR 1963).

B

4 d3 *(57)*

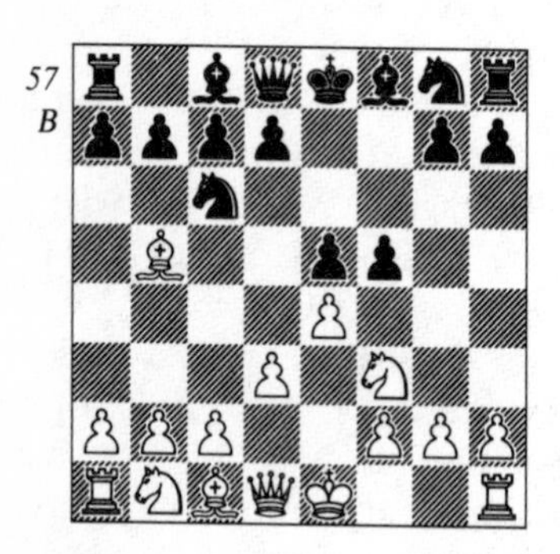
57
B

A more restrained method of development, which allows White to avoid many sharp opening variations. Practice has shown that Black has no particular difficulties.

4 … fe

Other possibilities:

(a) **4 … ♘f6** 5 ef ♗c5 6 0–0 0–0 7 ♗e3! ♕e7 8 ♘c3 ♘a5 9 d4 ed 10 ♗xd4 a6 11 ♖e1 ♕d6 12 ♗f1 and White has a lasting positional advantage (Heilemann–Ballbé, corr. 1967).

(b) **4 … d6** 5 0–0 ♗e7 6 ef ♘f6 7 d4 e4 8 d5 a6 9 ♗a4 ef 10 dc b5 11 ♗b3 fg 12 ♖e1 ♗xf5 13 ♘c3 ♗g6 14 ♗g5 ♔f8 15 ♕f3 and White's advantage is clear (Usov–Shechtman, Leningrad 1960).

5 de ♘f6
6 0–0 d6 *(58)*

Worthy of consideration is 6 … ♗c5 7 ♘c3 d6 8 ♗e3 ♗b6 9 ♘d5 0–0 10 ♗g5!? ♔h8 11 a4!? (Khalifman–Inkiov, Moscow 1989). With 11 … ♘e7! 12 a5 ♗c5 Black could have obtained complete equality.

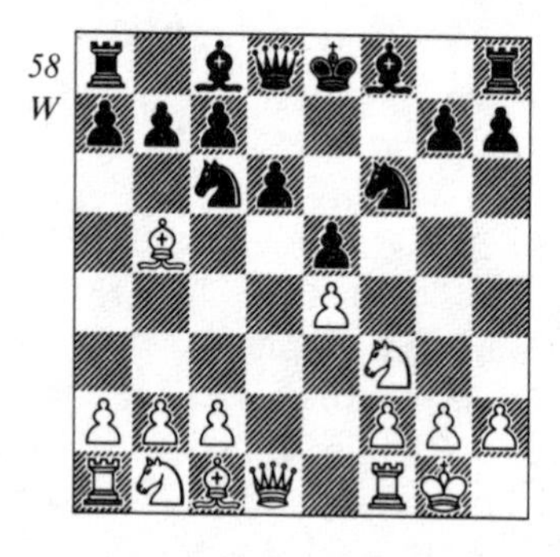
58
W

In this position the following lines are possible:

(a) **7 ♘c3** ♗e7 8 ♕d3 (after 8 ♘d5 ♘xe4 — also possible is 8 … ♗g4 9 ♘e3 ♗d7 10 ♗c4 ♘a5 — 9 ♘xe7 ♕xe7 10 ♕d5 ♘f6!, or 8 ♗c4 ♗g4 9 ♗e3 ♕d7 10 a3 h6 11 ♗e2 g5 12 ♘d2 ♗e6; Black has equal chances) 8 … ♗g4 9 h3 ♗xf3 10 ♕xf3 0–0 11 ♕d1 ♔h8

12 ♗e3 ♕e8 (12 ... ♕d7!?) 13 ♘d5! and White's position is preferable (Pilnik–Rubinetti, Mar del Plata 1971).

(b) **7 ♕d3** ♗e7 8 ♕c4 ♕d7 9 ♗a4 a6 10 ♗b3 ♗d8 11 ♗d2 b5 12 ♕d3 a5 13 a4 ♘b4 14 ♕e3 ba 15 ♗xa4 c6 16 h3 ♖b8 17 ♖d1 ♗b6 18 ♕e2 ♕c7 19 ♗xb4 with pressure for White (Vasyukov–Bebchuk, Moscow 1964).

(c) **7 ♗g5** ♗e7 8 ♗xf6 ♗xf6 9 ♕d5 ♗d7 10 ♘c3 ♕c8 11 ♖ad1 ♘d8 with roughly equal chances (Wolf–Spielmann, 1928).

C

4 d4!?

A very sharp continuation which in many variations leads to 'irrational' gambit play.

4 ... fe

After 4 ... ed 5 e5 there arises a position which is analogous to the Deferred Schliemann variation 1 e4 e5 2 ♘f3 ♘c6 3 ♗b5 a6 4 ♗a4 f5 5 d4 ed 6 e5. And after 4 ... ♘xd4 5 ♘xd4 ed 6 ♕xd4 fe 7 0–0 ♘f6 8 ♗g5 c6 9 ♗xf6 ♕xf6 10 ♕xe4+ ♗e7 11 ♘c3 White has a strong initiative.

5 ♘xe5

After 5 ♗xc6 dc 6 ♘xe5 ♕h4 7 0–0 ♗d6! 8 f3 ef 9 ♘xf3 ♕h5 10 ♖e1+ ♘e7 Black has an excellent position (analysis by Taimanov and Furman).

5 ... ♘xe5

6 de c6 *(59)*

7 ♘c3!?

It was precisely this piece sacrifice which enlivened interest in this

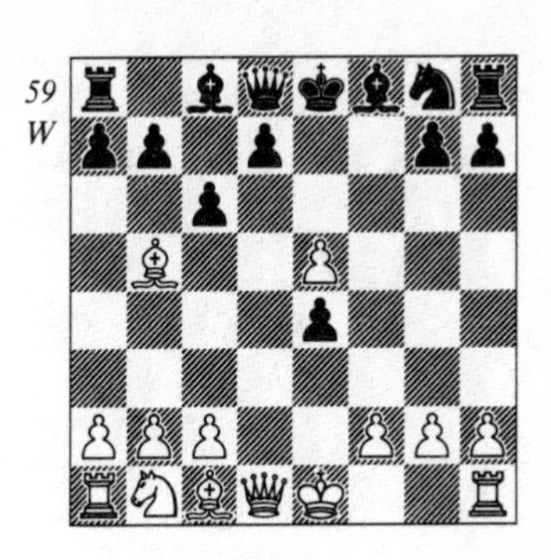

variation. Other possibilities offer fewer prospects:

(a) **7 ♗c4** ♕a5+ 8 ♘d2 ♕xe5 9 ♗xg8 ♖xg8 10 ♕e2 d5 11 f3 ♗e6 with an extra pawn for Black (Kholmov–Bronstein, USSR Ch. 1949).

(b) **7 ♗e2** ♕a5+ 8 ♗d2 ♕xe5 9 ♗h5+ ♔d8 10 ♗c3 ♕g5 11 0–0 ♘f6 12 f4 ef 13 ♗xf3 ♗c5+ 14 ♔h1 ♔c7 15 ♘d2 d5 and here Black stands better (Franz–Fichtl, Erfurt 1955).

7 ... cb

Another possibility is 7 ... ♕e7!? 8 0–0 (8 ♗f4 cb 9 0–0 ♕c5 10 ♘xe4 ♕c6 11 ♖e1 b6 12 ♕f3 ♗e7 is in Black's favour; Golubtsov–Anyukin, USSR 1986) 8 ... cb (8 ... ♕xe5+? 9 ♘xe4 ♔d8) 9 ♘xe4 ♕e6 10 ♖e1 ♔d8 11 ♕f3 ♘h6 with unclear play.

8 ♘xe4 d5

8 ... ♗e7 9 ♕d5! is dangerous for Black.

9 ed ♘f6 *(60)*

A critical position, with the following possibilities:

(a) **10 ♕d4** ♗e7 (10 ... ♘xe4 11 ♕xe4+ ♔f7 12 ♗f4 ♕e8 13 ♗e5

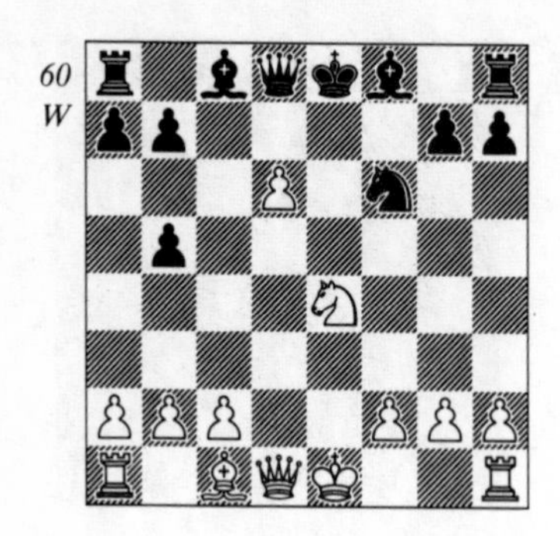

♕e6 14 ♕f4 ♔g8 15 0–0–0, or 10 … ♔f7 11 ♗g5 ♗f5 12 ♗xf6 gf 13 ♕d5+ gives White slightly better chances) 11 ♗g5 (interesting is 11 ♗f4 0–0 12 ♗xe5! ♗f6 13 de ♕xe7 14 ♘d6 ♘g4 with equal chances — Khachian) 11 … h6 12 ♗h4 ♗f5 13 0–0–0 (Diaz–Rodriguez, Cuba 1982). After 13 … g5!? 14 ♖he1 ♔f7 15 ♘xg5+ hg 16 ♖xe7+ ♔g6 17 ♗xg5 ♔xg5 18 ♕e3+, play is unclear.

(b) **10 0–0** ♘xe4! 11 ♕h5+ g6 12 ♕e5+ ♔f7 13 ♕xh8 ♕f6 14 ♕xh7+ ♗g7 15 ♗h6!? with an initiative for White (Keres).

(c) **10 ♗g5** ♕a5+ 11 ♘c3 b4 12 ♗xf6 gf 13 ♘d5 b3+! 14 c3 ♗e6 15 ♘c7+ ♔d7 16 0–0 ♗xd6 17 ♘xe6 ♕e5! 18 g3 ♕xe6 with equal chances (Piskov–Yandemirov, USSR 1984).

4 Bird's and Irregular Defences

In this chapter we discuss other, less common, systems for Black after 1 e4 e5 2 ♘f3 ♘c6 3 ♗b5:

A **3 … ♘d4** (Bird's Defence)
B **3 … g6**
C **3 … ♘ge7**
D **3 … others**

A

3 … ♘d4

This knight thrust also has a long history. It was introduced into practice more than a hundred years ago by the English master, Bird. As a rule, the struggle revolves around the square d4, which is both a strength and a weakness in Black's position. Until recently White was considered to have the better chances. Nevertheless interest in Bird's Defence has noticeably risen in the last few years.

4 ♘xd4

Definitely the most testing reply. The following should also be considered:

(a) **4 ♗c4** ♗c5 (4 … b5? 5 ♗xf7+! ♔xf7 6 ♘xd4 ed 7 ♕h5+ and 8 ♕d5+) 5 ♘xd4 ♗xd4 6 c3 ♗b7 7 ♕h5 ♕e7 with equality.

(b) **4 ♗a4** ♗c5 5 0–0 ♘xf3+ 6 ♕xf3 ♘e7 7 d3 0–0 8 ♗e3 ♗b6 9 ♘c3 d6 10 ♖ad1 and here the game is level (Réti–Spielmann, Budapest 1913).

4 … ed *(61)*

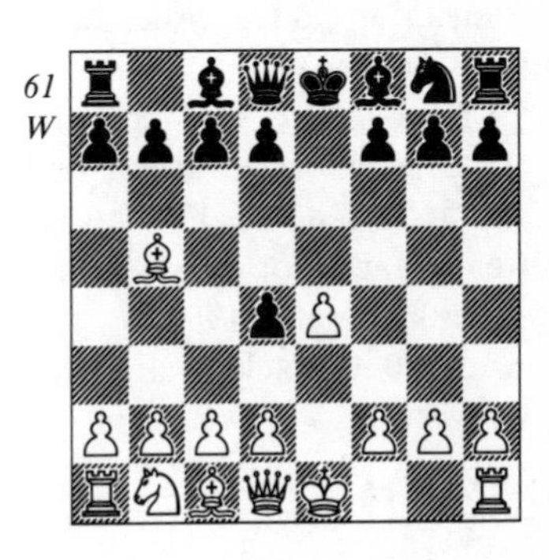
61
W

5 0–0

This is the common continuation.

An alternative is 5 d3 (5 c3? ♕g5). For example:

(a) **5 … c6** 6 ♗c4 d5 7 ed cd 8 ♗b5+ ♗d7 9 ♗xd7+ ♕xd7 10 0–0 ♗c5 transposes to variation A21, note to White's 9th move.

(b) **5 … g6** 6 c3 ♗g7 7 0–0 ♘e7 8 cd ♗xd4 9 ♘c3 c6 10 ♗c4 d6 11 ♗e3 and here Black has difficulties (Tarrasch–Blackburne,

St. Petersburg 1914). Note that 5 ... ♗c5 6 0–0 leads to variation A2.

Recently the move 5 ♗c4 has sometimes been adopted, with the following variations:

(a) **5 ... d6** 6 c3 ♘f6 7 0–0 ♗e7 8 ♖e1 c6 9 cd d5 10 ed ♘xd5 11 ♘c3 ♘b6 12 d3 0–0 13 ♕f3! ♗f6 14 ♗e3 ♗e6 (14 ... ♗xd4? 15 ♗xd4 ♕xd4 16 ♕xf7+!) 15 ♗xe6 fe 16 ♕g4 ♕d7 17 ♘e4 ♖ae8 18 ♘c5 with a material advantage for White (Aseev–Guseinov, USSR 1989).

(b) **5 ... c6** 6 0–0 d5 transposing to variation A11, note (a) to Black's 6th move.

(c) **5 ... ♘f6** 6 ♕e2 ♗c5 7 e5 0–0 8 0–0 d5 9 ef dc 10 ♕h5(?) b6 11 fg ♖e8 12 d3 cd 13 ♗a6 with better chances for Black (Short–Ivanchuk, Linares 1989).

After 5 0–0 Black's main choice is between:

A1 5 ... c6
A2 5 ... ♗c5

A1

5 ... c6

The following lines are also possible:

(a) **5 ... ♘e7** 6 ♖e1 (also of interest is 6 ♕h5, or 6 c3 ♘c6 7 ♕a4) 6 ... g6 7 c3 ♘c6 8 d3 ♗g7 9 c4 0–0 10 ♘d2 and White has slightly better chances (Keres).

(b) **5 ... g6** 6 d3 ♗g7 7 ♘d2 ♘e7 8 f4 and here White's position is preferable (Capablanca–Blackburne, St. Petersburg 1914).

After 5 ... c6 White has a choice between:

A11 6 ♗c4
A12 6 ♗a4

A11

6 ♗c4 *(62)*

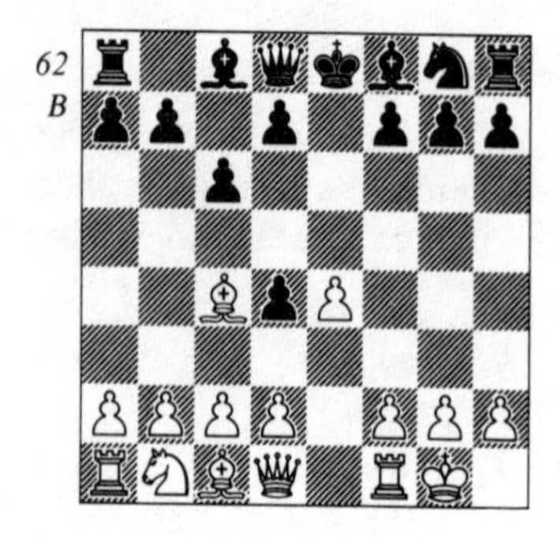

6 ... ♘f6

Other possibilities:

(a) **6 ... d5** 7 ed cd 8 ♗b5+ (8 ♖e1+ ♗e7 9 ♗b5+ ♔f8!?) 8 ... ♗d7 with the following variations:

(a) **9 ♖e1+** ♘e7 10 ♗xd7+ ♕xd7 11 ♕h5 (also not bad is 11 c3 0–0–0 12 cd ♘c6 13 d3 ♗d6 14 ♘c3) 11 ... ♖c8 (11 ... 0–0–0!? 12 ♕xf7 ♘c6 13 ♕xd7+ ♔xd7 14 d3 ♘b4 15 ♘a3 ♖c8 16 ♗f4 ♘xc2 17 ♘xc2 ♖xc2 with excellent play for Black; Rozentalis–Guseinov, USSR 1989) 12 d3! ♖c6 (12 ... ♖xc2? 13 ♘d2 ♖c6 14 ♘f3 ♖e6 15 ♖xe6 ♕xe6 16 ♗g5 is dangerous for Black) 13 ♗d2! (also good is 13 ♘d2) 13 ... ♖g6 14 c4! (14 ♕e5 ♔d8 15 ♕xd4 ♘c6, or 15 ♕b8 ♕c8 16 ♕xa7 ♖xg2+!) 14 ... ♔d8 15 ♘a3 ♕g4 (after 15 ... ♕f5 16 ♕xf5 ♘xf5 17 ♖e5, or 15 ... a6 16 ♖c1, Black has quite a few difficulties) 16 ♕xg4 ♖xg4 17 ♘b5 dc 18 ♘d6 is in White's favour (analysis by Boleslavsky and Suetin).

(a2) **9 ♕e2** ♘e7 (9 ... ♗e7) 10 b3! ♗xb5 11 ♕xb5+ ♕d7 12 ♕d3 0–0–0 (interesting is 12 ... ♘c6!? 13 ♖e1+ ♗e7 14 ♗a3 0–0 15 ♗xe7 ♖fe8! with a good game) 13 ♗b2 ♘c6 14 ♗d4 h5 15 ♘c3! ♘b4 16 ♕f3 ♘xc2 17 ♗xa7 ♘xa1 18 ♘d5! and White wins (Oll–Guseinov, USSR 1988).

(a3) **9 ♗xd7+** ♕xd7 10 0–0 ♗c5 transposing to variation A21 note to White's 9th move.

(b) **6 ... ♘e7** 7 ♖e1 ♘g6 8 d3 ♗e7 9 c3 dc 10 ♘xc3 0–0 11 d4 with a clear advantage to White (Panov–Vasiliev, USSR 1947).

7 ♖e1

Let us also consider the following variations:

(a) **7 ♕f3** (after 7 ♕e2 d6 8 e5?! de 9 ♕xe5+ ♗e7 10 ♖e1 b5! 11 ♗b3 a5 12 a4 ♖a7! Black seizes the initiative — Geller–Kholmov, USSR Ch. 1949; and after 7 e5?! d5 8 ed ♗xd6 9 ♖e1+ ♔f8! 10 d3 ♕c7 11 h3 b5 12 ♗b3 c5 13 ♘d2 ♗b7 Black stands better — Kholmov) 7 ... d5 8 ed cd 9 ♗b5+ ♗d7 10 ♗xd7+ ♕xd7 11 d3 ♖c8 12 ♘d2 with some pressure for White (Klaman–Tolush, Leningrad 1951).

(b) **7 d3** d5 8 ♘xd5 9 ♖e1+ ♗e7 10 ♗g5 0–0 11 ♗xe7 ♘xe7 12 ♘d2 and White is slightly better (Klaman).

7 ... d6

8 c3 *(63)*

Note that 8 d3 ♗e7 9 ♘d2 (9 ♗g5?! 0–0 10 ♘d2 ♘g4 11 ♗xe7 ♕xe7 gives White no advantage; Kuporosov–Zakharov, USSR 1986) 9 ... 0–0 10 ♘f3 promises White slightly better chances.

63
B

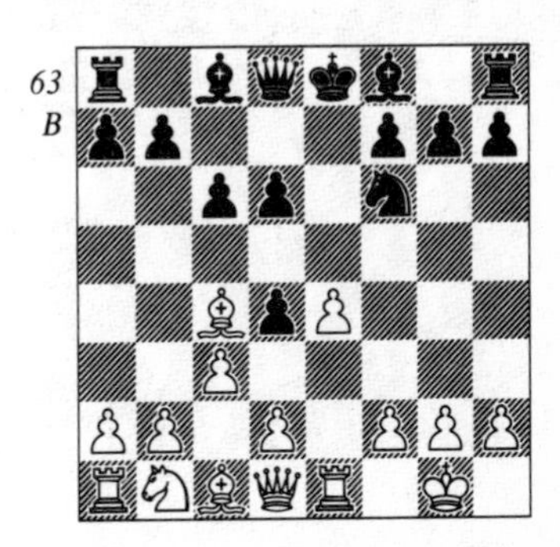

In this position the following variations are possible:

(a) **8 ... ♘g4!?** 9 ♕e2 b5 (in White's favour is 9 ... de? 10 ♘xc3 ♕h4 11 h3 ♘e5 12 d4! ♘xc4 13 ♕xc4 ♗e7 14 d5! ♗d7 15 ♕b3!; Geller–Szabó, Budapest 1973) 10 ♗d3 ♕f6!? 11 h3 dc 12 hg cb 13 e5! ba 14 ef+ ♗e6 15 ♗xb5 ♖c8 with complete equality for Black (Peters–Gibbons, Philadelphia 1979).

(b) **8 ... ♕b6** 9 ♕b3 ♕xb3 10 ♗xb3 dc 11 bc ♗e7 12 e5 de 13 ♖xe5 ♘d7 14 ♖e3 ♔f8 15 d4 ♘b6 and White's position is preferable (Lipnitsky–Tolush, USSR 1962).

Note also that after 8 ... dc 9 ♕b3 ♕c7 10 a4; or 8 ... ♗e7 9 cd d5 10 ed ♘xd5 11 ♘c3 ♘b6 12 d3 0–0 13 ♗e3, Black has to fight for equality.

A12

6 ♗a4 *(64)*

Smyslov has often advocated this move. In this position too, Black has certain difficulties.

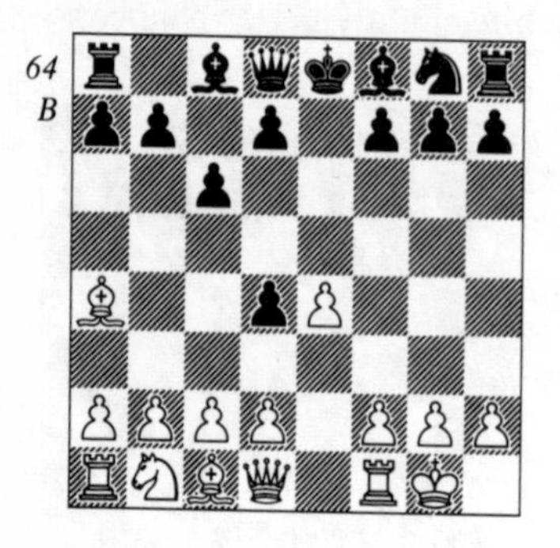

The following variations are possible:

(a) **6 … ♘f6** 7 d3 (7 c3) 7 … d5 (after 7 … d6 8 ♘d2 or 8 c3 White has the better chances) 8 ♗g5 (also not bad is 8 ed!? ♘xd5 9 ♖e1+ ♗e7 10 ♗g5) 8 … de 9 de ♗e7 10 e5!? ♘d5 11 ♗xe7 ♘xe7 12 ♗b3 0–0 13 ♘d2 with a minimal advantage to White (Aronin–Tolush, Leningrad 1951).

(b) **6 … g6** 7 c3 ♗g7 8 cd d5 9 ed ♘e7 10 dc 0–0 (Georgadze–Gurevich, Batumi 1969).

(c) **6 … d5** 7 ed ♕xd5 8 ♗b3 ♕f5 9 ♖e1+ ♗e7 10 d3 ♗d7 11 ♘d2 (Ciocaltea–Rossetto, Belgrade 1962).

(d) **6 … ♗c5** 7 c3 ♘e7 8 d3 0–0 9 ♘d2 dc 10 bc d5 11 d4 ♗b6 12 ♗a3 ♖e8 13 ♗c2 ♗c7 14 e5 ♘f5 15 ♕b1! (Smyslov–Lutikov, USSR Ch. 1960).

In all these cases White has the better chances.

A2

5 … ♗c5

This continuation is now in fashion. The main variations are:

A21 6 d3
A22 6 ♗c4
A23 6 c3

A21

6 d3

Let us first consider the following variations:

(a) **6 e5?!** c6 7 ♗c4 d5 8 ed ♗xd6 9 d3 ♘e7 10 ♘d2 0–0 11 ♘e4 ♘d5 12 ♖e1 ♗f5 13 ♕f3 ♗g6 14 ♘d6 ♕xd6 15 ♗d2 ♖ae8 with equality (Yurtaev–Klaric, USSR 1989).

(b) **6 b4** ♗xb4 (6 … ♗b6!?) 7 ♗b2 ♘e7 8 ♗xd4 0–0 9 ♕c1!? c5 10 ♕b2 cd 11 ♕xb4 (Plaskett–Kupreichik, Hastings 1984/5). With 11 … ♘c6! 12 ♕a4 a6 13 d3 ♖b8 14 ♗xc6 dc Black gets an excellent game.

(c) **6 ♕h5** ♕e7 7 d3 ♘f6 8 ♕h4 c6 9 ♗c4 d5 10 ed ♘xd5 11 ♗g5 f6 12 ♗d2 ♗e6 with equal play (Kuzmin–Malanyuk, USSR 1986).

6 … c6

After 6 … ♘e7 7 ♕h5! ♗b6 8 ♗g5 0–0 9 ♘d2 White's position is preferable.

7 ♗c4

After 7 ♗a4 ♘e7 8 f4 (interesting is 8 ♕h5!? d5 9 ♘d2 0–0

10 ♘f3 f6 11 ed ♘xd5 12 ♖e1; Anand–Lau, Moscow 1989) 8 ... f5 9 ♕h5 g6 10 ♕h6 ♘g3! the game is level (Blatny–Malanyuk, Warsaw 1989).

7 ... d5

8 ed

After 8 ♗b3 ♘e7 9 ♗g5 f6 10 ♗h4 0–0 11 ♘d2 ♔h8 12 ♔h1 a5 13 a4 ♗e6?! 14 f4 with slight pressure for White (Arakhamia–Ioseliani, USSR 1986).

8 ... cd

9 ♗b3

After 9 ♗b5+ ♗d7 (also interesting is 9 ... ♔f8!? 10 c3 ♘e7 11 cd ♗xd4 12 ♘c3 g6 13 ♗h6 ♔g8 14 ♖e1 ♗e6 with excellent play for Black; Sigurjonsson–Kupreichik, Winnipeg 1986) 10 ♗xd7+ ♕xd7 11 ♘d2 ♘e7 12 ♘b3 ♗b6 13 ♗g5 f6 the game is level (Lanc–Tseshkovsky, Trnava 1986 and Ljubojevic–Salov, Rotterdam 1989).

9 ... ♘e7 *(65)*

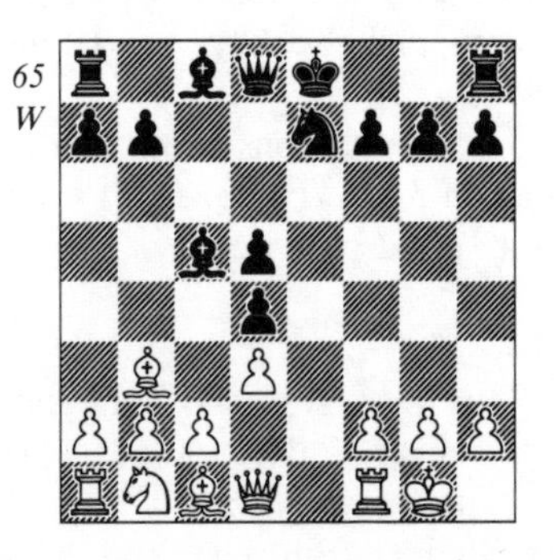

Here the following continuations have been tried:

(a) **10 c4** 0–0 11 cd ♘xd5 12 ♘d2 ♘e3 13 fe de 14 ♕h5 ed+ 15 ♕xc5 dc♕ 16 ♖axc1 ♗e6! with equality (Dvoiris–Balashov, USSR Ch. 1986).

(b) **10 ♗g5** (10 ♗f4!?) 10 ... f6 11 ♗f4 0–0 12 ♘d2 ♔h8 13 ♖e1 a5 14 a4 ♗b4 15 h3 g5 16 ♗h2 ♖a6! with excellent play for Black (Belyavsky–Tseshkovsky, USSR Ch. 1986).

(c) **10 ♖e1** 0–0 11 ♘d2 a5 12 a4 ♗b4! (Anand–Tseshkovsky, Calcutta 1986), and Black has full equality.

A22

6 ♗c4

One of the 'youngest' theoretical variations:

6 ... d6 *(66)*

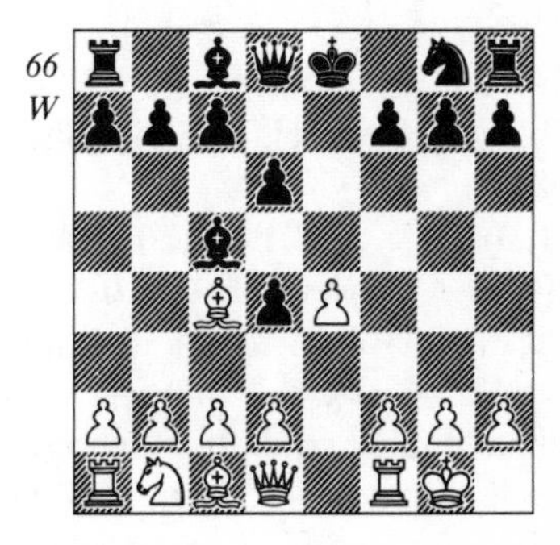

And now:

(a) **7 d3** ♕h4!? (7 ... c6 8 ♕h5!? ♕d7 9 ♗g5 h6 10 ♘d2 g6 11 ♕h4 ♕g4 12 f4 — Oll–Guseinov, Uzhgorod 1988; or 7 ... ♘e7 8 f4 d5 9 ♗b3 a5 10 a4 0–0 11 f5 ♖a6 12 ♘d2 ♗a7 13 ♘f3 c5 14 ♗g5 — Mautauzis–Barcza, Thessaloniki OL 1988; or 7 ... ♘f6 8 ♗g5 h6 9 ♗h4 g5 10 ♗g3 ♗g4 — 10 ...

♘g4 11 h3 ♘e5 12 ♗b3 ♗e6 13 ♕h5! — 11 f3 ♗e6 12 ♘d2 ♕d7 13 ♘b3! ♗b6 14 ♗f2 — Ghinda; in all cases White has the better chances) 8 ♘d2 ♘f6 9 f4 ♗e6 10 ♘f3 ♕h5 11 ♗b3 ♗xb3 12 ab ♗b6 13 h3 0–0–0 14 ♘g5 ♕xd1 15 ♖xd1 ♖de8!? with unclear play (Tseshkovsky–Klaric, Sochi 1989).

(b) **7 c3**, with the following lines:

(b1) **7 … ♘e7** 8 cd ♗xd4 9 ♕a4 ♘c6 10 ♗b5 ♗f6!? 11 ♗xc6 bc 12 ♕xc6 ♗d7 with unclear play (Ehlvest–Lalic, St. John 1988).

(b2) **7 … ♕f6** 8 ♘a3 ♗xa3 9 ♕a4 ♗d7 10 ♕a3 ♘e7 11 ♕b3 (also good is 11 ♗e2 0–0 12 d3) 11 … 0–0 12 ♕b7 (or 12 cd ♕xd4 13 d3!) 12 … ♗c6 13 ♕c7 ♖fc8 14 ♕a5 ♗e4 15 d3 ♖c5 16 ♕a6 with better chances for White (Ehlvest–Kupreichik, Kuibyshev 1986).

(b3) **7 … c6** 8 b4 ♗b6 9 ♕b3 ♕f6 10 ♗b2 ♘h6 11 ♘a3 0–0 12 ♖ae1 ♘g4 13 cd ♗xd4 14 ♗xd4 ♕xd4 15 ♕c3 ♕xc3 16 bc b5 with approximate equality (Schmittdiel–Tukmakov, Dortmund 1988).

(b4) **7 … ♘f6** 8 cd ♗xd4 9 ♕a4+ ♔f8 10 ♗xf7 c5 11 ♗b3 ♘e4 12 ♘c3 and White's chances are clearly better (Romanishin).

A23

6 c3 c6 *(67)*

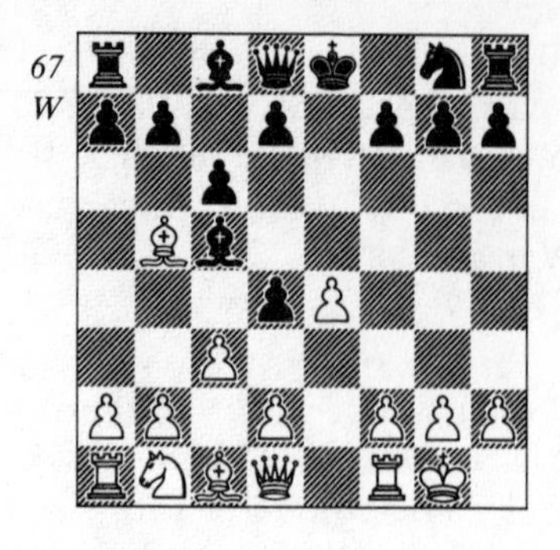

And now:

(a) **7 ♗c4** d5 (7 … d6 8 d3 ♕f6 9 a4 a5 10 ♘d2 ♘e7 11 ♘b3 0–0 12 ♘xc5 dc 13 ♕h5 — Zapata–Delaune, St. John 1988) 8 ed cd 9 ♗d3 ♕h4 10 ♗b5 ♔f8 11 b3!? ♘f6 12 ♗a3 ♗xa3 13 ♘xa3 a6 14 ♗d3 ♗g4 15 f3 ♗d7 16 ♘c2 with a minimal advantage to White (Zapata–Klaric, Sochi 1989).

(b) **7 ♗a4** ♘e7 8 d3 d5 (8 … ♗b6 9 cd ♗xd4 10 ♔f1 0–0 11 f4; Hübner–Nunn, Brussels 1986) 9 ♘d2 bc 10 bc 0–0 11 d4 with slight pressure for White (Hübner–Martz, Chicago 1982).

(c) **7 ♗d3!?** d5 8 ed ♕xd5 9 b4 ♗e7 10 ♖e1 ♘f6 11 b5 ♗e6 12 bc bc 13 ♕a4 0–0 14 ♕d4 ♕xd4 15 cd ♖fd8 and chances are equal (Timman–Belyavsky, Tilburg 1986).

These variations show that the plan of 5 … ♗c5 appears to offer quite good prospects.

B

3 … g6

This was first played in the game Loyd–From, Paris 1867. After that it was occasionally adopted by Steinitz, Pillsbury and Alekhine, but then the variation disappeared from tournament practice for some time. That it is now again in fashion is due in no small part to Smyslov.

White has two main plans:

B1 4 c3
B2 4 d4

The line 4 0–0 ♗g7 5 c3 has no independent significance, since it transposes to the first variation. Not very promising is 4 ♘c3 ♗g7 (also quite good is 4 … ♘d4) 5 d3 ♘ge7 6 ♗g5 h6 7 ♗h4 g5! 8 ♗g3 d6 9 h3 a6 10 ♗a4 b5 11 ♗b3 ♘a5 with full equality for Black (Rajna–Smyslov, Szolnok 1975).

B1

4 c3 d6

If 4 … ♗g7 then 5 d4 ed (5 … ♘ge7 6 d5!, followed by d5–d6, and Black has difficulties) 6 cd ♘ce7 7 ♘c3 ♘f6 8 e5 ♘fd5 9 ♘xd5 ♘xd5 10 ♕b3 and White has a strong initiative (Keres).

Often played is 4 … a6. After 5 ♗a4 there arises a position of the Steinitz Defence Deferred. The following variations are also possible:

(a) **5 ♗c4** d6 6 d4 ♗g7 7 ♗g5 ♘f6 8 ♘bd2 0–0 9 de de 10 ♕e2 h6 11 ♗h4 ♕e7 12 0–0 with slight pressure for White (Rozentalis–Georgadze, Minsk 1986).

(b) **5 ♗xc6** dc 6 0–0 ♗g7 7 d4 ed 8 cd ♘e7 (8 … ♗g4) 9 ♘c3 ♗g4 10 ♗e3 0–0 11 h3 ♗xf3 12 ♕xf3 f5 (12 … ♗xd4!?) 13 ♗g5 ♕d7 14 ♗xe7 ♕xe7 15 e5 ♖ad8 16 ♖ad1 c5! with equality (Chandler–Spassky, Vienna 1986).

5 d4

Not very promising for White is 5 ♗xc6+ bc 6 d4 f6 7 de de! with a level game.

5 … ♗d7 *(68)*

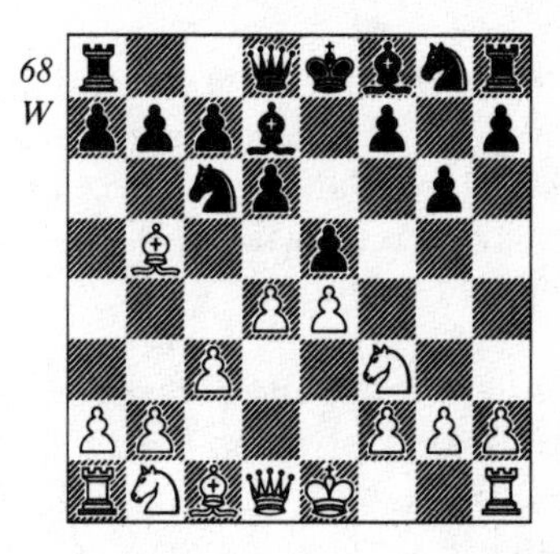

In this position the following variations are possible:

(a) **6 0–0** ♗g7 7 ♕b3 (after 7 de de — 7 … ♘xe5 8 ♘xe5 de 9 ♕b3! — 8 ♕e2 ♘ge7 9 ♖d1 0–0 10 ♗g5 ♕e8 11 ♘a3 a6 12 ♗a4 ♔h8 13 ♖d2 ♖d8 14 ♖ad1 ♗c8 the game is level; Hartston–Smyslov, Teesside 1975) 7 … ♘a5 8 ♕a4 c6 9 ♗e2 b5 10 ♕c2 ♘e7 11 ♗e3 0–0 12 de de 13 a4! ♕c7 14 b4 with advantage to White (Kupreichik–Smyslov, USSR Ch. 1976).

(b) **6 de** de 7 ♕e2 ♗g7 8 ♗e3 ♘ge7 9 ♘bd2 a6 10 ♗c4 ♕c8 11 0–0 0–0 12 b4 gives White some initiative (Tal–Smyslov, Biel 1976).

(c) **6 ♕b3!?** ♘a5 7 ♕a4 c6?! (7 … ♘c6 8 0–0 and then ♖d1 with an initiative for White) 8 ♗e2 b5 9 ♕c2 ♗g7 10 0–0 ♘e7 11 de! de 12 a4 a6 13 ♖d1 ♕c8 14 ♗e3

♘b7 15 c4 with pressure for White (Dolmatov–Kholmov, Sochi 1988). Note also that 6 ♗xc6 ♗xc6 7 de de promises White nothing.

B2

4 d4

An old and natural continuation. White immediately attacks Black's foundations in the centre. Practice has shown that Black has sufficient resources.

4 ... ed

After 4 ... ♘xd4 5 ♘xd4 ed 6 ♕xd4 ♕f6 7 e5 (after 7 ♕d3 ♗g7 8 ♘c3 c6, or 7 ♗e3 ♗g7 8 c3 ♕xd4 9 ♗xd4 ♘f6, chances are equal) 7 ... ♕b6 8 ♕d3! a6 9 ♗c4 ♕a5+ 10 ♘c3 ♕xe5+ 11 ♗e3 d5 12 0–0–0! White's initiative is extremely dangerous.

5 ♗g5 *(69)*

After 5 ♘xd4 ♗g7 6 ♘xc6 bc 7 ♗c4 ♘e7 8 ♘c3 d6 9 0–0 ♗e6 10 ♗b3 0–0 11 ♗e3 c5 Black has a good game (Lasker–Pillsbury, Hastings 1895).

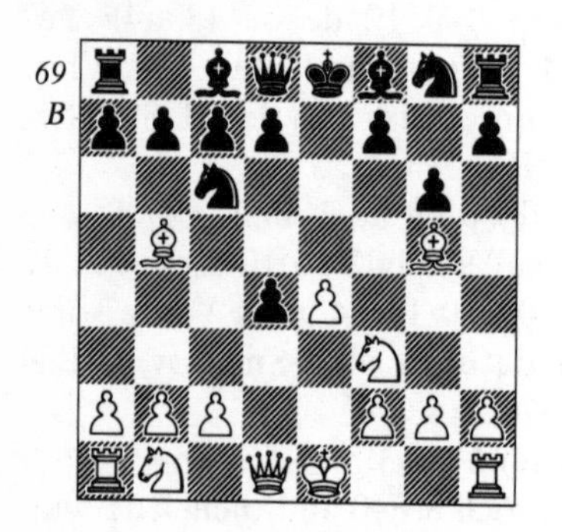

5 ... ♗e7

After 5 ... f6 6 ♗h4 (also good is 6 ♗f4 ♗g7 7 h4!? ♕e7 — 7 ... ♘h6; 7 ... a6 — 8 0–0 ♘e5 9 ♘xd4 ♘h6 10 ♘c3 c6 11 ♗e2 0–0 12 ♕d2 ♔f7 13 h5!; Kovalev–Maryasin, USSR 1986) 6 ... ♗g7 7 0–0 (or 7 ♘xd4 ♘ge7 8 ♗c4) 7 ... ♘ge7 8 ♗c4 ♘a5 9 ♕xd4 ♘ec6 10 ♕d5 ♘xc4 11 ♕xc4 d6 12 ♘c3 ♗g4 13 ♘d4!? ♘xd4 14 ♕xd4 g5 15 ♗g3 h5 16 h3 ♗e6 17 f4 with definite pressure for White (Nunn).

6 ♗xe7

After 6 h4!? (interesting is 6 ♗f4) 6 ... h6 7 ♗f4 ♘f6 8 ♘xd4 ♘xe4 9 0–0 ♗xh4 10 ♕d3 ♘d6 chances are roughly equal (Akopian).

6 ... ♘gxe7

After 6 ... ♕xe7 7 0–0 ♘f6 (7 ... ♕b4?! 8 ♗d3 d6 — 8 ... ♕xb2!? — 9 a3 ♕b6 10 ♘bd2 ♗g4 11 b4 a6 12 ♘c4 White has the better chances; Serper–Dreev, Minsk 1986) 8 ♗xc6 dc 9 ♕xd4 with a minimal advantage to White.

7 ♘xd4

7 0–0 ♘f6 8 e5 ♘h5 9 ♖e1 0–0 10 ♘d2 ♖d8 leads to a level game (Timoshenko–Georgadze, USSR 1989).

7 ... d5

Or 7 ... 0–0 8 ♘c3 a6 9 ♘xc6 bc 10 ♗d3 d5 with equal chances (Matanovic–Trifunovic, Skopje 1956).

8 ♘c3 de

And now:

(a) **9 ♘xe4** 0–0 10 ♗xc6 ♘xc6 11 ♘xc6 bc 12 0–0 ♗f5 13 ♖e1 ♖e8 with equality (Boleslavsky–

Trifunovic, Belgrade 1956).

(b) **9 ♗xc6+** ♘xc6 10 ♘xc6 ♕xd1+ 11 ♖xd1 bc 12 ♘e4 ♗f5 13 0–0!? (Nunn–Salov, Skelleftea 1989). With 13 … ♗xe4 14 ♖fe1 f5 15 f3 ♔e7 16 fe f4 17 ♖d3 Black could have obtained an acceptable position, although White has somewhat better chances.

C

3 … ♘ge7

This old continuation was revived by Larsen and nowadays is enjoying renewed popularity. The following lines are possible:

(a) **4 ♘c3** g6 (after 4 … ♘g6 5 d4 ed 6 ♘xd4 ♗c5 7 ♗e3 ♗xd4 8 ♗xd4 0–0 9 ♗e3 White has a clear positional advantage) 5 d4 ed (or 5 … ♗g7 6 ♗g5 h6 7 ♗e3 ed 8 ♘xd4 0–0 9 ♕d2 and 0–0–0) 6 ♘d5 ♗g7 7 ♗g5 (after 7 ♗f4 ♘xd5 8 ed ♘e7 9 d6 cd 10 0–0 0–0 11 ♗xd6 ♖e8 Black has an excellent game; Zaitsev–Dreev, Moscow 1989) 7 … h6 8 ♗f6 ♗xf6 9 ♘xf6+ ♔f8 10 0–0 ♔g7 11 ♘d5 ♖e8 12 ♖e1 d6 13 ♕d2 with a minimal advantage to White (Lanka–Banas, Trnava 1989).

(b) **4 c3** g6 (4 … d5?! 5 ♕e2! — Suetin) 5 0–0 ♗g7 6 d4 ed 7 cd d5 8 ed ♘xd5 9 ♖e1 ♗e6 10 ♗xc6 (in the game Mokry–Banas, Vienna 1988, play continued: 10 ♗g5 ♕d6 11 ♘c3 — 11 ♘d2 — 11 … 0–0 — 11 … ♘xc3 12 bc 0–0 and ♗d5 — 12 ♘e4 ♕b4 13 ♗xc6 bc 14 ♕c1 ♖fe8 — 14 … ♗xd4?! — 15 ♗d2 ♕b6 16 ♘c5 ♗f5 17 ♘e5 with pressure for White) 10 … bc 11 ♗g5 ♕d6 12 ♘bd2 (also possible is 12 ♘c3 ♘xc3 13 bc 0–0 14 ♕d2 c5 15 ♗h6 cd 16 ♗xg7 ♔xg7 17 ♘xd4; Zaid–Khermlin, USSR 1968) 12 … 0–0 13 ♕c1 ♖fe8 14 ♘e4 ♕b4 15 ♗d2 ♕b5 16 ♘e5 ♗f5 17 ♘c5 with some pressure for White (Gelfand–Dreev, Moscow 1989). Worse is 17 ♘g3?! ♘e7 18 ♗h6 ♗xh6 19 ♕xh6 f6! when Black has the better chances (Geller–Dreev, USSR 1989).

D

Some rare third moves for Black:

(a) **3 … ♕f6** 4 ♘c3 ♘ge7 (after 4 … ♘d4 5 ♘xd4 ed 6 ♘d5 ♕g5 7 ♘xc7+ ♔d8 8 ♘xa8 ♕xb5 9 d3 b6 10 ♗f4 d6 11 a4 ♕c6 12 ♕h5 g6 13 ♕b5 ♕xa8 14 a5! White has a big advantage — Alekhine) 5 d3 ♘d4 6 ♘xd4 ed 7 ♘e2 c6 8 ♗a4 d5 9 0–0 g6 10 b4 ♕d6 11 a3 ♗g7 12 ♗b2 and White's prospects are clearly better (Bogolyubov–Ed. Lasker, New York 1924).

(b) **3 … ♕e7** 4 ♘c3 ♘d8 5 d4! c6 6 de cb 7 ♘d5 ♕c5 8 ♗e3 ♕c4 9 b3 ♗b4+ 10 c3 ♗xc3+ 11 ♘d2 ♕xe4 12 ♘xc3 ♕xg2 13 ♕f3 with an advantage to White (Shakhmaty v SSSR No. 3, 1982).

(c) **3 … ♗b4** 4 c3 ♗a5 5 ♘a3 (after 5 0–0 ♘ge7 6 d4 ed 7 cd d5! 8 ed ♕xd5 9 ♘c3 ♗xc3 10 ♗xc6+ ♘xc6 11 bc 0–0 the chances are equal) 5 … ♗b6 (worse is 5 … d6 6 ♘c4 ♗b6 7 d4 with pressure for White) 6 ♘c4 ♘f6 7 ♗xc6 bc 8 ♘cxe5 ♘xe4 9 ♕e2 d5 10 d3 ♗a6 11 c4?! f6! with sharp play and chances for both sides.

5 Exchange Variation

This 'evergreen' system occurs after 1 e4 e5 2 ♘f3 ♘c6 3 ♗b5 a6:

4 ♗xc6 dc

One may say without the slightest hesitation that the Exchange Variation has existed ever since the beginning of theory in the Spanish Opening. The idea behind it consists in White's obtaining a pawn majority on the kingside, in return for which Black is given the advantage of the two bishops. Adherents of the Exchange Variation include two former World Champions — Emanuel Lasker and, many years later, Bobby Fischer. Nowadays the system where White plays 5 0–0 is the centre of attention.

Before considering the main variations, let us look at the reply 4 … bc. Practice has shown that Black has serious difficulties after this move. For example: 5 ♘c3 (also good is 5 d4 ed 6 ♕xd4 ♕f6 7 e5 ♕g6 8 0–0, or 5 ♘xe5 ♕g5 6 ♘f3 ♕xg2 7 ♖g1 ♕h3 8 d4 ♘f6 9 ♖g3 ♕h5 10 ♘c3) 5 … d6 6 d4 f6 7 ♗e3 ♘e7 8 ♕d3 ♗e6 9 0–0–0 ♘g6 10 h4 h5 11 ♘d2! (Padevsky–Daskalov, Bulgaria 1972).

After 4 … dc White has two main alternatives:

A 5 ♘c3
B 5 0–0

A

5 ♘c3 *(70)*

White achieves nothing after either 5 ♘xe5 ♕d4! or 5 d3 ♗c5. After 5 d4 ed 6 ♕xd4 ♕xd4 7 ♘xd4 ♗d7 8 ♗e3 0–0–0 9 ♘c3 ♖e8 10 0–0–0 ♗b4 11 ♘de2 f5 12 ef ♗xf5 13 a3 ♗d6 Black has a good game (Smyslov–Keres, USSR Ch. 1940).

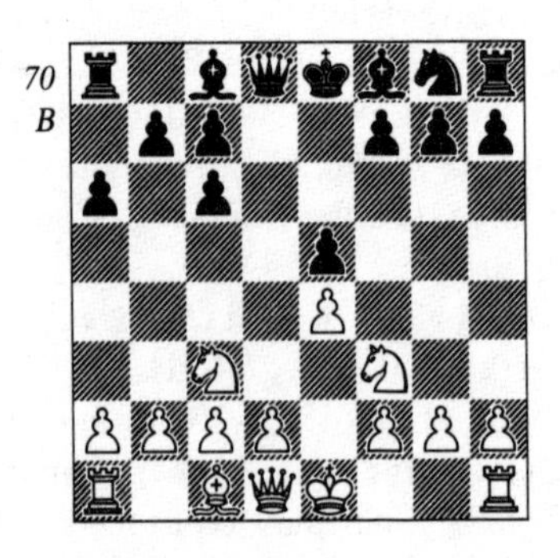
70
B

5 … f6

Another possibility for Black is 5 … ♕d6 (White has the better chances after: 5 … ♘f6 6 ♘xe5;

or 5 … ♗d6 6 d4; or 5 … ♗c5 6 ♘xe5 ♕g5 7 d4 ♕xg2 8 ♕f3 ♕xf3 9 ♘xf3; or 5 … ♗b4 6 ♘xe5 ♕g5 7 ♘f3 ♕xg2 8 ♖g1 ♕h3 9 ♖xg7) 6 d4 (6 d3) 6 … ed 7 ♘xd4 (7 ♕xd4 ♗g4!) 7 … ♕g6 8 ♕f3 ♗g4 9 ♕g3 0–0–0 10 h3 ♗d7 with equality (Goldenov–Bronstein, USSR Ch. 1952).

6 d4

6 d3(?) ♗d6 7 ♗e3 c5 8 ♘e2 ♘e7 etc. is passive.

6 … ed

7 ♕xd4

After 7 ♘xd4 c5 8 ♘de2 ♕xd1+ 9 ♘xd1 ♗e6 10 ♗f4 (10 ♘e3 ♗d6 11 ♗d2 ♘e7 is not dangerous for Black) 10 … 0–0–0 11 ♘e3 ♗c6 (after 11 … ♘e7 12 ♖d1! ♖xd1+ 13 ♔xd1 ♘c6 14 ♗g3 ♘d4 15 b3 ♗e7 16 c3 ♘b5 17 ♔c2 ♖e8 18 ♖d1 ♗f8 19 ♘f4 White has the better chances; Sorokin–Magerramov, USSR 1989) 12 f3 ♘e7 and Black has no particular worries (Lasker–Schlechter, London 1899).

7 … ♕xd4

8 ♘xd4

After 8 … ♗d7 (or 8 … ♗d6 9 ♘de2 ♘e7 10 ♗f4 ♘g6 11 ♗xd6 cd 12 0–0–0 ♔e7) 9 ♗e3 0–0–0 10 0–0–0 ♘e7 11 h3 ♘g6 12 ♘b3 ♗b4 13 ♘e2 ♖he8 Black has no difficulties (Bronstein–Smyslov, Zürich 1953).

B

5 0–0 *(71)*

Now Black has a wide choice:

B1 5 … ♗g4

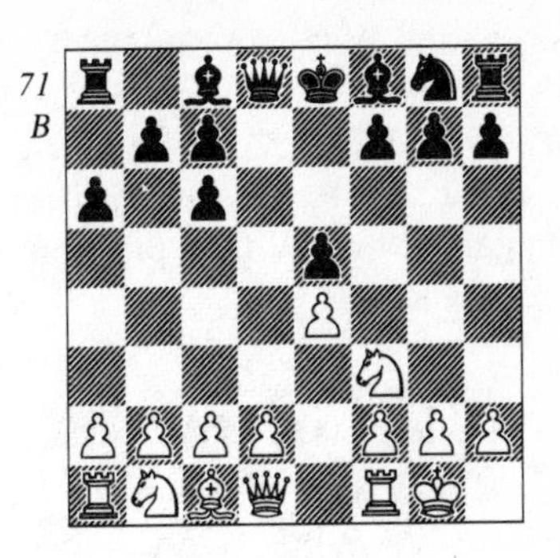
71
B

B2 5 … f6

B3 5 … ♘e7

B4 5 … ♕d6

Other moves are rarely seen:

(a) **5 … ♕e7** 6 d4 ed 7 ♕xd4 ♕f6 8 ♕a4 (also good is 8 ♕xf6 ♘xf6 9 ♗f4!) 8 … ♗g4 9 e5 ♕g6 10 ♘g5 ♗f5 11 ♕b3.

(b) **5 … ♕f6** 6 d4 ed 7 ♗g5 ♕g6 8 ♕xd4 ♗d6 9 ♘bd2 ♗e6 10 ♖e1 ♘e7 11 ♘c4! ♖ad8 12 ♘xd6 cd 13 e5! (analysis by Gipslis).

(c) **5 … ♗d6** 6 d4 ed 7 ♕xd4 f6 8 e5!? fe 9 ♘xe5 ♕e7 10 ♖e1 ♗e6 11 ♘f3 0–0–0 12 ♗g5 ♘f6 13 ♗xf6 gf 14 ♕e3 (Strain–Roring, corr. 1972).

(d) **5 … ♗e7** 6 d4 or 6 d3 ♕d6 7 ♘bd2.

In all these variations White has the better chances.

B1

5 … ♗g4

6 h3 h5!? *(72)*

After 6 … ♗xf3 7 ♕xf3 ♕d7 8 d3 ♗d6 9 ♘d2 ♘e7 10 ♘c4 0–0 11 ♗e3 f5 12 ef ♖xf5 13 ♕e2 ♘g6 14 ♘d2 ♖af8 15 ♘e4 (Nunn–

Korchnoi, Wijk aan Zee 1985), or 6 … ♗h5?! 7 g4 ♗g6 8 ♘xe5 ♕h4 9 ♕f3 f6 10 ♘xg6 hg 11 ♔g2 0–0–0 12 d3 (Panteleev–Khristov, Bulgaria 1965), White's position is preferable.

72
W

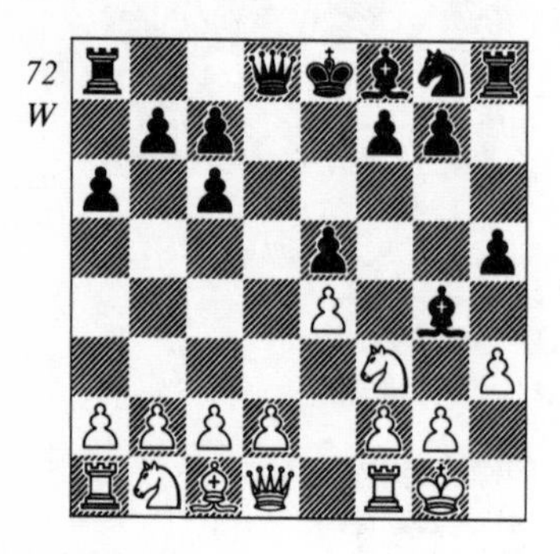

7 d3

White has nothing but problems after 7 d4 ♗xf3 8 ♕xf3 ♕xd4 9 ♖d1 ♕c4, or 7 ♖e1 ♕f6 8 hg?! hg 9 ♘xe5 ♕xe5 10 ♕xg4 ♘f6 11 ♕f3 0–0–0. After 7 c3 ♕d3 (also good is 7 … ♕f6 8 d4 ♗xf3!, or 7 … ♗c5) 8 ♖e1 (a drawing line is 8 hg hg 9 ♘xe5 ♗d6 10 ♘xd3 — 10 ♘xg4? ♘f6! — 10 … ♗h2+) 8 … ♗xf3 9 ♕xf3 ♕xf3 10 gf 0–0–0 11 ♔f1 ♗e7 12 ♔e2 ♗g5 Black has full equality.

7 … ♕f6 *(73)*

And now:

(a) **8 ♘bd2** ♘e7 9 ♖e1 (or 9 ♘c4 ♗xf3 10 ♕xf3 ♕xf3 11 gf ♘g6 12 ♗e3 0–0–0) 9 … ♘g6 10 d4 ♗d6 11 hg hg 12 ♘h2 ♖xh2 13 ♕xg4 ♕h4 (after 13 … ♖h4?! 14 ♕f5 ♘e7 15 ♕xf6 gf 16 c3 White stands better — Gipslis) 14 ♕xh4 ♖xh4 15 ♘f3 ♖h8 16 ♗e3 f6 17 g3 0–0–0 with equality (Mohrlok–Bilyap, Vrnjacka Banja 1967).

73
W

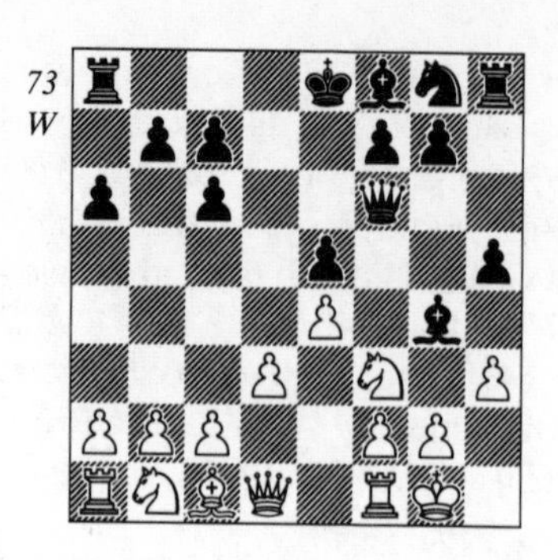

(b) **8 ♗e3** ♗xf3 9 ♕xf3 ♕xf3 10 gf ♗d6 11 ♔h1 f6 12 ♘d2 ♘e7 and Black has no difficulties (Ljubojevic–Spassky, Tilburg 1978).

(c) **8 hg?** hg 9 ♘g5 ♕h6 10 ♘h3 ♕h4! with an irresistible attack for Black.

B2

5 … f6

This positional continuation is perhaps the most solid.

6 d4

Black has two main replies: to maintain the tension in the centre with 6 … ♗g4; or to clarify the situation immediately with 6 … ed.

B21 6 … ♗g4
B22 6 … ed

B21

6 … ♗g4 *(74)*

And here there is a choice:

B211 7 c3
B212 7 de

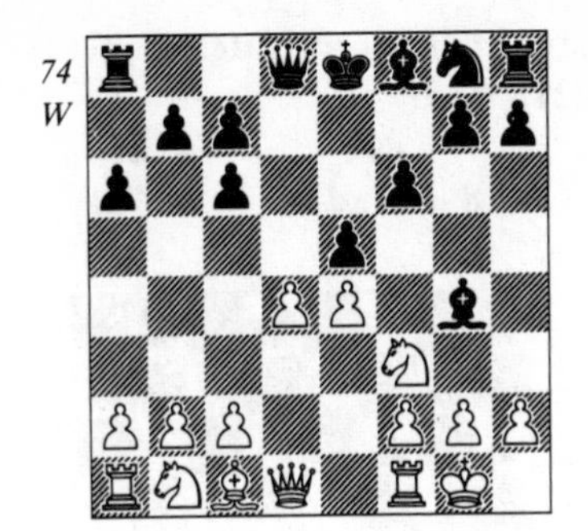

74
W

B211

7 c3 ♗d6

Other possibilities:

(a) **7 … ed** (7 … ♘e7 8 ♗e3!) 8 cd ♕d7 9 h3 ♗e6 10 ♘c3 0–0–0 11 ♗f4 ♘e7 12 ♖c1 ♘g6 13 ♗g3 with a clearly better position for White (Fischer–Gligoric, Havana OL 1966).

(b) **7 … ♕d7** 8 h3 ♗xf3 9 ♕xf3 ed 10 cd ♕xd4!? 11 ♖d1 ♕c4 12 ♗f4 ♗d6 13 ♗xd6 cd 14 ♖xd6 ♘h6! 15 ♘a3 ♕b4 16 ♖ad1 0–0 17 ♖1d2 ♘f6 with equality (Timman–Belyavsky, Linares 1988).

After 7 … ♗d6 White has the following lines:

B2111 8 ♗e3
B2112 8 ♘bd2
B2113 8 de

Also to be considered is 8 h3. For example: 8 … ♗h5 9 ♖e1 ♕e7 10 ♗e3 ♘h6 11 ♘bd2 ♔f7 12 ♕b3 ♘d8 13 de fe 14 ♗g5 ♕e6 15 ♗xd8 ♕xb3 16 ♘xb3 ♖xd8 with equal chances (Hort–Gligoric, Sousse 1967).

B2111

8 ♗e3 ♕e7

The following moves have also been tried:

(a) **8 … ♘e7** 9 ♘bd2 ♕d7 10 de (10 ♕b3 ♗e6!; 10 ♘c4 ♘g6!) 10 … fe 11 h3 (also good is 11 ♘c4 ♘g6 12 h3 ♗e6 13 ♕e2 0–0 14 ♘g5!; Petrushin–Kharitonov, Smolensk 1986) 11 … ♗e6 12 c4 ♘g6 13 c5 ♗e7 14 ♕c2 0–0 15 ♖fd1 ♗f6 16 ♘g5! with a dangerous initiative for White (Gerasimov–Savon, Kiev 1967).

(b) **8 … ♘h6** 9 de (also good is 9 ♗xh6) 9 … fe 10 h3 ♗h5 11 ♘bd2 ♘f7 12 ♕b3 ♕c8 13 c4 c5 14 ♕a4+ with pressure for White (Tatai–Westerinen, Amsterdam 1970).

(d) **8 … ♕d7** 9 h3 ed 10 cd ♗e6 11 ♘c3 and here Black has difficulties.

9 ♘bd2 0–0–0!
10 ♕c2 *(75)*

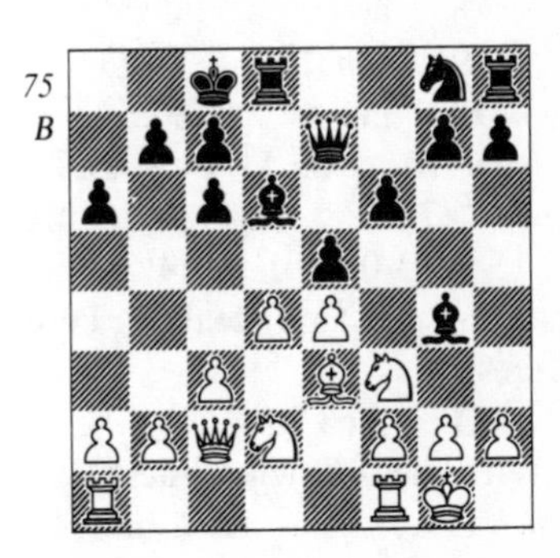

75
B

And now:

(a) **10 … ed** 11 cd ♖e8 12 e5 ♗b4 13 h3 ♗e6 14 ♘e4 ♕f7 15 a3 ♗b3 16 ♕b1 ♗f8 with equal chances (Smyslov–Geller, USSR Ch. 1973).

(b) **10 ... Qe8** 11 de fe 12 c4 Qe6 13 c5 Be7 14 b4 Nf6 15 a4 Nd7 16 b5 (Dementiev–Klovan, USSR 1971). Here, and after either 10 ... Nh6 11 de Bxe5 12 Nxe5 fe 13 Nc4, or 10 ... g5(?) 11 de Bxe5 12 Nxe5 fe 13 Nc4, White clearly has the better chances.

B2112

8 Nbd2

And now:

(a) **8 ... Nh6** 9 h3 Be6 10 Nb3! Nf7 11 Na5 Qc8 12 Nh2 c5 13 de fe 14 Qe2 b5 15 f4 with sharp play and chances for both sides (Kopylov–Kuuskmaa, corr. 1970).

(b) **8 ... Qe7** 9 Nc4! 0–0–0 10 h3 Bh5 11 Na5 Qd7 12 Be3 Ne7 13 Qb3 b6 14 Qc4 b5 15 Qe2 and Black's position is difficult (Belyavsky–Radulovic, Ohrid 1972).

B2113

8	**de**	**fe**
9	**Qb3!?**	**Bxf3**
10	**gf**	**Qc8**

After 10 ... b6 11 Qc4 Qd7 12 Be3 Ne7 13 Kh1 Ng6 14 Rg1 b5 15 Qb3 0–0–0 16 a4! White's chances are noticeably better (Keres).

11 Be3

With the following lines:

(a) **11 ... Nh6** 12 Nbd2 Nf7 13 Kh1 0–0 14 Rg1 Kh8 with complicated play (Dzhindzhikhashvili–Razuvaev, Tbilisi 1973).

(b) **11 ... Ne7** 12 Nd2 Qh3 13 Qxb7 0–0 14 Qb3+ Kh8 (Gipslis–Plachetka, Lublin 1972). By playing 15 Kh1, White could have maintained better chances.

B212

7	**de**	**Qxd1**
8	**Rxd1**	**fe** *(76)*

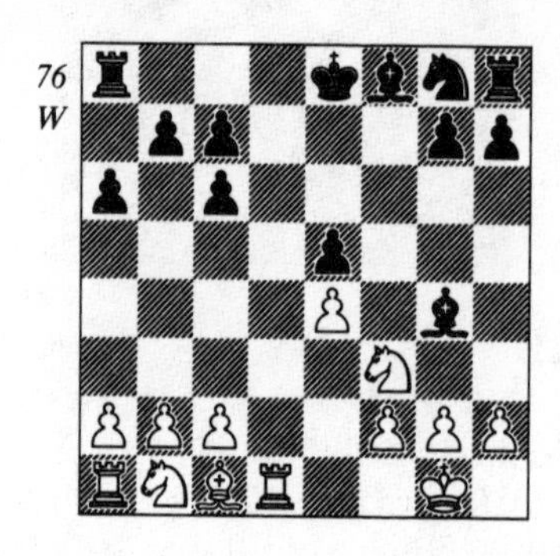

76
W

After 8 ... Bxf3 9 gf de 10 Be3 (10 f4 Nf6! 11 f3 Bd6 12 Nc3 ef with equality) 10 ... Bd6 11 Nd2 Ne7 12 Nc4 0–0–0 13 Rd3! b5 14 Na5 Bb4 15 Nb3 Rxd3 16 cd Ng6 17 Kf1! Rf8 18 Ke2 Nf4+ 19 Bxf4 Rxf4 20 Rg1 and White stands clearly better (Fischer–Rubinetti, Buenos Aires 1970).

9 Rd3! Bd6

An alternative is 9 ... Bxf3. For example:

(a) **10 Rxf3** Nf6 11 Nc3 Bb4 (interesting is 11 ... h6 12 Rd3 Bc5) 12 Bg5 Bxc3 13 bc (after 13 Rxc3 Nxe4 14 Re3 Nxg5 15 Rxe5+ Kf7 16 Rxg5 Rhd8 the game is level) 13 ... Rf8! 14 Bxf6 Rxf6 15 Rxf6 gf 16 Rd1 Ke7 17 Rd3 Rf8 18 Kf1 a5 19 g4 Rg8 20 h3 b5 21 Ke2 Ke6 22 Kf3 with a minimal advantage to White (Fischer–Smyslov, Monte Carlo 1967).

(b) **10 gf** Nf6 (10 ... Bd6) 11

♘d2 b5 12 a4 ♗d6 13 ♘b3 c5 14 ♘a5 c4 15 ♖d1 and White's position is preferable (Gipslis).

10 ♘bd2 *(77)*

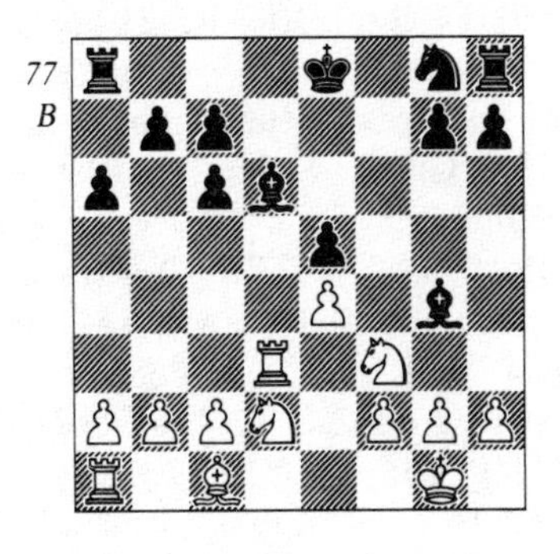

And now:

(a) **10 ... ♘f6** 11 ♘c4 (after 11 b3 0–0–0 12 ♗b2 ♗xf3 13 ♘xf3 ♘xe4 14 ♖e3 White stands slightly better) 11 ... 0–0 (after 11 ... ♘xe4 12 ♘fxe5! ♗e6 13 f3 ♗xe5 14 ♘xe5 ♘c5 15 ♖e3! 0–0–0 16 ♖e1 and White stands better; Adorjan–Harandi, Graz 1972) 12 ♘fxe5 ♗e2! 13 ♖e3 ♗xc4 14 ♘xc4 ♗c5 15 ♖e1 ♖ae8 16 ♗e3 ♗xe3 17 ♖xe3 ♖xe4 18 ♖xe4 ♘xe4 19 ♖d1 ♘d6! with equal chances (Ribli–Matanovic, Bath 1973).

(b) **10 ... b5** 11 b3 ♘e7 12 ♗b2 ♘g6 13 g3 0–0 14 ♔g2 c5 15 c4 ♖ab8 16 a4!? bc 17 ♘xc4 ♗xf3+ 18 ♖xf3 ♖xf3 19 ♔xf3 ♖xb3+ and Black has good chances of equality (Timman–Kasparov, match 1985).

B22

6 ... ed
7 ♘xd4

In this critical position Black has a choice between:

B221 7 ... c5
B222 7 ... ♘e7

B221

7 ... c5

7 ... ♗d6 is met fairly often. For example:

(a) **8 ♕h5+** g6 9 ♕f3 ♗xh2+ 10 ♔xh2 ♕xd4 11 ♖d1 ♕c4 12 ♗f4 ♕f7 13 ♕b3 ♕xb3 14 ab ♗e6 15 ♗xc7 ♘h6 16 ♘c3 0–0 17 ♘a4 ♖ae8 18 ♘c5 with pressure for White (Hecht–Gligoric, Teesside 1972).

(b) **8 ♘c3** ♘e7 9 ♕h5+ ♘g6 10 ♘f5 0–0 11 ♖d1 ♘e5 12 f4 ♘f7 13 ♘xd6 cd 14 a4 a5 15 ♗e3 ♕e7 16 ♖e1 and here White has the better chances (Barczay–Portisch, Sousse 1967).

Note that Black has no particular difficulties after 8 ♗e3 ♘e7 9 ♘d2 0–0 10 ♘c4 ♘g6, or 8 ♘f5?! ♗xf5 9 ef ♕d7 10 ♖e1+ ♔e7 11 ♕h5+ ♔f8.

After 7 ... c5 White has a choice between:

B2211 8 ♘b3
B2212 8 ♘e2

B2211

8 ♘b3 ♕xd1
9 ♖xd1

And now:

(a) **9 ... ♗d6** 10 ♘a5 ♘h6 (10 ... b5? 11 c4 ♘e7 12 ♗e3 favours White; Fischer–Portisch, Havana OL 1966) 11 ♗xh6 gh 12 ♘c4 ♗e7 13 ♘c3 ♔f7 14 ♘d5 ♗e6 with equal chances (Bagirov–Keres, Moscow 1967).

(b) **9 … ♗d7** 10 a4 (10 ♗f4) 10 … 0–0–0 11 ♗e3 b6 (Fischer–Anastasopoulos, Athens 1969). After 12 a5! c4 13 ab! cb 14 cb White has a dangerous attack.

(c) **9 … ♗g4!?** 10 f3 ♗e6 11 ♗f4 c4 12 ♘d4 0–0–0 13 ♘c3 ♗f7 14 ♘f5 ♖xd1+ 15 ♖xd1 ♘e7 16 ♘e3 ♘g6 17 ♗g3 ♗c5 18 ♔f2 ♖d8 with roughly equal chances (Vitolins–Romanishin, Kiev 1987).

B2212

8 ♘e2

With the following variations:

(a) **8 … ♕xd1** 9 ♖xd1 ♗d7 10 ♘c3 0–0–0 11 ♗f4 ♘e7 12 ♗g3 ♘c6 13 ♘d5 ♘e5 14 f4 ♘f7 with chances for both sides (Ljubojevic–Romanishin, Riga 1979).

(b) **8 … ♗e6** 9 ♘bc3 ♗d6 10 ♗f4 ♘e7 11 ♕d3 ♗xf4 12 ♘xf4 ♕xd3 13 ♘xd4 (Ljubojevic–Gligoric, match 1979). With 13 … b6 14 ♘f4 ♔f7 Black could have achieved approximate equality.

B222

7 … ♘e7(?!)
8 ♗e3

8 ♘c3 ♘g6 9 f4 c5 is not dangerous for Black, but an interesting line is 8 ♘a3!? ♘g6 9 ♘c4 ♕e7 (or 9 … ♗c5 10 ♗e3 0–0 11 ♘f5 ♗xe3 12 ♘cxe3 ♕xd1 13 ♖fxd1; Rytov–Klovan, USSR 1971) 10 ♖e1 ♕f7 11 ♕e2 c5 12 e5! cd 13 ef+ ♔d7 14 ♗g5 b6 (Shmit–Romanovsky, USSR 1971). By playing 15 h4!? White was able to maintain his initiative.

8 … ♘g6

And now:

(a) **9 ♕h5!?** ♗d6 10 ♘f5 0–0 11 f4! ♗xf5 12 ♕xf5 ♕e7 13 ♘d2 ♖ad8 14 ♖ae1 ♖fe8 15 c3 b5 16 g3 a5 17 ♖f2 ♕f7 18 b3 ♗f8 19 ♗d4 with better chances for White (Gipslis–Savon, USSR Ch. 1969).

(b) **9 ♘d2** ♗d6 10 ♘c4 (also good is 10 c3 0–0 11 ♕b3+ — or 11 f4 — 11 … ♔h8 12 ♘f5) 10 … 0–0 11 ♕d3 ♘e5 12 ♘xe5 ♗xe5 13 f4! ♗d6 14 f5 ♕e7 15 ♗f4 ♗xf4 16 ♖xf4 ♗d7 17 ♖e1 with strong pressure for White (Fischer–Unzicker, Siegen OL 1970).

(c) **9 ♘c3** ♗d6 10 ♘f5! 0–0 11 ♕g4 (not bad is 11 ♕h5 or 11 ♘xd6 cd 12 ♕d2) 11 … ♗e5 12 ♖ad1! ♕e8 13 ♗d4 ♗e6 14 f4 and White's position is preferable (Friedgood–Unzicker, Nice OL 1974).

B3

5 … ♘e7!? *(78)*

A 'patent' of Keres's.

78
W

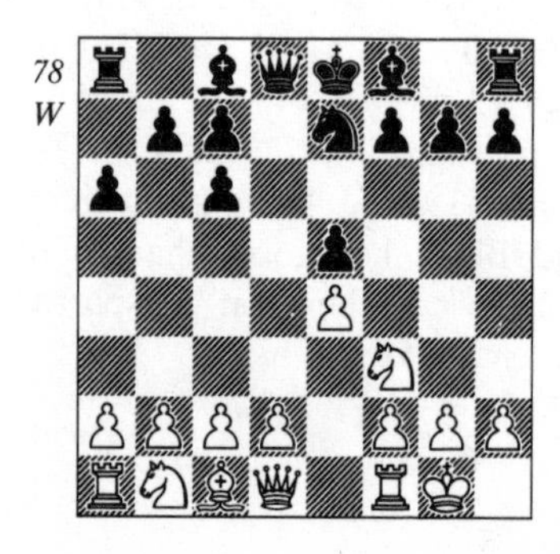

6 ♘xe5

The most common continuation. We note the following variations:

(a) **6 d4** ed 7 ♘xd4 c5 8 ♘b3 ♕xd1 9 ♖xd1 ♘g6 with equality (Keres).

(b) **6 c3** ♕d3 7 ♖e1 ♘g6 8 ♖e3 ♕d6 9 d4 ♗g4 10 ♖d3 ♕f6 11 h3 ♗xf3 12 ♖xf3 ♕h4 13 ♕b3 0–0–0 with excellent play for Black (Kholmov).

6 ... ♕d4
7 ♕h5 g6
8 ♕g5

An interesting alternative is 8 ♘f3 ♕xe4 9 ♘c3.

8 ... ♗g7
9 ♘d3

After 9 ♘f3 ♕xe4 10 ♖e1 ♕b4 11 d4 (after 11 c3 ♕d6 12 d4 h6 13 ♕e3 ♗e6, or 11 b3 h6 12 ♕e3 ♗e6 13 ♗a3 ♘d5, Black has at least equal chances) 11 ... ♗e6 12 c3 h6 13 ♕g3 ♕a5 14 b4 ♕a4 15 ♕xc7 ♘d5 16 ♕g3 0–0 17 ♗f4 ♗f5 any difficulties are White's (Tseitlin–Zaitsev, Odessa 1972).

9 ... f5
10 e5 *(79)*

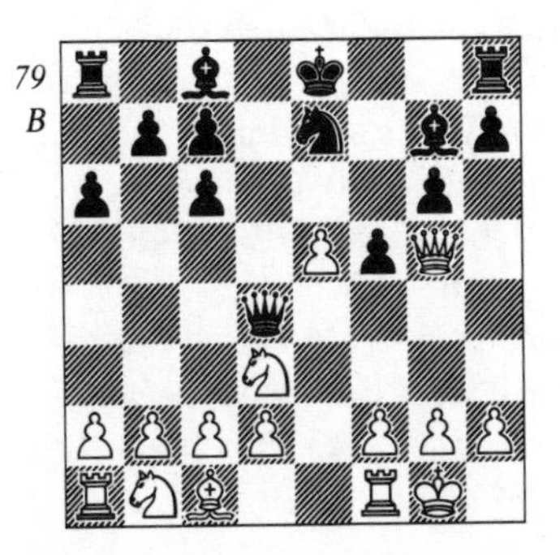

And now: 10 ... c5 11 b3!? h6 (after 11 ... ♕xa1?! 12 ♘c3 b6 13 ♗b2 ♕xf1+ 14 ♔xf1 White has the better chances) 12 ♕e3 f4! 13 ♕xd4 cd 14 ♗b2 ♗f5 15 ♘xf4 ♗xe5 16 ♘e2 0–0–0 17 d3 ♖he8! with full equality for Black (Martin–Medina, Olot 1973).

B4

5 ... ♕d6 *(80)*

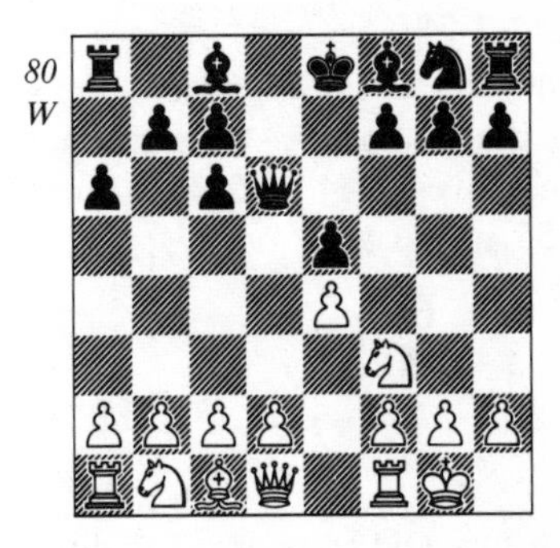

Black's plan involves castling long. Let us consider the following variations:

(a) **6 d4** ed 7 ♘xd4 ♗d7 8 ♗e3 0–0–0 9 ♘d2 ♘h6! 10 h3 ♕g6 11 ♕f3 f5 12 ♖ad1 fe 13 ♕xe4 ♘f5 14 ♘c4 ♖e8 15 ♘e5 ♖xe5 with equality (Naidenov–Sergiev, corr. 1982).

(b) **6 d3** f6 7 ♗e3 ♗g4 (after 7 ... ♗e6 8 ♘bd2 c5 9 ♘c4 ♕c6 10 ♘fd2 ♘e7 11 a4 b6 12 f4! with better chances for White — Schneider–Romanishin, Buenos Aires OL 1978) 8 ♘bd2 ♘e7 9 b4 ♘g6 10 h3 ♗e6 11 d4 ♕d7 12 a3 ♗e7 13 c4 0–0 14 ♕e2 ♕e8 15 ♖fd1 ♕f7 with full equality for Black.

6 Deferred Schliemann and Bayonet Attack

In this chapter we consider two unusual and slightly risky systems for Black after the standard opening moves 1 e4 e5 2 ♘f3 ♘c6 3 ♗b5 a6 4 ♗a4.

A 4 … f5
B 4 … b5

A

4 … f5 *(81)*

A rare and comparatively little-studied continuation known as the Deferred Schliemann, which is associated with sharp play, sometimes involving gambits. Although White has a number of lines giving him good prospects, until now no direct refutation of this system has been found.

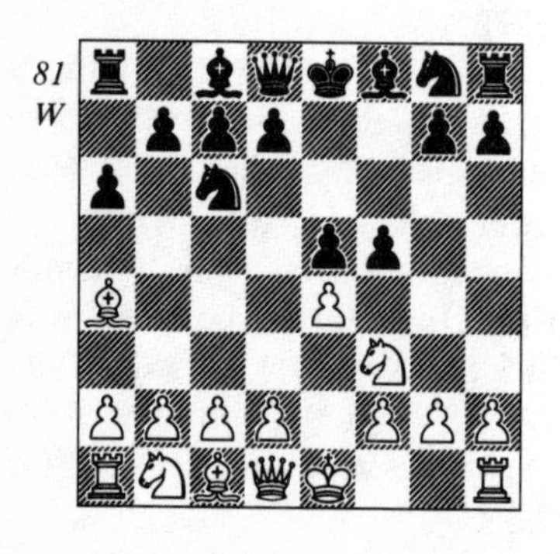
81
W

5 d4

This natural pawn advance in the centre poses the most difficult problems for Black. White has little to gain from 5 ♗xc6 dc 6 ♘xe5 ♕d4; or 5 ♕e2 fe 6 ♕xe4 b5! 7 ♗b3 ♘f6; or 5 d3 fe 6 de ♘f6.

But 5 ♘c3 is a serious alternative. For example, 5 … b5 6 ♗b3 b4 7 ♘d5 (after 7 ♘b1 fe 8 ♘xe5 ♕g5! 9 ♘xc6 dc 10 d3 ♕xg2 11 ♕h5+ g6 12 ♕e5+ ♘e7 13 ♕xe4 ♕xe4 14 de ♗g7 Black has equal chances) 7 … fe 8 d4! ef 9 ♕xf3 ♗e7 10 ♗g5 ♘f6 11 de ♘xd5 12 ♗xd5 ♘xe5 13 ♕e4 c6 14 ♕xe5 cd 15 0–0 ♔f8 16 ♗xe7+ ♕xe7 17 ♕xd5 ♖b8 18 ♖fe1 ♕f6 19 ♕c5+ with perpetual check (analysis by Moiseev).

5 … ed

In White's favour is 5 … fe 6 ♘xe5 ♕h4 7 0–0 ♘f6 8 ♘c3 ♘d8 9 f3 b5 10 ♗b3 d6 11 ♘d5 etc.

6 e5

After 6 ♘xd4 ♘xd4 7 ♕xd4 c5 8 ♕e5+ ♕e7 9 ♕xe7+ ♗xe7 10 ♗b3 fe 11 ♘c3 ♘f6 Black has a good game.

6 ... ♝c5

After 6 ... ♝b4+ 7 c3 dc 8 ♘xc3 (8 bc) 8 ... ♘ge7 9 0–0 d5 10 ed ♛xd6 11 ♛e2 0–0 12 ♗g5 ♝xc3 13 bc h6 14 ♖ad1 White has strong pressure (Nei–Vinogradov, Tallinn 1962).

7 0–0

Interesting complications arise after 7 c3!? dc 8 ♘xc3 ♘ge7 9 ♗b3 d5! 10 0–0 (or 10 ♘xd5 ♘xd5 11 ♗xd5 ♘b4) 10 ... ♝e6 11 ♖g5 ♝g8 12 ♕h5+ (12 e6 ♘d4 13 ♕h5+ g6 14 ♕h6 ♘xe6 15 ♘xe6 ♝xe6 16 ♕g7 ♜g8 17 ♕xh7 ♛d7 with good play for White) 12 ... g6 13 ♕h6 ♘xe5 14 ♘e2 ♘c6 15 ♕g7 ♛e7 16 ♕xh8 0–0–0 with excellent counterchances for Black.

7 ... ♘ge7

8 ♗b3

Other possibilities:

(a) **8 ♕e2** b5 9 ♗b3 ♘a5 10 ♘bd2 ♝b6 11 ♘g5 ♘xb3 12 ♕h5+ g6 13 ♕h6 ♘c5! 14 ♕g7 ♜f8 15 ♘xh7 ♘e6 with advantage to Black.

(b) **8 c3** dc 9 ♘xc3 (or 9 ♗b3!? d5 10 ♘xc3 ♘a5 11 ♗xd5 c6 12 ♗b3 ♛xd1 13 ♗xd1 b5?! 14 ♖b1 ♝b6 15 e6! 0–0 with an initiative for White; Romanishin–Pytel, Jurmala 1983) 9 ... d5 10 ♗g5! ♚f8 11 ♖c1 ♝a7 12 ♗xc6 bc 13 ♘e2 c5 14 ♘f4 c6 (Watson–Nunn, London 1984). After 15 b4! or 15 e6 White has good winning chances.

(c) **8 ♘g5?!** h6 9 ♕h5+ h6 10 ♕h4 ♘d5!

8 ... d5

9 ed ♛xd6

10 ♖e1 *(82)*

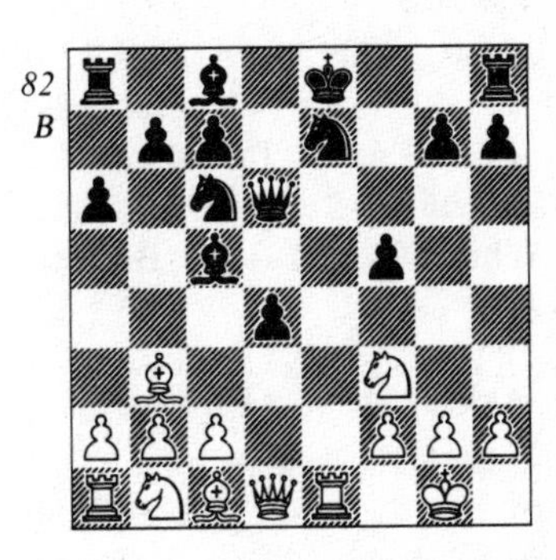

82
B

And now:

(a) **10 ... h6** 11 ♘bd2 (after 11 a4 ♝d7 12 ♘bd2 0–0–0 13 ♘c4 ♛f6 14 ♘ce5 ♘xe5 15 ♘xe5 ♝e8! Black has no worries) 11 ... b5 (after 11 ... ♛f6 12 ♘c4 ♚f8 13 ♘ce5 g5 14 c3 dc 15 bc ♚g7 16 ♘f7, or 11 ... ♘a5 12 ♘e5 ♘xb3 13 ♕h5+ g6 14 ♘xg6 ♘xa1 15 ♘xh8+ ♚d7 16 ♘c4!, Black's position is bad — it is necessary to control the c4 square!) 12 a4 ♝b7 (worse is 12 ... ♜b8 13 ab ab 14 ♘f1 ♚d8 15 c3 ♝d7 16 cd ♝xd4 17 ♖e2 f4 18 ♖d2 ♝g4 19 ♘xd4 ♝xd1 20 ♘xc6+ ♘xc6 21 ♖xd6+ cd 22 ♗xd1 with a decisive advantage to White; Masseev–Andreev, corr. 1960/1) 13 ab ab 14 ♖xa8 ♝xa8, with the following variations:

(a1) **15 ♕e2** d3?! 16 cd ♚d8 17 d4 ♘xd4 18 ♘xd4 ♝xd4 19 ♘f3 (Keres).

(a2) **15 ♖e6** ♛d7 16 ♕e2 d3! 17 cd ♚d8 18 d4! ♘xd4 19 ♘xd4

♗xd4 20 ♘f3 ♗xf3 21 ♕xf3 (Balashov).

In both cases Black has certain difficulties.

(b) **10 … b5** 11 a4 ♖b8 12 ab ab 13 ♗g5 ♔f8 14 ♘bd2 ♗d7 15 ♗xe7+ ♘xe7 16 ♘e5 ♗e8 17 ♘d3 ♗b6 18 ♖e6 with advantage to White (Klovan–Toth, Budapest 1970).

(c) **10 … ♗d7** 11 ♘bd2 b5 12 a4 ♖b8 13 ab ab 14 ♘g5 ♘d8 15 ♕h5 ♕g6 16 ♕xg6+ hg 17 ♘df3 ♗d6 18 ♘e5 and here White stands clearly better (Fuchs–Gragger, Tel Aviv 1964).

B

4	**…**	**b5**
5	**♗b3**	**♘a5** *(83)*

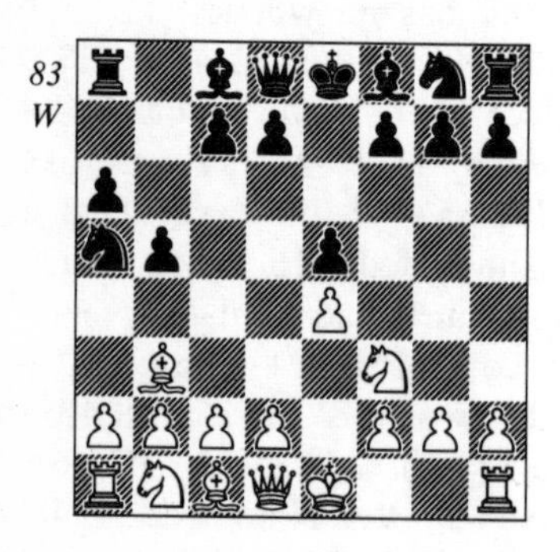

83
W

The investigation of this system, usually known as the Bayonet Attack, only began comparatively recently — in the 1950s. Black aims to exchange off White's active bishop quickly, for the sake of which he makes certain concessions in the centre. Practice has shown that it is not easy for Black to equalise.

White has two main continuations:

B1 6 0–0
B2 6 d4

Note that after 5 … ♗b7 6 d4 d6 7 c3 ♗e7 8 0–0 ♘f6 9 ♖e1, or 5 … ♗c5 6 a4! ♖b8 7 ab ab 8 0–0 d6 9 c3 ♗g4 10 ♗d5!, Black has difficulties.

B1

6	**0–0**	

White achieves nothing after either 6 ♗xf7+?! ♔xf7 7 ♘xe5+ ♔e7 8 ♘c3 ♕e8! when Black has the better chances, or 6 ♘xe5 ♘xb3 7 ab ♕g5 8 ♘f3 ♕xg2 9 ♖g1 ♕h3 10 ♘c3 ♗b7 11 d4 d6 with equality.

6	**…**	**d6**
7	**d4**	

A critical position, where Black has a choice between three moves.

B11 7 … f6
B12 7 … ♘xb3
B13 7 … ed

B11

7	**…**	**f6**

And now:

(a) **8 ♗e3** ♘xb3 (after 8 … ♘e7 9 de fe 10 ♘c3 ♘xb3 11 ab ♕d7 12 ♕d2 ♘g6 13 ♘d5, or 8 … ed 9 ♘xd4 c5 10 ♗b5, Black has serious difficulties) 9 ab ♘e7 10 c4 ♗b7 and Black has a constrained but solid position. There may follow 11 ♘c3 b4 (also possible is 11 … c6) 12 ♘d5 a5 with complicated play (Suetin).

(b) **8 ♗xg8** ♖xg8 9 ♘h4 (9 a4!?)

9 ... ♕d7 10 ♘c3 ♕g4 11 ♘f3 ♗b7 12 a4 b4 13 ♘d5 0–0–0 14 ♖e1 (14 ♘xb4 c5!) 14 ... f5! with excellent counterplay for Black (Ostojic–Johannessen, Amsterdam 1969). Worthy of consideration is 8 ♘h4.

B12

7 ... ♘xb3
8 ab f6 *(84)*

84
W

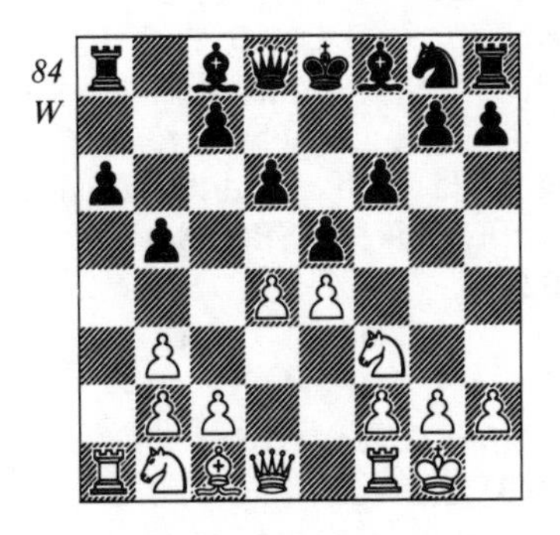

9 c4

Other possibilities:

(a) **9 ♘c3** ♕b7 10 ♘h4 (also not bad is 10 ♕e2 ♘e7 11 de de 12 ♖d1 ♕c8 13 ♕e3) 10 ... ♕d7 (or 10 ... ♘e7 11 de de 12 ♕f3 ♕d7 13 ♖d1 ♕e6 and Black's defence holds; Anand–Agdestein, Baguio 1987) 11 f4 0–0–0 12 ♘f3 ♘e7 13 de de 14 ♕xd7+ ♖xd7 15 fe b4 16 ♘a4 ♘g6 17 ef ♗xe4 and chances are roughly equal (Unzicker–Taimanov, Moscow 1956).

(b) **9 ♘h4** ♘e7 (9 ... ♕d7) 10 f4 ♗b7 11 d5 c6 12 c4 ef 13 ♖xf4 g5 14 ♕h5+ ♔d7 15 ♖xf6 with advantage to White (Arnason–Agdestein, Gausdal 1987).

(c) **9 ♕e2** g6 10 ♖d1 ♗g7 11 ♘c3 ♗d7 12 de fe 13 ♗g5 ♘f6 14 ♘d4 0–0 15 ♘e1 and White's position is preferable (Troianescu–Bilek, Hungary 1958).

9 ... b4

After 9 ... ♗b7 10 ♘c3 ♘e7 11 ♕e2 c6 12 ♖d1 ♕c7 13 ♗e3 White has a positional advantage (Fischer–Johannessen, Havana OL 1966).

After 9 ... b4 the following variations are possible:

(a) **10 ♘h4** ♘e7 (10 ... g6 11 f4 ef 12 ♗xf4 ♗g7 13 ♘f3 ♘e7 14 ♕d2 a5 15 ♗h6 is to White's advantage; Spassky–Sakharov, Leningrad 1960) 11 ♗e3 g6 12 ♕d2 ed 13 ♗xd4 ♗g7 14 ♗e3 a5 15 ♗h6 0–0 16 ♗xg7 ♔xg7 17 ♕e3 with pressure for White (Ernst–Agdestein, Gausdal 1987).

(b) **10 ♘e1!?** ♗b7 11 d5 c5 12 dc ♗xc6 13 ♘c2 a5 14 ♕d3 ♕c7 15 ♘e3 with better chances for White (Ivkov–Johannessen, Halle 1963).

(c) **10 ♗e3** ♘e7 11 ♘bd2 ♘g6 12 c5 ♗e7 13 cd cd 14 ♘c4 with pressure for White.

(d) **10 ♕d3** c5 11 dc dc 12 ♕xd8+ ♔xd8 13 ♗e3 ♔c7 14 ♘e1 a5 15 ♘d3 ♔c6 16 f4 ef 17 ♗xf4 ♘e7 18 ♘d2 ♘g6 19 ♗g3 ♗e7 20 ♖fd1 ♗g4 21 ♘f3 ♖hd8 22 ♘f2 ♖xd1 23 ♖xd1 ♗e6 with good chances of equality (Timman–Agdestein, Belgrade 1989).

B13

7 ... ed
8 ♘xd4 ♗b7 *(85)*

Other continuations:

(a) **8 … ♘xb3** 9 ab ♗b7 10 c4 b4 11 ♖e1 ♕d7 12 ♘d2 ♘e7 13 ♘f1 g6 14 ♘e3 ♗g7 15 ♘d5 with a clear advantage for White (Garcia–Evans, Havana 1964).

(b) **8 … ♗d7** 9 ♗d2 ♘xb3 10 ab g6 11 ♖e1 ♗g7 12 ♗c3! ♘f6 13 e5 de 14 ♖xe5+ ♔f8 and here White has an advantage (Keres). Also good is 9 ♕e1!? ♘xb3 10 ab ♗e7 11 e5!

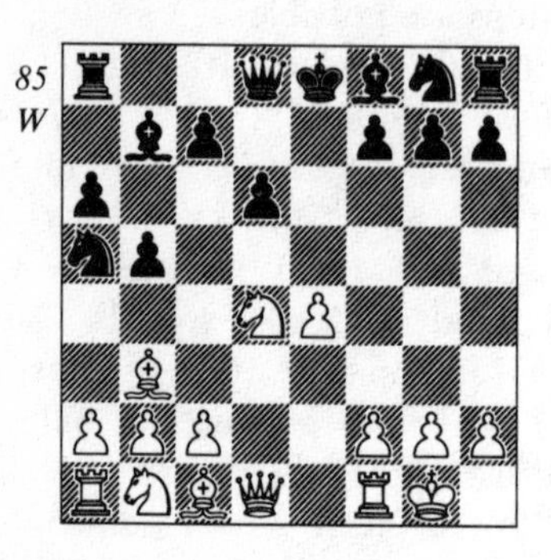

85
W

After 8 … ♗b7 the following variations are possible:

(a) **9 c4** c5 (9 … ♘xc4 10 ♗xc4 bc 11 ♘c3! ♘f6 12 ♗g5 ♗e7 13 ♘f5 is in White's favour) 10 ♘f5 (also good is 10 ♘c2 ♘f6 11 ♘c3) 10 … g6 11 ♘g3!? (11 ♘e3) 11 … ♗g7 12 ♘c3 b4 13 ♘d5 ♘f6 14 ♗a4+ ♔f8 15 a3 ♘xc4 16 ♘xf6 ♗xf6 17 ab with an initiative for White (Tseshkovsky–Kupreichik, Minsk 1985).

(b) **9 ♕e1** c5 10 ♗d2 ♘xb3 11 ♘xb3 ♗e7 12 ♘a5 ♖a7 13 a4 b4 14 ♘xb7 ♖xb7 15 ♕e2 ♖b6 16 ♖d1 ♘f6 17 ♗g5 0–0 18 ♘d2 d5 19 ed ♘xd5 20 ♗xe7 ♕xe7 21 ♕xe7 ♘xe7 22 ♘c4 with a clear advantage to White.

(c) **9 ♗d2** ♘xb3 (9 … c5 10 ♗d5!) 10 ♘xb3 (ab g6 11 c4 ♗g7 12 ♗c3 ♘f6 13 cb 0–0 14 ba?! — 14 f3 — 14 … ♗xe4 15 ♖e1 ♕c8 16 ♘d2 ♗d5 17 ♘c4 ♖xa6 18 ♖xa6 ♕xa6 with equal chances; A. Sokolov–Kupreichik, USSR Ch. 1985) 10 … ♘f6 11 ♖e1 ♗e7 12 ♘a5 ♖b8 13 ♘xb7 ♖xb7 14 ♕f3 ♕c8 15 ♘c3 c6 16 ♘e2 0–0 17 ♘d4 ♖e8 18 ♘f5 ♗f8 19 ♗g5 ♘d7 20 ♕g3 ♘c5 21 f3 ♘e6 22 ♗e3 d5 with equality (Ehlvest–Kupreichik, USSR 1984).

B2

6	**d4**	**ed**
7	**♕xd4**	**♘e7**

After 7 … ♘xb3 8 ab ♘e7 9 ♘c3 (also good is 9 0–0 or 9 ♗g5!?) 9 … ♘c6 10 ♕d3 ♗b4 11 0–0 ♗xc3 12 bc 0–0 13 c4 bc 14 ♕xc4 ♕f6 15 ♗a3 White has the better chances (Teschner–van den Berg, Dortmund 1957). Interesting is 7 … ♗b7!?

8	**♗g5**	**d6**

Worthy of consideration is 8 … ♘xb3 9 ab f6 10 ♗h4 ♗b7 11 0–0 d5!? 12 e5 ♘f5 13 ♕f4 ♘xh4 14 ♕xh4 ♕d7 15 e6 ♕d6 16 ♖e1 ♗e7 17 ♘c3 0–0–0 with unclear play (Sokolov–Johannessen, Belgrade 1962).

9	**e5**	**c5**
10	**♕d2**	**♘xb3**

After 11 ab de 12 ♕xd8+ ♔xd8 13 ♘xe5 ♗e6 chances are equal (Suetin).

7 Deferred Steinitz and Other Deferred Defences

Apart from the commonly played 4 … ♘f6, Black also has several other alternatives after 1 e4 e5 2 ♘f3 ♘c6 3 ♗b5 a6 4 ♗a4 which we shall deal with in this chapter. First we analyse the Deferred Steinitz, before moving on to other plans.

A 4 … d6
B 4 … others

A 4 … d6

Along with the modern Closed Systems and the Open Defence, the Steinitz Defence Deferred is acknowledged as one of the most important systems in the Spanish Opening. The strategic *leitmotif* of Black's play here is the support and consolidation of the important strongpoint in the centre, e5. The main systems are:

A1 5 c3
A2 5 0–0
A3 5 ♗xc6+

Alternatives are:

(a) **5 c4** (the Duras System), with the following lines:

(a1) **5 … ♗g4** 6 ♘c3 ♘f6 (worse is 6 … ♘e7? 7 h3 ♗xf3 8 ♕xf3 ♘g6 9 ♘d5 with pressure for White; but worthy of attention is 6 … g6 7 d3 ♗g7 8 ♘d5 h6) 7 h3 ♗xf3 8 ♕xf3 ♗e7 9 d3 0–0 10 ♗e3 ♘d7! 11 ♘d5 ♘c5! 12 ♗xc5 dc 13 ♗xc6 bc 14 ♘xe7 ♕xe7 with a strong position for Black (Goldenov–Yudovich, USSR Ch. 1947).

(a2) **5 … ♗d7** 6 ♘c3 g6 7 d4 ed (7 … ♗g7 8 ♗g5 f6 9 ♗e3 ♘ge7 10 d5! favours White) 8 ♘xd4 ♗g7 9 ♘xc6 bc 10 0–0 ♘f6 (10 … ♘e7 11 c5!) 11 c5!? dc 12 ♗e3 ♕e7 13 f3 0–0 14 ♕d2 ♖fd8 15 ♕f2 ♗f8 with near equality (Keres).

(b) **5 d4** b5 6 ♗b3 ♘xd4 7 ♘xd4 ed, and now:

(b1) **8 c3** dc (8 … ♗b7 9 cd!? ♘f6 — 9 … ♗xe4?! 10 0–0 ♗e7 11 ♖e1 ♗b7 12 ♘c3 favours White — 10 f3 ♗e7 11 0–0 0–0 12 ♘c3 c5 13 ♗e3; 8 … d3? 9 a4! promises White some initiative) 9 ♘xc3 (9 ♕d5 ♗e6 10 ♕c6+ ♗d7 11 ♕d5 leads to a draw, and 9

♕h5 ♕d7 10 ♘xc3 ♘f6 11 ♕e2 ♗e7 12 0–0 0–0 13 ♖d1 ♕e8 14 ♗f4 ♗g4 favours Black) 9 ... ♘f6 (9 ... ♗b7!?) 10 0–0 ♗e7 11 ♖e1 0–0 12 ♗g5 ♗b7 and White still has to prove the correctness of the pawn sacrifice.

(b2) **8 ♗d5** ♖b8 9 ♗c6+ ♗d7 10 ♗xd7+ ♕xd7 11 ♕xd4 ♘f6 12 ♘c3 ♗e7 13 0–0 0–0 14 a4 ♖fe8 15 ♕d3 b4 16 ♘d5 a5 17 b3 ♘xd5 18 ed ♗f6 and Black has an excellent position (Hort–Keres, Oberhausen 1961). Note also that neither 5 ♘c3 ♗d7 6 0–0 g6 nor 5 d3 b5 6 ♗b3 ♘a5 is very promising for White.

A1

5 c3

Here Black's main choice is between:

A11 5 ... ♗d7
A12 5 ... f5

In White's favour are 5 ... b5 6 ♗c2! ♘f6 7 d4, and 5 ... ♗g4 6 h3!

A11

5 ... ♗d7
6 d4

This is the initial move of a system where Black has a choice between:

A111 6 ... ♘f6
A112 6 ... ♘ge7
A113 6 ... g6

A111

6 ... ♘f6
7 0–0

Often 7 ♘bd2 is played here, preventing 7 ... ♘xe4. After 7 0–0 there is again a choice of continuations:

A1111 7 ... ♗e7
A1112 7 ... ♘xe4
A1113 7 ... g6

A1111

7 ... ♗e7
8 ♖e1

White has few prospects after 8 d5 ♘b8 9 ♗c2 ♗g4 10 c4 ♘bd7 11 ♘c3 ♘f8 12 h3 ♗d7 13 ♘e1 g5!? 14 ♗xg5 ♖g8 15 f4 ef 16 ♗xf4 ♗xh3 with excellent play for Black (Bogolyubov–Alekhine, match 1929).

8 ... 0–0
9 ♘bd2 *(86)*

Passive is 9 h3(?) ed 10 cd d5! with a comfortable game for Black.

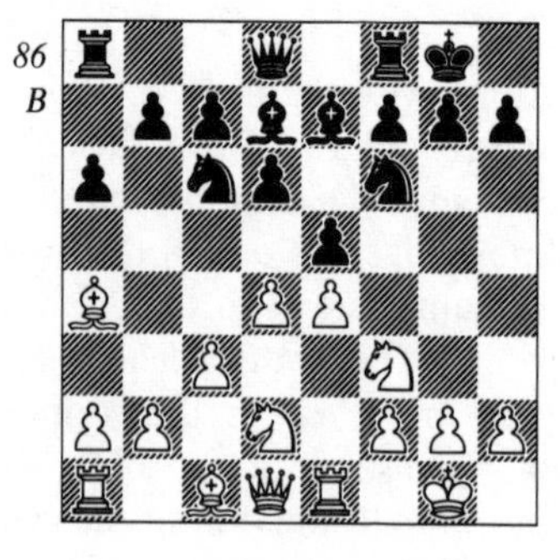

After 9 ♘bd2 the most important plans for Black are:

A11111 9 ... ed
A11112 9 ... ♗e8
A11113 9 ... ♖e8

A11111

9 ... ed

This is a rare example in this system of where, for the sake of creating active play for his pieces, Black gives up the centre.

To White's advantage are both 9 ... b5 10 ♗b3 ed 11 cd ♘b4 12 d5!, and 9 ... ♕e8 10 ♗xc6 ♗xc6 11 de de 12 ♘xe5.

10 cd ♘b4

11 ♗xd7

After 11 d5 ♘d3 12 ♖e3 ♗xa4 13 ♕xa4 ♘c5, or 11 ♘f1 ♗xa4 12 ♕xa4 d5!, or 11 ♗b3 c5 12 ♘f1 ♗b5, Black gets a comfortable game.

11 ... ♕xd7 *(87)*

Interesting is 11 ... ♘xd7!?

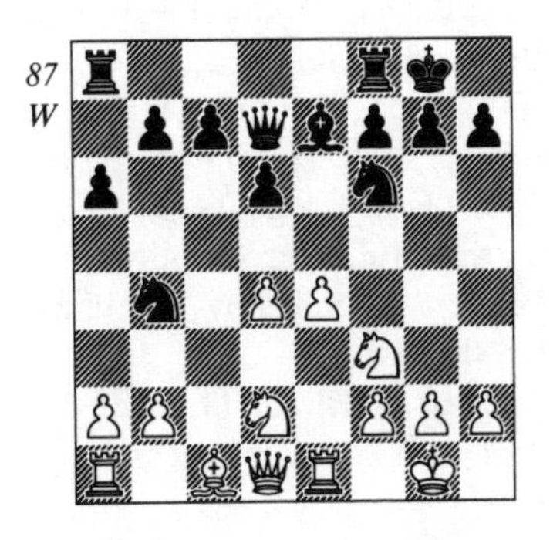

Here White's choice is between:

A111111 12 ♘f1
A111112 12 ♕b3
A111113 12 d5

A111111

12 ♘f1

After 12 ♘b1?! (interesting is 12 ♘b3!?) 12 ... d5 13 ♘e5 ♕d6 14 a3 ♘c6 15 ♘xc6 ♕xc6 16 e5 ♘e4 Black has full equality (Suetin).

12 ... c5

The variation with 12 ... d5 has a dubious reputation: 12 ... d5?! 13 ♘e5 ♕e6 14 a3 ♘c6 15 ♘xc6 ♕xc6 16 e5 ♘e4 17 ♘e3 ♕d7 (17 ... f5? 18 ♕b3 ♖ad8 19 ♘xf5) 18 f3 ♘g5 19 f4 ♘e4 20 f5 is clearly in White's favour.

13 a3 ♘c6

14 d5 ♘e5 *(88)*

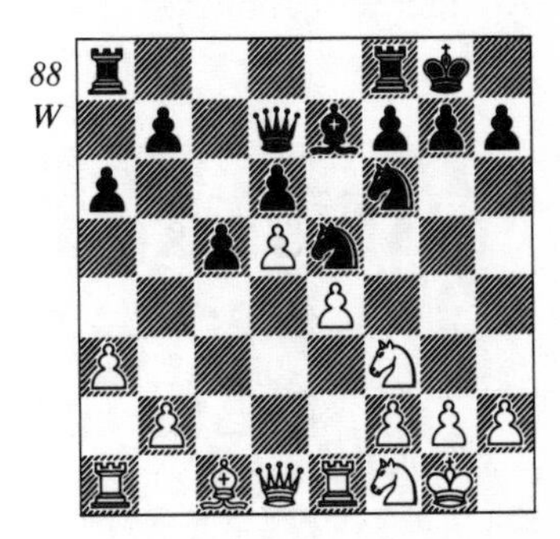

And now:

(a) **15 ♘xe5** de 16 ♘g3 (16 ♘e3?! ♘xe4 17 ♘c4 ♕f5 18 ♕c2 ♘d6 19 ♕xf5 ♘xf5 20 ♖xe5 ♘d6! 21 ♖xe7 ♘xc4 22 ♖xb7 ♖fd8 leads to a level game — Bronstein) 16 ... ♘e8 17 f4 ♗d6! 18 ♘f5 f6 19 g3 (19 ♕f3!?) 19 ... g6 20 ♘h6+ ♔h8 21 f5 c4 22 h4 ♗c5+ 23 ♔g2 (Averbakh–Smyslov, USSR Ch. 1951). With 23 ... ♘d6 Black was able to maintain the equilibrium.

(b) **15 ♘g3!?** ♖ad8 16 ♘f5 ♖fe8 17 ♘xe5 de 18 ♕f3! with pressure for White (Lilienthal–Sokolsky, Yerevan 1954).

A111112

12 ♕b3

This manoeuvre has undergone a certain crisis-period but has again become topical.

12 ... a5

After 12 ... c5 13 a3 (13 ♘c4!?) 13 ... ♘c6 14 d5 ♘e5 15 ♘xe5 de 16 ♘c4, or 12 ... d5 13 ♘e5 ♕e6 14 a3 ♘c6 15 ed (also good is 16 ♘xc6) 15 ... ♘xd5 16 ♘df3 ♕d6 17 ♗d2, White stands clearly better.

13 a3

An interesting move is 13 ♘f1!?

13 ... ♘a6 *(89)*

89
W

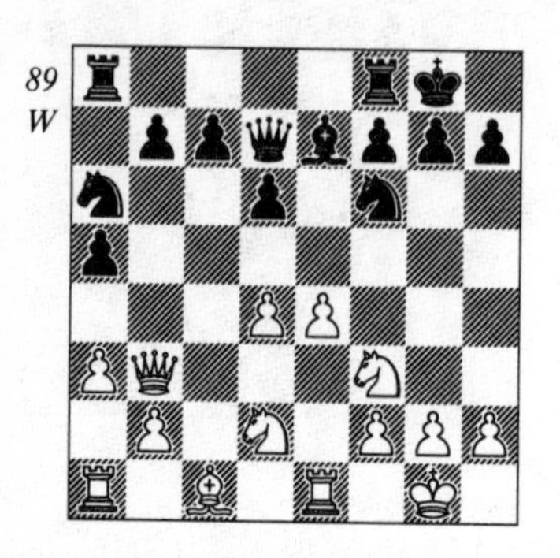

After which:

(a) **14 ♘c4!** a4 (14 ... d5? 15 ed ♘xd5 16 ♘xa5!) 15 ♕c2 d5 16 ed ♘xd5 17 ♘e3 ♘xe3 18 ♗xe3 ♖fe8 19 ♖ac1 ♗f6 20 ♖ed1 ♕b5 21 ♘d2. After carrying out the manoeuvre ♘d2–c4–e3, White will have the better position (Zuidema–Smyslov, Skopje OL 1972).

(b) **14 ♘f1** d5 15 e5 ♘e4 16 ♘1d2 a4 17 ♕d3 ♘xd2 18 ♗xd2 (Smyslov–Keres, USSR 1941). By playing 18 ... c5! Black was able to obtain good counterplay.

A111113

12 d5

A rare continuation and one which does not offer good prospects. After 12 ... a5 (worse is 12 ... ♘d3 13 ♖e3 ♘xc1 14 ♖xc1 with pressure for White — ♖ec3 and ♕b3 etc.) 13 ♘f1 ♖e8 14 a3 ♘a6 15 ♘g3 g6 a sharp position arises, with chances for both sides.

A11112

9 ... ♗e8?!

The so-called 'Kecskemét Variation', introduced into practice by Alekhine in 1927. It is no longer topical. The following variations are possible:

(a) **10 ♗xc6** ♗xc6 11 de de 12 ♘xe5 ♗xe4 13 ♕b3! ♗c6 14 ♘xc6 bc 15 ♕a4 with obvious advantage to White (Kirjavainen–Böök, Helsinki 1972).

(b) **10 ♗b3** ♘d7 11 ♘f1 ♗f6 (11 ... ♔h8 and f7–f6) 12 ♘e3 ♘e7 13 ♘g4 ♘g6 14 g3! ♗e7 15 h4 with a dangerous initiative for White (Smyslov–Lyublinsky, USSR 1949).

(c) **10 ♘f1?!** ed! 11 cd d5 12 e5 ♘e4 with equal chances.

A11113

9 ... ♖e8

An idea similar to that in the Kecskemét Variation: Black intends to consolidate his strongpoint on e5. Practice has confirmed that, here too, Black has substantial difficulties:

(a) **10 ♘f1** h6 (in White's favour is 10 ... ♗f8 11 ♗g5 h6 12 ♗xf6 ♕xf6 13 de ♘xe5 14 ♘xe5 ♗xa4 15 ♘g4!) 11 ♘g3 (interesting is 11 d5 ♘a7?! 12 ♗c2) 11 ... ♗f8 12 h3 (White has somewhat better play after 12 Bd2!? or 12 a3) 12 ... Na5 13 Bc2 c5 14 b4 cb 15 cb Nc6 16 a3 ed 17 Bb2 Rc8 18 Nxd4 Ne5 19 Bb3 and White stands better (Matulovic–Portisch, Palma de Mallorca 1971).

(b) **10 a3** Bf8 11 b4?! d5! 12 Bb3 Bg4 13 h3 Bh5 14 de Nxe5 15 de Nxe5 15 g4 Nxf3+ 16 Nxf3 de 17 gh ef 18 Rxe8 Qxe8 19 Qxf3 Qe1+ 20 Kg2 with equal chances (Fischer–Gligoric, Zagreb 1959).

(c) **10 h3** Bf8 11 Bc2 g6 12 Nf1 Bg7 13 Ng3 Qe7 14 Be3 Na5 15 b3 c5 with a secure position for Black.

(d) **10 Bxc6** Bxc6 11 de de 12 Nxe5 Bxe4 13 Qb3!? and White's position is preferable (Suetin).

A1112

7 ... Nxe4

This early opening-up of the centre is risky for Black. Practice has shown that White has the better chances.

8 Re1 *(90)*

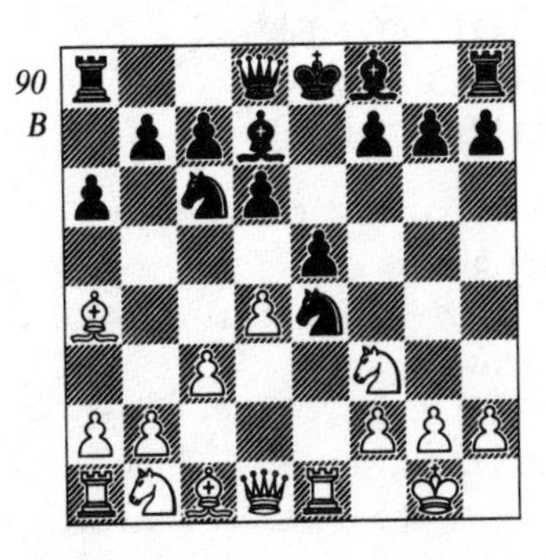

And now:

(a) **8 ... Nf6** 9 Bxc6 (also good is 9 de de 10 Nxe5 Nxe5 11 Rxe5+ Be7 12 Bf4) 9 ... Bxc6 10 de de 11 Qxd8+ Raxd8 12 Nxe5 Be4 13 Nbd2 (13 Bg5!? Be7 14 Nd2) 13 ... Be7 14 Nxe4 Nxe4 15 Bh6! gh (bad is 15 ... Nxf2? 16 Bxg7 Rg8 17 Bf6 Rd2 18 Kf1 Nd1 19 Nd3 Rg6 20 Bxe7 Rxd8 21 Bc5+ and White wins; Geller–Veltmander, USSR 1954) 16 Rxe4 0–0 17 Nc6! bc 18 Rxe7 Rd2 and Black has drawing chances.

(b) **8 ... f5** 9 de de 10 Nbd2 Nxd2 11 Bxc6! Nxf3 12 Bxf3 Bd6 13 Bxb7 Rb8 14 Bd5! with a positional advantage to White (Boleslavsky).

A1113

7 ... g6 *(91)*

A suggestion of Keres's. Black's intention is to strengthen the e5-square. The following variations arise:

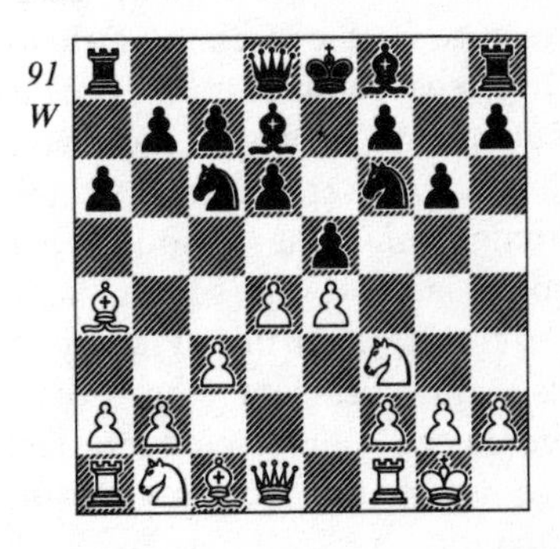

(a) **8 Bxc6** (interesting is 8 de Nxe4 9 Nbd2!) 8 ... Bxc6 9 de Nxe4 10 Nbd2 Be7 11 Nxe4 Bxe4 12 ed Qd6 13 Qxd6 cd 14 Re1 Bd5 15 Bg5 Be6 16 Re3 h6 17 Bxe7 Kxe7 18 Nd4 Kf6 19 Rf3+ Ke7 20 Re1 and White has an advantage in the ending (Geller–Zhukhovitsky, USSR Ch. 1969).

(b) **8 ♖e1** ♕e7 (possible is 8 ... b5 9 ♗c2 ♗g7 10 de ♘xe5 11 ♘xe5 de 12 ♗g5 h6 13 ♗h4 ♕e7 with a solid defence for Black; Shamkovich–Keres, Riga 1968; but not good is 8 ... ♗g7 9 ♗xc6! ♗xc6 10 de ♘xe5 11 ed ♕xd6 12 ♕xd6 cd 13 ♘g5 0–0 14 ♖xe4! with clearly better play for White) 9 ♘bd2 (also not bad is 9 ♗g5 ♗g7 10 ♘bd2) 9 ... ♗g7 10 ♘f1 (10 a3!?; 10 ♗xc6 ♗xc6 11 ♘c4!?) 10 ... h6 11 ♘e3 0–0 12 ♗b3 ♕d8 13 ♕d3 ♖e8 14 de ♘xe5 15 ♘xe5 de 16 ♖d1 ♕e7 with equal chances (Tal–Zhukhovitsky, USSR Ch. 1969).

A112

6 ... ♘ge7

One of the most complicated systems in the Steinitz Defence Deferred, commonly known as Rubinstein's System. Black intends to transfer the knight to g6, securely strengthening the e5-square and taking aim at the square f4. A certain defect of this system consists in the fact that Black renounces his counterattack against e4 and weakens the d5-square.

White has a rather wide choice of plans, with three main alternatives. Other possibilities on White's 7th move are given later.

A1121 7 ♗b3
A1122 7 0–0
A1123 7 ♘bd2
A1124 7 others

Note that nowadays Rubinstein's System frequently arises after a different move-order, e.g.: 3 ... ♘ge7 4 c3 a6 5 ♗a4 d6 6 d4 ♗d7; or 3 ... a6 4 ♗a4 ♘ge7 5 c3 d6 6 d4 ♗d7.

A1121

7 ♗b3 h6 *(92)*

92
W

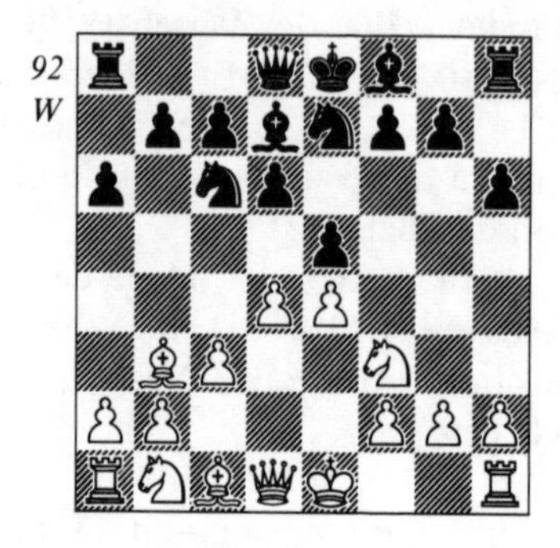

Parrying the threat 8 ♘g5. Now White has a wide choice:

A11211 8 ♕e2
A11212 8 ♘bd2
A11213 8 ♘h4
A11214 8 0–0

Let us first consider two other variations:

(a) **8 ♘g1!?** (Suetin), with the following lines:

(a1) **8 ... ♘g6** 9 ♘ge2 ♕h4 (interesting is 9 ... ♘h4 10 0–0 g5!) 10 ♕d3 ♘a5 11 ♗c2 ♗e7 12 ♘bd2 ♗c5 13 d5 0–0 14 ♕g3 h6 with good counterplay for Black (Nezhmetdinov–Keres, Vilnius 1958).

(a2) **8 … ♘a5** 9 ♗c2 ♘g6 10 ♘e2 ♗e7 11 0–0 ♗g5 12 f4 (the basic idea in this variation!) 12 … ♘xf4 13 ♘xf4 ef 14 ♗xf4 0–0 15 ♕f3 ♕f6 16 ♘d2 (Suetin–Uusi, Minsk 1957).

(a3) **8 … ed** 9 cd d5 10 e5 ♗f5 11 ♘e2 ♘b4 12 0–0 ♘ec6 13 a3 ♘d3 14 ♘c3 ♘xc1 15 ♖xc1 ♗e6 16 ♘f4 (Gipslis–Kaminsky, Sverdlovsk 1957).

In both cases White has slightly better chances.

(b) **8 ♗e3** ♘g6 (interesting is 8 … g5?! 9 ♗xg5 — 9 de ♘xe5! 10 ♘xe5 de 11 h4 with better chances for White; Keres — 9 … hg 10 ♘xg5 ♘d5! 11 ♘xf7 ♔xf7 12 ♗xd5 ♔e8 with unclear play) 9 ♘bd2 ♗e7 10 ♘f1 0–0 11 ♘g3 ♖e8 12 0–0 ♗g5 with equal chances.

A11211

8 ♕e2

A continuation with scope for investigation. For the time being, it is not easy for Black to solve his problems.

8 … ♘g6

9 ♕c4! *(93)*

It is this manoeuvre which places Black in a difficult position. The following variations are possible:

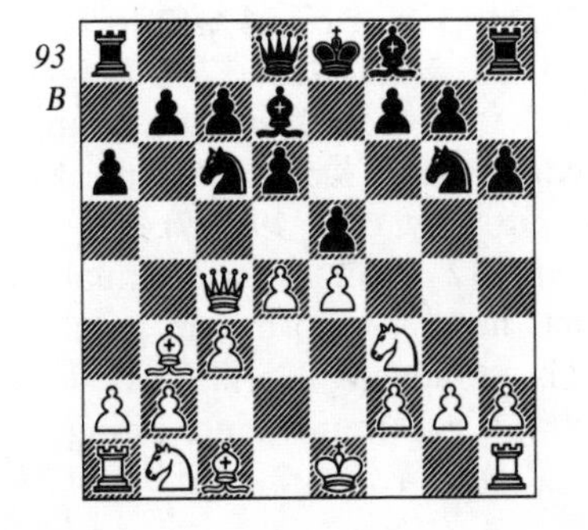

93
B

(a) **9 … ♕e7** 10 d5 b5 11 ♕e2 ♘a5 12 ♗c2 c6 13 b4 ♘c4 14 dc ♗xc6 15 a4 ♕b7 16 0–0 ♗e7 17 ♘a3 ♘xa3 18 ♖xa3 0–0 with approximate equality.

(b) **9 … ♕f6** 10 d5 b5 11 ♕e2 ♘a5 12 ♗d1 ♗e7 13 g3 0–0 14 h4 ♗g4 15 h5 ♘h8 16 ♕d3 (Euwe).

(c) **9 … ♗e6** 10 d5 ♘a5 11 ♕a4+ c6 12 de b5 13 ef+ ♔d7 14 ♕b4! d5 15 ♘xe5+ ♘xe5 16 ♕d4 (Fischer). In both cases White has the better chances.

A11212

8 ♘bd2 ♘g6

It is risky to play 8 … g5?! 9 de (also not bad is 9 ♘c4 ♘g6 10 ♘e3 ♗g7 11 ♘f5 ♗f6 12 h3 — Suetin) 9 … de 10 ♘c4 ♘g6 11 h4 g4 12 h5! with an initiative for White (Keres).

9 ♘c4 ♗e7

And now:

(a) **10 0–0** ♗g5 (worse is 10 … 0–0 11 ♘e3 ♖e8 12 ♖e1 ♗f8 13 ♗c2 ♘h4 14 ♘xh4 ♕xh4 15 ♘d5 with advantage to White; Bronstein–Keres, USSR Ch. 1948) 11 ♘e3 ♗xe3 12 ♗xe3 0–0 (interesting is 12 … ♕f6 — for example: 13 ♘e1 ♘a5 14 ♗c2 ♗b5 with satisfactory play for Black) 13 ♘d2 ♘a5 14 ♗c2 ♗b5 15 ♖e1 ♘c4 16 ♘xc4 ♗xc4 17 ♕f3 ♗e6 18 b3 ♕e7 19 ♕g3 with equal play (Keres–Bondarevsky, USSR Ch. 1950).

(b) **10 ♘e3** ♗g5, and now:

(b1) **11 ♘d5** ♗xc1 12 ♖xc1 ♗g4 with equal chances (Keres).

(b2) **11 ♘xg5** hg 12 g3 (12 ♕f3) 12 ... ♗h3 (in the game Sax–Portisch, Skelleftea 1989, 12 ... ed!? 13 cd ♔f8 14 0–0 ♗h3 15 ♕f3 ♕d7 16 ♖d1 ♖e8 was played, with quite good counterplay for Black) 13 ♗a4 (after 13 ♕f3 ♕d7 14 ♘f5 ed! 15 cd 0–0–0 16 ♗xg5 ♗xf5 17 ♕xf5 ♘xd4 18 ♕xd7 ♖xd7 19 ♗d1 ♖e8 Black has good counterplay) 13 ... ♔f8 14 d5 ♘e7 15 ♕f3 ♕c8 16 ♗d2 ♔g8 17 ♗c2 ♕d7 18 0–0–0 ♖f8 with roughly equal play (analysis by Boleslavsky and Suetin).

(b3) **10 ♗e3!?** ♗g5 11 ♘xg5 hg 12 ♕d2 ♘f4 13 f3 ♕e7 14 0–0–0 0–0–0 15 g3 ♘h3 16 ♗c2 g6 17 d5 ♘b8 18 ♘a5 b6 19 ♘c4 ♔b7 20 ♗d3 with somewhat better chances for White (Pulkkinen–Likhela, Espoo 1989).

A11213

8 ♘h4!?

This dynamic continuation was introduced into practice by Smyslov. White aims for a quick attack on the kingside. The threat of 9 ♕f3 or 9 ♕h5 is clear. Black has a choice between:

A112131 8 ... ♘a5
A112132 8 ... ed

A112131

8 ... ♘a5

In White's favour is 8 ... ♘c8(?) 9 ♘f6 g6 10 ♘g3 ♗g7 11 0–0 cd 12 f4! (Geller–Keres, USSR Ch. 1950). Bad for Black is 8 ... g5? 9 ♕h5! ♖h7 10 ♗xg5!

9 ♗c2 g5

In White's favour is 9 ... g6 10 0–0 ♗g7 11 f4! Also after 9 ... c5 10 dc dc 11 ♕f3! ♘g6 12 ♘f5 ♕f6 13 ♘d2 ♘e7 14 0–0 g6 15 ♘xe7 ♗xe7 16 ♕e3 White has the better chances (Tal–Keres, USSR Ch. 1973).

10 ♘f5 ♘xf5
11 ef ♘c6 *(94)*

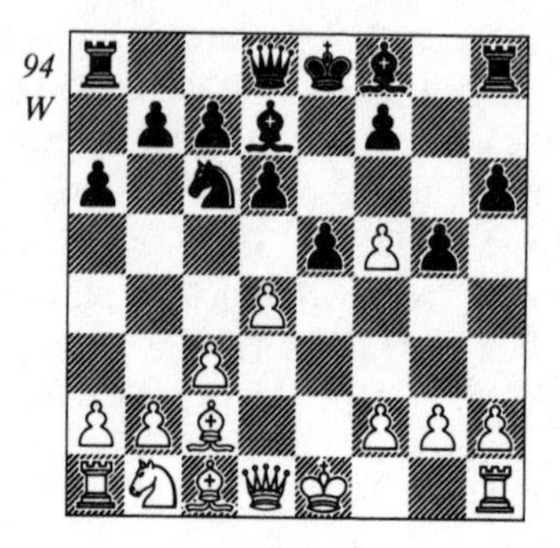

94
W

With the following variations:

(a) **12 0–0** ♗g7 13 d5 (also good is 13 de — for example: 13 ... ♘xe5 14 f4 gf 15 ♗xf4 ♕e7 16 ♘d2 0–0–0 17 ♘e4 d5? 18 f6! with a decisive attack for White; Suetin–Aratovsky, Leningrad 1951) 13 ... ♘e7 14 ♕f3 f6 15 c4 h5! 16 ♗xg5 ♕c8! 17 ♘c3 fg 18 f6 0–0 19 ♕xh5 ♖xf6 with double-edged play (Konstantinopolsky–Aratovsky, corr. 1955/7).

(b) **12 ♗e3!?** This continuation has not yet been met in practice. The following variations show that it is extremely interesting:

(b1) **12 ... ♗g7** 13 d5 ♘e7 14

♕f3 f6 15 h4 0–0 16 g4! c6 17 c4 b5 18 ♘c3 bc 19 ♗e4 and then 0–0–0.

(b2) **12 ... ♕f6** 13 d5 ♘e7 14 g4 ♘xd5 (14 ... h5 15 ♘d2) 15 ♕xd5 ♗c6 16 ♗a4! ♗xa4 17 ♕xb7 ♕d8 18 ♕e4! ♗d7 19 c4 ♖b8 20 b3.

(b3) **12 ... ed** 13 cd ♘e7 14 ♕f3 ♗c6 15 ♗e4 ♗xe4 16 ♕xe4 ♗g7 17 h4! ♕d7 18 ♕f3 ♘c6 19 ♘c3 ♘xd4 20 ♗xd4 ♗xd4 21 ♘d5.

In all cases White's chances are substantially better (analysis by Boleslavsky and Suetin).

A112132

8 ... ed

9 cd

9 0–0!? d3!?

9 ... ♘xd4!?

This forced variation was worked out in the 1950s by a group of Ukrainian players.

10 ♕xd4 ♘c6

11 ♕d5 ♕xh4

12 ♕xf7+ ♔d8

13 ♘c3 ♘e5

14 ♕d5 *(95)*

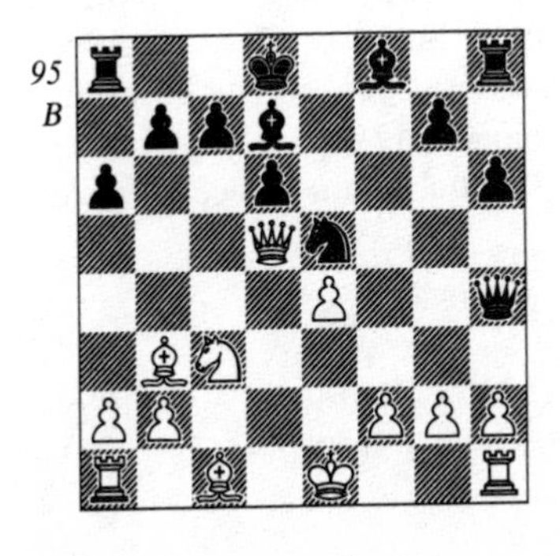

95
B

And now:

(a) **14 ... ♗c6** 15 ♕d4 ♗e7 16 0–0 ♗f6 17 ♕d1 ♗xe4 18 ♘xe4 ♕xe4 19 ♗d5 ♕b4 20 ♗d2 with double-edged play and equal chances (Tukmakov).

(b) **14 ... ♕g4** 15 ♗e3! ♗c6 16 ♕d4 ♕xg2 17 0–0–0 and White has excellent compensation for the sacrificed pawn.

(c) **14 ... g5?!** 15 ♗e3 ♕g4 16 h3 ♕xg2 17 0–0–0 ♕f3 (17 ... ♗g7 18 ♖hg1 ♕f3 19 ♕xb7 ♗c6 20 ♖xd6+!) 18 ♖hg1 ♕h5 19 f4 gf 20 ♗xf4 with a strong initiative for White (Suetin–Ciocaltea, Debrecen 1961).

A11214

8 0–0

With the following possible variation: 8 ... ♘g6 9 ♘e1 ♘a5 (9 ... ♗e7 10 f4!) 10 f4 ♘xb3 11 ♕xb3 ef 12 ♗xf4 ♖b8 and Black has more than adequate defensive resources. For example: 13 ♗xd6 (13 ♗xh6 ♗e6 14 d5 ♗g4 15 ♗e3 ♕h4!) 13 ... ♗e6 14 d5 ♕xd6 and Black repels the threats (Boleslavsky).

A1122

7 0–0 ♘g6 *(96)*

Worthy of consideration is 7 ... h6 and if 8 ♘bd2 then 8 ... g5!? 9 de de 10 ♖e1 ♘g6 with pressure for Black on the kingside (Rubinstein).

Here the following variations may arise:

(a) **8 ♘bd2** ♗e7 9 ♖e1 h6 (also possible is 9 ... 0–0 10 ♘f1 ♗g4 — 10 ... ♘h4!? — 11 ♗xc6 ♘h4 12

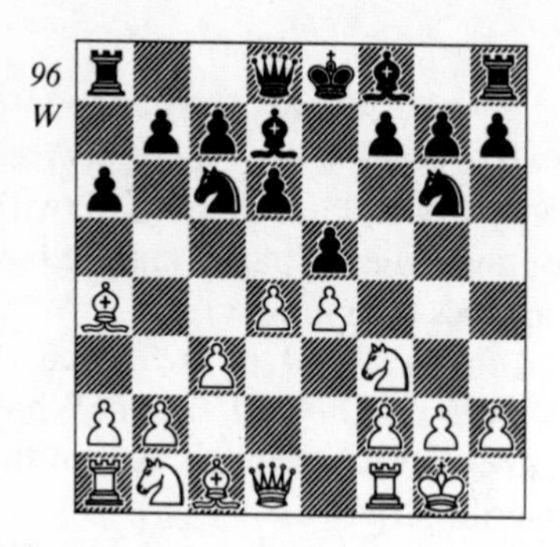
96
W

♘bd2 bc with roughly equal play; Matanovic–Petrosian, Leningrad 1957) 10 h3 0–0 11 a3 ♗f6 12 ♘f1 ♘h4 13 ♘xh4 ♗xh4 14 ♘e3 ♗g5 15 ♘d5 and White stands a little better (Planinc–Ivkov, Ljubljana/ Portoroz 1973).

(b) **8 ♗e3** ♗e7 9 ♘bd2 0–0 10 a3 ♔h8 11 ♖e1 ed 12 cd f5! 13 ef ♗xf5 14 ♖c1 d5 15 ♗xc6 bc 16 ♖xc6 ♗d6 and Black has sufficient compensation for the pawn (Boleslavsky–Tarasov, USSR Ch. 1957).

Note that after either 8 d5 ♘b8 9 c4 ♗e7 10 ♘c3 h6 11 ♗e3 ♗g5, or 8 c4 ♗e7 9 ♘c3 0–0 10 ♗e3 ♗g4, Black has complete equality.

A1123

7 ♘bd2 ♘g6

Also possible is 7 … g6. For example: 8 de de 9 h4 ♗g7 10 h5 ♘c8 and Black has a strong defence (Keres).

8 ♘f1

With the following variations:

(a) **8 … ♘h4** 9 ♘xh4 ♕xh4 10 ♘g3 (or 10 ♗c2 ed 11 cd f5!) 10 … g6 11 0–0 ♗h6 12 ♗xh6 ♕xh6 13 de de 14 ♕d5 ♕g7 with equality (Boleslavsky–Bondarevsky, Rostov 1960).

(b) **8 … ♗e7** 9 ♘e3 ♗g5! 10 0–0 ♗xe3 11 ♗xe3 0–0 12 ♗c2 ♕e7 13 ♕d2 ♔h8 14 ♖ae1 ♗g4 15 ♗d1 f5 and in this position Black is not worse (Unzicker–Ciocaltea, Moscow OL 1956).

A1124

We shall briefly consider the following variations:

(a) **7 ♗e3** ♘g6 8 h4!? ♗e7 (8 … ♗g4!?) 9 h5 ♘h4 10 ♘xh4 ♗xh4 11 d5 ♘b8 12 ♗xd7+ ♘xd7 13 ♕g4 ♗f6 14 h6 g6 and Black's position is sufficiently solid (Keres).

(b) **7 h4!?** ed! cd d5 9 e5 ♗g4 with counterplay for Black.

(c) After **7 de** Black's simplest reply is 7 … ♘xe5.

A113

6 … g6

Alekhine's system is also one of the most active methods of opposing White's activity in the opening. In many variations of this system, play resembles that in the King's Indian Defence. In some lines Black organises a counterattack on the kingside by means of f7–f5.

White's main choice is between:

A1131 7 0–0
A1132 7 ♗g5

Quite often played is 7 de de 8 0–0, which transposes to variation A11311.

A1131

7 0–0 ♗g7

A critical position, where White has a choice between:

A11311 8 de
A11312 8 ♖e1

A11311

8 de de *(97)*

Recently the reputation of the move 8 … ♘xe5 has begun to change. For example: 9 ♘xe5 de 10 f4 ♗xa4 (after 10 … ♘e7 11 f5 — 11 fe ♘c6 12 ♗f4 ♕e7 13 ♘d2 0–0–0 14 ♗xc6 ♗xc6 15 ♕e2 h6 16 ♕e3 g5 17 ♗g3 h5 18 ♘f3 h4 with good play for Black; Taborov–Bronstein, Daugavpils 1978 — 11 … gf 12 ef ♘d5 13 ♕xd5 ♗xa4 14 ♕xb7 ♗xb5 15 f6 Black's position is bad; Geller–Salov, Moscow 1986) 11 ♕xa4 b5! (but not 11 … ♕d7? 12 ♕xd7+ ♔xd7 13 fe!; Fine–Alekhine, AVRO 1938) 12 ♕b3 ef 13 ♗xf4 ♘f6 14 ♘d2 0–0 15 ♖ae1 ♘d7 with approximate equality (Geller–Smyslov, Sochi 1986).

After 8 … de White has the following choice:

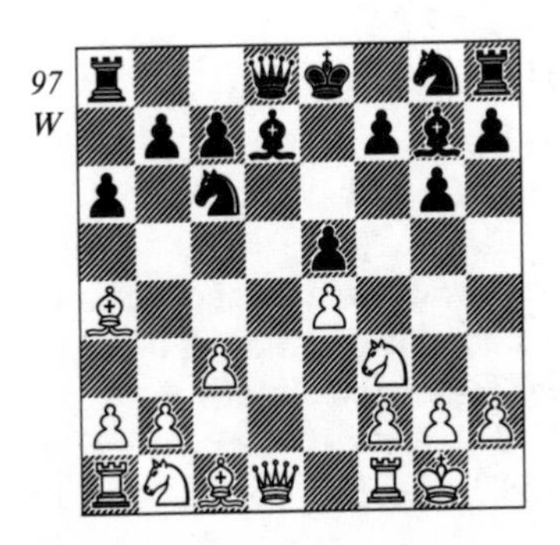

97
W

(a) **9 ♗e3** ♘f6 10 ♘bd2 0–0 (or 10 … ♕e7 11 b4 b6 12 ♗b3!? h6 13 a4 ♘g4 14 ♘c4 a5! 15 b5 — 15 ♗c1!? — 15 … ♘xe3 16 ♘xe3 ♘b8 with roughly equal play; Sokolov–Yudasin, USSR 1988) 11 ♗c5 (11 ♖e1 ♖e8 12 ♗g5 h6 13 ♗h4 ♕e7 14 ♘f1 ♖ad8 15 ♘e3 g5 16 ♗g3 ♘xe4!? 17 ♘d5 ♕d6 18 ♖xe4 ♗f5 19 ♖d4! ♘xd4 20 ♘xd4 ♗e4 21 ♗xe8 ♕xd5 22 ♗xf7+ ♔xf7 23 ♕h5+ ♔g8 with equal chances; Lutikov–Vasyukov, Moscow 1958) 11 … ♖e8 12 ♖e1 b6 13 ♗a3 ♕c8 14 ♗c2 ♕b7 15 ♕e2 ♖ad8 16 ♖ad1 with complicated play (de Firmian–Zsu. Polgar, 1986).

(b) **9 ♗g5** ♘ge7 (9 … ♘f6? 10 ♗xc6 ♗xc6 11 ♘xe5 ♕xd1 12 ♖xd1 ♘xe4 13 ♗f4 is in White's favour) 10 ♘bd2 0–0 11 ♘b3 ♕e8 12 ♘c5 ♗c8 13 b4 h6 14 ♗xe7 ♕xe7 15 ♗xc6 bc 16 ♘bd2 ♖d8 17 ♕e2 with a minimal advantage to White (Ulybin–Kamsky, USSR 1988).

A11312

8 ♖e1 ♘ge7

And now, 9 ♗e3 0–0 10 ♘bd2 ♕e8? (10 … h6) 11 ♗b3 b6 12 de de 13 ♘c4 ♔h8 14 ♕c1! ♗g4 15 ♘g5 h6 16 h3 ♗d7 17 ♘f3 ♔h7 18 a4! with definite pressure for White (Karpov–Spassky, Bugojno 1986).

Let us briefly consider rarer continuations on White's 8th move.

(a) **8 ♗e3** ♘f6 9 ♘bd2 0–0 10 h3 ♘h5!? 11 ♖e1 h6 12 ♘f1 ♔h7 with roughly equal chances (Hulak–Kovacevic, Yugoslavia 1986).

(b) **8 d5** ♘b8 (also not bad is 8 … ♘ce7 9 ♗xd7+ ♕xd7 10 c4 ♘f6 11 ♘c3 0–0) 9 c4 ♘f6 10 ♘c3 0–0 11 ♗xd7 ♘bxd7 12 ♘e1 ♕e7 13 ♗g5 c5 with full equality for Black (Lutikov–Bronstein, Moscow 1959).

(c) **8 ♗b3!?** ♘f6 9 ♘g5 0–0 10 f4 ♕e7 fe de 12 d5 ♘a5 13 ♗c2 ♘c4 with roughly equal chances (Ehlvest–Karolyi, Tallinn 1985).

A1132

7	**♗g5**	**f6**

The most topical plan. Possible is 7 … ♗e7, after which White may play 8 ♗e3!?

8	**♗e3**	**♘h6**
9	**0–0**	

Interesting is 9 b4!? ♗g7 10 ♗b3 ♕e7 11 0–0 ♘f7 12 ♗d5!? (Romanishin–Torre, Brussels 1986).

9	**…**	**♗g7**
10	**h3**	**♘f7**
11	**♘bd2**	**0–0**

And now:

(a) **12 ♖e1** ♕e7 13 b4 ♔h8 14 ♗c2 ♘cd8 15 ♘f1 ♘e6 16 ♕d2 ♘fg5! with counterplay for Black (Sokolov–Spassky, Montpellier 1985).

(b) **12 ♗c2** ♕e7 13 ♖e1 ♔h8 14 ♕b1 ♘cd8 15 b4 ♘e6 16 a4 ♗h6 and here Black has no particular difficulties (Belyavsky–Smyslov, Montpellier 1985).

A12

5	**…**	**f5!?**

The move 5 … f5 entered into practice in 1928, when Capablanca adopted it with success at a tournament in Budapest. At the present time this active system, the Siesta Variation, is extremely topical.

6	**ef**

The continuation 6 d4 fe ceased to be played a long time ago, as White hardly has anything better than 7 ♘xe5 de 8 ♕h5+ ♔e7 9 ♗xc6 bc 10 ♗g5+ ♘f6 11 de ♕d5 12 ♗h4 ♔d7 13 ♕g5 h6! 14 ♕f5+ ♔e8 15 ♕g6+ ♕f7 16 ♕xf7+ ♔xf7 17 ef gf with equality (Capablanca).

6	**…**	**♗xf5** *(98)*

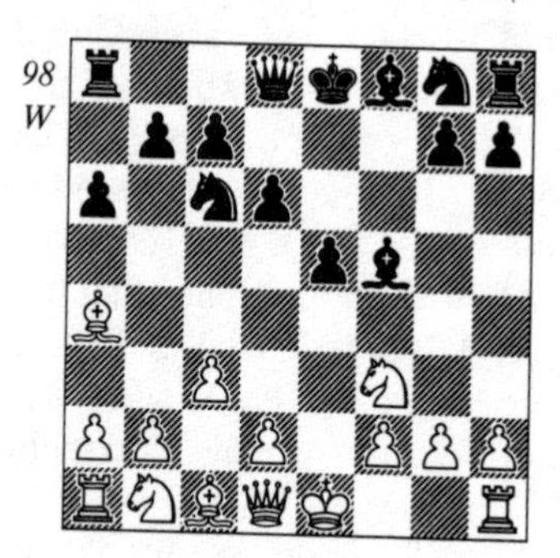

White has a choice between:

A121 **7 d4**
A122 **7 0–0**

A121

7	**d4**	**e4**
8	**♘g5**	

Interest flared up and died away in a gambit variation: 8 0–0!? ef 9 ♕xf3 ♘e7 (possible is 9 … ♗d7 10 ♖e1 ♗e7) 10 ♖e1 ♕c8 11 h3 ♔d8!? 12 ♗b3 d5 13 ♗g5 h6!

14 ♕xd5+ ♕d7 with better chances for Black (Keres). White also gets nothing after 8 ♗g5 ♗e7 9 ♘h4 ♗e6 10 ♗xe7 ♘xe7 11 ♕h5+ g6 12 ♕h6 ♘g8! etc.

But an interesting line is 8 d5 ef 9 dc b5 10 ♕xf3 ♗xb1 11 ♗b3 ♗g6 (11 … ♕e7+ 12 ♔d1! ♗e4 13 ♕h3 and then ♖e1) 12 0–0 ♘f6 13 ♗h6! d5 14 ♖fe1+ ♗e4 (14 … ♘e4 15 ♖ad1!) 15 ♖ad1 ♗e7 16 ♖xe4 de 17 ♖xd8+ ♗xd8 18 ♕g3 and Black's position is bad (Karklins–Nance, USA 1989).

8 … d5

On 8 … ♘f6 or 8 … h6 there follows 9 ♕b3!

9 f3 e3

The alternative is 9 … h6!? 10 fe hg 11 ef ♗d6 with good counterplay for Black. Moves that have been tried here are: 12 ♘d2, 12 ♕d3, 12 ♕e2+ and 12 ♕g4?!, but on each occasion Black has obtained at least an equal game. It is not impossible that, as information on 9 … h6 increases, it will become the main line.

10 f4

10 ♗xe3? h6 11 ♘h3 ♗xh3 12 gh ♕h4+ favours Black.

10 … ♗d6 *(99)*

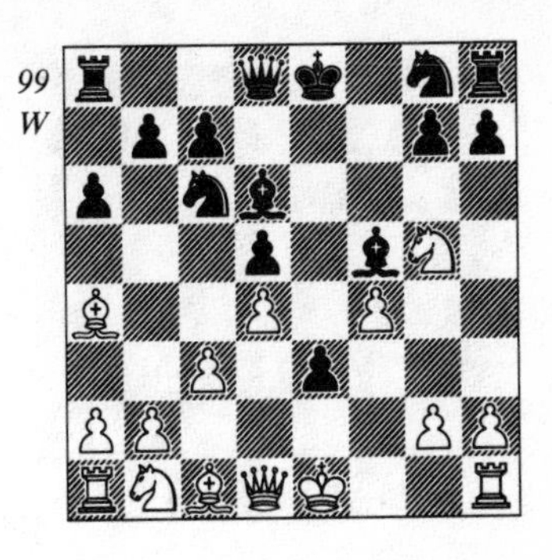
99
W

Worthy of consideration is 10 … ♘f6, after which White apparently should play 11 ♘f3 and then ♘e5.

After 10 … ♗d6 the following variations arise:

(a) **11 ♕h5+!** g6 (11 … ♗g6 12 ♕f3 ♕f6 13 ♕xe3+ ♘e7 14 ♕e6! favours White) 12 ♕f3 ♕f6 13 ♕xe3 ♘e7 (13 … ♔d7?! 14 0–0 ♖e8 15 ♕g3 h5 16 ♘a3 ♘h6 17 ♘f3 is in White's favour) 14 0–0. Black has lively piece play for the pawn, but one defect of his position is that his pieces have no access to the square g6. White's chances are somewhat better.

(b) **11 ♕f3** ♕f6 12 ♕xe3+ ♘e7 13 ♗xc6 (preferable is 13 0–0 0–0 14 ♘f3 ♗e4 15 ♘g5 ♗f5) 13 … bc 14 0–0 0–0 15 ♘d2? (essential was 15 ♘f3) 15 … ♘g6 16 g3 ♖ae8 17 ♕f2 ♗d3 with a clear advantage to Black (Euwe–Keres, World Ch. tournament 1948).

(c) Note also that after **11 ♗xe3** ♘f6 (also good is 11 … ♕e7 12 ♕e2 ♘h6!) 12 0–0 0–0 Black has excellent counterplay.

A122

7 0–0

This variation was not popular for long, although in the 1950s it was considered almost a refutation of the system with 5 … f5.

7 … ♗d3 *(100)*

And now:

8 ♖e1 ♗e7 (worse is 8 … e4 9 ♕b3 ♖b8 10 ♕e6+ ♕e7 11 ♕d5

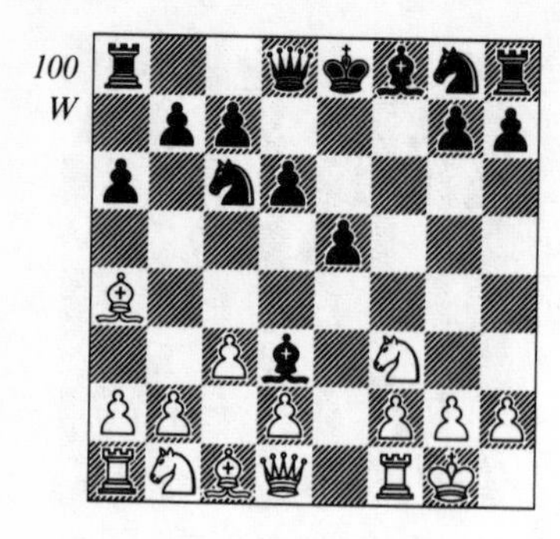
100
W

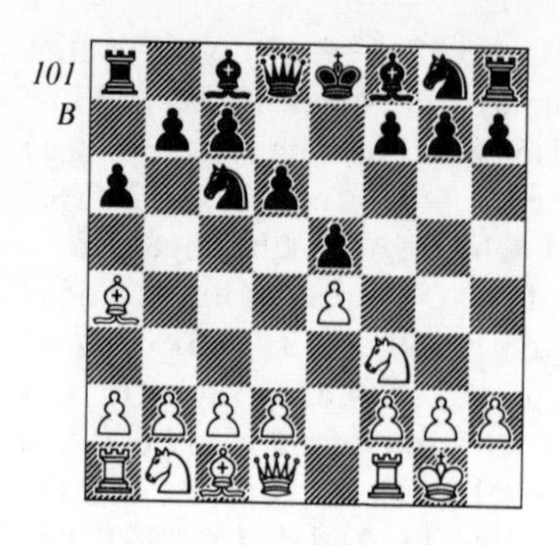
101
B

♘f6 12 ♗xc6+ bc 13 ♕xc6 ♔d8 14 ♘d4 and White stands better). Now:

(a) **9 ♕b3** (or 9 ♖e3 e4 10 ♘e1 ♗g5! 11 ♖h3 ♘f6 12 ♘xd3 ed 13 ♖xd3 0–0 14 ♖h3 ♕e7 15 ♘a3 ♖ae8 16 ♘c2 ♘e4 with full equality for Black; Smyslov–Lutikov, USSR Ch. 1961) 9 ... ♖b8 10 ♕d5 e4 11 ♗b3 ♘h6 12 ♘g5 ♘e5 13 ♘xe4 ♖f8 14 ♘g3 c6 15 ♕d4 c5 16 ♕d5 c4 with excellent counterplay for Black (Radchenko).

(b) **9 ♗c2** ♗xc2 10 ♕xc2 ♘f6 11 d4 ed (11 ... 0–0 12 de ♘xe5 13 ♘xe5 de 14 ♘d2 ♗c5 15 ♘b3 ♗b6 16 ♗e3 is better for White — Keres) 12 cd 0–0 13 ♘c3 ♔h8 14 ♘g5 ♘xd4! 15 ♕d3 h6 16 ♕xd4 hg 17 ♗xg5 ♕d7 with equal chances (Glek–Vorotnikov, USSR 1986).

A2

5 0–0 *(101)*

The fate of this system largely depends on the evaluation of the sharp variation beginning with 5 ... ♗g4, around which most investigation has revolved.

5 ... ♗g4

The move 5 ... ♗d7 has become less popular, although objectively there is no clear advantage for White. For example: 6 d4 b5 (in White's favour is 6 ... ♘ge7 7 d5 ♘b8 8 c4) 7 ♗b3 ♘xd4 (also possible is 7 ... ed 8 c3 d3!? 9 ♕xd3 ♘f6) 8 ♘xd4 ed 9 c3 d3 (9 ... dc 10 ♕h5 g6 11 ♕d5 ♗e6 12 ♕c6+ ♗d7 13 ♕xc3 gives White a strong initiative) 10 ♕xd3 (10 a4!) 10 ... ♘f6 11 ♕g3 ♘h5 12 ♕f3 ♘f6 13 ♖e1 ♗e7 14 ♘d2 0–0 15 ♘f1 ♘g4 16 ♕e2 ♗h4 with approximate equality (Gufeld–Bondarevsky, USSR Ch. 1963).

We shall briefly consider the rarer continuations on Black's 5th move in reply to 5 0–0. In White's favour is 5 ... g5?! 6 d4 g4 7 ♗xc6+ bc 8 ♘e1 ed 9 ♕xd4 ♕f6 10 ♕a4! ♘e7 11 ♘c3 ♗d7 12 ♕a5! (Suetin–Bondarevsky, USSR Ch. 1963); or 5 ... f5 6 d4 fe 7 ♘g5 ed 8 ♕xd4 ♘f6 9 ♘xe4 ♗d7 10 ♖e1! White also stands better after 5 ... g6 6 d4 ♗g7 7 ♗g5 ♘e7 8 ♘c3, or 5 ... ♘e7 6 d4 b5 7 ♗b3 ♘xd4 8 ♘xd4 ed 9 c3 dc 10 ♕h5 ♘g6 11 ♘xc3 ♗e7

12 f4! etc.

6 h3 h5!? *(102)*

The alternative is 6 ... ♗h5 7 c3 (interesting is 7 c4 ♘f6 8 ♘c3 ♗e7 9 d3 ♘d7 10 ♗e3 0–0 11 ♘d5 ♗g6 12 g4! with an initiative for White; Vasyukov–Bakulin, Moscow 1961). And now:

(a) **7 ... ♘f6** 8 d4 (8 d3) 8 ... b5 (after 8 ... ♘d7 9 ♗e3 ♗e7 10 ♘bd2 0–0 11 a3 ♗f6 12 g4! White has the better chances) 9 ♗b3 ♗e7 10 ♗e3 0–0 11 ♘bd2 d5 12 g4 ♗g6 13 ♘xe5 ♘xe5 14 de ♘xe4 15 f4 ♘xd2 16 ♕xd2 ♗e4 17 ♖ad1 and White has clearly better prospects.

(b) **7 ... ♕f6** 8 g4 ♗g6 9 d4 ♗xe4 10 ♘bd2 ♗g6 (10 ... ♗d3 11 ♗xc6+ bc 12 ♖e1 0–0–0 13 ♖e3 ♕g6 14 ♘h4 is in White's favour — Smyslov–Medina, Tel Aviv OL 1964; White is also better after 10 ... ♗xf3 11 ♘xf3 e4 12 ♘g5 d5 13 f3 ♕d6 14 ♕e1!) 11 ♗xc6+ bc 12 de de 13 ♘xe5 ♗d6 14 ♘xg6 ♕xg6 15 ♖e1+ ♔f8 16 ♘c4 with a clear advantage to White (Fischer–Geller, Bled 1961).

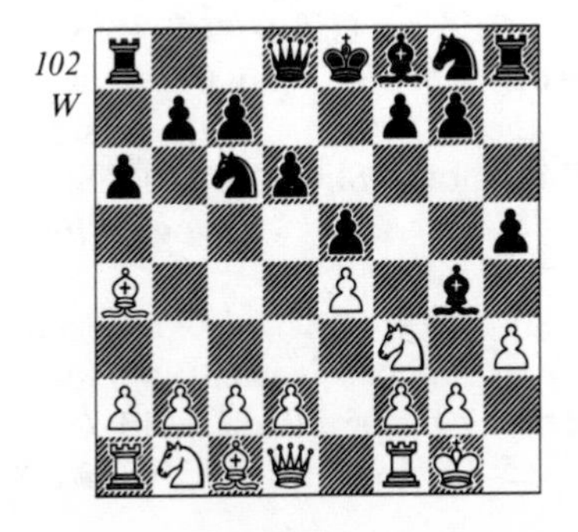

102
W

7 d4

Let us also consider the following variations:

(a) **7 c4** ♕f6 (7 ... b5?! 8 cb ♘d4 9 ba+ c6 10 ♘xd4 ♗xd1 11 ♗xc6+ ♔e7 12 ♘f5+ ♔f6 13 ♗xa8 ♕xa8 14 ♖xd1 d5! leads to unclear and sharp play) 8 ♕b3 0–0–0 9 ♗xc6 bc, and now:

(a1) **10 hg** hg 11 ♘h2 ♕h4! 12 ♕g3 ♕xg3 13 fg d5! 14 ♘xg4 ♗c5+ with dangerous counterplay for Black (Suetin).

(a2) **10 ♘h2** ♗d7 11 d4 ed 12 ♘f3 ♖e8 13 ♗g5 ♕g6 14 ♘bd2 c5 with roughly equal play (Suetin).

(b) **7 ♗xc6+** bc 8 d4 ♕f6 9 ♘bd2 ♗e6 10 ♘b3 ♕g6 11 ♘g5!? (11 ♕b3 f6!) 11 ... ♗c8 12 de f6?! 13 ef gf 14 ♕d4! with better prospects for White (Kozlov–Vorotnikov, USSR 1979).

7 ... b5

After 7 ... ♕f6 8 de de 9 hg hg 10 ♗g5 ♕e6 11 ♕d5 (or 11 ♘h4 ♗e7 12 ♗b3! ♕c8 13 ♕d5 ♘d8 14 ♕xe5 ♖h5 15 f4) 11 ... gf 12 ♕xe6+ fe 13 ♗xc6+ bc 14 gf White has the advantage.

8 ♗b3 ♘xd4

8 ... ♗xf3 9 ♕xf3 ♕f6 10 ♕c3! is good for White.

9 hg hg

10 ♘g5 ♘h6 *(103)*

A very sharp and problematic position has arisen, where the following variations are possible:

(a) **11 c3** ♘xb3 12 ab ♗e7 13 ♕d5 ♖c8 14 ♖xa6 (14 f4!?) 14 ... ♗xg5 15 ♕c6+ ♔f8 16 ♗xg5 ♕xg5 17 ♖a8 ♖d8 18 ♘d2 g6 19

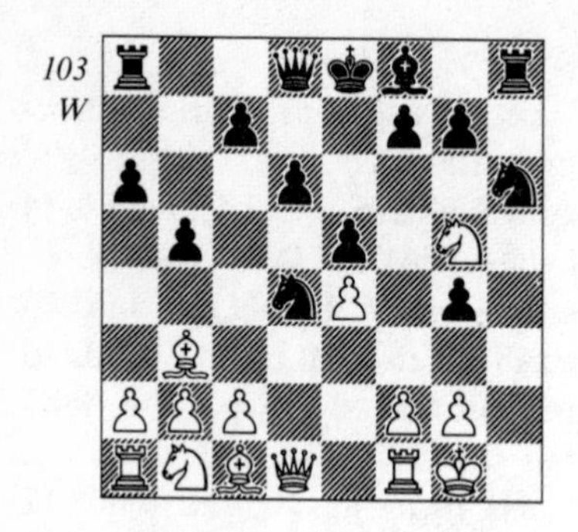
103
W

♖xd8+ ♕xd8 20 ♖a1 ♔g7 21 ♘f1 g3! with sharp counterplay for Black (Parma–Mestrovic, Sarajevo 1971).

(b) **11 f4** d5 (interesting is 11 … gf!? 12 ♖xf3 ♘xf3+ 13 ♕xf3 ♕f6) 12 ♗xd5 ♗c5 13 ♗e3 ♕d6! 14 b4 ♗b6 15 c4 bc 16 ♘a3 ♘df5 17 ♗f2 g3 with sufficient counterplay for Black (Ciric–Scholl, Amsterdam 1970).

(c) **11 g3** ♕f6!? 12 c3 (12 f4 gf 13 ♘xf3 ♕g6! is good for Black) 12 … ♘xb3 13 ♕xb3 ♗e7 14 a4 (14 ♕d5!?) 14 … ♕g6 15 ab ♗g5 16 ♖xa6 ♖d8 with unclear play (Marjanovic–Chermek, Bled 1989).

A3

5 ♗xc6+ bc

In exchanging his active bishop, White counts on an advantage in space and in some lines wishes to make use of Black's pawn weaknesses on the queenside. But Black has certain trump cards — his cluster of pawns in the centre may later on become mobile.

6 d4 f6

After 6 … ed 7 ♘xd4 a position arises which is characteristic of the Steinitz Defence. Also possible is 7 ♕xd4, for example: 7 … c5 8 ♕d3 g6 9 ♘c3 ♗g7 10 ♗g5! ♕d7 11 0–0–0.

Worthy of consideration is 6 … ♗g4 (Lutikov). For example: 7 de de 8 ♕xd8+ (8 ♘bd2 f6 9 ♕e2) 8 … ♖xd8 9 ♘bd2 f6 and it is hard for White to make use of his opponent's pawn weaknesses.

7 ♗e3

Besides this move there are some well-known continuations:

(a) **7 ♘c3** ♖b8 8 ♗e3!? ♖xb2 9 ♕d3 ♖b8 10 0–0 ♘e7 with roughly equal chances.

(b) **7 c4** ♘e7 8 ♘c3 ♘g6 (interesting is 8 … c5!? 9 dc dc 10 ♕xd8+ ♔xd8) 9 ♗e3 ♗e7 10 ♕a4 ♗d7 11 c5 ♕b8 12 0–0–0 ♕b7 13 ♖d2 ♖b8 14 de de 15 g3 ♘f8 16 ♘h4 g6 17 ♕c2 ♗e6 with double-edged and roughly equal play (Spassky–Smyslov, Leningrad 1958). There is a curious variation 8 ♕a4 ♗d7 9 c5 ♘g6 10 ♗e3 ♗e7 11 h4!? h5 which requires examination.

7 … ♘e7

Possible is 7 … ♖b8 8 b3 (8 ♘bd2) 8 … ♘e7 9 ♘c3 ♘g6 10 ♕d3 ♗e7 11 0–0–0 a5 with chances for both sides (Matanovic–Sliwa, Sofia 1958).

8 ♘c3 ♘g6 *(104)*

And now:

(a) **9 ♕d2** ♗e7 (also not bad are 9 … a5 or 9 … ♗e6) 10 0–0–0 ♗e6 11 h4 h5 12 de fe 13 ♘g5 ♗xg5 14 ♗xg5 ♕b8 15 b3 ♕b4

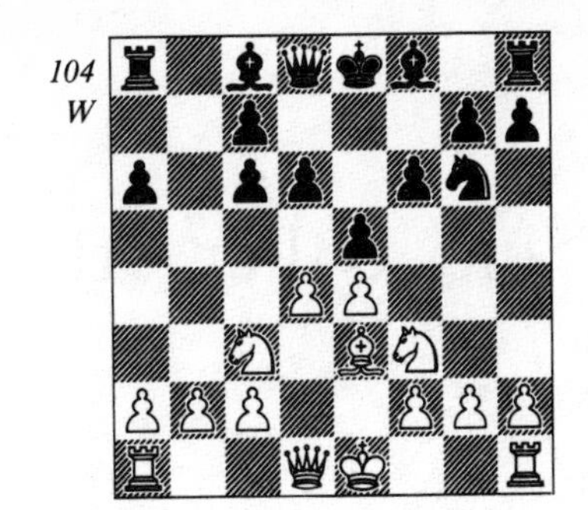
104
W

with good play for Black (Ivkov–Smyslov, Belgrade 1956).

(b) **9 ♕d3** ♗e7 10 0–0–0 a5 11 h4 h5 with slightly better play for White.

(c) **9 ♕e2** a5 10 ♕c4 ♕d7 11 0–0–0 ♗a6 12 ♕b3 ♗e7 13 h4 h5 and chances are equal.

B

In concluding this chapter of the book we shall briefly consider some rare continuations.

(a) **4 ... ♘ge7** 5 c3 (or 5 ♘c3 d6 6 d4 ed 7 ♘xd4 ♗d7 8 ♗b3 ♘xd4 9 ♕xd4 ♘c6 10 ♕e3 and Black has a strong defence) 5 ... b5 (better is 5 ... d6, transposing to the Steinitz Defence Deferred) 6 ♗b3 d5(?) 7 ♕e2 ♗e6 8 ♘g5 ♘g6 9 d3 and Black's position is bad (Suetin–Klaric, Sochi 1977).

(b) **4 ... ♗e7?!** 5 0–0 d6 6 c4 ♘f6 7 d4 0–0 8 ♘c3 with pressure for White.

(c) **4 ... ♗c5?!** 5 c3 b5 6 ♗c2 d5 7 d4! and here Black has difficulties.

(d) **4 ... g6** 5 d4 ♘xd4 6 ♘xd4 ed 7 ♕xd4 ♕f6 8 e5 ♕e7 9 ♘c3 with a marked advantage to White.

(e) **4 ... ♘d4?!** 5 ♘xe5 b5 6 ♗b3 ♕g5 7 ♘g4 d5 8 h3 h5 9 d3 ♕g6 10 ♘e3 with better chances for White.

(f) **4 ... ♗b4** 5 c3 ♗a5 6 0–0 ♘ge7 7 d4 ed 8 cd d5 9 ed ♕xd5 10 ♘c3 and White has a noticeable lead in development.

8 Centre Attack and Other 5th Moves

In this chapter we shall look at the popular Centre Attack and other White 5th moves apart from the usual 5 0–0 after the sequence 1 e4 e5 2 ♘f3 ♘c6 3 ♗b5 a6 4 ♗a4 ♘f6.

A 5 d4
B 5 ♘c3

Let us also briefly consider the following variations:

(a) **5 ♕e2**. This continuation is met very rarely nowadays. The following variations are possible: 5 ... b5 6 ♗b3 ♗c5 (also good is 6 ... ♗e7 7 a4 ♖b8 8 ab ab 9 d4 d5! 10 c3 ♘xe4 11 ♘xe5 ♘xe5 12 de 0–0 13 0–0 ♗f5 with equal play; Spassky–Kholmov, Leningrad 1954) 7 a4 ♖b8 8 ab ab 9 ♘c3 0–0 (or 9 ... b4 10 ♘d5 0–0 11 d3 ♘xd5 12 ♗xd5 ♘d4 13 ♘xd4 ♗xd4 14 0–0 c6 with equality) 10 d3 d6 11 ♗g5 ♗b4 (or 11 ... h6 12 ♗xf6 ♕xf6 13 ♘d5 ♕d8 14 0–0 b4; Bogolyubov–Eliskases, match 1939) 12 0–0 ♗xc3 13 bc h6 14 ♗h4 ♕e7 with full equality for Black (Spielmann–Eliskases, match 1932).

(b) **5 d3**. A very old continuation, which was adopted by Anderssen and Steinitz. Nowadays, however, it is usually resorted to in order to avoid the main lines. It is reliable but passive: 5 ... d6 (5 ... b5 6 ♗b3 ♗e7 7 c3 d5!? or 7 ... d6 with level chances) 6 c3 g6 (also good is 6 ... ♗e7 7 ♘bd2 0–0 8 h3 b5 9 ♗c2 d5) 7 ♘bd2 (7 0–0 ♗g7 8 d4 0–0 9 d5 ♘e7 10 ♖e1 c6 11 dc bc 12 c4 ♕c7 13 ♘c3 ♗e6 14 ♕e2 c5 gives Black full equality; Stein–Korchnoi, USSR 1965) 7 ... ♗g7 8 ♘f1 0–0 9 ♘g3 b5 10 ♗c2 d5 11 ♕e2 ♗b7 12 0–0 ♖e8 with equality (Treybal–Grünfeld, Teplitz–Schönau, 1922).

(c) **5 ♗xc6** dc 6 d3 (after 6 ♘c3 ♗g4 7 h3 ♗h5 8 d3 ♘d7 9 ♗e3 ♗b4 10 ♗d2 ♕e7 Black is no worse; Flohr–Euwe, Semmering 1937) 6 ... ♗d6 7 ♘bd2 ♗e6 (also possible is 7 ... c5 8 ♘c4 ♘d7 9 a4 b6 10 0–0 0–0; Korchnoi–Suetin, USSR 1965) 8 ♕e2 ♘d7 9 ♘c4 f6 10 d4 ♗g4 11 de ♘xe5 12 ♘cxe5 ♗xe5 with equal play (Flohr–Keres, Hastings 1937/8).

A

5 **d4** *(105)*

An early attack against the centre, which leads to lively piece play. Such a method of fighting for the initiative has long been known, but its detailed elaboration began only in the 1950s. Objectively this move can hardly give White the advantage, but a number of variations lend themselves to concrete calculation. Note that this plan frequently arises after 5 0–0 ♗e7 6 d4.

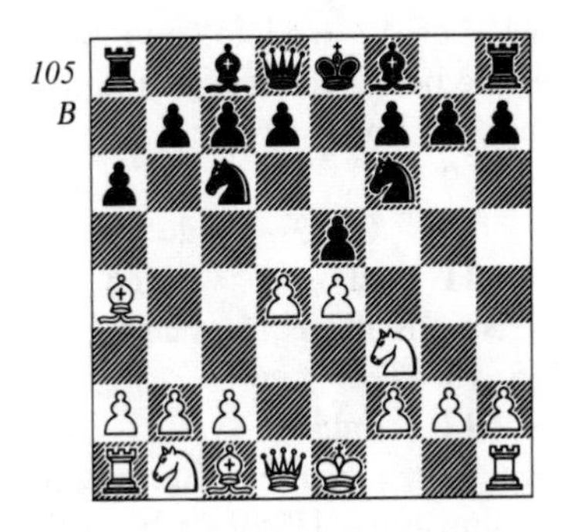

105
B

5 … ed

Other variations:

(a) **5 … ♘xe4** 6 ♕e2 b5 7 ♕xe4 d5 8 ♕e3 ba 9 ♘xe5 ♘xe5 10 0–0 ♗e6 11 de ♕d7 12 ♘c3 ♗b4 13 ♕g3 0–0 14 ♗h6 f6 15 ♗f4 c5 16 ♖ad1 with pressure for White (Kholmov–Khasin, USSR Ch. 1961).

(b) **5 … ♘xd4** 6 ♘xd4 ed 7 e5 ♘e4 8 ♕xd4 ♘c5 9 ♘c3 ♗e7 10 ♕g4.

(c) **5 … b5** 6 ♗b3 ed 7 e5 ♘e4 8 ♗d5 ♗b4+ 9 c3 dc 10 0–0 cb 11 ♗xb2. In both cases White has a dangerous initiative.

6 0–0 ♗e7 *(106)*

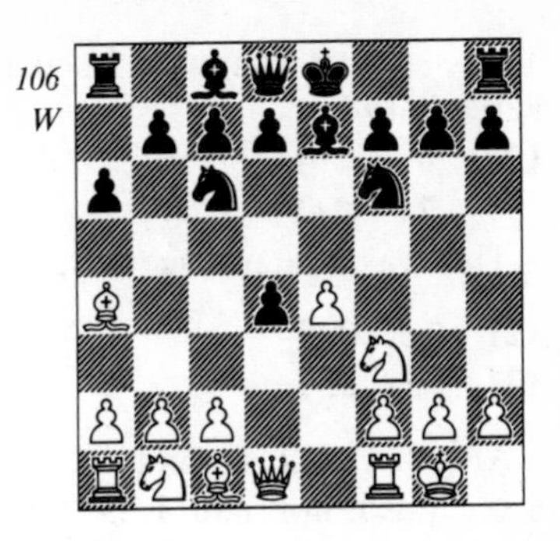

106
W

A critical position, in which White has two main plans:

A1 7 e5
A2 7 ♖e1

A1

7 e5 ♘e4
8 ♘xd4

White has few prospects after 8 ♖e1 ♘c5 9 ♗xc6 dc 10 ♘xd4 0–0 11 ♘c3 f5; or 8 b4?! 0–0 9 a3 b5 10 ♗b3 d5 etc.

8 … 0–0

Also not bad is 8 … ♘xd4 9 ♕xd4 ♘c5 10 ♘c3 0–0 11 ♗g5 ♗xg5 12 ♕xc5 ♗e7 13 ♕e3 d5; or 8 … ♘c5 9 ♘f5 0–0 10 ♕g4 g6 11 ♗xc6 dc 12 ♘xe7+ ♕xe7 13 ♕g3 ♖e8 with equal chances.

9 ♘f5 d5
10 ♗xc6 bc
11 ♘xe7+ ♕xe7
12 ♖e1

And now:

(a) **12 … f6** 13 f3 ♘g5! 14 ♘c3 ♗f5 15 ef ♕xf6 and Black is not worse (Keres).

(b) **12 … ♗f5!?** 13 f3 ♘c5 14 b3 ♘e6 15 ♗a3 c5 16 ♘c3 ♖fd8 17 ♕d2 ♕h4 with chances for both sides (Mnatsakanyan–Smejkal, Yerevan 1976).

A2

7 ♖e1

This was a later discovery.

A21 7 … 0–0
A22 7 … b5

After 7 … d6 8 ♘xd4 ♗d7 9 ♗xc6 (also not bad is 9 ♘xc6 ♗xc6 10 ♗xc6+ bc 11 ♘c3) 9 … bc 10 ♗f4 a position arises which is characteristic of the Steinitz Defence.

A21

7 … 0–0
8 e5 ♘e8 *(107)*

Worse is 8 … ♘d5 9 ♘xd4 ♘xd4 10 ♕xd4 ♘b6 11 ♗b3 d5 12 ed ♗xd6 (12 … ♕xd6 13 ♕e4!) 13 ♗f4 ♕h4 14 g3 ♕g4 15 h3 ♕f3 16 ♖e3! ♕c6 17 ♖c3 ♕d7 18 ♖d3! with advantage to White (Kholmov–Gurgenidze, USSR 1961).

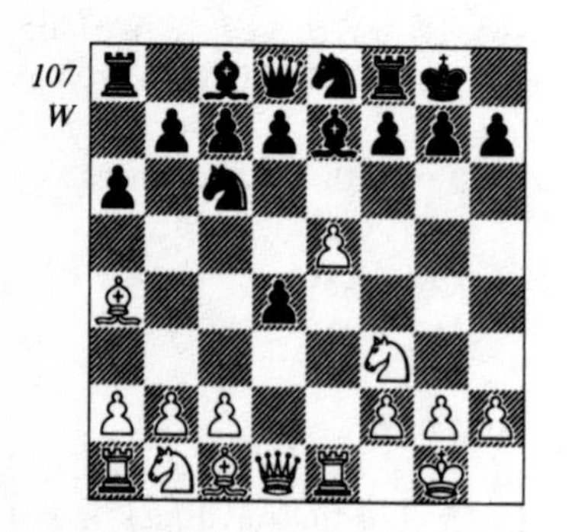
107
W

9 c3!?

Other possibilities for White briefly:

(a) **9 ♗f4** b5 10 ♗b3 d5 11 c3 (or 11 ♘xd4 ♘xd4 12 ♕xd4 c6 13 ♕b3 ♘c7 14 c3 g6 15 ♘d2 ♗f5 with chances for both sides; Capelan–Gligoric, Berlin 1971) 11 … ♗g4 12 h3 ♗h5 13 g4 ♗g6 14 ♘xd4 ♘xd4 15 cd c6 16 ♗e3 f5 17 f4 ♘c7 18 ♘c3 ♕d7 and Black has a solid position (Grünberg–Vogt, East Germany 1978).

(b) **9 ♘xd4?!** ♘xd4 10 ♕xd4 b5 11 ♗b3 c5 12 ♕e4 ♖b8 13 c4 ♗b7 14 ♕e2 b4 15 ♘d2 ♘c7 16 ♘e4 ♘e6 17 ♕d3 f5! and Black has the better chances (Kholmov–Smyslov, Sochi 1974).

9 … dc
10 ♘xc3 d6
11 ed ♘xd6

Also possible is 11 … cd 12 ♘d5 ♗f6 13 ♗e3 ♗e6.

12 ♘d5

In the game Georgadze–Romanishin, USSR Ch. 1978, there followed: 12 … ♗e6 13 ♗xc6 bc 14 ♘xe7+ ♕xe7 15 ♕c2 ♗f5 16 ♖xe7 ♗xc2 17 ♗f4 ♘f5 with equal chances.

A22

7 … b5
8 e5

After 8 ♗b3 d6 9 ♗d5 ♘xd5 10 ed ♘e5 11 ♘xd4 0–0 12 ♘c3 ♖e8! 13 a4 b4 14 ♘e4 ♗b7 15 ♘f5 ♕d7 16 ♘xe7+ ♖xe7 the game is level (Timman–Spassky, match 1983).

8 … ♘xe5 *(108)*

And now:

(a) **9 ♖xe5** d6 (also possible is 9 … ba 10 ♘xd4 0–0 11 ♘c3 ♖e8 12 ♗g5 ♗b7 13 ♘f5! ♗f8 14

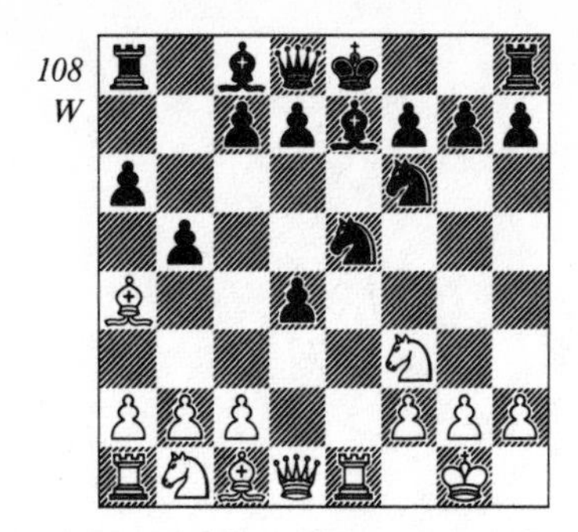
108
W

♕d4 c5 15 ♕f4 ♖xe5 16 ♘h6+ with some initiative for White; Machulsky–Geller, USSR 1981) 10 ♖e1 (10 ♖xe7+? ♕xe7 11 ♗b3 c5 favours Black; double-edged play arises after 10 ♖g5?! ba 11 ♕xd4!?) 10 … ba 11 ♘xd4 (or 11 ♗g5 0–0 12 ♕e2 ♖e8 13 ♗xf6 gf 14 ♘xd4 ♗b7! 15 ♕h5 ♗f8 16 ♘c3 ♖e5 17 ♘f5 ♕e8 with equal chances; Machulsky–Timoshchenko, Krasnoyarsk 1981) 11 … ♗d7 12 ♕f3 0–0 13 ♘c6 ♗xc6 14 ♕xc6 d5! 15 ♗g5 a3 16 ♘xa3 ♕d6 17 ♕xd6 ♗xd6 18 ♖ad1 ♖ab8 19 ♗xf6 gf 20 ♖xd5 ♖fd8 with excellent play for Black (Khasanov–Kaidanov, Tashkent 1985).

(b) **9 ♘xe5** ba 10 ♕xd4 0–0 11 ♕xa4 ♖b8 12 a3 ♖b6 13 ♘c3 ♖e6 14 ♗g5 c6 with equal chances for both sides (Chiburdanidze–Romanishin, Frunze 1985).

B

5 ♘c3 *(109)*

There was a time when this continuation was considered virtually the main line, but nowadays it is hardly ever played.

5 … b5

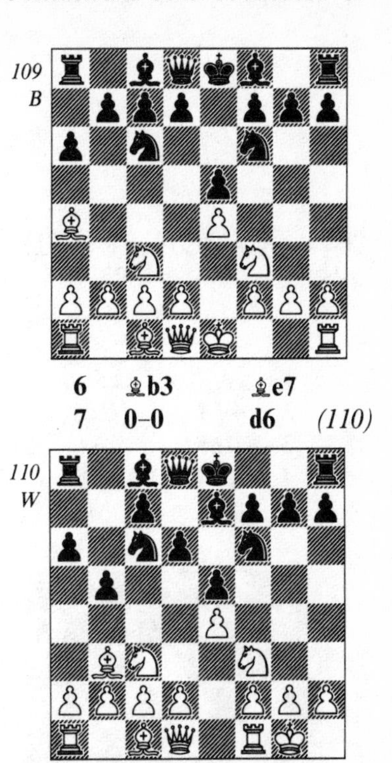
109
B

6 ♗b3 ♗e7
7 0–0 d6 *(110)*

110
W

And now, **8 ♘d5!?** with the following lines:

(a) **8 … ♘a5** 9 ♘xe7 ♕xe7 10 d4 ♗b7 11 ♗g5 0–0 (11 … ♗xe4? 12 ♘xe5! ♘xb3 13 ab de 14 ♖e1 ed 15 ♗xf6 ♕xf6 16 ♖xe4+ ♔d7 favours White; Keres–Spassky, Amsterdam 1956) 12 de de 13 ♕e1 ♘xb3 14 ab (Keres–Euwe, match 1939/40). By playing 14 … h6 15 ♗xf6 ♕xf6 16 ♕e3 ♕c6 17 ♖fe1 f6 18 b4 ♕c4 Black is able to obtain equality.

(b) **8 … ♘xe4** 9 d4 ♗b7 10 ♖e1 ♘a5 11 de ♘xb3 12 ab de 13 c4 ♘f6 14 ♘xe7 ♕xd1 15 ♖xd1 ♗xf3 16 gf ♔xe7 with satisfactory play for Black (Karaklajic–Keres, Belgrade 1956).

9 Open Variation

1	**e4**	**e5**
2	**♘f3**	**♘c6**
3	**♗b5**	**a6**
4	**♗a4**	**♘f6**
5	**0–0**	**♘xe4** *(111)*

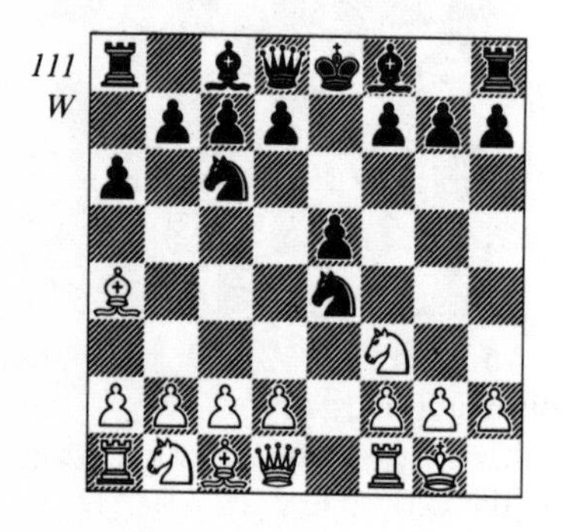
111
W

This is one of the most interesting areas of opening theory. By capturing the pawn on e4, Black aims to create space for his pieces. At the same time he has to reckon with a certain weakness of his pawn structure on the queenside. A lively strategic conflict arises which is frequently seen in the games of top grandmasters and club players alike.

6 d4

The main continuation. After 6 ♖e1 (6 ♗xc6 dc 7 ♖e1 ♘c5 is not dangerous for Black) 6 ... ♘c5! 7 ♘c3 ♗e7 8 ♗xc6 dc, or 6 ♕e2 ♘c5 7 ♗xc6 dc 8 d4 ♘e6 9 de ♘d4 10 ♘xd4 ♕xd4 11 h3 ♗e7 12 ♘d2, Black has no difficulties.

6 ... b5

Let us briefly consider the following variations:

(a) **6 ... ed** 7 ♖e1 d5 (the 'Riga Variation') 8 ♘xd4 (besides this classical variation, no less effective is 8 c4! dc 9 ♘xc3! ♗e6 10 ♘d4 ♕d7 11 ♘xc6 ♘xc3 12 bc bc 13 c4! and Black has enormous difficulties) 8 ... ♗d6 9 ♘xc6 ♗xh2+ 10 ♔h1 ♕h4 11 ♖xe4+! de 12 ♕d8+ ♕xd8 13 ♘xd8+ ♔xd8 14 ♔xh2 ♗e6 15 ♗e3 f5 16 ♘c3 ♔e7 17 g4! g6 18 ♔g3 with a clear advantage to White (Capablanca–Ed. Lasker, New York 1915).

(b) **6 ... ♗e7?!** — the Walbrodt Variation, which until recently had not been studied very deeply. The following variations arise:

(b1) **7 ♖e1** f5 (not without interest is 7 ... b5!? 8 ♖xe4 d5 9 ♘xe5 ♘xe5 10 ♗xb5+ ab 11 ♖xe5 0–0 12 ♘c3, when there arises a formation analogous to the Marshall Attack) 8 de 0–0 9 ♗b3+ (worthy of consideration is 9 ♘c3!? ♘xc3 10 bc d6 11 ed ♕xd6 12 ♕e2 ♗f6 13 ♕c4+ ♔h8 14 ♗f4 — Boleslavsky) 9 … ♔h8 10 ♘c3! (also good is 10 ♗d5) 10 … ♘xc3 11 bc h6 12 a4 (also not bad is 12 ♗d5 d6 13 ed ♗xd6 14 ♘g5!) 12 … a5? (better is 12 … b6) 13 ♖b1 b6 14 ♗d5 ♗b7 15 ♘d4 with an onslaught from White (Geller–Kurajica, Wijk aan Zee 1977).

(b2) **7 ♕e2** f5 8 de 0–0 9 ♖d1 (interesting is 9 ♘c3!? ♘xc3 10 bc ♔h8 11 c4 ♘a5 12 ♕d3 b6 13 ♗e3 f4 14 ♗d4 ♗b7 15 ♗c3 ♗xf3 16 ♕xf3 ♘xc4 17 ♗b3 ♘a5 18 ♗d5 c6 19 ♗e4 with advantage to White — Christiansen–Smyslov, Copenhagen 1985) 9 … ♕e8 10 ♗b3+ ♔h8 11 ♘bd2 ♘c5! 12 ♘c4 with pressure for White (Lasker–Walbrodt, Nürnberg 1896).

7 ♗b3 d5 *(112)*

Let us consider the following continuations:

(a) **7 … ed?!** — the Trifunovic Variation. Practice has shown that Black gets a difficult game:

(a1) **8 ♘xd4** ♘xd4 9 ♕xd4 ♘f6 (9 … ♘c5 10 ♗xf7+!) 10 ♗g5 ♗b7 11 ♖e1+.

(a2) **8 ♖e1** d5 9 ♘c3! ♗e6 (9 … dc?! 10 ♗xd5 ♗b7 11 ♗xe4! ♗e7 12 ♕e2) 10 ♘xe4 de 11 ♖xe4! ♗e7 12 ♗xe6 fe 13 ♘xd4! (Fischer–Trifunovic, Bled 1961).

In both cases Black's position is bad.

(b) **7 … ♗e7** — the Smyslov Variation, which has also not been studied very much. The following variations may arise: 8 ♘xe5 (or 8 de ♘c5 9 ♗d5 ♗b7 10 ♘c3 0–0 11 ♗e3 d6 and Black has good chances of equality; on 8 ♕e2 there follows 8 … d5 9 de ♘a5!) 8 … ♘xe5 9 de ♗b7 10 ♕g4 0–0 (Tal–Smyslov, USSR Ch. 1977). After 11 f3 (11 ♘c3 ♘xc3 12 ♗h6 ♗f6! 13 ef ♕xf6 14 ♗g5 ♕d4!) 11 … ♘g5 12 f4? (better is 12 ♘c3 and if 12 … ♔h8 then 13 f4!) 12 … ♘e4 13 f5 ♔h8 Black has a good game.

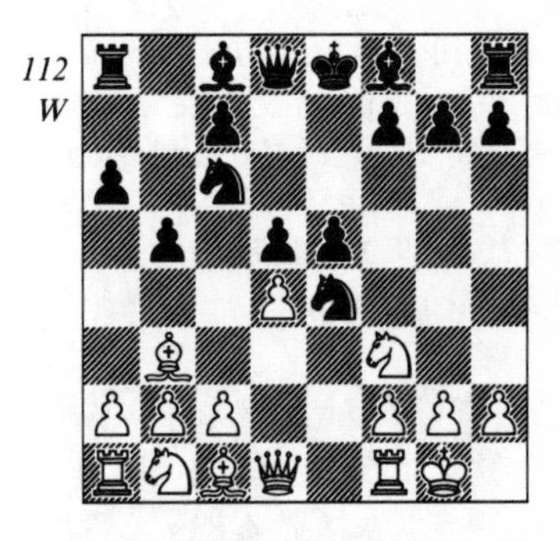
112
W

In this position White has two main variations to choose from:

A 8 de
B 8 ♘xe5

We shall also consider continuations which are rare nowadays:

(a) **8 a4?!** ♘xd4! 9 ♘xd4 ed 10 ab ♗c5 11 c3 0–0 12 cd ♗b6 (also not bad is 12 … ♗d6 13 ♘c3 ♗b7) 13 ♘c3 ♗b7 14 ba ♖xa6 15 ♖xa6 ♗xa6 16 ♖e1 ♗b7 17 ♘a4 ♕f6 with full equality for Black (Lasker–Schlechter, match 1910).

(b) **8 c4?!** dc (or 8 … ♗g4!? 9 cd ♘xd4 10 ♖e1 f5 11 h3 ♘xf3+ 12 gf ♕h4!) 9 ♕e2 cb 10 ♕xe4 ♗b7 (Larsen). This situation favours Black.

(c) **8 ♘c3?!** (Puc) 8 … ♘xc3 9 bc e4 10 ♘g5 ♗f5 11 f3 e3 12 f4 ♕d7 13 ♕f3 ♖d8 14 ♕xc3+ ♗e7 15 h3 0–0 16 g4 ♗xg5 17 fg ♗e6 with excellent play for Black (Shatskes–Zhuravlev, Riga 1962).

A

8 de

The main line of the system.

8 … ♗e6 *(113)*

First let us consider a forgotten variation with 8 … ♘e7. After 9 a4 ♖b8 10 ab ab 11 ♘d4 ♘c5 (11 … c5 12 ♘xb5!) 12 ♗g5 ♕d7 13 ♖a7! ♖b7 14 ♖a8! Black has a difficult position.

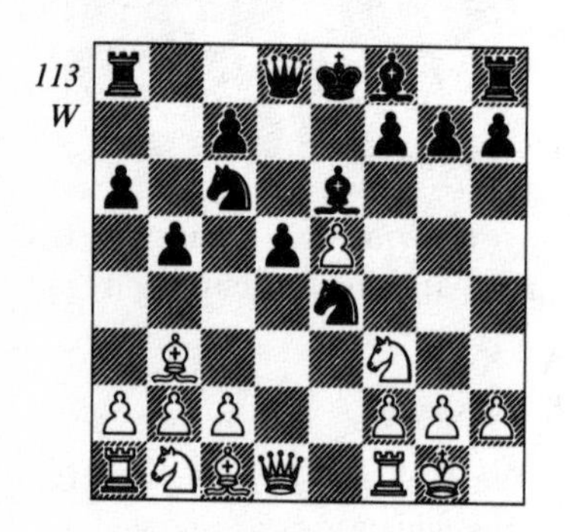

In this critical position White has a wide choice, but mainly:

A1 9 c3
A2 9 ♘bd2
A3 9 ♕e2

It is also necessary to take the following lines into consideration:

(a) **9 ♗e3**. This objectively rather harmless move is nowadays quite fashionable. Frequently play transposes to a system considered later (9 c3 ♗e7 10 ♗e3). We shall briefly consider the following variations:

(a1) **9 … ♗e7** 10 ♘bd2 ♘xd2 (or 10 … ♘c5 11 ♘g5?! — 11 ♘d4; 11 c3 ♘d3! — 11 … 0–0 12 ♕h5 ♗xg5 13 ♗xg5 ♕d7 14 ♖ae1 ♖fe8 with equal play; Dvoiris–Kaidanov, Vilnius 1984) 11 ♕xd2 ♕d7 12 a4 0–0 12 ♖fd1 ♖ad8 14 ab ab 15 c3 ♕c8 16 ♕d3 ♕b7 17 ♗c2 g6 18 h3 ♗f5 and Black has a solid defence (Grushevsky–Khermmen, Moscow 1977).

(a2) **9 … ♗c5** 10 ♕d3 0–0 11 ♘bd2 ♗xe3 12 ♕xe3 ♘xd2 13 ♕xd2 ♘e7 14 ♕c3 a5 15 a4 b4 16 ♕c5 ♕d7 17 ♘d4 c6! and here Black's position is not bad (Lobron–Yusupov, Sarajevo 1984).

(a3) **9 … ♘a5** 10 ♘d4 ♕d7 11 ♕e1 ♘xb3 12 ab ♗e7 13 b4 c5 14 ♘xe6 fe 15 f3 with complicated play (Kupreichik–Sdutsky, Moscow 1979).

(b) **9 a4** b4 10 a5 ♘c5 11 ♗g5 ♕d7 12 ♘bd2 h6 13 ♗f4 ♗e7 with equality.

(c) **9 ♘c3?!** ♘xc3 10 bc ♘e7 11 ♗a3 a5 12 ♗xe7 ♗xe7 13 a4 c5 14 ab 0–0! with better chances for Black.

A1

9 c3

White creates space for his 'b3' bishop to manoeuvre, at the same time strengthening the d4 square. Black has a choice of:

A11 **9 ... ♗e7**
A12 **9 ... ♗c5**
A13 **9 ... ♘c5**

Unattractive is 9 ... g6(?) 10 a4 ♗g7 11 ab ♘xe5 12 ♘xe5 ♗xe5 13 ♘bd2, and even more so 9 ... g5? 10 ♘bd2 ♘c5 11 ♗c2 g4 12 ♘d4 ♘xe5 13 f4! gf 14 ♘2xf3 ♗d6 15 ♘xe5 ♗xe5 16 ♘xe6 ♘xe6 17 ♕h5! (Keres).

A11

9 ... ♗e7 *(114)*

One of the main systems. Aiming to complete his development as quickly as possible, Black intends in some lines to begin an offensive on the queenside.

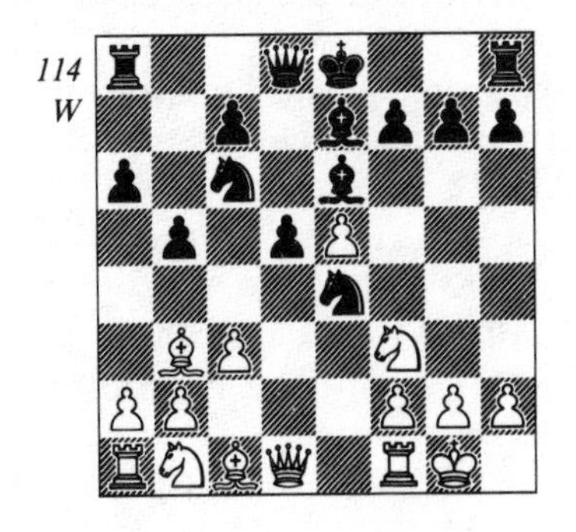

Now White has the following choice:

A111 **10 ♘bd2**
A112 **10 ♗c2**
A113 **10 ♖e1**
A114 **10 ♗e3**

Let us also consider the following variations:

(a) **10 ♕e2** 0–0 (or 10 ... ♘c5 11 ♗c2 d4!? 12 ♖d1 ♗c4 13 ♕e1 d3 14 ♘a3 ♕c8 15 ♗b1 ♗d5! with excellent counterplay for Black) 11 ♘d4?! ♕d7 13 f3 ♘c5 13 ♗c2 f6! 14 ef ♗xf6 15 ♘xe6 ♕xe6 16 ♕xe6+ ♘xe6 17 ♗b3 ♖ad8 18 ♖fd1 ♘e7 19 ♘bd2 ♔f7 and Black has full equality (Korchnoi–Suetin, USSR 1960).

(b) **10 ♗f4** ♘c5 (also good is 10 ... g5!? 11 ♗e3 g4 12 ♘fd2 ♘c5) 11 ♗c2 ♗g4 12 h3 ♗h5 13 ♕e2 ♘e6 14 ♗h2 ♗c5 15 ♘bd2 ♘e7 16 ♖ad1 ♕c8 17 ♘b3 ♗b6 18 ♔h1 c5 with excellent play for Black (Petrosian–Korchnoi, Moscow 1965).

(c) **10 a4** (the Alekhine Variation) 10 ... b4 11 ♘d4 ♘xe5 12 f4 ♗g4! 13 ♕c2 c5 14 fe cd 15 cd 0–0 16 ♘d2 (16 ♕d3 ♗h5!) 16 ... ♗e2 17 ♖e1 ♖c8 18 ♕b1 ♗h5 19 ♘xe4 ♗g6 20 ♗c2 de or 20 ... b3!? with sufficient counterplay for Black.

A111

10 ♘bd2 0–0

Again White has a choice:

A1111 **11 ♗c2**
A1112 **11 ♕e2**
A1113 **11 ♖e1**

A1111

11 ♗c2 f5

Briefly the other possibilities:

(a) **11 ... ♗f5** 12 ♘d4 ♘xd4 13 cd c5 (13 ... f6!?) 14 ♘xe4 ♗xe4 15 ♗xe4 de 16 d5 ♖e8 17 ♖e1

(17 f4!) 17 ... ♕d7 18 d6 ♗f8 and Black's defence holds (Geller–Korchnoi, Budva 1967).

(b) **11 ... ♘c5** 12 ♘d4 ♕d7 13 ♖e1.

(c) **11 ... ♘xd2** 12 ♕xd2 f6 13 ♕d3 g6 14 ef ♗xf6 15 ♗h6 ♖e8 16 ♖fe1 (Suetin–Korchnoi, Moscow 1966). In both cases White stands better.

After 11 ... f5 White has another choice of alternatives:

A11111 12 ♘b3
A11112 12 ef

A11111

12 ♘b3

This is now the main continuation, forcing Black to solve problems which are not so simple. Note an original idea which occurred in the game Ciric–Leverett, Gausdal 1982: 12 ♘d4!? ♘xd4?! 13 cd c5 14 dc ♘xd2 15 ♗xd2 ♗xc5 16 ♖c1 with a comfortable formation for White.

12 ... ♕d7
13 ♘fd4!

13 ♘bd4 ♘a5!? 14 ♘xe6 ♕xe6 15 ♘d4?! ♕xe5 16 f3 ♗d6 17 g3 f4! 18 fe fg 19 ♘f3 g2! 20 ♔xg2 ♖xf3 led to a draw in the game Boleslavsky–Zagorovsky, Gorky 1954.

13 ... ♘xd4

We shall also consider:

(a) **13 ... ♖ad8** 14 ♘xc6 ♕xc6 15 ♘d4 ♕d7 16 f3 ♘c5 17 ♖e1! ♘b7 18 b4 c5 19 bc ♘xc5 20 a4! ba 21 ♗xa4 ♘xa4 22 ♕xa4 and then ♗a3, with marked pressure for White (analysis by Boleslavsky and Suetin).

(b) **13 ... ♘c5** 14 ♘xc6 ♕xc6 15 ♘d4 ♕d7 16 ♖e1 ♖ad8 17 f3 and again Black has certain difficulties (Suetin).

14 ♘xd4

On 14 cd there could follow 14 ... f4 or 14 ... a5.

14 ... c5

And now:

(a) **15 ♘xe6** ♕xe6 16 f3 ♘g5 17 a4 (17 ♗xg5 ♗xg5 18 f4 ♗e7 19 a4 ♖ad8 20 ab ab 21 ♔h1 c4! 22 ♕e2 d4! with counterplay for Black — Boleslavsky; 17 ♖e1!?) 17 ... g6 18 ♗xg5 ♗xg5 19 f4 ♗e7 20 ♕f3 b4 21 ♖ad1 ♖ad8 22 cb c4 23 b3 ♗xb4 24 bc bc 25 ♔h1 a5 with sufficient counterplay for Black (Balashov–Korchnoi, Bad Lauterberg 1979).

(b) **15 ♘e2** ♖ad8 16 ♘f4 ♕c6 17 ♕h5 (17 a4) 17 ... ♗c8 with approximate equality (Bogolyubov–Euwe, match 1928).

A11112

12 ef ♘xf6
13 ♘b3

After 13 ♘g5 ♗g4 14 f3 ♗c8 15 ♖e1 ♗d6! Black has excellent play.

13 ... ♗g4
14 ♕d3 ♘e4

Also not bad is 14 ... ♗h5.

15 ♘bd4 ♘xd4
16 ♘xd4 ♗d6

And now:

(a) **17 h3** (17 ♘xb5? ♗xh2+ 18 ♔xh2 ♕h4+ 19 ♔g1 ♖f5 is bad for White) 17 ... ♕h4 18 ♘xb5

Nxf2! 19 Bg5! Nxd3 20 Bxh4 ab 21 Bxd3 Bd7 with equality (Ragozin–Ravinsky, Moscow 1947).

(b) **17 Bb3** Kh8! 18 h3 Qh4 19 f4 Nc5 20 Qe3 Rac8 21 Nf3 Bxf3 22 Qxf3 Ne4 23 Be3 Ng5! is in Black's favour (Gipslis–Suetin, Tallinn 1959).

A1112

11 Qe2 *(115)*

This solid system has an extremely steady reputation, although it is seldom played. This is due to the rather static nature of the positions which arise.

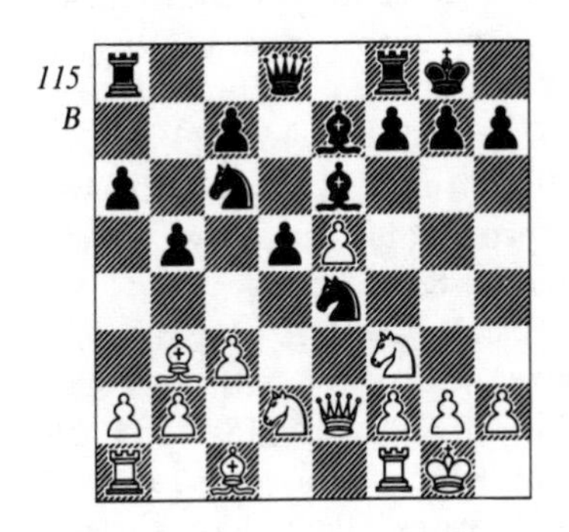

115
B

11 ... Nc5

Let us also consider the following variations:

(a) **11 ... Nxd2** 12 Qxd2 Na5 (12 ... Qd7!? — Larsen) 13 Bc2 c5 (13 ... Nc4 14 Qd3 g6 15 Nd4 — also good is 15 Bh6 Nxb2 16 Qe3! Re8 17 Nd4 Qd7 18 f4 with an attack for White — 15 ... Nxe5 16 Qg3! and White has a dangerous attack) 14 Qd3 g6 15 Bh6 Re8 16 Rad1 with a strong initiative for White (Vasyukov–Lukic, Uppsala 1956).

(b) **11 ... Bf5** 12 Rfd1 (worthy of consideration is 12 Nd4 Nxd4 13 cd) 12 ... Nc5 13 Nd4 Nxd4 14 cd Bd3 15 Qg4 Nxb3 16 Nxb3 Bc2 17 Bh6 Bg6 18 Be3 with better chances for White (Larsen).

12 Nd4

12 Bc2 d4! is good for Black.

12 ... Nxb3
13 N2xb3

In the event of 13 Nxc6 Nxc1 14 Raxc1 Qd7 15 Nxe7+ Qxe7 16 f4 f5 17 ef (or 17 a3 c5 18 Nf3 Rfd8 19 Rfd1) 17 ... Qxf6 18 Qe3 Bf5 19 Qd4 White has a minimal advantage, but the position has been abruptly simplified, alleviating Black's defence.

13 ... Qd7

After 14 Nxc6 Qxc6 15 Be3 Bf5 16 Rfd1 Rfd8 (also possible is 16 ... Qf6 and then f7–f6) 17 f3 Bf8 18 Qf2 a5 19 Rd2 b4 with sufficient counterplay for Black (Keres–Unzicker, match 1956).

A1113

11 Re1 Nc5 *(116)*

After 11 ... Nxd2 12 Bxd2 Na5 13 Bc2 c5 14 h3 Qd7 15 Bg5 Nc6 16 Qd3 g6 17 Qd2 White has strong pressure on the dark squares (Kholmov–Nei, USSR Ch. 1963).

12 Nd4!?

In the event of 12 Bc2 d4 13 cd Nxd4 14 Nxd4 Qxd4, or 12 Nf1 Nxb3 13 ab d4! 14 Nxd4 Nxd4 15 cd c5, Black even stands slightly better.

12 ... Nxd4

116
W

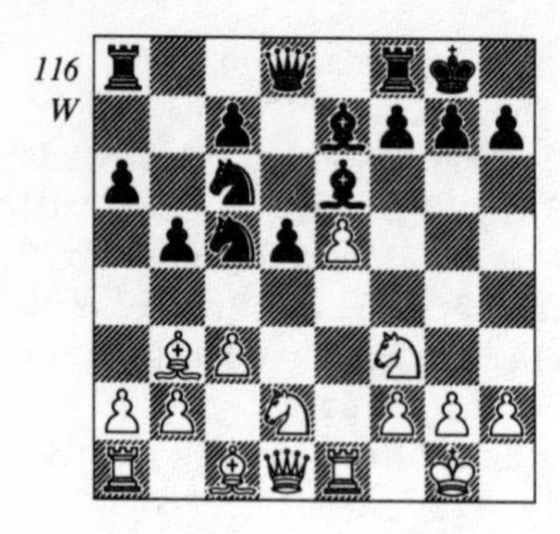

13	**cd**	**♘d3!**
14	**♖e3**	**♘f4**

After 15 ♗c2 c5! 16 ♖e1 (or 16 ♘b3 c4 17 ♘d2 f5!) 16 … c4 17 ♘f1 ♘g6! 18 ♕h5 ♕d7 Black stands better (Vasyukov–Suetin, USSR Ch. 1965).

A112

10	**♗c2**	**0–0**

After 10 … ♗g4 11 h3 ♗h5 (11 … ♗xf3? 12 gf!) 12 g4 ♗g6 13 ♗b3 ♘a5 14 ♗xd5 c6 15 ♗xe4 ♗xe4 16 ♕xd8+ ♖xd8 17 ♘bd2 ♗d5 18 ♖e1 White has the advantage (Fischer–Olafsson, Havana OL 1966). In the event of 10 … ♘c5?! 11 ♘d4! ♘xe5?! 12 ♕h5! ♘g6 13 f4! White has a strong initiative.

11 **♕e2** *(117)*

117
B

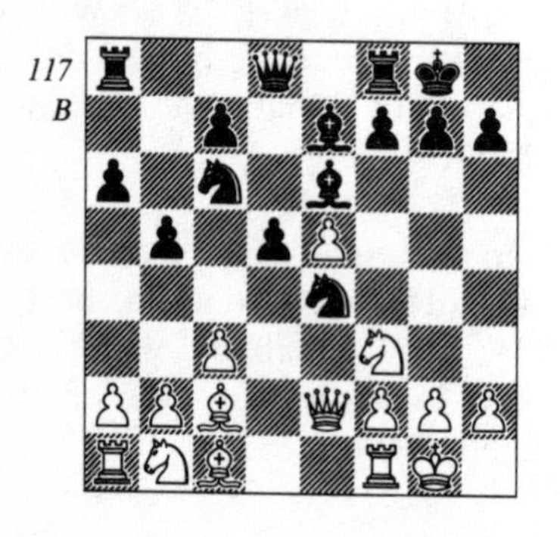

In this critical position Black has a rather pleasant choice:

(a) **11 … f5!?** 12 ef ♖xf6 13 ♘g5 ♗c5 14 ♗xe4 (worthy of consideration is 14 ♘xe6 ♖xe6 15 ♘d2 ♘g5 16 ♕d3 ♘e5 17 ♕g3! — analysis by Boleslavsky and Suetin; in White's favour is 14 ♘xe4 de 15 ♘d2 e3!) 14 … de 15 ♘xe4 ♗c4 16 ♘xf6+ ♕xf6 with full equality for Black.

(b) **11 … ♘c5** 12 ♘d4 ♕d7 13 ♘bd2 f6 (interesting is 13 … ♗g4 14 ♕e3 — 14 f3 — 14 … ♘e6 15 ♘2b3 ♘exd4 16 cd ♘b4 17 ♗b1 ♗f5 18 ♗d2 ♗xb1 19 ♗xb4 ♗xb4 20 ♖ab1 a5 with chances to equalise; Suetin–Szukszta, Polanica Zdroj 1958) 14 ef ♗xf6 15 ♘xe6 ♘xe6 16 ♘f3 ♘c5 17 ♖d1 ♖ae8 18 ♗e3 ♕d6 with approximate equality (Stein–Savon, Kiev 1963).

(c) **11 … ♕d7!?** 12 ♗xe4 de 13 ♕xe4 ♗d5; or 12 ♖d1 f5 13 ♘bd2 ♔h8 14 ♘b3 ♗f7 15 ♘bd4 ♗h5 (Tal–Keres, Moscow 1967). In both cases Black has a strong initiative.

A113

10	**♖e1**	**0–0**
11	**♘d4?!** *(118)*	

And now:

(a) **11 … ♘xe5** 12 f3 ♗d6 (worse is 12 … c5 13 fe! cd 14 ed ♗g4 15 ♕xd4 ♗f6 16 ♖xe5 ♗xe5 17 ♕xe5 with advantage to White) 13 fe ♗g4 14 ♕c2! c5 15 ♗xd5 cd 16 ♗xa8 ♕h4 17 ♖f1 d3 18 ♕f2 ♕xf2+ 19 ♖xf2 ♖xa8 with good counterchances for

118
B

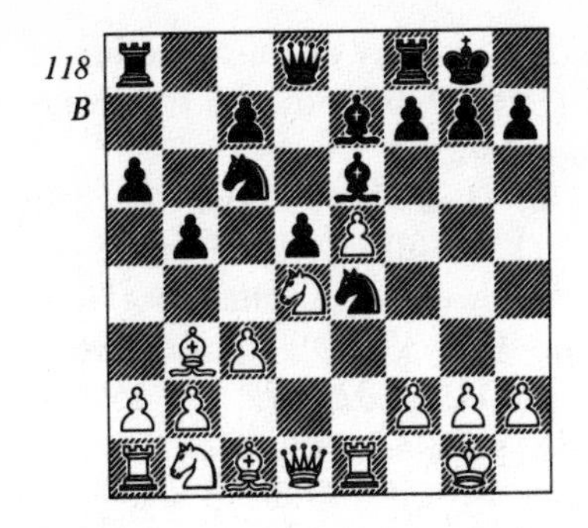

Black (Teichmann–John, Breslau 1913).

(b) **11 … ♘xd4** 12 cd ♗h4 13 ♖f1 f5 14 f3 ♘g3 15 hg ♗xg3 16 f4 ♕h4 17 ♖f3 ♕h2+ 18 ♔f1 ♕h1+ 19 ♔e2 ♕xg2+ 20 ♔d3 g5 21 ♕e2 ♕h3 22 ♕f2 with advantage to White (Maróczy–Weenink, Scheveningen 1923).

A114

10 ♗e3 0–0

Let us consider other possibilities for Black:

(a) **10 … ♕d7** 11 ♘bd2 ♘xd2 (White has better chances in the event of 11 … ♖d8 12 h3 0–0 13 ♖e1; or 11 … 0–0 12 ♗c2 f5 13 ef ♘xf6 14 ♕b1 ♔h8 15 ♘g5 ♗g8 16 ♗f5) 12 ♕xd2 ♘a5 13 ♗g5 c5 14 ♗xe7 ♕xe7 15 ♘g5 ♘xb3 16 ab 0–0 17 f4! with an initiative for White (Sokolov–Yusupov, Montpellier 1985).

(b) **10 … ♘c5** 11 ♗c2 ♗g4 (interesting is 11 … ♘d7!? 12 ♘d4 ♘dxe5 13 f4 ♘c4 14 ♘xc6 ♘xe3 15 ♘xd8 ♘xd4 16 ♘xe6 ♘e3 17 ♘xc7+ ♔d7 18 ♘xa8 ♘xc2 with equality — Tal–Timman, Montpellier 1985) 12 ♘bd2 ♘e6 13 ♕b1 ♗h5 14 a4 (worthy of consideration is 14 ♗f5!? ♗g6 15 ♖d1 0–0 16 a4 ♕d7 17 ab ab 18 ♖xa8 ♖xa8 19 ♘f1 ♖d8 20 ♘g3 b4! — Jansa–Bernal, Thessaloniki OL 1984; or 14 ♖d1!? ♕d7 15 ♗f5 ♗g6 16 g4 0–0 17 ♘e4 ♖ad8; Malanyuk–Agzamov, USSR 1983 — with complicated play in each case) 14 … b4 15 a5 ♗g6 16 ♘b3 bc 17 bc ♕b8 18 ♕a2 0–0 19 ♗xg6 hg (Gligoric–Szabó, Zürich 1953). By playing 20 ♖fb1! White created pressure on the queenside.

(c) **10 … ♘a5(?)** 11 ♘d4! 0–0 12 f3 ♘c5 13 ♗c2 ♘c4 14 ♗c1 ♘xe5 15 b4 ♘b7 16 f4 ♘c4 17 ♕d3 g6 18 f5! with an attack for White (Keres).

11 ♘bd2 *(119)*

119
B

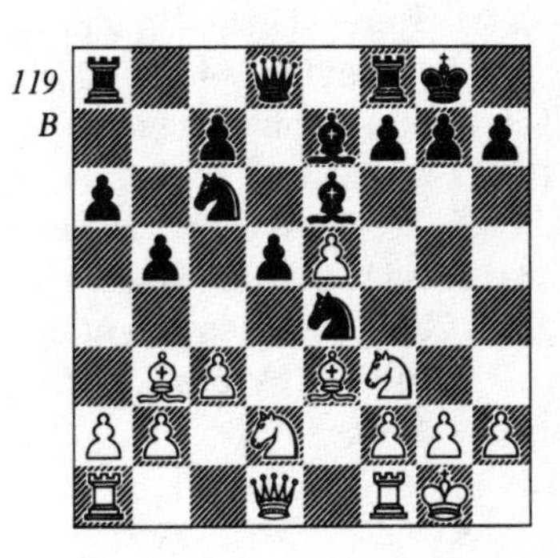

11 … ♘xd2

Let us also consider the following variations:

(a) **11 … ♕d7** 12 ♖e1 (sharp play ensues after 12 ♗c2 f5 13 ef ♘xf6 14 ♕b1 ♗g4 15 h3 ♗xf3 16 ♘xf3 and then ♘g5) 12 … ♘xd2 13 ♕xd2 ♘a5 14 ♗c2 ♘c4 15 ♕d3 g6 16 ♗h6 ♘xb2 17 ♕d4!

♖fe8 18 ♘g5 ♘c4 19 ♖ad1 ♘a3 20 ♗d3 c5 21 ♕f4 ♕c6 22 ♖e3 with a dangerous initiative for White (Gligoric–Unzicker, Tel Aviv OL 1964).

(b) **11 … ♗g4** 12 ♘xe4 de 13 ♕d5! ♕xd5 (13 … ef 14 ♕xc6 fg 15 ♕xg2 ♕d7 16 ♗g6! gh 17 f3 ♖ae8 18 ♖ae1 h5 19 ♔h1 ♕c6 20 ♖e4 with a strong attack for White; Nunn–Heidrich, West Germany 1985) 14 ♗xd5 ef 15 ♗xc6 fg 16 ♔xg2 (16 ♖fc1!) 16 … ♖ad8 17 a4 f6 18 ab ab 19 ♗xb5 fe 20 ♗c4+ with a clear advantage to White (Alekhine–Teichmann, match 1921).

12 ♕xd2

And now:

(a) **12 … ♕d7** 13 ♗g5 ♖ad8 14 ♖fe1 (Keres–Unzicker, Zürich 1959). By playing 14 … ♖fe8! Black built a strong defence.

(b) **12 … ♘a5** 13 ♗c2 ♘c4 14 ♕d3 g6 15 ♗h6 ♘xb2 16 ♕c3 ♖e8 17 ♘d4 ♕d7 18 f4 ♘c4 19 ♕g3 c5 20 f5! with a strong attack for White (Averbakh–Zak, Moscow 1947).

A12

9 … ♗c5

Nowadays this is a very popular system, brimming with tactical complications. A counterattack on the kingside serves as the *leitmotif* of Black's operations in a number of variations. White has two main plans:

A121 10 ♘bd2
A122 10 ♕d3

Also worthy of consideration is 10 ♕e2 0–0, with the following variations:

(a) **11 ♗e3** ♕e7 (also not bad is 11 … f6) 12 ♗xc5 ♕xc5 13 ♘bd2 with equal chances (Gligoric–Unzicker, Oberhausen 1961).

(b) **11 ♘bd2** ♗f5! 12 e6!? fe (also possible is 12 … ♘a5 13 ef+ ♔h8 14 ♗d1 ♗b6) 13 ♘xe4 de 14 ♘g5 ♕f6! 15 ♘xe4 ♕e5 16 ♗c2 ♖ad8! 17 ♗g5 ♗xe4 18 ♕xe4 ♕xg5 19 ♕xe6+ ♔h8 20 ♕xc6 ♖d2! with good play for Black (Sapundzhiev).

A121

10 ♘bd2 0–0
11 ♗c2

In this position Black has a rich choice of continuations:

A1211 11 … f5
A1212 11 … ♘xf2
A1213 11 … ♗f5
A1214 11 … ♘xd2

A1211

11 … f5

Now we need to give separate consideration to the continuations:

A12111 12 ♘b3
A12112 12 ef

A12111

12 ♘b3 ♗b6 *(120)*

Analogous variations are reached after 12 … ♗a7. On the other hand, Black is worse after 12 … ♗e7 13 ♘fd4 ♕d7 14 ♘xc6 ♕xc6 15 a4! with pressure for

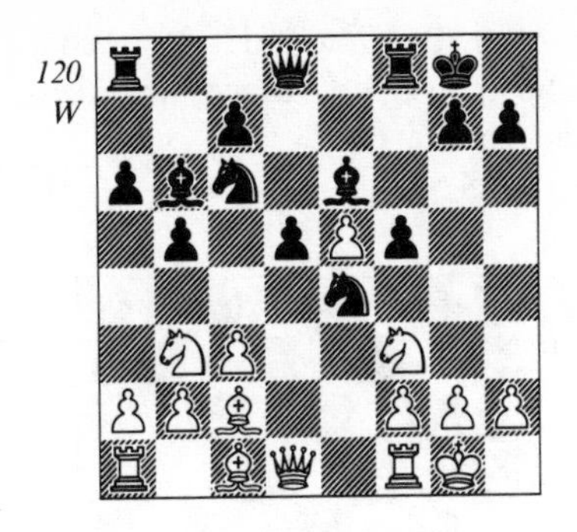

120
W

White (Teichmann–Zoege, Hamburg 1905).

13 ♘fd4

After 13 a4 ♕d7! 14 ♘bd4 ♘xd4 15 ♘xd4 a5 16 ♘e2 d4! 17 cd cd 18 ♘f4 ♗c4 Black has a good game (Suetin–Nei, USSR Ch. 1966/7).

13 … ♘xd4
14 ♘xd4 *(121)*

Black gets excellent counterplay after 14 cd f4 15 f3 ♘g3 16 hg fg 17 ♕d3 ♗f5 18 ♕xf5 ♖xf5 19 ♗xf5 ♕h4 20 ♗e6+ ♔h8 21 ♖d1 ♕h2+ 22 ♔f1 ♕h1+ 23 ♔e2 ♕xg2+ 24 ♔d3 ♕xf3+ 25 ♗e3 ♕e4+ 26 ♔d2 c5 (analysis by Boey).

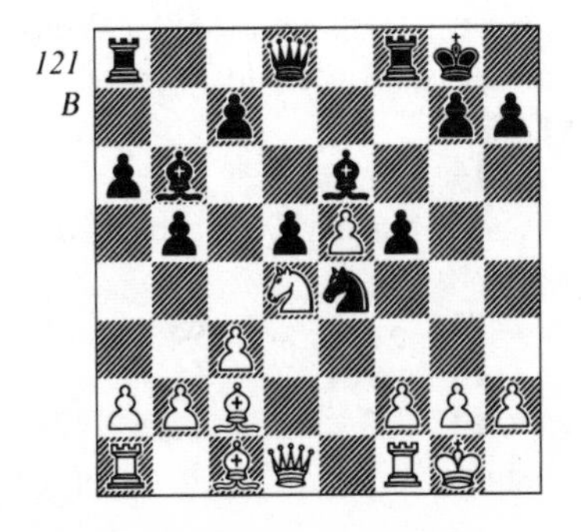

121
B

14 … ♗xd4

An integral part of Black's plan. After 14 … ♕d7 15 f3 ♘c5 16 ♔h1 ♘b7 17 ♗e3 c5 18 ♘xe6 ♕xe6 19 a4! ♘a5 20 ♗f2 ♔h8 21 ♖e1 ♖a7 22 ♕e2! White stands clearly better (Stein–Keres, Moscow 1967). After 14 … ♗xd4 White has a choice between:

A121111 15 cd
A121112 15 ♕xd4

A121111

15 cd f4
16 f3 ♘g3 *(122)*

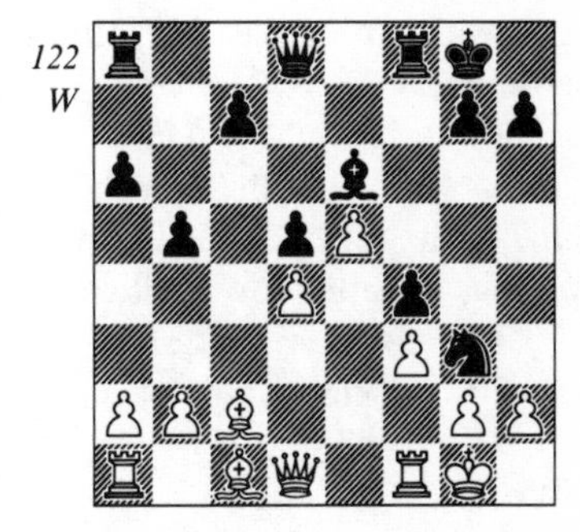

122
W

This position was subjected in the 1940s and 1950s to truly 'X-ray' analysis. Nowadays it is mainly just an adornment to the textbooks. But it is quite possible that it is merely taking a temporary 'breather'.

17 hg

The alternative is 17 ♖f2, with the following consequences: 17 … ♕h4 18 ♕d3 ♖f5 19 ♗xf4 ♖xf4 20 hg (or 20 ♕c3!? ♘e4!? 21 ♗xe4 de 22 ♕c6 ♖af8 23 ♕xe6+ ♔h8 24 ♕xa6 ef 25 g3 ♕g4 26 ♕xb5 h5! with excellent counterplay for Black; Bannik–Altshuler, corr. 1964) 20 ... ♕xg3 21 ♕xh7+ ♔f7 22 ♖ad1 (in Black's favour is 22 ♕h5+ ♔e7 23 ♖d1!? — 23 ♕g6! with unclear play — 23 ... ♖h4 24 ♕g6 ♖ah8 25 ♔f1 ♖g4! 26 ♕d3 ♖h1+ 27 ♔e2 ♖e4+!! 28 ♕xe4 de 29 ♖xh1 ♗c4+ 30 ♔e3 g5!) 22 ... ♖h4 23 ♕d3 c5 with very sharp play, in which the chances are roughly equal (Napolitano–Sapundzhiev, corr. 1970/2).

17 ... fg

18 ♕d3

Bad is 18 ♖e1 ♕h4 19 ♗e3 ♗g4! with an irresistible attack for Black.

18 ... ♗f5

18 ... ♕h4 19 ♕xh7+ ♕xh7 20 ♗xh7+ ♔xh7 21 ♗g5, followed by ♗h4, is better for White.

19 ♕xf5 ♖xf5

20 ♗xf5 ♕h4

21 ♗h3

Worse is 21 ♗e6+ ♔h8 22 ♗h3 ♕xd4+ 23 ♔h1 ♕xe5 24 ♗d2 ♕xb2 25 ♗f4 d4 26 ♗xc7 d3 27 ♗xg3 d2 28 ♖ad1 ♖e8! with a good game for Black.

21 ... ♕xd4+

22 ♔h1 ♕xe5

23 ♗d2

23 ♖b1!? is interesting.

23 ... ♕xb2

After 23 ... c5 24 ♗c3 — 24 ♖e1!? — 24 ... d4 25 ♖ae1 ♕f4 26 ♖e4 ♕h6 27 ♗e1 Black's position is bad.

24 ♗f4 d4

25 ♗xg3

After 25 ♗xc7 d3 26 ♗e6+ ♔h8 27 ♗xg3 d2 Black has excellent counterplay.

25 ... d3 *(123)*

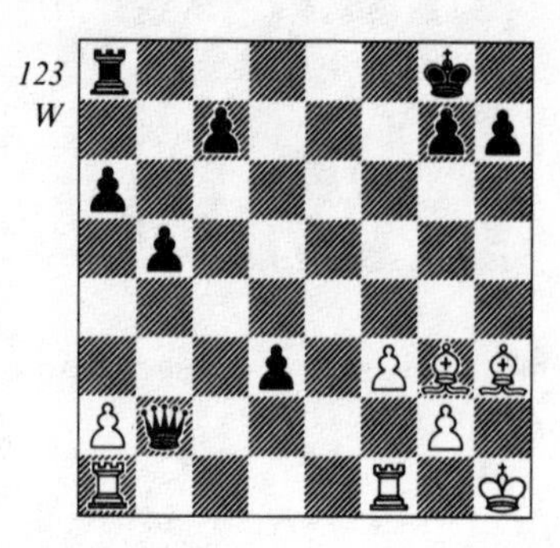
123
W

And now:

(a) **26 ♖ad1** d2 27 ♗e6+ (after 27 ♖f2 ♖d8 28 ♗f4 ♕xa2 29 ♖fxd2 ♖xd2 30 ♖xd2 ♕c4! Black has plenty of counterplay) 27 ... ♔f8 28 ♗xc7 ♔e7 29 ♗d5 ♖f8 30 ♗a5 b4 (or 30 ... ♖f5 31 ♖xd2 ♖h5+ 32 ♔g1 ♕a3 33 ♖e1+) 31 ♖f2 ♖f6 32 ♖e2+ ♔f8 33 ♖e4! and White's threats are extremely real.

(b) **26 ♗xc7** (26 ♗e6+ ♔h8 27 f4 ♖d8 28 f5 d2 favours Black) 26 ... d2 27 ♗a5 ♖e8 28 a3 ♖e2 29 ♗b4 g5! with good counterplay for Black (Miller–Veltmander, USSR 1946).

A121112

15 ♕xd4

A comparatively little-studied position.

15 ... c5

16 ♕d1 f4

17 f3 ♘g5 *(124)*

After 17 ... ♘g3? 18 hg fg 19

♕d3 ♗f5 20 ♕xf5 ♖xf5 21 ♗xf5 ♕h4 22 ♗h3 Black does not have compensation for the loss of material.

124
W

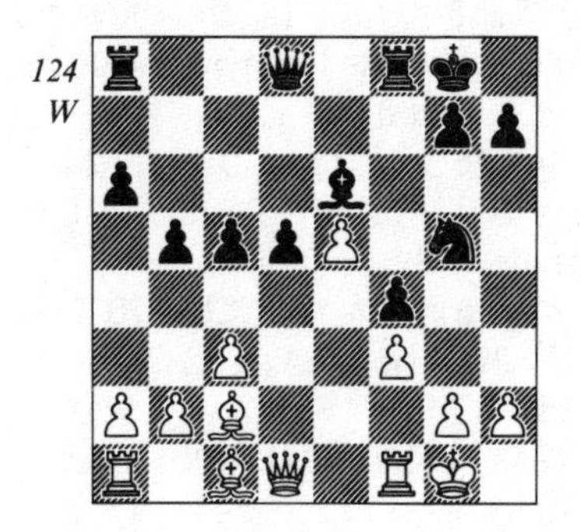

In this critical position the following variations arise:

(a) **18 b4** (Barden) 18 … ♕b6 19 bc ♗xc5+ 20 ♕d4 ♕xd4+ 21 cd ♗c8 22 ♗b3 ♗b7 and then ♘e6, with a secure blockade for Black on the light squares (Suetin).

(b) **18 a4** b4 19 cb (19 h4? ♘h3+! 20 hg ♕xh4 21 ♖f2 ♗xh3 22 ♖h2 ♖ae8 with a draw; Averbakh–Szabó, Zürich 1953) 19 … cb 20 ♕d4 ♗f5 21 ♗b3 ♘e6 22 ♕xd5 ♕b6+ 23 ♔h1 ♖ad8 24 a5! ♕a7 25 ♕c6 is in White's favour (Keres). It seems that 16 … ♕e7 is better, since if 17 a4 then 17 … ♖ad8, intending d5–d4. Also worthy of consideration are 16 … c4 and 16 … a5.

A12112

12 ef ♘xf6

13 ♘b3

But not 13 ♘g5? ♗g4 14 ♗xh7?! ♔xh7 15 ♕xg4 ♘xg5 16 ♘b3 ♖xf2! 17 ♘xc5 ♖xf1+ 18 ♔xf1 ♕f8+ 19 ♗f4 ♕xc5 with advantage to Black (Levenfish).

13 … ♗b6

Worse is 13 … ♗d6? 14 ♘g5! ♗c8 15 ♘xh7 or 15 ♗xh7+.

14 ♘g5

After 14 ♘bd4 ♘xd4 15 ♘xd4 ♗g4 16 ♕d3 c5 17 ♘f5 ♕d7!, or 14 ♗g5 (14 a4 ♗g4!) 14 … ♕d7 15 ♕d3 ♘e4 16 ♗h4 ♗f5!, Black has excellent play.

14 … ♗g4

Also possible is 14 … ♕d7 15 ♘xe6 ♕xe6 16 ♘d4 ♘xd4 17 cd ♘e4 18 ♗e3 ♖f6 19 ♖e1 c6 20 f3 ♘d6 and Black has a strong defence (Malyshev–Druganov, corr. 1954).

15 ♗xh7+ ♔h8

16 ♕c2 *(125)*

125
B

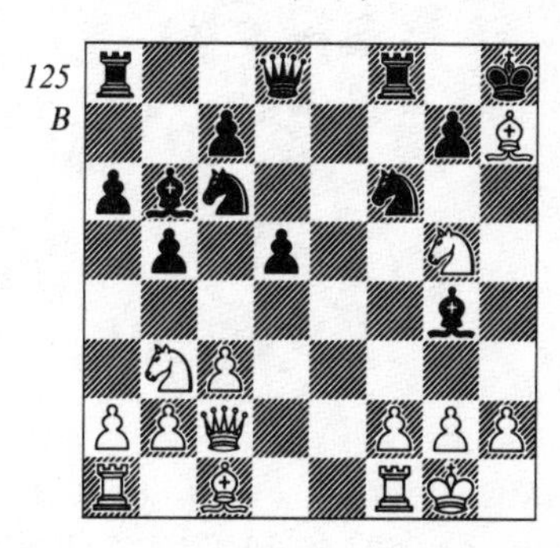

Here the following variations are possible:

(a) **16 … ♘h5** 17 ♗g6 ♘f4 18 ♗xf4! ♖xf4 19 ♘f7+ ♖xf7 20 ♗xf7 ♘e5 21 ♗h5! ♗xh5 22 ♕f5 ♘f3+ 23 gf ♕h4 24 ♘d4 and Black does not have compensation for the loss of the exchange (Moskalenko–Vladimirov, USSR 1962).

(b) **16 … ♘e5** 17 h3 ♕d6 18 ♕d4 is also in White's favour.

(c) **16 … ♕d6** 17 ♔h1 (17 h3? ♗xh3! 18 gh ♘g4!) 17 … ♘e5 18 f3 with unclear play.

A1212

11 … ♘xf2!?

Going straight for the weak f2 point! Ensuing play is subject to concrete calculation and is filled with combinational motifs. This variation is known internationally as the Dilworth Variation, after the English player who played and analysed it extensively.

12 ♖xf2 f6 *(126)*

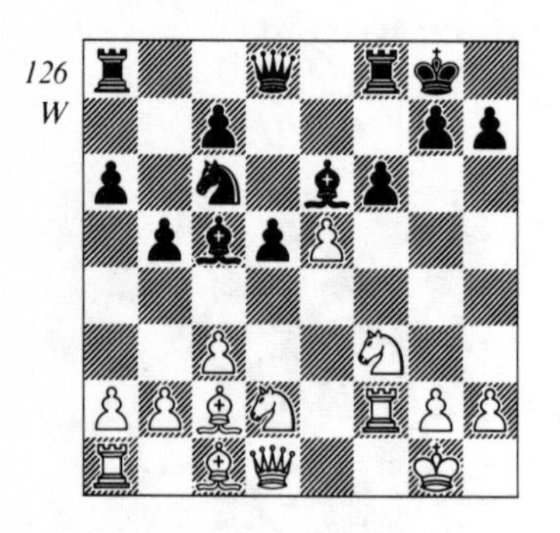

13 ef

After 13 ♘f1 ♗xf2+ 14 ♔xf2 fe, or 13 ♕e2 fe 14 ♘b3 ♗xf2+ 15 ♕xf2 ♗f5 15 ♗xf5 ♖xf5 17 ♕c5 ♕d6, Black has at least equal chances.

13 … ♗xf2+

Worse is 13 … ♕xf6?! 14 ♕f1 ♗g4 15 h3! (also good are 15 ♕d3! and 15 ♘d4! ♕h4 16 ♘2f3 ♘xf3+ 17 ♖xf3) 15 … ♗xf3 (15 … ♗h5 16 ♕d3!) 16 ♘xf3 ♘e5 17 ♗d1 (Keres), in each case with advantage to White.

14 ♔xf2 ♕xf6

15 ♔g1

Also frequently played is 15 ♘f1 ♘e5 (15 … d4? 16 ♔g1! favours White; Short–Popovic, Belgrade 1987), and now:

(a) **16 ♗e3** (Larsen) 16 … ♖ae8 17 ♗d4 (Short–Yusupov, Belgrade 1989 went 17 ♗c5 ♘xf3+ 18 gf ♖f7 19 ♗d3 ♗h3! 20 ♘g3 h5! 21 ♗f1! ♗g4 22 ♗g2 h4 23 ♘f1 h3?! — ♕g6!? — 24 ♗h1 ♖e4 25 ♘g3 ♖f4 with roughly equal play) 17 … ♕h4+ 18 ♔g1 ♘xf3+ 19 gf ♕g5+ 20 ♘g3 ♗h3 21 a4 g6 22 ab ab 23 ♗f2 with a minimal advantage to White (Tseshkovsky–Chekhov, Rostock 1985).

(b) **16 ♔g1** ♘xf3+ 17 gf ♕xf3 18 ♕xf3 ♖xf3 19 ♗d1 (19 ♗e3!?) 19 … ♖f7 20 ♘g3 ♗h3 21 ♗e2 ♖e8 22 ♗d2 c5 with better chances for Black (Morovic–Yusupov, Tunis 1985).

15 … ♖ae8

And now:

(a) **16 ♘f1** ♘e5 17 ♗e3 ♘xf3+ 18 ♕xf3 ♕xf3 19 gf ♖xf3 (19 … ♗h3 20 ♔f2) 20 ♗f2! ♗h3 21 ♘g3 g6 22 ♖d1 (22 a4!?) 22 … c6 23 ♖d2 (Matanovic–Wade, Palma de Mallorca 1966). After 23 … ♔g7 24 ♗d3 White has only a minimal advantage.

(b) **16 h3** ♘e5 17 ♘xe5 ♕xf2+ (or 17 … ♕xe5 18 ♘f3 ♕g3 19 ♕e1! ♕xe1+ 20 ♘xe1 ♗f5 21 ♗g5 ♖xe1+ 22 ♖xe1 ♗xc2 23 b4 with a minimal advantage to

White; Lyukmanev–Shikhirev, corr. 1988) 18 ♔h2 ♕f4+ 19 ♔h1 ♕xe5 20 ♘f3 ♕g3 21 ♕d3 ♗f5 22 ♕xd5 ♗e6 (Piasetski–Leveille, Canada 1972). By playing 23 ♕d3 White was able to maintain the equilibrium.

(c) **16 ♕f1** ♗f5 17 ♗xf5 ♕xf5 18 ♘b3 (18 b3 d4!; Ljubojevic–Yusupov, Tilburg 1987) 18 ... ♘e5 19 ♘bd4 ♘xf3+ 20 ♘xf3 ♕c2 with counterplay for Black (Medina–Mocete, corr. 1946/7).

A1213

11 ... ♗f5

One of the fashionable variations in which interest has risen in recent years, named the Flohr–Larsen Variation. Black strives for lively piece play, rich in tactical subtleties.

12 ♘b3 *(127)*

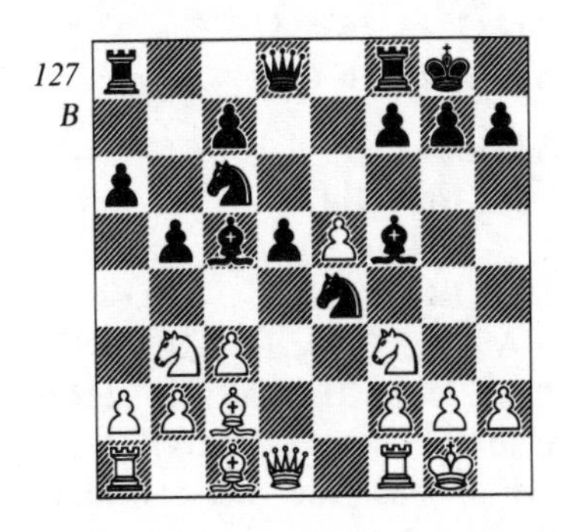

In this critical position Black has two lines to choose from:

A12131 12 ... ♗g4
A12132 12 ... ♗g6

After 12 ... ♗xf2+?! 13 ♖xf2 ♘xf2 14 ♔xf2 ♗xc2 15 ♕xc2 f6 16 e6 ♕d6 17 ♗e3 ♕xe6 18 ♘bd4 ♘xd4 19 ♘xd4 White has the better chances (Morovic–Murey, Thessaloniki OL 1984).

A12131

12 ... ♗g4
13 h3

Other possibilities:

(a) **13 ♘xc5** (13 a4 ♗a7!) 13 ... ♘xc5 14 ♖e1 (14 ♗e3 ♘e4!?) 14 ... ♖e8 (also possible is 14 ... ♗h5!? 15 ♗g5 ♗xf3 16 ♕xf3 ♕xg5 17 ♕xd5 ♖ae8! with counterplay for Black according to Korchnoi's analysis) 15 ♗f4 (or 15 ♗e3 ♘e6 16 ♕d3 g6 17 ♗h6 ♘e7 18 ♘d4 ♗f5 19 ♘xf5 ♘xf5 with equal chances; Fischer–Larsen, Santa Monica 1966) 15 ... ♗h5! 16 ♗g3 (interesting is 16 ♕d2 ♗xf3 17 gf ♕d7 18 ♖ad1 ♘e7 19 ♗g3 ♖ab8 20 f4 ♕h3 21 f5! with an attack; Klovan–Semenyuk, corr. 1975) 16 ... ♗g6 17 ♘d4 ♕d7 18 f3 ♖ac8 19 ♖d1 with a positional advantage to White (Karpov–Smyslov, Leningrad 1977).

(b) **13 ♕e1** (13 ♕e2 f5!) 13 ... ♗xf3 14 gf ♘xe5 15 ♔g2 ♕h4! 16 ♘xc5 ♘xf3! 17 ♔xf3 ♕h5+ 18 ♔e3 ♘xc5 with an attack for Black (analysis by Suetin).

13 ... ♗h5

After 14 g4 ♗g6 15 ♗xe4! de 16 ♘xc5 ef 17 ♗f4 ♕xd1 (or 17 ... ♕e7 18 ♕d5 ♘a5 19 b4 ♘c4 20 ♕xf3 ♘xe5 21 ♗xe5 ♕xe5 22 ♘d7!) 18 ♖axd1 ♘d8 19 ♖d7 ♘e6 20 ♘xe6 fe 21 ♗e3 ♖ac8 22 ♖fd1 ♗e4 23 ♗c5 ♖fe8 24 ♖7d4 ♗d5

25 b3 a5 26 ♔h2 with advantage to White (Karpov–Korchnoi, 14th game, World Ch. 1978).

A12132

12 ... ♗g6 *(128)*

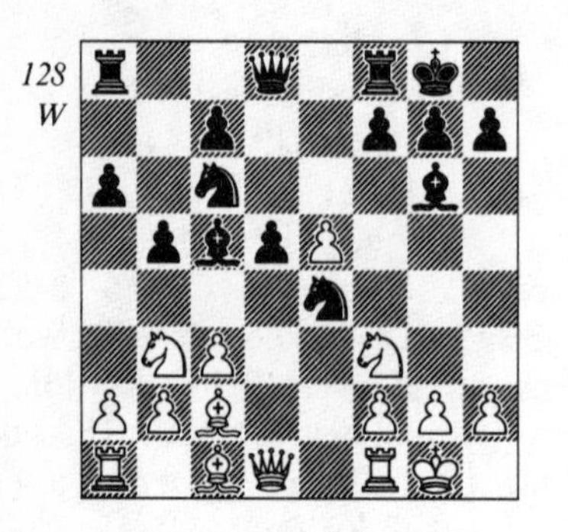

Until quite recently this reply was almost entirely unexplored. But now the theory of this line is growing very rapidly.

13 ♘fd4

Other lines:

(a) **13 a4** ♗b6 14 ♘bd4 ♘xd4 15 ♘xd4 ♕d7 16 ♗e3 ♘c5 17 a5 ♗a7 18 f4 ♗xc2 19 ♘xc2 f6 20 ef ♖xf6 21 ♔h1 c6 with equal chances (van der Wiel–Korchnoi, Wijk aan Zee 1983).

(b) **13 ♗f4?!** ♗b6 14 a4 ♕d7 15 ab ab 16 ♖xa8 ♖xa8 17 ♘fd4 b4 18 ♗d3 bc 19 ♗xb5 ♘xf2! 20 ♖xf2 ♘xd4 21 ♗d7 ♘b3 22 bc ♖a1 23 ♕xa1 ♘xa1 24 ♗c6 ♗e4 25 c4 ♘c2 26 ♗d2! and Black's position is even slightly preferable (Short–Timman, Tilburg 1988).

13 ... ♗xd4
14 cd a5
15 ♗e3

Interesting is 15 ♗d3!? and if 15 ... a4 then 16 ♗xb5 ab 17 ♗xc6 ♖a6 18 f3 ♖xc6 19 fe ba 20 ♖xa2 ♗e4.

15 ... a4 *(129)*

After 15 ... ♘b4? 16 ♗b1 a4 17 ♘d2 a3 18 ♕c1! Black has great difficulties (Karpov–Savon, Moscow 1971).

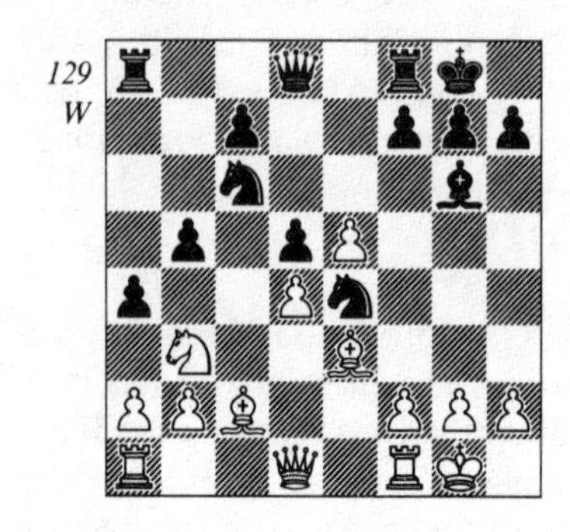

In this position White has two lines:

A121321 16 ♘d2
A121322 16 ♘c1

A121321

16 ♘d2 a3
17 ♘xe4 ab
18 ♖ab1 ♗xe4

After 18 ... de 19 ♖xb2 ♕d7 20 ♖xb5 ♘xd4 21 ♖c5 ♖fd8 22 ♕xd4 ♕xd4 23 ♗xd4 ♖xd4 24 ♗b3 White has the better chances (Raaste–Norry, Espoo 1989). After 19 ... ♕d7 20 ♗d3 ♗xd3 21 ♕xd3 ♖fb8 (interesting is 21 ... b4!? 22 ♗d2 ♖fb8 23 ♖fb1 ♕g4 with equal chances; Hübner–Korchnoi, Lucerne OL 1982) 22 ♖fb1 b4 23 ♖c1 ♖b6 24 ♕b1 h6 25 h3 with definite pressure for

White (Popovic–Timman, Sarajevo 1984).

A121322

16 ♘c1 a3

After 16 ... ♘b4 (16 ... f6!?) 17 ♗b1 a3 18 b3 c5 19 dc! White has the advantage (Tseshkovsky–Geller, USSR Ch. 1980/1).

After 16 ... a3 the following variations may arise:

(a) **17 b3** (17 ♖b1 f6 18 f3 fe! is good for Black; Unzicker–Korchnoi, Beer-Sheva 1984) 17 ... f6 18 ef ♕xf6 19 ♘e2 ♕e7!? (also possible is 19 ... ♘b4 20 ♗b1 ♖ae8) 20 ♖c1 ♘b4 21 ♗b1 ♖ae8 22 ♘c3!? ♘xc3 23 ♖xc3 ♗xb1 24 ♕xb1 c6 25 ♗c1 ♕e1 26 ♖e3 ♖xe3 27 ♗xe3 ♕xb1 28 ♖xb1 ♖e8 29 ♗d2 ♘c2 30 ♖c1 ♘xd4 with double-edged play (Speelman–Timman, London 1989).

(b) **17 ba!?** ♖xa3 18 ♗b3 ♘c3 19 ♕d2 b4 20 ♘d3 ♗xd3 21 ♕xd3 ♘a5 (21 ... ♕a8!?) 22 ♗c2 ♕h4 23 ♗c1 with complicated play (Short–Yusupov, Belfort 1988).

A1214

11 ... ♘xd2

A very old variation, in which Black has quite a few difficulties.

12 ♕xd2

12 ♗xd2 d4!

12 ... f6

Other replies are not very attractive: 12 ... ♘e7 13 b4 ♗b6 14 ♘g5 ♗f5 15 ♗xf5 ♘xf5 16 ♕d3 g6 17 ♕h3!; 12 ... ♕e7 13 ♕d3 g6 14 ♗h6 ♖e8 15 ♕d2; 12 ... ♕d7 13 ♕f4 with the threat 14 ♘g5! — in all cases Black has difficulties.

13 ef ♖xf6

14 ♘g5 ♗f5 *(130)*

Bad is 14 ... g6? 15 ♘xh7!, or 14 ... h6 15 ♘xe6 ♖xe6 16 ♕d3.

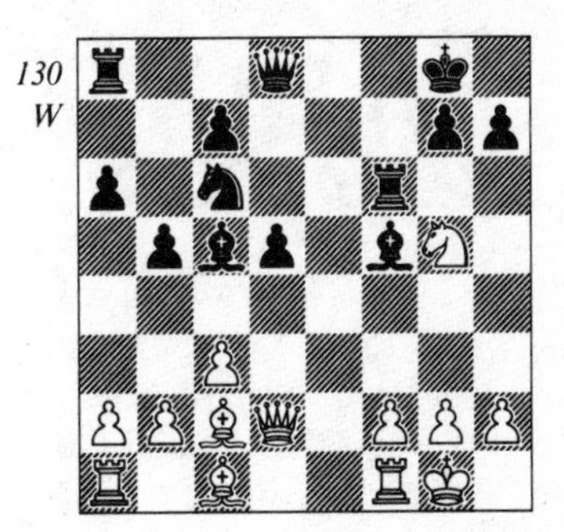
130
W

Here the following variations arise:

(a) **15 a4!** ♘e7 16 ♗xf5 ♘xf5 17 ♕d3! h6 18 ab! ab 19 ♖xa8 ♕xa8 20 ♕xb5 ♕f8 21 b4! hg 22 bc with advantage to White (Suetin–Antoshin, Sochi 1974).

(b) **15 b4** ♗b6 16 ♗b3 ♘e7 17 a4 c6 18 ♖e1 ♗g6 19 ♘f3 ♘f5 20 ♘e5 ♗e8 21 ♕a2 ba 22 ♗xa4 h6 23 ♗f4 a5 with equality (Karpov–Antoshin, USSR Ch. 1970).

(c) **15 ♗xf5** ♖xf5 16 ♘e6 ♕d6 17 ♘xc5 ♕xc5 18 ♕d3 ♖af8 and Black has no difficulties (Minic).

A122

10 ♕d3 *(131)*

This plan, the idea of which is to neutralise the pressure against the square f2, has in recent years acquired a new lease of life.

10 ... 0–0

Also possible is 10 ... ♘e7 11 ♗e3 (interesting is 11 ♘bd2 ♗f5

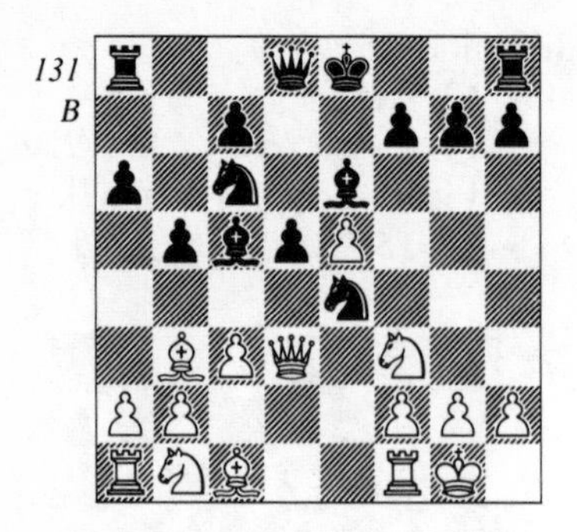

12 ♕e2 ♕d7 13 ♘xe4 ♗xe4 14 ♘g5 ♗f5 15 ♗e3 ♗xe3 16 ♕xe3 h6 17 ♘f3 0–0 with equal chances) 11 … 0–0 12 ♘bd2 ♗xe3 13 ♕xe3 ♘f5 14 ♕e2 ♘xd2 15 ♕xd2 c5 with equal play (Balashov–Yusupov, Toluca 1982). It looks extravagant to play 10 … f5 11 ef ♕xf6 12 ♗e3 0–0–0!? 13 a4 ♘a5 14 ♗d4 ♕h6 15 ♗c2 ♗d6 16 ♗e5! with advantage to White (Keres).

11 ♗e3

An alternative is 11 ♘bd2 f5 12 ef ♘xf6, with the following variations:

(a) **13 a4**, and now:

(a1) **13 … ♖b8** 14 ab ab 15 ♘g5 ♘e5 16 ♕g3 ♕d6 17 ♗c2 ♗d7 18 ♘b3 ♗b6 19 ♗f4 ♖be8 20 ♘d4 ♘h5 21 ♗xe5 ♖xe5 22 ♗xh7+ ♔h8 23 ♕h4 g6 24 f4 ♖xg5 25 ♕xg5 ♔xh7 (Sokolov–Timman, Reykjavik 1988). Here there followed: 26 f5! ♖xf5 27 ♖xf5 ♗xf5 28 g4 ♕e5 29 gf ♗xd4+ 30 cd ♕xd4+ 31 ♔h1 ♕e4 with equal chances.

(a2) **13 … ♗f7!?** 14 ♘g5 ♘e5 15 ♕g3 ♕d6 16 ♗c2 h6 17 ♘xf7 ♘xf7 18 ♘b3 ♕xg3 19 hg ♗b6 20 ♘d4 c5 21 ♘f5 with a small initiative for White (Sokolov–Yusupov, match 1986).

(b) **13 ♘g5** ♘e5 14 ♕g3 ♕d6 15 ♗c2 ♗d7 16 ♘b3 ♗b6 17 ♘d4 ♖ae8 18 ♗f4 ♘h5 19 ♗xe5 ♖xe5 20 ♗xh7+ ♔h8 21 ♕h4 g6 22 f4 ♗xd4+ with equality (Khalifman–Kaidanov, USSR 1986).

11 … f6

Also not bad is 11 … ♗xe3 12 ♕xe3 ♘a5 13 ♘bd2 ♘xd2 14 ♕xd2 ♕e7 15 ♗c2 ♘c4 with roughly equal play (Byrne–Martinovsky, USA 1988).

12 ef ♕xf6 *(132)*

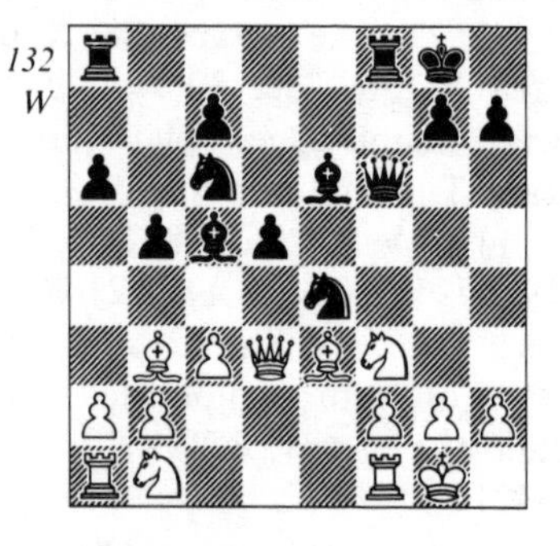

In this position the following variations are possible:

(a) **13 ♘bd2** ♘e5!? (or 13 … ♗xe3 14 ♕xe3 ♘xd2 15 ♕xd2 ♖ad8 with roughly equal play) 14 ♘xe5 ♕xe5 15 ♗d4 ♗xd4 16 cd ♕d6 17 ♖ae1 c5 18 ♘xe4 de 19 ♗xe6+ ♕xe6 20 ♖xe4 ♕xa2 21 dc ♕xb2 with approximate equality (Sapundzhiev).

(b) **13 ♗xd5?!** ♖ad8 14 ♗xe6+ ♕xe6 15 ♘d4 ♘xd4 16 cd ♗xd4

17 ♗xd4 c5 with positional advantage to Black (Panov).

A13

9 … ♘c5

Black's plan looks active. By trying to force the bishop away from b3, Black intends to transfer his own bishop to g4. In some lines Black prepares the counterthrust in the centre, d5–d4. However, all this is associated with a loss of time. White has to play forcefully, and an uncompromising struggle develops, in which calculation plays an important role.

Recently there has been much new interest in this variation, usually known as the Berlin Variation, in connection with the popularity of 9 ♘bd2 (9 … ♘c5 10 c3 ♗g4).

The main variations are:

A131 10 ♗c2
A132 10 ♘d4

A little-studied continuation is 10 ♗g5!? For example: 10 … ♕d7 11 ♗c2 h6 12 ♗h4 g5 13 ♗g3 ♗g7 14 ♖e1 ♖d8 15 ♘d4! with pressure for White (Vasyukov–Zaitsev, USSR Ch. 1969).

A131

10 ♗c2 ♗g4 *(133)*
11 ♖e1

The following lines should also be taken into consideration:

(a) **11 ♕e2** ♕d7 12 ♖d1 ♖d8 13 b4 ♘e6 14 a4 ♗e7 15 ab ab 16 ♗d3 ♗xf3 17 gf ♗g5! 18 ♗xb5 ♗xc1 19 ♖xc1 0–0 with double-edged play (Liberzon).

133
W

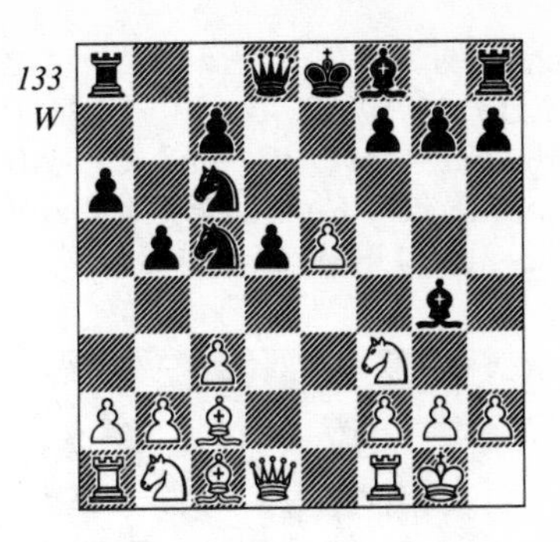

(b) **11 ♘bd2** ♕d7 12 h3 (also good is 12 ♖e1 d4?! 13 ♘e4 ♘xe4 14 ♗xe4 dc 15 ♕c2! with advantage to White) 12 … ♗h5 13 ♘b3 ♘e6 14 ♖e1 ♗e7 15 ♗f5 ♗g6 16 ♘fd4 0–0 17 ♗g4 ♘cxd4 18 cd a5 19 f4 with somewhat better chances for White (Nunn–Tal, Naestved 1985).

(c) **11 h3** ♗h5 12 ♗f4 d4!? 13 g4 d3 with excellent play for Black.

11 … ♗e7

Other continuations:

(a) **11 … d4?** 12 h3 ♗h5 13 e6 fe (or 13 … ♘xe6 14 ♗e4 ♕d7 15 a4 or 15 cd) 14 cd ♗xf3 15 ♕xf3 ♘xd4 16 ♕h5+ g6 17 ♗xg6+ hg 18 ♕xh8 ♘c2 19 ♗h6 with a dangerous attack for White (analysis by Bondarevsky and Suetin).

(b) **11 … ♘e6** 12 a4 ♘a5 13 ab ab 14 ♕d3 c6 15 ♘d4 ♘xd4 16 cd with better play for White (Bronstein–Makogonov, USSR Ch. 1947).

12 ♘bd2 *(134)*

After 12 ♗e3 ♘e6 13 ♗b3 ♘xe5 14 ♕xd5?! (better is 14 ♗xd5 c6 15 ♗e4 with equal chances) 14 … ♕xd5 15 ♗xd5 ♗xf3 16 ♗xf3 ♘xf3+ 17 gf f5 18 ♘d2 ♔f7 19 ♘b3 c5 with counterplay for Black (Tseshkovsky–Tal, USSR Ch. 1978).

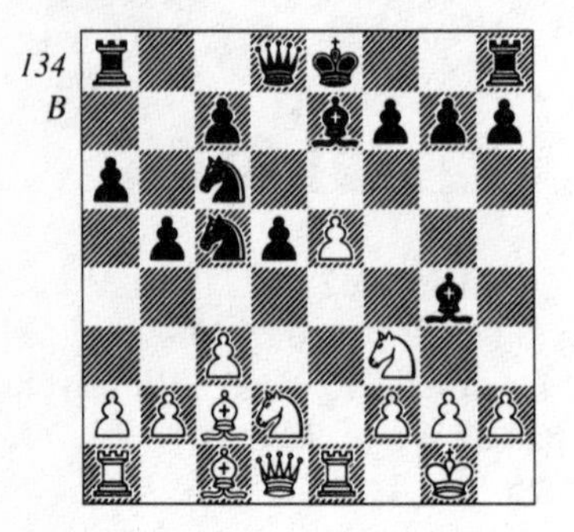

As the main variations we shall take:

A1311 12 … ♕d7
A1312 12 … 0–0

We shall first consider the following variations:

(a) **12 … d4!?** 13 ♘b3 (after 13 ♘e4?! d3 14 ♘xc5 dc 15 ♕xd8+ ♖xd8 16 ♘b3 ♗xf3 17 gf a5! Black stands better — Euwe) 13 … d3 14 ♗b1 ♘xb3 15 ab ♗f5 16 ♗e3 0–0 17 ♘d4 ♘xd4 18 cd ♗b4 19 ♖f1 c5 20 ♗xd3 cd 21 ♗f4 ♗xd3 22 ♕xd3 ♕d5 with roughly equal chances (Larsen).

(b) **12 … ♗h5** 13 ♘f1 0–0 14 ♘g3 ♗g6 15 ♗e3 ♕d7, and now:

(b1) **16 b4!** ♘a4 (16 … ♘e6 17 ♘f5!) 17 ♗xa4 ba 18 a3 ♖fd8 19 ♗g5 ♖e8 20 ♗xe7 ♖xe7 21 ♖a2 ♗e4 22 ♘xe4 de 23 ♕xd7 ♖xd7 24 e6! with a rather better ending for White (Geller–Agzamov, USSR Ch. 1985).

(b2) **16 h4** ♖ad8 17 h5 ♗xc2 18 ♕xc2 ♘e6 19 ♖ad1 f6 20 ef ♗xf6 21 h6! and here White stands a little better (Anand–Torre, Thessaloniki OL 1988).

A1311

12 … ♕d7

Now White has a choice of:

A13111 13 h3
A13112 13 ♘f1

A13111

13 h3

Let us consider the move 13 ♘b3. For example: 13 … ♘e6 14 h3 ♗h5 15 ♗f5 ♘cd8 16 ♗e3 a5 17 ♗c5 (or 17 g4!? ♗g6 18 ♕e2 a4 19 ♘bd4 ♖b8 20 ♘xe6 ♘xe6 21 ♘d4 c5 22 ♘xe6 fe 23 ♗xg6+ hg 24 ♖ad1 with an insignificant advantage to White; Sablotski–Kandaurov, corr. 1981) 17 … a4 18 ♗xe7 ♕xe7 19 ♘bd2 c6 20 b4 ♘g5 with double-edged play (Karpov–Korchnoi, 28th game, World Ch. match 1978).

13	**…**	**♗h5**
14	**♘f1**	**♖ad8**
15	**♘g3**	**♗g6**
16	**♘d4**	**♘xd4**

Interesting is 16 … 0–0!? 17 ♗f5?! ♘e6 18 ♗g4 ♘cxd4 19 cd c5 20 ♘f5 ♕a7! 21 ♘xe7+ ♕xe7 22 ♗e3 cd 23 ♗xd4 ♖c8 with excellent play for Black.

17	**cd**	**♘e6**
18	**♘f5**	**c5**
19	**♗e3**	**♕a7!**

Chances are roughly equal (de

Firmian–Agzamov, Warsaw 1983).

A13112

13 ♘f1 ♖ad8

Possible is 13 ... ♗h5 14 ♘g3 ♗g6 15 h4!? 0–0 16 h5 ♗xc2 17 ♕xc2 f5 18 ef ♗xf6 19 ♗e3 ♘e6 20 ♖ad1 ♖ad8 with roughly equal play (Mokry–Yusupov, Dubai OL 1986).

14 ♘e3 ♗h5 *(135)*

After 14 ... ♗xf3 15 ♕xf3 ♘xe5 16 ♕g3 ♘g6 17 ♘f5, or 14 ... 0–0 15 ♘xg4 ♕xg4 16 ♗e3, White has the better chances.

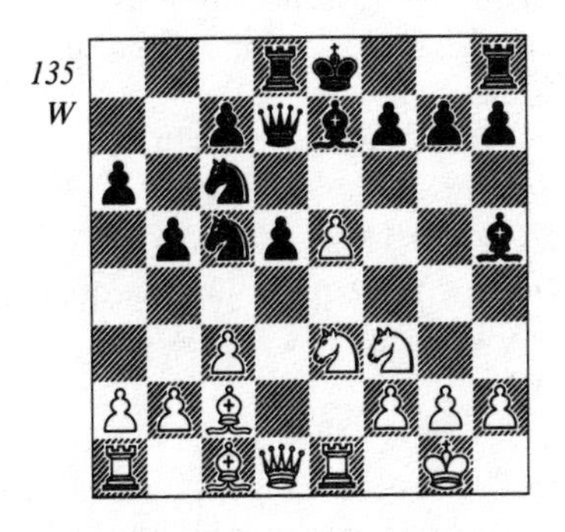
135
W

The following variations arise:

(a) **15 ♘f5** 0–0 (or 15 ... ♘e6 16 a4 b4 17 a5 ♘a7 18 ♘xe7 ♕xe7 19 ♕d3 ♘b5 20 ♗a4 cb 21 ♗xb5 cb 22 ♘d4 ♗g6 and chances are roughly equal; Aseev–Agzamov, Tashkent 1984) 16 ♘xe7+ ♘xe7, and now:

(a1) **17 ♗e3** ♘a4!? 18 ♕d3 ♘g6 19 e6 (after 19 b3 ♗xf3 20 ♗xf3 ♕h3 21 ♗d2 ♘c5 22 ♕f5 the chances are level; van der Wiel–Hjartarson, Rotterdam 1989, also interesting is 19 ♗c1!?) 19 ... fe 20 ♘e5 ♘xb2 21 ♘xd7 ♘xd3 22 ♘xf8 ♘xe1 23 ♗xg6 ♗xg6 (Marjanovic–Korchnoi, Belgrade 1987). After 24 ♘e6! chances would have been equal.

(a2) **17 b4** ♘e4! (17 ... ♘a4? 18 ♗xh7+!) 18 ♗xe4 de 19 ♕xd7 ♖xd7 20 ♘g5 ♗g6 21 e6 ♖xd3!? 22 ef+ ♗xf7 23 ♘e4 ♘d5 with approximate equality (Sokolov–Korchnoi, Tilburg 1987).

(b) **15 b4!?** ♘e6 16 ♘f5 d4?! (16 ... 0–0) 17 ♗e4 ♗g6 18 g4! h5 19 h3 ♔f8 20 a4! with better chances for White (Hjartarson–Korchnoi, match 1988).

A1312

12 ... 0–0

And now:

(a) **13 h3** ♗h5 14 ♘b3 ♘e6 15 g4!? ♗g6 16 ♗f5 ♕d7 17 ♗e3 ♘cd8 18 ♔h1 a5 (better is 18 ... ♘b7 and c5) 19 ♕e2 a4 20 ♘bd4 ♖b8 21 ♗d3 ♗xd3 22 ♕xd3 ♘c5 23 ♕f1 with somewhat better chances for White (Tseshkovsky–Agzamov, USSR Ch. 1981).

(b) **13 ♘f1** ♗h5 14 ♗e3!? (or 14 ♘g3 ♗g6 15 ♘f5 ♕d7 16 g4 ♖ad8 17 h4! ♘e4 18 ♘xe7+ ♘xe7 19 ♘h2 ♘c5 20 ♗e3 ♘e6 21 ♗b3 with better play for White; Kupreichik–Kaidanov, USSR 1986) 14 ... ♗g6 (interesting is 14 ... ♘xe5 15 ♗c5 ♘xf3+ 16 ♕xf3 ♗xf3 17 ♗xe7 ♕d7 18 ♗xf8 ♗xg2! 19 ♗c5 ♗xf1 20 ♔xf1 ♕h3+ 21 ♔g1 ♕g4+ 22 ♔h1 with a draw — Ivanchuk) 15 ♘g3 ♖e8 16 h4 ♗xc2 17 ♕xc2 ♘d7 18 ♗f4 and White's position is preferable (Ivanchuk–Tukmakov, New York 1988).

(c) **13 ♘b3**, and here:

(c1) **13 … ♕d7** 14 ♘xc5 ♗xc5 15 ♕d3 g6 16 ♗g5 ♗e7 17 ♗h6 ♖fd8 with good play for Black (Larsen).

(c2) **13 … ♘e6** 14 h3 (or 14 ♕d3 g6 15 ♘fd4 ♘cxd4 16 ♘xd4 ♘xd4 17 cd c5 18 ♕g3 ♕d7 19 dc ♗xc5 20 ♗g5 ♖fe8 21 ♗f6 ♖ac8 22 ♗b3 ♗f5 23 ♖ad1 d4 24 ♕f4; Chandler–Wedberg, Haninge 1988) 14 … ♗h5 15 ♗f5 ♘cd8 16 ♗e3 a5 17 ♘c5 ♕c6 18 ♘d3 ♗xf3 19 ♕xf3 g6 20 ♗g4 (Ehlvest–Hjartarson, Belfort 1988). In both cases White has the better chances.

A132

10 ♘d4!? *(136)*

White's main intention is to prevent Black's plan of playing ♗g4 and d5–d4, and for the sake of this he is willing to sacrifice a pawn.

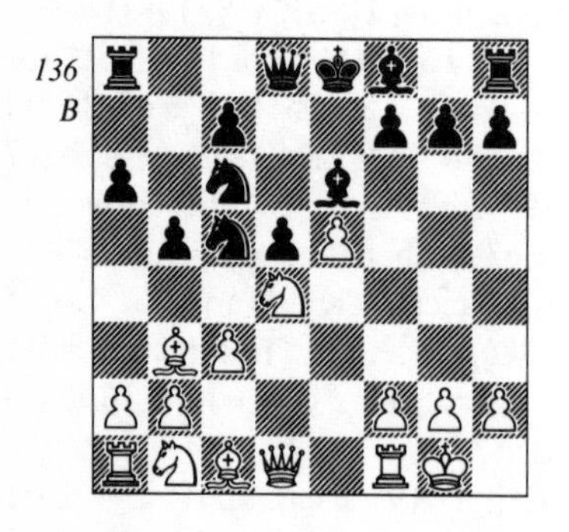

136
B

10 … ♘xe5

After 10 … ♘xd4 11 cd ♘xb3 12 ♕xb3 c5 11 dc ♗xc5 14 ♕g3, or 10 … ♘xb3 11 ♘xc6 ♕d7 12 ab ♕xc6 13 b4, or 10 … ♕d7 11 ♗c2, White's position is preferable.

11 f4 ♘ed3

After 11 … ♘c4 12 f5 ♗d7 13 ♕h5 ♘e4 14 ♘d2 ♘f6 15 ♕g5 ♗e7 16 ♕xg7 ♖g8 17 ♕h6 c5 18 ♘4f3 ♗xf5 19 ♘h4 Black has certain difficulties (Mukhin–Ruderfer, Riga 1972).

12 f5 ♗c8

And now:

(a) **13 ♘c6!?** ♕d6 14 ♕e2+ ♔d7 15 ♘d4 and it is not easy for White to demonstrate that he has compensation for the pawn (Larsen).

(b) **13 ♗c2** ♘xc1 14 ♖e1+ ♘e4 15 ♕xc1 ♗b7 16 ♘d2 ♗e7 17 ♘xe4 de 18 ♗xe4 ♗xe4 19 ♖xe4 0–0 with approximate equality (Euwe).

A2

9 ♘bd2

Until quite recently this variation had been overshadowed. But during the last few years its theoretical basis has developed at a fast pace and now this move has become one of the most popular. The ensuing struggle here is characterized by subtle manoeuvring and tactical sharpness.

9 … ♘c5

We shall briefly consider the following possibilities for Black:

(a) **9 … ♗e7** 10 ♘xe4 (10 c3 0–0 11 ♗c2 f5 transposes to A1111) 10 … de 11 ♗xe6 fe 12 ♘g5 ♗xg5 (also possible is 12 … ♕xd1) 13

♕h5+ g6 14 ♕xg5 0–0! 15 ♕g4 ♕d5 16 ♗f4 ♘xe5 17 ♕g3 ♘c4 18 b3 ♘d6 19 ♖ad1 ♕c5 20 ♗xd6 cd 21 ♕xd6 ♕xd6 22 ♗xd6 ♖ac8 with full equality for Black (Vogt–Chekhov, Potsdam 1985).

(b) **9 … ♗c5!?** 10 ♘xe4 (10 c3 0–0 11 ♗c2) 10 … de 11 ♗xe6 ♕xd1 12 ♖xd1 fe 13 ♘g5 0–0 14 ♘xe4 ♗b6 15 ♔f1? ♖f5 16 f3 ♖xe5 17 c3 ♖f8 18 ♔e2 ♖xe4! and Black obtained a clear advantage (Shmuter–Shulkis, USSR 1989).

10 c3 d4 *(137)*

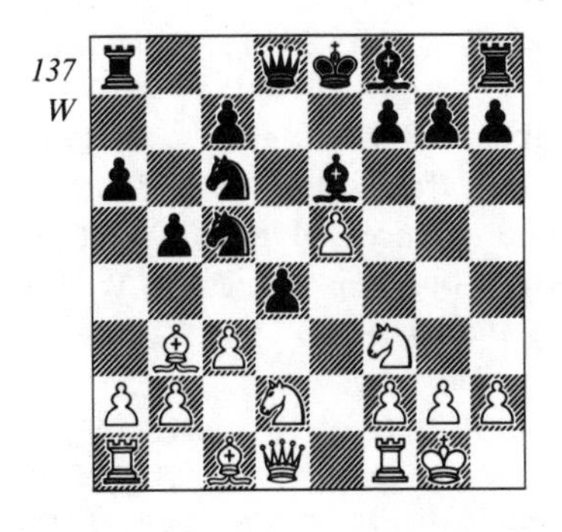

137
W

It is this continuation which is the subject of great analytical discussion. Note that the following lines are in White's favour: 10 … g6? 11 ♕e2 ♗g7 12 ♘d4 ♘xe5 13 f4 ♘c4 14 f5 gf 15 ♘xf5 ♖g8 16 ♘xc4 dc 17 ♗c2 ♘d3 18 ♗h6! with an irresistible attack for White (Karpov–Korchnoi, 8th game, World Ch. 1978); 10 … ♘xb3 11 ♘xb3 ♗e7 12 ♘fd4! and White dominates the centre; and 10 … ♘d3?! 11 ♕e2 ♘xc1 12 ♖axc1 ♘a5 13 ♘d4 ♘xb3 14 ab c5 15 ♘xe6 fe 16 ♕a4 (Kir. Georgiev–Ivanov, Montreal 1986).

As an alternative Black may play 10 … ♗g4, which usually leads to the variation A13, considered above. But such a move-order has its subtle side — for example: 11 ♗c2 ♘e6!? 12 ♖e1 ♗c5 13 ♘f1 ♗h5 (13 … ♕d7 14 ♘g3) 14 ♘g3 ♗g6 15 ♗b3! ♘e7 16 h4 h6?! (16 … h5!? and then c6 and ♘e7–f5) 17 h5 ♗h7 18 ♘d4 ♗xd4 19 cd 0–0 20 ♕g4 with an initiative for White (Kovalev–Kaidanov, USSR 1988).

11 ♗xe6

Sharp play ensues after 11 ♘g5!? ♕xg5 12 ♕f3 0–0–0 (after 12 … ♗d7 13 ♗xf7+ ♔e7 14 ♘b3! ♕xe5 15 ♘xc5 ♕xc5 16 ♖e1+, or 12 … ♔d7 13 ♗d5! 14 ♕xd5+ ♗d6 15 cd ♘xd4 16 ♘c4!, White has a very strong attack) 13 ♗xe6 fe 14 ♕xc6 ♕xe5 15 b4 ♕d5 16 ♕xd5 ed 17 bc dc 18 ♘b3 d4 19 ♗a3 ♗e7 20 ♗b4 ♗f6 21 a4 ♔d7! 22 ab ab 23 ♖a6? c6 (23 … ♖a8!) 24 ♖d1 ♔e6 25 ♖xc6+ ♔d5 26 ♖xf6 ♔c4! with equal chances (Timman–Smyslov, Bad Lauterberg 1979). Stronger is 23 ♖fd1! ♔e6 24 ♖ac1 ♔f7 25 ♔f1 ♖he8 26 ♖d3 ♖e4 27 g3 and Black has quite a few difficulties (Lilienthal).

11 … ♘xe6
12 cd

After 12 a4 dc 13 bc b4 14 cb (14 ♕c2 ♕d5 15 c4 ♕d7 16 ♘b3 ♖d8) 14 … ♘xb4 15 ♗a3 ♕d5 with equality (Romanishin–

Marin, Dresden 1988), or 12 ♘b3 dc 13 ♕c2 ♕d5! (Sax–Tal, Tallinn 1979), Black has no difficulties.

12 ... ♘cxd4

(138)

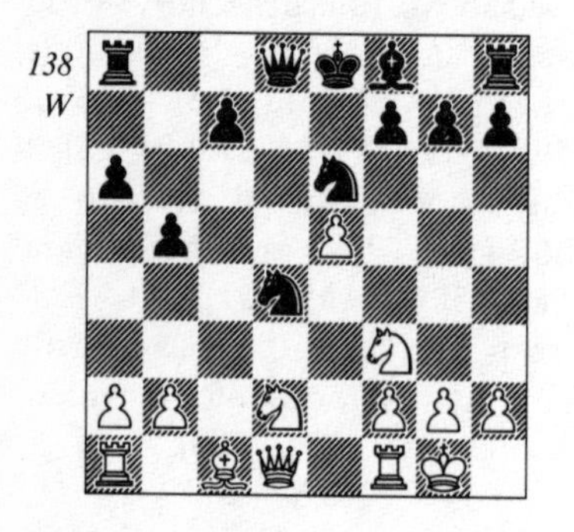

A critical position, where White has a choice of:

A21 13 ♘e4
A22 13 a4

A21

13 ♘e4 ♗e7

An alternative is 13 ... ♕d5 14 ♘xd4 ♘xd4 15 ♘c3 (also not bad is 15 ♖e1 ♗b4 16 ♘c3 ♕d8 17 ♗g5!; Malchinov–Odeev, USSR 1983) 15 ... ♕d7 (after 15 ... ♕c4 16 ♗e3 ♖d8 17 ♖c1 ♗c5 18 ♕g4 ♘e6 19 ♕xc4 bc 20 ♘d1! Black has difficulties; Ilovans–Moldobaev, USSR 1983) 16 ♗e3 ♗e7 17 ♘e4 (or 17 ♕h5 ♕e6 18 ♖ad1 ♖d8) 17 ... ♗a7 18 ♖c1 0–0 19 ♘c5 ♗xc5 20 ♖xc5 ♖fd8 21 ♗xd4 ♕xd4 22 ♕xd4 ♖xd4 23 ♖xc7 ♖d2 24 ♖fc1 ♖e8 (Belyavsky–Dorfman, USSR Ch. 1981).

14 ♗e3 ♘f5

Black has serious difficulties after 14 ... c5 15 b4!, or 14 ... ♘xf3+? 15 ♕xf3 0–0 16 ♖fd1 ♕e8 (somewhat better is 16 ... ♕c8) 17 ♘f6+! ♗xf6 18 ef ♕c8 19 fg ♖d8 20 h4! c5 21 ♖ac1 ♕c7 22 h5 (Karpov–Korchnoi, 14th game, World Ch. match 1981).

15 ♕c2 0–0
16 ♖ad1

An ineffectual continuation is 16 ♘f6+ ♗xf6 17 ♕xf5 ♗e7 18 ♖ad1 ♕c8 19 ♘d2 ♖d8 when Black has no difficulties (van der Wiel–Korchnoi, Sarajevo 1984); or 16 ♘eg5 ♗xg5 17 ♘xg5 g6 (not bad is 17 ... ♘xg5 18 ♕xf5 ♘e6 19 ♕e4 c5 20 f4 f5 21 ef ♕xf6 22 f5 ♗d4 23 ♕d5+ ♕f7 — Larsen) 18 ♘xe6 fe 19 ♖ae1 ♕d5 20 b3 ♖ac8 21 ♗c5 ♖fd8 with good chances of equality (Karpov–Korchnoi, 16th game, World Ch. match 1981).

16 ... ♘xe3
17 fe ♕c8 *(139)*

Interesting is 17 ... ♕e8?! 18 ♘d4 ♖d8 19 ♘xe6 ♖xd1!? 20 ♖xd1?! fe 21 ♕c7 ♕h5 22 ♖f1 with double-edged play (van der Wiel–Korchnoi, Wijk aan Zee 1984).

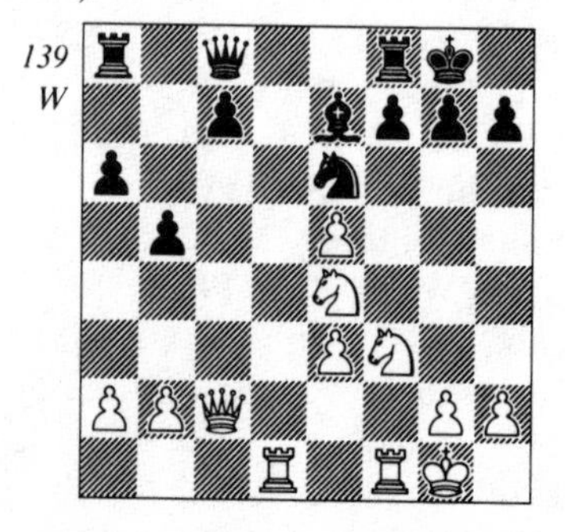

In this position the following variations are possible:

(a) **18 h3** ♖d8 19 ♘h2!? (19 ♖c1! — Karpov) 19 ... ♖xd1 20 ♕xd1 ♕e8 (20 ... ♘c5 21 ♕f3!) 21 ♕h5 ♘c5 22 ♘g3 a5 is good for Black (Tal–Korchnoi, Reykjavik 1987).

(b) **18 ♖d3!?** c5 19 ♘d6 ♕c7 (19 ... ♕b8) 20 ♖fd1 ♖fd8 21 ♖d5 ♗f8 22 b3 with a minimal advantage to White (Short–Belyavsky, Barcelona 1989).

Note also that after 18 ♘d4 ♘xd4 19 ed ♕e6 (Smirin–Mikhalchishin, USSR 1988), or 18 ♘g3!? ♖d8 19 ♘d4 ♘xd4 20 ed c6! (Sax–Hellers, Haninge 1989), chances are roughly equal.

A22

13 a4 ♗e7

Other possibilities for Black:

(a) **13 ... ♗c5** 14 ♘e4 ♗b6 15 ♘xd4 ♗xd4 16 ♘g5! 0–0 17 ab ♘xg5 18 ♗xg5 ♗xf2+ 19 ♖xf2 ♕xg5 20 ba ♕xe5 (Tischbierek–Chekhov, Potsdam 1985). Here, 21 ♕f1! gives White good chances.

(b) **13 ... ♖b8** 14 ab ab 15 ♘e4 ♗e7 16 ♘d6+ cd 17 ♘xd4 ♘xd4 18 ♕xd4 de 19 ♕xe5 0–0 20 ♗f4 ♖b7 with equal chances (Nunn–Timman, Amsterdam 1985).

14 ♘xd4 *(140)*

Interesting is 14 ab!? ♘xb5 (14 ... ab 15 ♖xa8 ♕xa8 16 ♘xd4 ♘xd4 17 ♕g4 ♘e6 18 f4! favours White) 15 ♕c2 (15 ♘b3!?) 15 ... 0–0 16 ♘b3 c5 17 ♗e3 ♕b6 18 ♖a4 ♖fb8 19 ♘a5 ♖c8 20 ♕e4 ♘bd4 21 ♘xd4 cd 22 ♗xd4 ♘xd4 with equal chances (Sax–Yusupov, Sofia 1984).

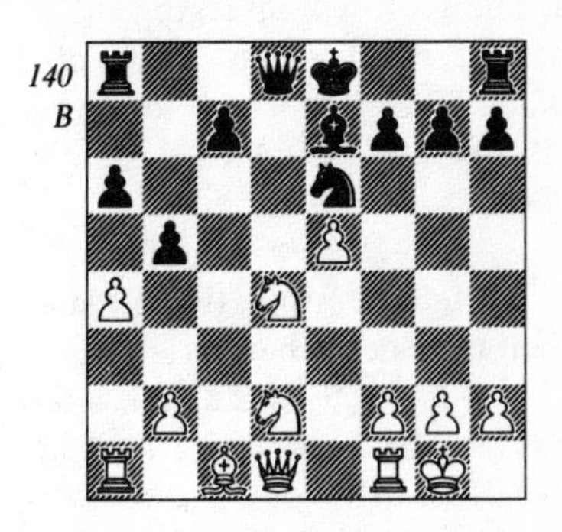

140
B

After 14 ♘xd4 the following variations are possible:

(a) **14 ... ♕xd4** 15 ab ♕xe5 16 ba 0–0 17 ♘f3 ♕b5 18 ♕a4 ♕xa4 19 ♖xa4 ♘c5 with equality (Psakhis–Dolmatov, USSR Ch. 1981).

(b) **14 ... ♘xd4** 15 ♘e4 0–0 (after 15 ... ♘e6 16 ♗e3 0–0 17 f4 ♕xd1 18 ♖fxd1 ♖fb8 19 ♖d7 White is clearly better; Karpov–Korchnoi, 18th game, World Ch. match 1981) 16 ab ♘xb5 17 ♗e3 ♕c8 18 ♕e2 ♕e6 19 f4 f6 20 ef ♗xf6 21 e5 with some pressure for White (Ivanchuk–Yusupov, Linares 1989).

A3

9 ♕e2

This plan, known as the Keres System, was tried with success at the World Championship Match Tournament in 1948 and was later popular, especially in the 1960s. Nowadays interest in it has fallen noticeably.

White's plan is to apply pressure

along the d-file. In a number of variations the pawn on c2 moves in one go to c4, attacking the d5 square. Practice has shown that Black has sufficient defensive resources and can create counterplay.

9 ... ♗e7

The main continuation. First we shall consider other variations:

(a) **9 ... ♗c5** 10 ♗e3 (an alternative is 10 ♘bd2 ♘xd2 11 ♗xd2 0–0 12 ♖ad1 ♗g4 13 ♗e3 d4 14 h3 ♗h5 15 g4 ♗g6 with double-edged play — Keres) 10 ... 0–0 (interesting is 10 ... ♗g4!? 11 ♖d1 ♘e7 12 c3 c6 13 ♗c2 ♕c7 and Black's defence holds; Ivanov–Aseev, USSR 1983) 11 ♖d1 (11 ♘bd2 ♘xd2 12 ♕xd2), and now:

(a1) **11 ... ♗xe3** (11 ... ♘a5) 12 ♕xe3 ♘e7 13 ♘bd2 ♘f5 14 ♕e2 ♘c5 15 c3 with slight pressure for White (Sokolov–Karaklajic, Sarajevo 1958).

(a2) **11 ... d4!?** 12 ♘c3! ♘xc3 13 bc de 14 ♖xd8 ef+ 15 ♔f1 ♖axd8 (Antunes–Flear, Pau 1988). With 16 ♗xe6 fe 17 ♘g5 White maintained his initiative.

(b) **9 ... ♘c5** 10 ♖d1 ♘xb3?! (10 ... ♗e7, transposing to the main line) 11 ab (11 cb!? ♕d7 12 ♘c3) 11 ... ♕c8 12 c4! ♘b4 13 cb ab 14 ♖xa8 ♕xa8 15 ♗d2 c6 16 ♘d4 ♘a6 17 b4! with pressure for White. Note that other lines favouring White are: 9 ... ♘a5 10 ♖d1 (also good is 10 ♘d4) 10 ... ♗c5 11 ♗e3 ♗xe3 12 ♕xe3 c5 13 c3 0–0 14 ♘e1! (Keres); or 9 ... g5? 10 c4! bc 11 ♗a4 ♗d7 12 e6! fe 13 ♗xc6 ♗xc6 14 ♘e5! (Boleslavsky–Stoltz, Stockholm 1948).

10 ♖d1

After 10 c4?! bc (also not bad is 10 ... ♘c5 11 cd ♗xd5 12 ♖d1 ♘xb3 13 ab 0–0 14 ♘c3 ♗xf3 15 gf ♕c8 16 ♘d5 ♗d8 — Larsen) 11 ♗a4 ♗d7 12 ♘c3 ♘c5 13 e6 fe 14 ♗xc6 ♗xc6 15 ♘e5 ♕d6 16 ♕h5+ g6 17 ♘xg6 hg 18 ♕xh8+ ♔d7 19 ♕g7 d4 Black's chances are clearly better (Abroshin–Radchenko, corr. 1954).

After 10 ♖d1 Black has a choice between:

A31 10 ... 0–0
A32 10 ... ♘c5

In White's favour is 10 ... ♘a5 11 ♘d4 c5 12 ♘f5! ♗xf5 13 ♗xd5 ♘g5 14 ♗xg5 ♗xg5 15 ♕f3!

A31

10 ... 0–0

For a long time this move was not popular, but Larsen restored its reputation.

11 c4

There has been little study of 11 ♗e3. For example: 11 ... ♘a5 12 ♘d4 c5 13 ♘xe6 fe 14 c3 ♘xb3 15 ab ♕e8 16 ♘a3 ♕g6 17 f3 ♘g5 18 ♔h1 ♘f7 19 ♗f2 ♖fc8 (19 ... ♔h8!?) 20 ♘c2 a5 21 ♘e3 with a minimal advantage to White (Ciric–Zuidema, Amsterdam 1967).

11 ... bc
12 ♗xc4 *(141)*

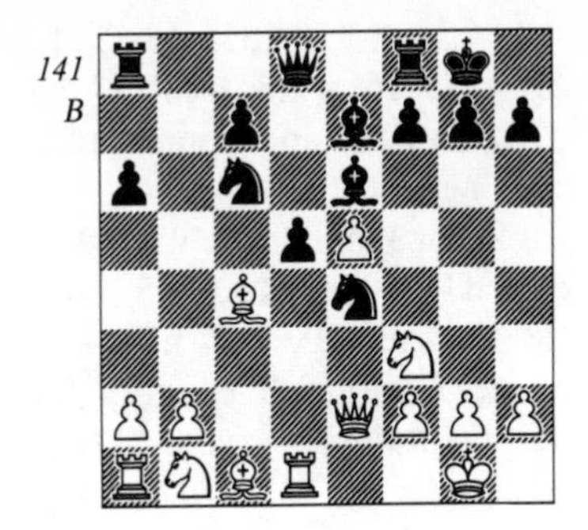
141
B

A critical position, where Black again has a choice of moves:

A311 12 ... ♗c5
A312 12 ... ♕d7

In White's favour is 12 ... dc?! 13 ♖xd8 ♖fxd8 14 h3 (also good is 14 ♘c3 or 14 ♗d2) 14 ... ♗d5 15 ♘c3 (Boleslavsky); or 12 ... ♘a5?! 13 ♗d3 ♘c5 14 ♗c2 ♘c6 15 a3! (Keres).

A311

12	**...**	**♗c5**
13	**♗e3**	**♗xe3**
14	**♕xe3**	**♕b8**
15	**♗b3**	**♘a5** *(142)*

After 15 ... ♕b6 16 ♕e2 ♖ad8 17 ♘c3 ♘xc3 18 bc ♕c5 (interesting is 18 ... ♘e7 19 ♖ab1 ♕a5 20 dc! — Petrosian) 19 h3! ♗c8 20 ♕d3 ♖fe8 21 ♖e1 g6 22 ♖ad1 a5 23 ♗a4 ♗d7 24 ♕xd5 with advantage to White (Hübner–Korchnoi, Solingen 1973).

After 15 ... ♘a5 the following variations arise:

(a) **16 ♘e1** ♕b6 (16 ... ♘xb3 17 ab ♕b6 18 ♕xb6 cb 19 b4!) 17 ♕xb6 cb 18 f3 ♘xb3 19 ab ♘c5 20 b4 ♘d7 21 ♘d3 (Karpov–

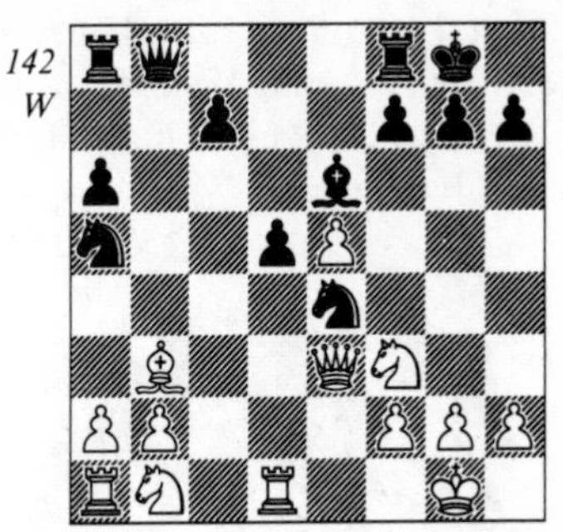
142
W

Korchnoi, 12th game, World Ch. 1978). After 21 ... a5 22 ba ba, or 21 ... ♗f5 22 ♘c3 ♘xd3 and ♘xe5, Black has good chances of equality.

(b) **16 ♘bd2** ♕a7 17 ♘d4 (after 17 ♘xe4!? ♕xe3 18 fe ♘xb3 19 ab de 20 ♘d4 ♖fb8, or 17 ♕xa7 ♖xa7 18 ♘xe4 ♘xb3 19 ab de 20 ♘d4 c5, chances are roughly equal; Vogt–Sznapik, Warsaw 1979) 17 ... ♘xd2 18 ♕xd2 ♕b6 19 ♗c2 c5! 20 ♘f5 ♗xf5 21 ♗xf5 ♖ad8 and here the game is level (Kavalek–Karpov, Montreal 1979).

A312

12	**...**	**♕d7**

A move introduced into practice by the Swedish master, Ekström.

13	**♘c3**	

Worse is 13 a3 ♘a5 14 ♗a2 c5 15 ♘bd2 ♘xd2 16 ♗xd2 ♘c6 17 ♗f4 c4 (Svensson–Ekström, corr. 1964); or 13 ♗xd5 ♗xd5 14 ♕xe4 ♗xe4 15 ♖xd7 ♖fd8 16 ♖xd8+ ♖xd8 17 ♘c3 ♗xf3 18 gf ♘e5 (Ekström) — in each case Black stands better.

13	**...**	**♘xc3**
14	**bc**	**f6**

After 14 … ♘a5 15 ♗d3 c5 16 ♗g5 f6 17 ef ♗xf6 18 ♗xf6 ♖xf6 19 c4 ♗g4 20 ♗e4 White has a clear advantage.

15 ef ♗xf6 *(143)*

143
W

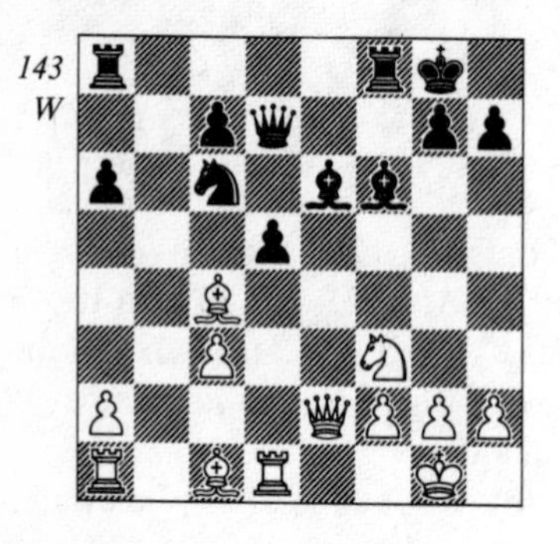

And now: 16 ♘g5 ♗xg5 17 ♗xg5 h6 18 ♗e3 ♘e5 19 ♗d3 ♕d6 20 h3 (after 20 ♖d4 c5 21 ♖f4 g5! 22 ♖xf8+ ♖xf8 23 h3 ♗xh3! 24 gh ♘f3+ 25 ♔f1 c4 26 ♗c2 ♕e6 27 ♔g2 ♘h4+ with a draw — Tal; or 20 ♗c5 ♕xc5 21 ♕xe5 ♕xf2+ 22 ♔h1 ♕f6 23 ♕xf6 ♖xf6 24 ♗xd5 ♗xd5 25 ♖xd5 and the game is level) 20 … c6 21 ♖d4? ♘g6 22 ♖ad1 ♕e5 23 ♖1d2 a5 24 ♖a4 ♖fe8 25 c4 dc 26 ♗xc4 ♕a1+ 27 ♖d1 ♕e5 28 ♕c2! with advantage to White (Kavalek–Bisguier, West Germany 1974).

A32

10 … ♘c5

This is the most solid system. We shall look in some detail at the crucial variations, 11 ♗xd5 and 11 c4, but first let us consider the following variations:

(a) **11 ♗e3** 0–0 12 c4 bc 13 ♗xc4 ♘a5 14 ♗xd5 ♗xd5 15 ♘c3 ♗xf3 16 ♕xf3 ♕e8! 17 b4 ♘d7 18 ba ♘xe5 and White stands a little better.

(b) **11 ♘c3** ♘xb3 12 cb!? 0–0 13 ♗e3 ♕d7 14 ♗g5 ♖ad8 15 ♖ac1 ♖fe8 16 ♗xe7 ♘xe7 17 h3 d4 18 ♘e4 ♗d5 with full equality for Black (Matulovic–Savon, Skopje 1968).

A321 11 ♗xd5
A322 11 c4

A321

11 ♗xd5 ♗xd5
12 ♘c3 ♗c4

In White's favour is 12 … ♘b4? 13 ♘e1 ♕d7 14 a3 ♕c6 15 ab ♗c4 16 ♕g4!

13 ♖xd8+ ♖xd8
14 ♕e3 b4
15 b3 ♗e6

15 … bc? 16 ♗a3!

16 ♘e4 ♖d1+
17 ♘e1 ♘d4 *(144)*

144
W

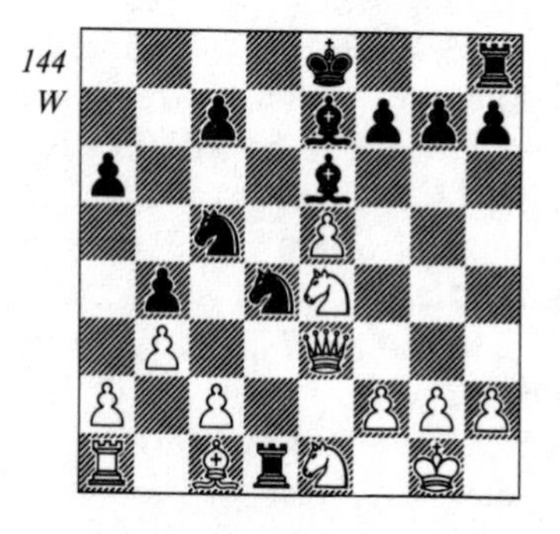

Now the following variations may arise:

(a) **18 ♗b2** ♘xc2 19 ♕e2 ♖xa1 20 ♗xa1 ♘xa1 21 ♘xc5 ♗xc5

22 ♘d3 ♗b6 (22 … ♗e7? 23 ♘f4!) 23 ♘xb4 0–0 (23 … a5 24 ♘c6 ♔d7 25 ♕b5 ♔c8) 24 ♘c6 ♔d7 25 ♕b5 ♔c8) 24 ♘c6 f6 25 h4 fe! 26 ♕xe5 ♖f6, and now:

(a1) **27 ♘d4** (or 27 g4 ♗xf2+ 28 ♔h1 ♗xh4 29 ♘e7+ ♔f8 30 ♘f5 ♗xf5 31 gf ♘xb3 32 ab ♖d6 — Suetin–Geller, USSR Ch. 1958) 27 … ♗f7 28 ♘f3 ♘c2 29 ♕e4 ♗g6 30 ♕d5+ ♔f8! (Suetin–Boleslavsky, USSR Ch. 1958). In both cases chances are equal.

(a2) **27 ♘d8** ♗f7 28 ♘xf7 ♔xf7 29 ♕xa1 ♖xf2 30 ♔h2 a5 31 ♕e5 h6 32 a4 (32 a3!) 32 … g6 33 ♕d5+ ♔g7 34 ♕e5+ ♔f7 25 h5 ♖f5! with equal chances (Timman–Yusupov, Montpellier 1985).

(b) **18 ♗d2!?** ♘xc2 19 ♕xc5 ♖xe1+ 20 ♖xe1 ♗xc5 21 ♖c1 ♗e7 (21 … ♗b6 deserves consideration) 22 ♖xc2 ♗f5! 23 ♖c4 ♗xe4 24 ♖xe4 c5 with equal chances; or in gambit style: 18 … ♖xa1 19 ♕xd4 ♘xe4 20 ♕xa1 ♘xd2 21 f3 0–0 22 ♕d1 ♖d8 23 ♘d3 ♘c4! 24 bc ♗xc4 also with roughly equal play.

A322

11 c4 d4!?

A recommendation of Keres and Tolush.

12 cb ♘xb3

Other possibilities:

(a) **12 … d3** 13 ♕f1 ♘xb3 (after 13 … ♗xb3 14 ab ♘b4 15 ♗d2! ♘xb3 — 15 … ♘c2 16 ♖a5! — 16 ♗xb4 — Boleslavsky; or 13 … ♘d4 14 ♘xd4 ♕xd4 15 ♗xe6 fe 16 ba 0–0 17 ♘c3 ♖xa6 18 ♗e3 ♕xe5 19 ♖ac1 and then 20 b4! — Suetin — White has the better chances) 14 ab ♘b4 (or 14 … ab 15 ♖xa8 ♕xa8 16 ♕xd3 0–0 17 ♕xb5 ♗g4 18 ♕e2 ♗c5 19 ♕e4! with advantage to White — Suetin) 15 ♗d2 ♘c2 16 ♖xa6 ♖xa6 17 ba ♗xb3 18 ♗c3 ♗c4 19 ♘bd2 ♗xa6 20 b3 0–0 21 ♘c4 ♕b8 22 ♕xd3 ♕xb3 23 ♘a5 ♗xd3 24 ♘xb3 ♗f5 25 ♘bd4 ♘xd4 26 ♘xd4 ♗d7 27 f4 c5 with equal chances (Rodriguez–Yusupov, Toluca 1982).

B

8 ♘xe5 ♘xe5
9 de *(145)*

145
B

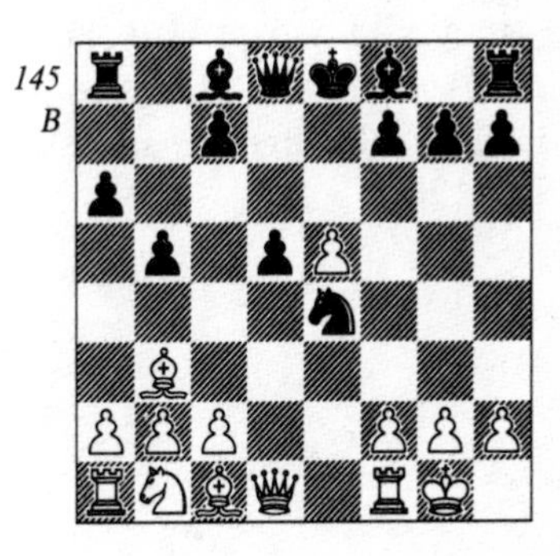

Objectively this is not dangerous for Black! But he does have to reckon with a possible attack by means of f2–f4–f5. There are two plans to choose from:

B1 9 … c6
B2 9 … ♗b7

B1

9 … c6

And now:

(a) **10 ♗e3** ♗e7 11 ♘d2 ♘xd2 12 ♕xd2 0–0 13 ♕c3 ♗b7 14 f4 a5 15 a3 b4 16 ♕d2 a4 with full equality for Black (Fischer–Addison, USA 1967).

(b) **10 c3** ♗e7 (also good is 10 ... ♗c5 11 ♘d2 ♘xd2 12 ♗xd2 ♗f5 13 ♕f3 ♕d7 14 ♗e3 ♗xe3 15 ♕xe3 0–0 with equality) 11 ♗e3 0–0 12 ♘bd2 ♘xd2 13 ♕xd2 ♗f5 14 ♖e1 ♕d7 15 ♖ad1 ♕e6 16 ♗g5 ♗c5 and chances are equal (Trifunovic–Donner, Wageningen 1957).

B2

9 ... ♗b7
10 c3

After 10 ♗e3 ♗c5 11 ♗xc5 ♘xc5 12 ♘d2 0–0 13 ♕h5 d4 14 f4 ♘xb3 15 ab ♕d5 Black has no difficulties (Savon–Shiyanovsky, USSR 1963).

10 ... ♗c5

And now:

(a) **11 ♘bd2** 0–0 (or 11 ... ♕h4!? 12 ♘xe4 de 13 e6! fe 14 ♗xe6 ♖d8 15 ♕e2 ♗d6 16 g3 ♕f6 17 ♗b3 ♖d7 18 a4 ♕f3 with equal chances; Sanakoev–Zelevinsky, Leningrad 1963) 12 ♘xe4 de 13 ♕g4 ♕e7 14 ♗f4 ♔h8 15 ♖ad1 f5 16 ♕g3 h6 with double-edged play (Vasyukov–Savon, Grozny 1969).

(b) **11 ♕e2** 0–0 12 ♗e3 ♕e7 13 f3 ♗xe3+ 14 ♕xe3 ♘c5 15 ♘d2 f5 16 f4 ♘fe6 17 ♘f3 c5 and Black is not worse (de Greiff–Milev, Havana 1962).

(c) **11 ♕g4!?** ♕e7 12 ♘d2 (12 ♕xg7 0–0–0!) 12 ... ♕xe5 13 ♘xe4 de 14 ♗f4 ♕f6 15 ♖ad1 0–0 16 ♗xc7 ♖ae8 with chances for both sides (Cherepkov–Bronstein, USSR Ch. 1961).

10 Rubinstein, Møller and Archangel Variations

In this chapter we deal with some of the less commonly seen Closed Systems, before moving on to the standard 5 ... ♗e7 which occupies Chapters 11–17. After 1 e4 e5 2 ♘f3 ♘c6 3 ♗b5 a6 4 ♗a4 ♘f6 5 0–0:

A 5 ... d6 (Rubinstein)
B 5 ... ♗c5 (Møller)
C 5 ... b5 (Archangel)

A

5 ... d6 *(146)*

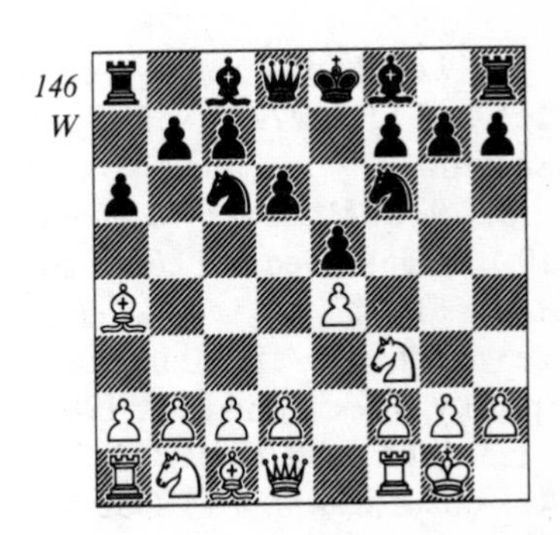

146
W

At the present time the Rubinstein System is rarely encountered. This variation combines motifs from the Steinitz Defence Deferred with schemes familiar from the Closed Systems. Of course we shall only consider here the lines which are unique to this variation. On the whole, Black has quite a few difficulties in this system.

The two most important continuations for White are:

A1 6 ♗xc6+
A2 6 ♖e1

A1

6 ♗xc6+

The most testing reply. The move 6 c3 was considered in the chapter dealing with the Steinitz Defence Deferred. White achieves nothing after either 6 c4 ♘xe4! 7 d4 ♗d7 8 ♖e1 ♘f6 9 de de 10 ♗xc6 ♗xc6 11 ♕xd8+ ♖xd8 12 ♘xe5 ♗e4 13 ♘d2 ♗b4! when Black has no difficulties (analysis by Hort and Pribyl), or 6 d4 b5 7 ♗b3 ♘xd4 8 ♘xd4 ed 9 c3 dc (or 9 ... ♗b7 10 cd ♗e7).

6 ... bc
7 d4 *(147)* **♘xe4**

Let us also consider the following variations:

(a) **7 ... ♗g4!?** 8 de ♘xe4, and now:

147
B

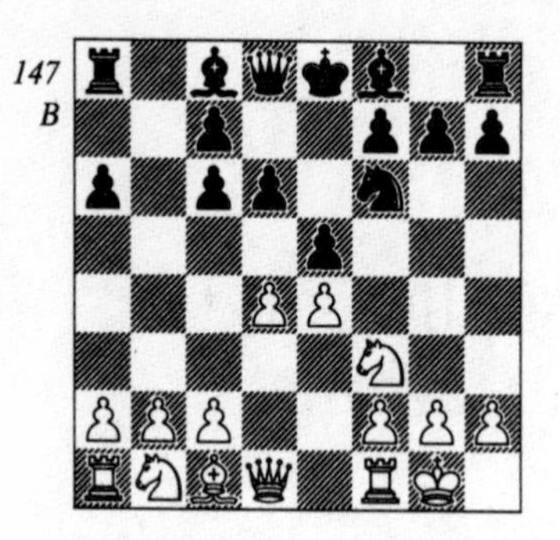

(a1) **9 ed** ♗xd6 10 ♕e2! ♕e7 11 ♖e1 ♘c5 12 ♕xe7+ ♗xe7 13 ♘e5 (Suetin).

(a2) **9 ♕e1!?** ♗xf3 10 gf ♘c5 (10 ... ♘g5) 11 ed+ ♘e6 12 ♕e4 ♕xd6 13 ♘c3 ♕d7 14 f4 g6 15 ♗e3 ♗d6 16 f5 (Ljubojevic–Spassky, Thessaloniki OL 1988).

(a3) **9 h3** ♗h5 10 c4!? ♗e7 11 ♖e1 d5 12 ♕a4 0–0 13 ♘d2 ♗c5 14 ♘xe4 de 15 ♘h2 f5 16 ♕xc6 ♗b4 17 ♖f1 ♗e2 18 a3 ♗xf1 19 ♘xf1 ♗e7 with double-edged play (Krogius–Borisenko, USSR 1953).

(b) **7 ... ♘d7** 8 ♘a3! f6 (or 8 ... a5 9 ♘c4 ♗a6 10 ♘xa5 ♗xf1 11 ♘xc6 with advantage to White) 9 ♘c4 a5 10 ♖e1 ♘b6 11 ♘e3 ♗e7 12 c4 ♗e6 13 a5! ♘c8 14 ♕a4 ♘a7 15 ♘c4 with pressure for White (Rauzer–Savitsky, USSR Ch. 1933).

(c) **7 ... ♗e7?!** 8 de?! (8 ♖e1!) 8 ... ♘xe4 9 ♘d2 ♘xd2 10 ♗xd2 ♗g4 11 ♗e3 d5 with a good game for Black (Gurgenidze–Spassky, USSR Ch. 1961).

8 ♖e1

After 8 ♕e2 f5 9 ♘bd2 ♘xd2 10 ♘xd2 ♗e7 (10 ... e4 11 f3 d5 12 fe fe 13 ♘xe4!) 11 de 0–0 (11 ... de 12 ♘c4!) 12 ♕c4+ ♔h8 13 ♕xc6 ♖b8 with roughly equal chances.

8	**...**	**f5**
9	**de**	**d5**
10	**♘d4**	

In the early 1940s Boleslavsky's move 10 ♘c3!? was fashionable. But after 10 ... ♗b4! 11 ♘d4 ♘xc3 12 bc ♗xc3 13 ♗a3 ♕h4 14 ♘xc6 ♗e6! Black has full equality (Botvinnik).

10 ... ♗c5 *(148)*

Bad is 10 ... c5? 11 ♘e2 c6 12 ♘f4 g6 13 c4! b4 14 ♕a4 ♗b7 15 f3 ♘g5 16 h4 ♘f7 17 e6! (Keres–Reshevsky, AVRO 1938), or 10 ... ♕h4? 11 g3 ♕h3 12 ♘c3 ♗c5 13 ♘ce2! and White's threats of 14 f3 or 14 ♘f4 are very unpleasant.

148
W

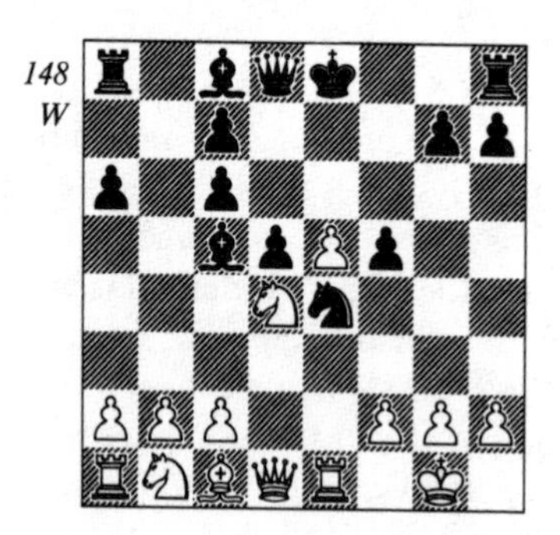

After 10 ... ♗c5 the following variations are possible:

(a) **11 c3** 0–0 12 f3 ♘g5 13 ♔h1 ♗xd4 14 ♗xg5 ♕xg5 15 cd ♖b8 16 b3 ♕h4 17 ♘c3 with positional advantage to White (Smyslov–Levenfish, USSR 1938).

(b) **11 f3!?** ♕h4 12 c3 ♘f2 13 g3

♕h5 14 ♔xf2! ♕xh2+ 15 ♔e3 and White has an advantage in material (Hort and Pribyl).

(c) **11 ♗e3?!** f4! 12 ♘xc6 fe 13 ♘xd8 ef+ 14 ♔f1 fe♕+ 15 ♔xe1 ♗f2+ 16 ♔f1 ♖f8 17 ♕xd5 ♗c5+ 18 ♔e1 ♗f2+ and Black has an excellent game (Euwe).

A2

6 ♖e1 b5

In White's favour is 6 … ♗g4?! 7 c3 ♘d7 8 h3! ♗h5 9 d4! White also has better chances after 6 … ♗d7 7 c4! ♗e7 8 ♘c3 0–0 9 ♗xc6 bc 10 d4 ed 11 ♕xd4 ♘g4 12 ♗f4 f6 13 c5! (Mestel–Bellin, British Ch. 1988).

7 ♗b3 ♘a5
8 d4 ♘xb3

8 … ed? 9 e5! de 10 ♘xe5 ♗e6 11 ♘xf7!

9 ab ♗b7 *(149)*

Passive is 9 … ♘d7?! 10 ♗d2 (also possible is 10 de ♘xe5 11 ♘d4) 10 … ♗b7 11 ♗a5 ♗e7 12 ♘c3 and Black has difficulties (Euwe).

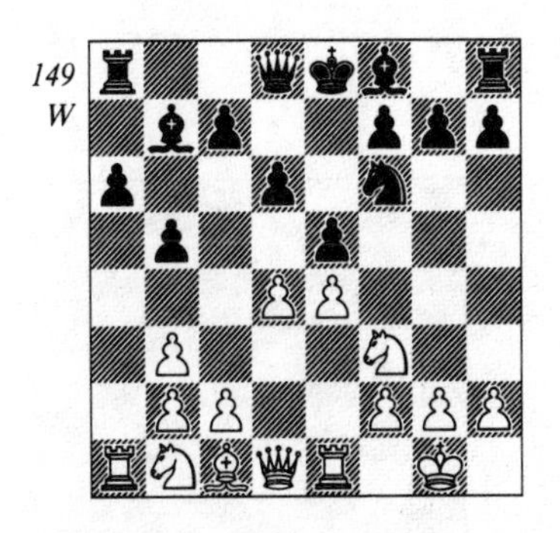
149
W

In this critical position the following variation may arise: 10 ♗g5 h6 11 ♗h4 (also not bad is 11 ♗xf6 ♕xf6 12 ♘c3 c6 13 ♕d3 ♕e7 14 de de 15 ♖ad1 f6 16 ♘h4) 11 … ♗e7 (sharp play ensues after 11 … g5 12 ♗g3 ♘xe4 13 ♘xe5!? de 14 ♗xe5 f6 15 ♕h5+ ♔d7 16 ♕g4+ ♔e8 17 ♗g3 ♔f7 18 ♖xe4 ♗xe4 19 ♕xe4 ♗d6) 12 ♘c3 b4 (12 … ♘d7) 13 ♗xf6 ♗xf6 14 ♘d5 a5 15 ♘xf6+ ♕xf6 16 de de 17 ♕d3 with a small advantage to White (Unzicker–Lehmann, West Germany 1953).

B

5 … ♗c5

The Møller system was rather popular in the 1930s and had a place in Alekhine's opening repertoire. Practice has shown, however, that Black has serious problems in this line, where play is governed by concrete calculation.

6 c3

The alternative is 6 ♘xe5 ♘xe5 (6 … ♘xe4? 7 ♘xc6 dc 8 ♕e2 ♕e7 9 ♖e1 ♘f6 10 d4 ♕xe2 11 ♖xe2+ ♗e7 12 ♗b3 favours White — Hort) 7 d4 ♘xe4 8 ♖e1 ♗e7 9 ♖xe4 ♘g6 10 c4 0–0 11 ♘c3 f5 12 ♖e2 f4 13 f3 with a minimal advantage to White (Kashdan–Milner-Barry, London 1932).

6 … ♗a7

The following lines favour White: 6 … b5 7 ♗c2 ♗a7 8 d4 ♕e7 9 a4; or 6 … 0–0 7 d4 ed 8 cd ♗b6 9 ♘c3; or 6 … ♘xe4 7 ♕e2!

7 d4 ♘xe4

7 … b5 8 ♗c2 or 8 ♗b3 ♕e7

9 ♗d5! is unattractive for Black (Suetin).

8 ♖e1

After 8 ♕e2 f5 9 ♘bd2 0–0 (possible is 9 … ♘xd2 10 ♘xe5 0–0 11 ♗xd2) 10 ♘xe4 fe 11 ♕xe4 d5 12 ♗b5 ♗e6 13 ♕e3 ♖f5 14 g4!? ♖xf3 15 ♕xf3 ed 16 ♖e1 ♗f7 with unclear play (Hort and Pribyl).

8 … f5

9 ♘bd2! *(150)*

The sharp variation 9 ♖xe4 fe 10 ♗g5 ♘e7 11 ♘xe5 0–0 12 ♘d2 d5 13 ♘xe4 ♗e6 14 ♘g3 probably favours Black — 14 … ♕d6 is better than 14 … h6 15 ♗xe7 (Sergeant–Milner-Barry, Margate 1935).

150
B

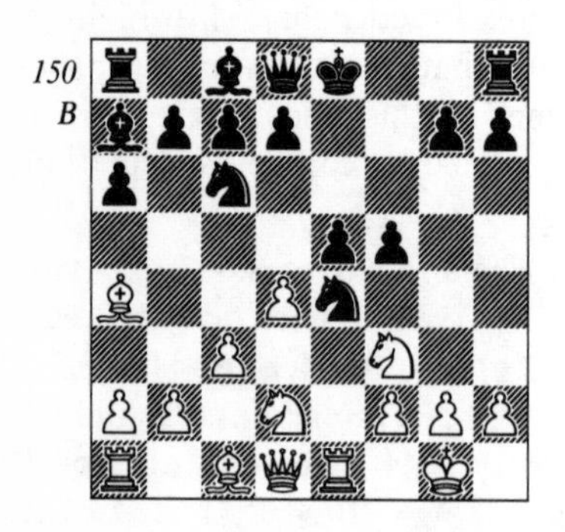

Now the following variations arise:

(a) **9 … 0–0** (9 … b5? 10 ♘xe4 fe 11 ♗g5 ♘e7 12 ♖xe4 d6 13 ♘xe5! is bad for Black) 10 ♘xe4 fe 11 ♗g5 ♕e8 12 ♖xe4 d6 13 de (also good is 13 ♗e3! ♗f5 14 ♖h4 ♕g6 15 ♗b3+ ♔h8 16 ♘g5 etc.) 13 … ♗f5 (13 … ♕g6 14 ♖f4 ♖xf4 15 ♗xf4 ♗g4 16 ♕b3+ and White has a clear advantage) 14 ♕d5+! (also good is 14 ♖f4!? or 14 ♖e1) 14 … ♗e6 15 ♕d2 ♕h5 16 ed ♗g4 17 ♗xc6 bc 18 d7 ♗xf3 19 gf ♕xf3 20 ♖f4 ♖xf4 21 ♕xf4 ♕xf4 22 ♗xf4 ♖d8 23 ♖d1 with a decisive advantage to White (Radchenko).

(b) **9 … ♘xd2** 10 ♗xc6 ♘xf3+ (10 … e4 11 ♗e5) 11 ♗xf3 e4 12 ♗xe4! fe 13 ♖xe4! ♔f7 14 ♕f3+ ♔g8 15 ♗g5 ♕f8 16 ♖f4 ♕e8 17 ♕d5+ ♕e6 18 ♖e1 with better chances for White (Böök).

C

5 … b5

6 ♗b3

Besides 5 … ♗e7, nowadays 5 … b5 is a very common continuation. This frequently amounts to a different move-order and transposes to the main line: 5 … b5 6 ♗b3 ♗e7 7 ♖e1 d6 8 c3. Here we shall consider the independent variations:

C1 6 … ♗b7
C2 6 … d6

C1

6 … ♗b7 *(151)*

151
W

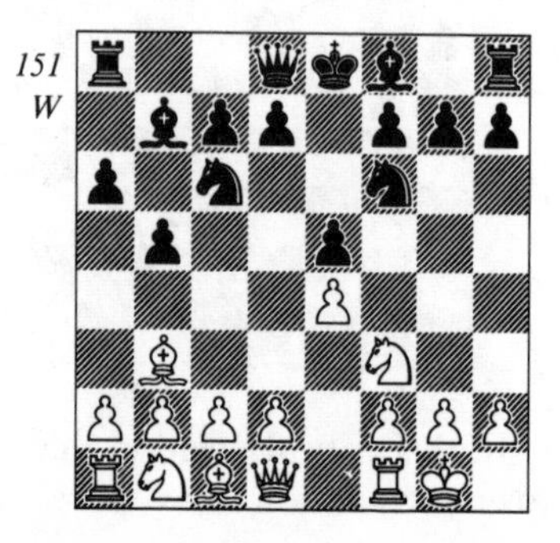

This interesting variation, elaborated a short while ago by a group of players from Archangel, has become very popular at the present time. It is actually a modern version of the Møller System. Black intends to play very actively, aiming primarily at a counter-attack. White has a large number of plans at his disposal — in some he aims to seize the centre, allowing counterplay, while in others he aims to limit Black's counterplay, contenting himself, as it were, with a small but lasting advantage.

We shall consider the following possibilities:

C11 7 Re1
C12 7 c3
C13 7 d3

First let us consider the following variations:

(a) **7 d4** Nxd4 8 Nxd4 (after 8 Bxf7+ Kxf7 9 Nxe5+ Kg8 10 Qxd4 c5 11 Qd1 Qe7 12 Nf3 Qxe4 13 Bg5 Qf5 Black has full equality; Vitolins–Kozlov, Riga 1982) 8 ... ed 9 e5 (after 9 c3 Nxe4 — also good is 9 ... d6 10 cd Be7 — 10 Re1 Be7 11 Qg4 0–0 12 Rxe4 Bxe4 13 Qxe4 Bf6 14 Bd2 Re8 15 Qf4 c5! 16 cd d5 17 Nc3 Bxd4 18 Rd1 Qf6 Black has a good game; Byrne–Smejkal, Leningrad 1973) 9 ... Ne4 10 c3 (10 Qf3 Qe7 11 Nd2 — 11 c3 0–0–0!? — 11 ... Nc5 12 Bd5 c6 13 Ne4! Nxe4 14 Bxe4 0–0–0 15 a4 b4 16 Bf4 g5 with chances for both sides; G. Garcia–Rodriguez, Havana 1983; worthy of consideration is 10 Qh5!? or 10 Re1 — Suetin) 10 ... dc?! (interesting is 10 ... Nc5!? 11 cd Nxb3 12 Qxb3 d6) 11 Qf3 d5 12 ed Qf6 13 d7+! Kxd7 14 Qg4+ Ke8 15 Nxc3! h5 16 Qe2 Qe5 17 Nxe4 Bxe4 18 f3 with a strong attack for White (van der Wiel–Martin, Biel 1985).

(b) **7 Nc3** Be7 8 d3 0–0 9 Bd2 d6 10 Nd5!? (after 10 a4 Na5 11 Ba2 b4 12 Ne2 d5 Black has full equality) 10 ... Nd7 11 a4 ba?! 12 Bxa4 Nc5 13 Bxc6 Bxc6 14 Be3 Nd7 15 c4 f5 16 ef Rxf5 17 d4 Bxd5 18 cd e4 19 Nd2 Nf6 20 Nxe4 Nxd5 21 Bd2 and White has the better chances (Geller–Dorfman, USSR Ch. 1976).

C11

7 Re1 Bc5

After 7 ... Be7 8 d4! Nxd4 9 Nxd4! ed 10 e5 Ne4 11 Qg4 c5 12 Qxg7 Rf8 13 Qxh7 c4 14 Rxe4 cb 15 ab Qb6 16 Bh6 0–0–0 17 Bxf8 Rxf8 18 Nd2 White has a marked advantage.

8 c3 d6 *(152)*

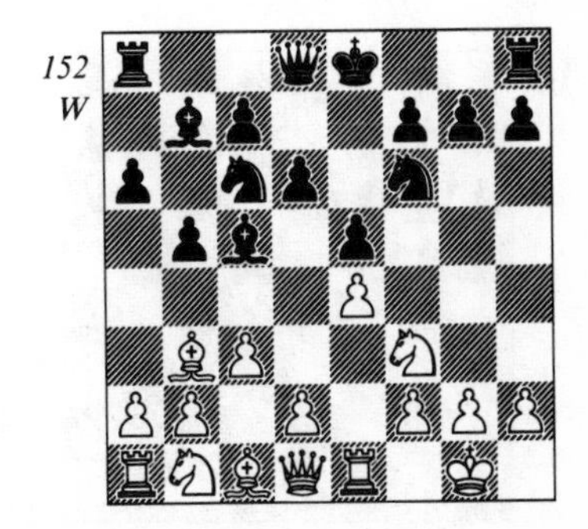

Not infrequently the continuation 8 ... 0–0 9 d4 ♗b6 10 ♗g5 h6 11 ♗h4 ♖e8 is seen, with the following variations:

(a) **12 ♕d3** (12 a4 d6 leads to the main variation) 12 ... d6 13 ♘bd2 ♘a5 14 ♗c2 c5 15 d5 c4! 16 ♕e2 ♔h7 17 b4 with somewhat better chances for White (Savon–Gipslis, Moscow 1970).

(b) **12 de** ♘xe5 13 ♘xe5 ♖xe5 14 ♘d2 with unclear play. The evaluation of this position depends on whether White will be able to advance his mobile pawn centre.

After 8 ... ♕e7 9 d4 ♗b6 10 a4 b4 11 ♗d5! ed 12 ♗g5 ♕d6 13 a5 ♗a7 14 e5 (Kupper–Müller, Freiburg 1971), and especially after 8 ... ♘g4? 9 d4 ed 10 h3! ♘xf2 11 ♔xf2 dc+ 12 ♔g3 ♗d6+ 13 e5 ♘xe5 14 ♘xe5 ♕e7 15 ♘xc3 0–0–0 16 ♘f5 ♗xe5+ 17 ♖xe5 ♕xe5 18 ♗f4 (Tringov–Radulov, Bulgaria 1966), Black has difficulties.

9 d4 ♗b6 *(153)*

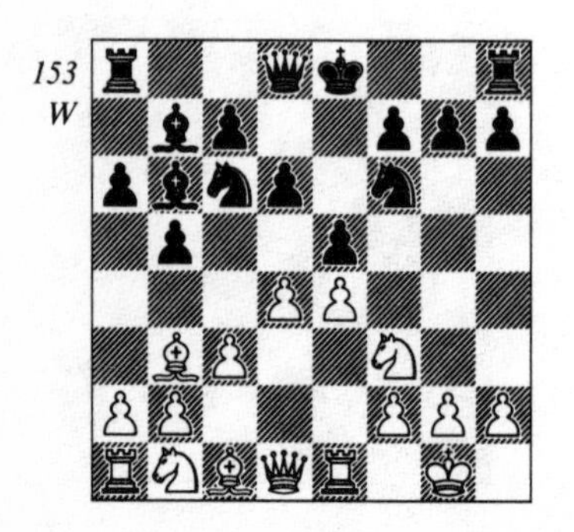

153
W

A critical position.

10 ♗g5

The following variations have also been played:

(a) **10 a3!?** (Suetin) 10 ... 0–0 11 ♗c2 ♘e7 12 ♘bd2 ♘g6 13 ♘f1 ed 14 cd ♖e8 15 ♘g3 c5 16 d5 c4 with good play for Black (Suetin–Smejkal, Sochi 1973).

(b) **10 ♗e3** 0–0 (also possible is 10 ... ed 11 cd ♘a5) 11 ♘bd2 h6 12 de de 13 ♗xb6 cb 14 ♕e2 ♕c7 15 ♘h4 ♘e7 16 ♖ad1 ♖ad8 17 ♘f5 ♖d7 18 ♘xe7+ ♖xe7 19 f3 ♕c5+ with equality (Spassky–Smejkal, Sochi 1973).

(c) **10 ♘h4!?** ♘e7 11 ♕f3 h6 12 ♘d2! ♕d7 13 ♘f1 ♕g4 14 ♕xg4 ♘xg4 15 f3 ♘f6 16 ♗e3 ed 17 ♗xd4 ♗xd4+ 18 cd g5 19 ♘f5 ♘xf5 20 ef+ with better chances for White (Kapengut–Kupreichik, Minsk 1973).

(d) **10 a4** h6 11 ♘a3 (11 ♘h4!? ♘e7 12 ♕d3 ♕d7 13 h3 0–0–0 14 ab ab 15 ♘a3; Arnason–Timman, Reykjavik 1987) 11 ... 0–0 (in White's favour is 11 ... ed 12 cd 0–0 13 ♗f4 ♘a5 14 ♗c2) 12 d5 ♘e7 13 ♘c2 c6 14 ab ab 15 ♖xa8 ♗xa8 16 ♘b4 cd 17 ♘d5 ♘exd5 18 ed ♗b7 with roughly equal play (Bozic–Petronic, Bela Crkva 1989).

(e) **10 ♕d3!?** h6 11 a4 0–0 12 ♘bd2 cd 13 ♘xd4 ♘xd4 14 cd ♖e8 15 ♗c2 ♖e6 16 e5?! ♘d5! with advantage to Black (Medina–Mikhalchishin, Barcelona 1984).

10 ... h6
11 ♗h4

Now Black has a choice:

C111 11 ... 0-0
C112 11 ... ♛d7

C111

11 ... 0-0 *(154)*

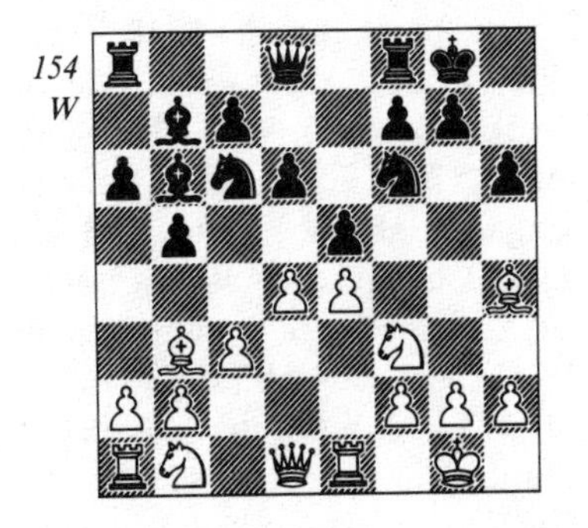

154 W

Less well-known is 11 ... ♛e7 12 a4 0-0-0!? For example: 13 ab ab 14 ♘a3 g5 15 ♗g3 ♘a7 16 ♗c2 h5 17 h4 gh 18 ♗xh4 (interesting is 18 ♘xh4 ♖dg8 19 ♘f5) 18 ... ♖dg8 19 ♛e2 ♛e6 20 g3 ♖g4! with roughly equal play; or 13 ♛d3 g5 14 ♗g3 ed 15 ab ab 16 ♛xb5 ♘a7 17 ♛f5+ ♚b8 18 e5!? ♘h5 with double-edged play (Sax–Harandi, Rio de Janeiro 1979).

12 a4

The move 12 ♛d3!? has become popular. For example: 12 ... g5! (or 12 ... ♛e7 13 ♘bd2 ♚h8 14 ♘f1 ♖g8!? with complicated play — Suetin) 13 ♘xg5!? (13 ♗g3 ♘e7 14 h4 ♘h5! 15 hg ♘xg3 16 fg c5! with unclear play) 13 ... hg 14 ♗xg5 ed 15 ♛g3 (*tr. note* 15 e5! ♘xe5 16 ♖xe5 Diaz–Valdes, Cuba 1988) 15 ... ♚g7 16 f4 ♖g8 17 e5 dc+ 18 ♚h1 de 19 fe ♘xe5! (also good is 19 ... ♘h5 20 ♛g4 ♘d4! 21 ♘xc3 ♚f8 22 ♗h6+ ♚e7 23 ♗g5+ ♚f8 with approximate equality — Perez–Valdes, Pinal del Rio 1988) 20 ♖xe5 ♛d4! 21 ♗e3 ♛g4 22 ♖g5+ ♚f8! and play turns out in Black's favour (Diaz–Valdes, Cuba 1987).

12 ... ♛e7

Let us consider the following variations:

(a) **12 ... ♖e8** 13 ab ab 14 ♖xa8 ♗xa8 15 ♛d3 (also good is 15 d5 ♘b8 16 ♗xf6! ♛xf6 17 ♘a3) 15 ... ed (15 ... b4!) 16 cd ♘a5 17 ♗xf6 ♛xf6 18 ♗c2 ♘c6 19 e5! de 20 ♘c3 ♖b8 21 ♛h7+ ♚f8 (Bednarski–Sznapik, Poland 1970). By playing 22 d5! ♘e7 23 ♛h8+ ♘g8 24 ♗h7 ♚e7 25 ♖xe5+ ♚d7 26 ♗f5+ White was able to obtain a clear advantage.

(b) **12 ... ed** 13 ab ab 14 ♖xa8 ♗xa8 15 cd ♖e8 16 ♘c3 g5 17 ♗g3 (interesting is 17 ♗xg5! hg 18 ♘xg5 ♖e7 19 ♛f3! — Suetin) 17 ... ♘a5 18 d5! b4 (Enklaar–Planinc, Amsterdam 1973). After 19 ♗a4 ♖e7 20 ♘a2 ♘xe4 21 ♘xb4 f5 22 ♘c6! White has a considerable advantage.

(c) **12 ... g5?!** 13 ♗g3 (13 ♘xg5 hg 14 ♗xg5 ed 15 ♛f3 ♚g7 16 ♛g3!? leads to unclear play) 13 ... ♖e8 14 ab ab 15 ♖xa8 ♗xa8 16 h4 g4 17 ♘h2 with difficulties for Black.

13 ab ab
14 ♖xa8 ♖xa8

After 15 ♘a3 ♘a5 16 ♗xf6

♕xf6 17 ♘xb5 ♘xb5 18 ♕xb3 White has somewhat better prospects.

C112

11 ... ♕d7

With castling long in mind, Black allows his pawn structure on the kingside to be weakened, in order, after the g-file is opened (12 ♗xf6 gf), to make use of it for a counter-attack.

12 a4 0–0–0

13 ab ab *(155)*

With the following variations:

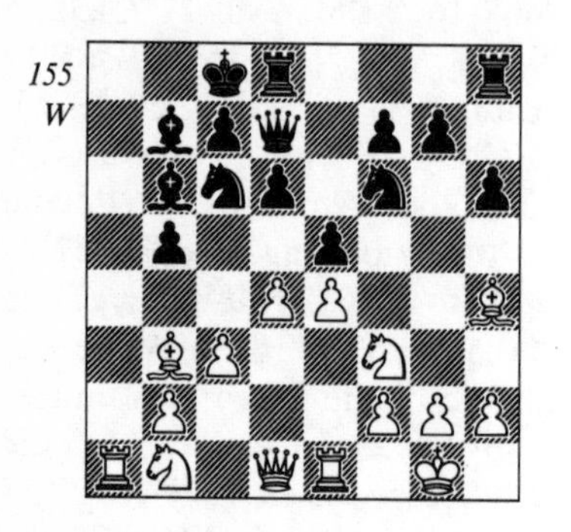

155
W

(a) **14 ♗xf6** gf 15 ♗d5!? (Suetin) 15 ... ♖hg8 (after 15 ... f5?! 16 ♕d3! ed 17 ♕xb5 fe 18 ♘xd4! ♘b8 19 ♗xb7+ ♔xb7 20 ♖e4 White has a clear advantage; Rogers–Flear, Szirak 1986) 16 ♔h1 ♘e7 17 ♗xb7+ ♔xb7 18 ♘bd2 ♘g6 19 ♘f1 ♘f4 20 ♘e3 f5 21 ef e4 22 ♘d2 ♕c6 23 ♕c2 ♘d3 24 ♖f1 d5 25 f3 h5 26 fe de 27 ♘b3 ♕h6 28 ♕e2 with a small advantage to White (Klovan–Malanyuk, USSR 1984).

(b) **14 ♘a3** g5 15 ♗g3 h5 (an unclear position is reached after 15 ... ed!? 16 ♘xb5 ♖de8 17 ♘bxd4 ♘xd4 18 ♘xd4 ♘xe4 19 ♗a4 c6 20 ♗c2 ♘xg3 21 fg ♖xe1+ 22 ♕xe1 with slightly better chances for White — Euwe) 16 h4 (16 de!? h4 17 ef hg 18 hg ♖h6 19 ♗d5! favours White) 16 ... gh 17 ♗xh4 ♖h6 18 ♘g5! (after 18 de ♘xe5 19 ♘xe5 de 20 ♕xd7+ ♖xd7, or 18 ♘c2 ♖g8 19 ♘g5 ♖hg6 20 ♗xf7 ♖xg5 21 ♗xg8 ♖xg8 22 ♗xf6 ♕h3 23 g3 ed; Chepurnoi–Katuryan, corr. 1984, chances are roughly equal) 18 ... ♖g6 19 ♘xb5 d5 20 ed ed 21 ♕f3 and White has the better chances.

C12

7 c3

Nowadays this continuation is fashionable. The variations that arise make for a sharp struggle requiring accurate calculation.

7 ... ♘xe4

After 7 ... ♗e7 8 d4 d6 9 ♘bd2 White has transposed to an advantageous version of the Closed System. But worthy of consideration is 7 ... h6. For example: 8 d4 d6 9 ♕e2!? g6 (or 9 ... ♗e7 10 ♖d1 ♘d7 11 ♘bd2 0–0 12 ♘f1 ♖e8 13 ♘g3 ♗f8; Petrushin–Malanyuk, USSR 1984) 10 a4 ♗g7 11 de de 12 ab ab 13 ♖xa8 ♕xa8 14 ♘a3 0–0 15 ♘xb5! ♘a5 16 ♗c2 ♗xe4 17 ♘xc7 ♕c6! 18 ♗xe4 ♘xe4 19 ♘a6 ♕c4 (Popovic–Tal, Subotica 1987). In both cases Black has quite good counterplay.

8 d4 *(156)*

After 8 ♖e1 ♘c5 9 ♗d5 ♗e7 10 ♘xe5 ♘xe5 11 ♗xb7 ♘ed3! 12 ♗xa8 ♘xe1 13 ♕xe1 ♕xa8 14 ♕e2 0–0 Black has no problems.

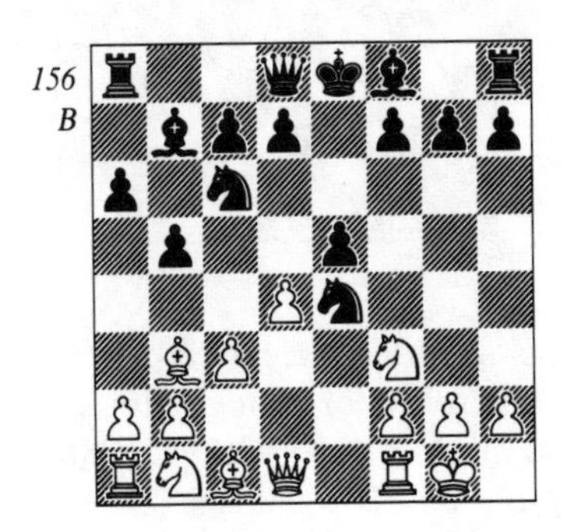
156
B

In this position Black has two main lines:

C121 8 ... ♗e7
C122 8 ... ♘a5

C121

8 ... ♗e7

Note that after 8 ... d5 9 ♖e1 ♗e7 10 de ♘a5 11 ♗c2 c5 12 ♘bd2 0–0 13 ♕e2, and especially after 8 ... ed? 9 ♖e1 d5 10 ♘g5!, White has clearly the better chances.

9 ♖e1 d5

After 10 de ♘a5 11 ♗c2 0–0 12 ♘bd2 ♘c4 13 ♘xc4 (13 ♕e2!) 13 ... bc 14 ♗e3 ♕c8 15 ♕e2 ♕e6 16 ♗xe4 de 17 ♘d2 ♕xe5 18 ♘xc4 ♕f5 19 b4 ♗f6 chances are equal (Suetin–Tseshkovsky, Sochi 1974).

C122

8 ... ♘a5
9 ♗c2

In the event of 9 ♘xe5 ♘xb3 10 ♕xb3 ♕f6 (after 10 ... ♘d6 11 ♗f4 — 11 c4 f6! 12 c5 fe 13 cd ♗xd6 14 de ♗c5 15 ♗e3 ♕e7 and the game is level — 11 ... ♗e7 12 ♘d2 White's position is preferable — Zaitsev) 11 f3 ♘c5 12 ♕d1 (12 ♘g4!?) 12 ... ♘e6 13 a4 ♗d6 14 ♕e2?! c5! Black gets a good game (Anand–Mikhalchishin, Moscow 1989).

9 ... ed *(157)*

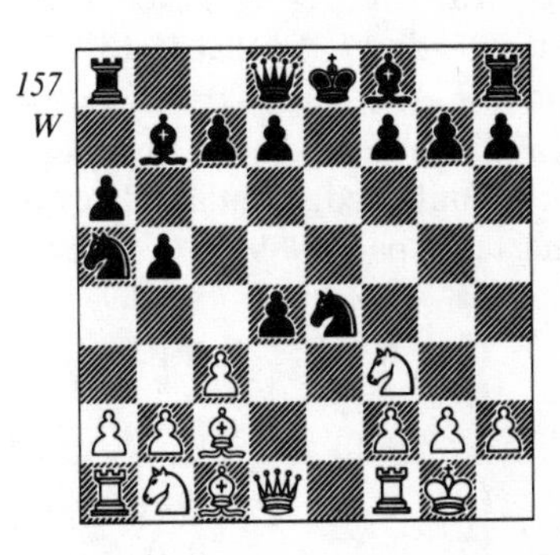
157
W

10 b4!?

White gets nothing after 10 cd d5 11 ♖e1 ♗e7. After 10 ♕e2 d5 11 ♘xd4 c5 12 ♘b3 ♘xb3 13 ab ♗e7 14 ♖e1 the game is approximately level (Mortensen–Rodriguez, Lucerne OL 1982). Interesting is 10 ♖e1 d5 11 ♘xd4 (11 ♘g5!?) 11 ... c5 12 ♘f5 g6 13 ♘g3 ♗e7 14 ♗h6 ♘c4 with somewhat better chances for White.

10 ... ♘c4
11 ♗xe4 ♗xe4
12 ♖e1 d5
13 ♘xd4

After 13 ♕xd4 ♗e7 14 ♕xg7 ♗f6 15 ♕h6 ♖g8 16 a4 ♔d7!?, or 16 ... ♕e7 17 ♘bd2 ♘xd2

18 ♗xd2 0–0–0, Black has quite good counterplay.

13 … ♗d6

Let us consider the following variations:

(a) **13 … ♔d7** 14 ♕g4+ f5 15 ♘xf5 ♗xf5 16 ♕xf5+ ♔c6 17 ♘d2 ♘xd2 18 ♗xd2 ♕d7 19 ♖e6 ♗d6 20 ♖ae1 ♖ae8! with roughly equal play (Edistratov–Kulikov, USSR 1986).

(b) **13 … c5** 14 bc ♗xc5 15 f3 0–0 16 fe de 17 ♖xe4 ♕d5 18 ♖h4 ♖fe8 19 ♘d2 ♖ad8 20 ♘2b3 ♗b6 21 ♕d3 h6 22 ♕g3 ♔f8 23 ♖g4 g5 with double-edged play (Hazai–Raaste, Espoo 1989).

14 f3 ♕h4
15 h3 ♕g3
16 ♘f5

16 fe? ♕h2+ 17 ♔f1 ♗g3!

16 … ♕h2+
17 ♔f2 0–0–0
18 fe de
19 ♕g4

After 19 ♘xd6 ♖xd6 20 ♕g4 ♔b8 21 ♗f4 ♖f6 chances are roughly equal.

19 … ♘e5

Or 19 … ♔b8 20 ♕xe4 ♖he8 21 ♕xe8 ♖xe8 22 ♖xe8+ ♔b7 23 ♘xd6 ♘xd6 24 ♖e1 ♘f5 25 ♘d2 ♕g3+ 26 ♔f1 ♘h4 with roughly equal chances (Kindermann–Mainka, Dortmund 1988).

20 ♕xe4 ♖he8 *(158)*

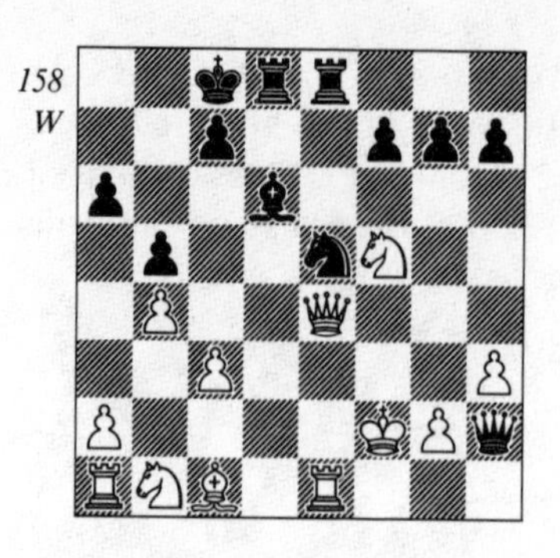

And now:

(a) **21 ♘d2** ♕f4 22 ♘xd6 ♖xd6 23 ♖xe4 with better chances for White.

(b) **21 ♘xd6?!** ♖xd6 22 ♗f4 ♘g4+! 23 hg ♖xe4 with plenty of counterplay for Black (Moiseev–Yakovich, USSR 1986). Also interesting is 21 ♗g5! g6 22 ♘d2 (Abramovic–Flear, Brussels 1986).

C13

7 d3

This is also a fashionable continuation and one which limits Black's chances of a counterattack.

7 … ♗e7

Other continuations briefly:

(a) **7 … ♗c5** 8 ♘c3 (also good is 8 ♗e3) 8 … d6 9 a4 b4 10 ♘d5 ♘xd5 11 ♗xd5 0–0 12 c3 a5 13 d4 ed 14 ♘xd4 ♕d7 15 ♗e3 ♗xd4 16 cd with somewhat better play for White (Plachetka–Grabczewski, Kecskemét 1975).

(b) **7 … h6!?** 8 c3 g6 9 a4 ♗g7 10 ab (10 ♘a3!?) 10 … ab 11 ♖xa8 ♗xa8 12 ♘a3 ♕b8 13 ♘h4! with some pressure for White (Lau–Flear, 1980).

After 7 … ♗e7 White has a choice of:

C131 8 c4!?
C132 8 a4

C131

8 c4!?

A recommendation of Matanovic's. In the game Vasyukov–Rantanen, Belgrade 1988, there occurred: 8 ♖e1 0–0 9 ♘bd2 ♖e8 10 ♘f1 ♗f8 11 c3 ♘a5 12 ♗c2 d5 13 ♕e2 c5 14 ♘g3 d4 15 cd cd (15 ... ed!?) 16 ♗d2 ♖c8 17 ♖ec1! with better chances for White.

8 ... bc

After 8 ... b5 9 ♗a4! d6 10 d4 0–0 11 d5 White stands better.

9 ♗xc4 0–0

10 ♘c3 d6 *(159)*

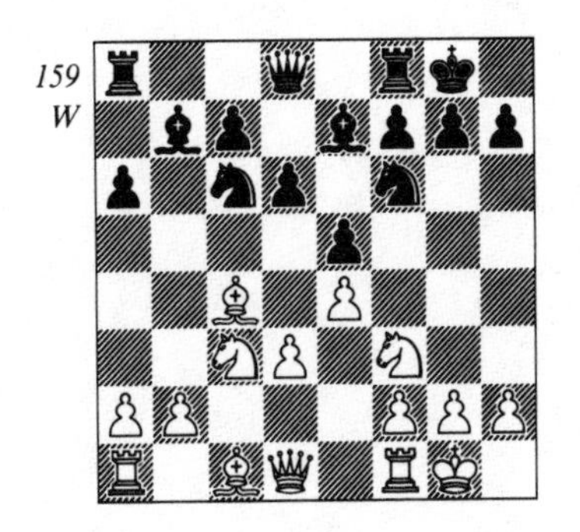

159
W

And now:

(a) **11 ♕a4!?** ♘d7 12 ♘d5 ♘c5 11 ♕a3 ♘e6 14 ♗e3 ♔h8 15 ♖ac1 ♘cd4?! (correct is 15 ... f5! 16 ♘xe7 ♕xe7 17 ♗d5 ♘cd8 18 ♗xb7 ♘xb7 with equal play) 16 ♘xd4 ♘xd4 17 ♗xd4 ed 18 ♘xe7+ ♕xe7 19 b4! with a small advantage to White (Mestel–Flear, British Ch. 1986).

(b) **11 a3** ♘d4 (also possible is 11 ... ♘a5 12 ♗a2 c5 13 ♗g5 ♘c6 14 ♗xf6 ♗xf6 15 ♗d5 ♖b8; Romanishin–Karpov, Brussels 1986) 12 ♘xd4 ed 13 ♘d5 ♘xd5 14 ed ♕d7 15 ♕f3 ♗f6 and chances are equal (Oll–Malanyuk, USSR 1984).

C132

8 a4 d6

8 ... 0–0 9 ♘c3 b4 10 ♘d5 ♘a5 11 ♘xe7+ ♕xe7 12 ♗a2 d5 13 ed ♗xd5 14 ♖e1 ♗xa2 15 ♖xe5 ♗e6 16 ♖xa5 c5 17 d4 cd 18 ♗g5 ♖fd8 19 ♕d2 b3! with equality (Oll–Khermlin, corr. 1985).

After 8 ... d6 the following variations are possible:

(a) **9 c3** 0–0 10 ♘bd2 ♘d7 11 ♖e1 ♘c5 with equal play.

(b) **9 ♘c3** ♘a5 10 ♗a2 b4 11 ♘d5 (or 11 ♘e2 ♖b8 12 ♘g3 0–0 13 c3 b3 14 ♗b1 c5 and Black is no worse; Kupreichik–Yakovich, USSR 1986) 11 ... ♘xd5 12 ed b3 13 ♕e1 ♗xd5 14 ♕xa5 ♗xf3 15 ♗xb3 ♗b7 16 f4 ef 17 ♕b4 with some pressure for White (Ehlvest–Yakovich, USSR 1986).

C2

6 ... d6

7 c3

Tempting, but dangerous, is 7 ♘g5?! d5! 8 ed ♘d4 9 ♖e1 ♗c5 10 ♖xe5+ ♔f8 11 c3 ♘g4 12 cd ♗xd4 13 ♘f3 ♗xe5 14 h3 h5 15 hg hg 16 ♘xe5 ♕h4 17 ♔f1 ♕f6 with advantage to Black (Keres). Black also gets excellent play after 7 a4 ♗b7 8 ♖e1 ♗e7 9 c3 ♘a5 10 ♗c2 c5 11 d4 cd 12 cd 0–0 13 ab ab 14 de de 15 ♘xe5 ♗d6 16 ♘g4 ♘xe4 17 ♘d2 ♖e8 (Kupreichik–Podgaets, USSR 1985).

7 ... ♗e7
8 d4 ♗g4
9 h3!?

After 9 ♗e3 0–0 10 h3 ♗h5 11 ♘bd2 Black must play 11 ... ♘d7 or 11 ... ♘a5, but not 11 ... d5?! 12 g4 ♗g6 13 ♘xe5 ♘xe5 14 de ♘xe4 15 f4! and Black's position is bad.

9 ... ♗xf3

After 9 ... ♗h5 10 d5 ♘a5 11 ♗c2 c6 12 dc there arises a variation which is good for White, with an awkwardly–placed black bishop on h5.

10 ♕xf3

10 g5 ♘a5 11 ♗c2 ♘h5 12 f4 (there threatened 12 ... ♗g5) 12 ... ♘xf4 13 ♗xf4 ef and Black has an excellent game.

10 ... ed

After 11 ♕g3! 0–0 (11 ... ♕d7!? 12 ♕xg7 0–0–0) 12 ♗h6 ♘e8 13 ♗d5 ♕d7 14 ♕g4! ♕xg4 15 hg gh 16 ♗xc6 dc 17 ♘xc3 ♖b8 18 ♘d5 White has more than adequate compensation for the pawn (Gligoric–Rossetto, Portoroz 1958).

11 Worrall Attack and Delayed Exchange Variations

In this chapter we look at some of the less common alternatives after the usual sequence 1 e4 e5 2 ♘f3 ♘c6 3 ♗b5 a6 4 ♗a4 ♘f6 5 0–0 ♗e7. These are:

A 6 ♕e2
B 6 ♗xc6
C 6 ♖e1

A

6 ♕e2

A plan which has long been known: White's queen defends the e4-square and the rook heads for the d-file. However, this is associated with a loss of time, which allows Black to obtain full equality. Nowadays it is hardly ever played.

6 … b5

Or 6 … d6 7 c3 (7 ♗xc6+ bc 8 d4) 7 … ♗d7 8 d4 0–0 9 ♗c2 ♖e8 with a solid position for Black.

7 ♗b3 *(160)*

Now, as in the main line with 6 ♖e1, Black has two alternatives:

A1 7 … 0–0
A2 7 … d6

160
B

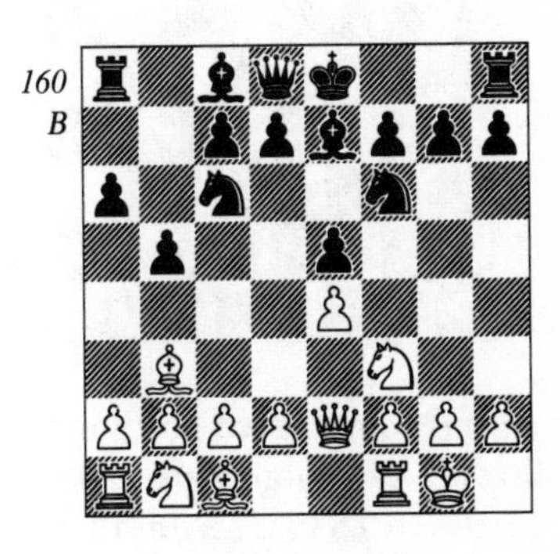

A1

7 … 0–0
8 c3

An alternative is 8 a4, with the following variations:

(a) **8 … b4!** 9 a5 d6 10 c3 ♖b8 11 ♗c4 d5! with good counterplay for Black (Tringov–Smyslov, Amsterdam 1964).

(b) **8 … d5!?** 9 d3 (9 ab de!) 9 … ♗g4 10 c3 d4 11 h3 ♗xf3 12 ♕xf3 dc 13 ♘xc3 b4 with equality (Keres–Unzicker, Moscow 1956).

(c) **8 … ♗b7** 9 c3 d5 10 d3 ♖e8 11 ♖e1 ♘a5 12 ♗c2 b4! with counterplay for Black (Filipovich–Geller, Warsaw 1969).

8	**...**	**d5!?**
9	**d3** *(161)*	

Interesting is 9 ed ♗g4! 10 dc e4 11 d4 ef 12 gf ♗h3 13 ♖e1 ♖e8 14 ♗g5 ♘d5! with excellent play for Black (Foltys–Keres, Salzburg 1943).

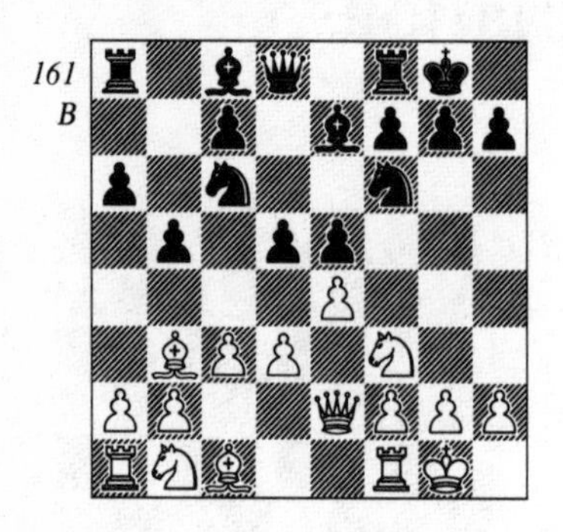

161
B

In this complicated position the following variations may arise:

(a) **9 ... ♖e8** (9 ... ♕d6) 10 ♖e1 (10 ed ♘xd5 11 ♘xe5 ♘xe5 12 ♕xe5 ♗b7 and Black has excellent play for the pawn) 10 ... ♗b7 11 ♘bd2 ♕d7 (11 ... ♗f8 12 ♘f1 ♘a5 13 ♗c2 c5) 12 ♘f1 ♖ad8 13 ♗g5 ♘a5 14 ♗c2 de 15 de ♘c4 16 ♘e3 ♘xe3 (16 ... ♘xb2? 17 ♘xe5 ♕e6 18 ♘xf7!; Keres–Geller, Budapest 1952) 17 ♕xe3 ♘g4 18 ♕e2 ♗xg5 19 ♗xg5 h6 with equality (Filip).

(b) **9 ... ♗b7!?** 10 ♖d1 ♖e8 11 ♘bd2 ♗f8 12 ♘f1 ♘a5 13 ♗c2 c5 with good play for Black (Hübner–Geller, Sousse 1970).

(c) **9 ... d4** 10 cd ♘xd4 (10 ... ♗g4? 11 de ♘d4 12 ♕e3 ♗xf3 13 ef! ♗xf6 14 gf ♗g5 15 ♕xd4 favours White) 11 ♘xd4 ♕xd4 12 ♗e3 ♕d6 13 ♘d2 ♖d8 14 ♖ac1 with somewhat better play for White.

Note that after 9 ... de 10 de ♗g4 11 h3 ♗h5 12 ♗g5 ♘e8 13 ♗xe7 ♗xf3 14 ♕xf3 ♕xe7 15 ♖d1 (Alekhine–Junge, Cracow 1942), or 9 ... ♗g4 10 h3 ♗xf3 11 ♕xf3 d4 (Keres–Brinkmann, Madrid 1943), White has the better chances.

A2

7	**...**	**d6**
8	**a4**	

An alternative is 8 c3, with the following variations:

(a) **8 ... ♘a5** 9 ♗c2 c5 10 d4 (or 10 a4 ♖b8 11 ab ab 12 d4 ♘c6) 10 ... ♕c7 11 ♖fd1 0–0 12 ♗g5 ♗g4 13 de de 14 ♘bd2 ♖fd8 15 ♘f1 ♘h5 with sufficient counterplay for Black (Alekhine–Keres, Salzburg 1942).

(b) 8 ... 0–0 9 d4 ed 10 cd ♗g4 11 ♖d1 d5 12 e5 ♘e4 13 ♘c3 ♘xc3 14 bc ♘a5 15 ♗c2 ♕d7 with good counterplay for Black (Réti–Stoltz, match 1929).

8	**...**	**♗g4**

Worthy of consideration is 8 ... ♗e6!? 9 ♗xe6 fe 10 ab ab 11 ♖xa8 ♕xa8 12 ♕xb5 ♘xe4 13 d4 0–0 14 d5 ♖xf3! 15 gf ♘d4 and Black has more than adequate compensation for the exchange (Averkin–Krivoruchkin, USSR 1968). In White's favour are both 8 ... b4 9 ♕c4!, and 8 ... ♖b8 9 ab ab 10 c3 ♗g4 11 h3! ♗h5 12 d3.

9	**c3**	**0–0**

On 9 ... b4 it is best to play 10 d3 0–0 11 ♘bd2 etc.

10 h3

After 10 ab ab 11 ♖xa8 ♕xa8 12 ♕xb5 ♘a7! 13 ♕e2 ♕xe4 14 ♕xe4 ♘xe4 15 d4 ♗xf3 16 gf ♘g5 Black has an excellent game (Fine–Keres, AVRO 1938).

10 ... ♘a5

Also not bad is 10 ... ♗xf3 11 ♕xf3 ♘a5 12 ♗c2 c5, or 10 ... ♗d7.

11 ♗c2

11 ♗xf7+!? ♖xf7 12 hg ♘b3! 13 ♖a3 ♘xc1 14 ♖xc1 ♘xg4 leads to double-edged play (Keres).

11 ... ♗e6
12 ab ab
13 d4 ♗c4
14 ♗d3 ♗xd3
15 ♕xd3 *(162)*

162
B

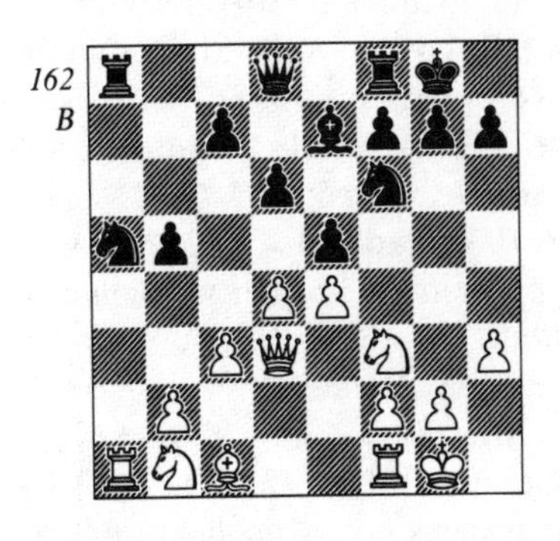

And now:

(a) **15 ... ♘b3** 16 ♖xa8 ♕xa8 17 ♗g5 ♕a4 18 ♘a3 ♖b8 (Vasyukov–Ravinsky, Moscow 1957).

(b) **15 ... ♘c4** 16 ♖xa8 ♕xa8 17 h3 ♕a2! 18 bc bc 19 ♕e3 ♕xb1 20 de ♘xe4 21 ♖e1 ♘c5 22 ♗a3 ♕b5 23 ♗xc5 ♕xc5 24 ♕xc5 dc 25 ♖d1 ♖d8 (Vukovic). In both cases chances are equal.

B

6 ♗xc6

In aiming for pressure against e5, White at the same time somewhat constrains Black's pawn mass on the queenside. Black has sufficient resources.

6 ... dc

After 6 ... bc 7 ♖e1 d6 8 d4 play transposes to Rubinstein's Defence.

White has three main methods of development to choose from:

B1 7 d3
B2 7 ♘c3
B3 7 ♕e1

B1

7 d3 ♘d7

After 7 ... ♗g4 8 h3 ♗xf3 (8 ... ♗h5? 9 g4 ♘xg4 10 hg ♗xg4 11 ♔g2, and then ♖h1, favours White) 9 ♕xf3 ♕d6 10 ♘d2 0–0–0 11 ♘c4 ♕e6 12 ♕g3 or 12 ♕e2, followed by f2–f4, White has the better chances.

8 ♘bd2 0–0

An alternative is 8 ... f6 or 8 ... c5 9 ♘c4 ♗d6.

9 ♘c4 f6

Also possible is 9 ... ♗f6 10 b3 ♖e8 11 ♗b2 c5.

10 ♘h4

A different plan is 10 b3 ♘c5 11 ♗b2 and then ♘c4–e3, but after 10 d4 ed 11 ♘xd4 ♘e5! Black gets excellent play.

10 ... ♘c5 *(163)*

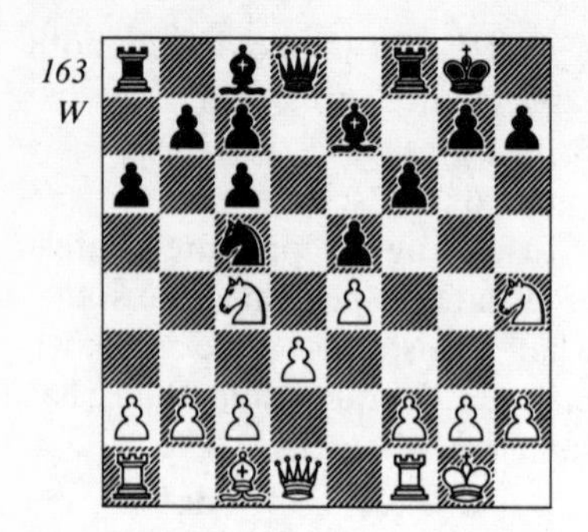
163
W

And now:

(a) **11 ♘f5** ♗xf5 12 ef ♕d7 13 ♕g4 b5 14 ♘e3 ♖fe8 15 b3 ♕d4! 16 ♗d2 ♕xg4 17 ♘xg4 ♘b7 and Black has a strong defensive position (Gheorghiu–Portisch, Moscow 1967).

(b) **11 f4** ef 12 ♖xf4, when Black may force a draw with the move 12 … g5.

(c) **11 ♗e3!** b6 12 ♕f3 g6 13 ♕g3 ♔h8 14 f4 ef 15 ♖xf4 ♖g8 16 ♖f2 ♗e6 17 b3 ♘d7 18 ♘f3 c5 19 ♖af1 b5 20 ♘cd2 ♗d6 21 ♗f4 with a minimal advantage to White (Malanyuk–Podgaets, USSR 1984).

B2

7 ♘c3

White intends to open up the centre by means of d2–d4. For example: 7 … ♘d7 8 d4 ed 9 ♕xd4 0–0 10 ♗f4 ♘c5 11 ♕e3 ♘e6 12 ♖ad1 ♕e8 13 ♗g3 ♗c5 14 ♕e1 f6 15 ♘h4 g6 16 ♔h1 with an initiative for White (Tal–Szabó, Leipzig OL 1960). Therefore Black must modify his plan.

7 … ♗g4

And now:

(a) **8 d3** ♘d7 9 ♕e2 ♗d6 10 h3 ♗xf3 11 ♕xf3 ♘c5 with equal chances (Nezhmetdinov–Bannik, USSR Ch. 1956).

(b) **8 h3** ♗h5 9 g4! (9 ♕e2 ♕c8! 10 d3 h6 11 ♘d1 ♘h7 with full equality for Black; Tal–Keres, Bled 1961) 9 … ♗g6 (9 … ♘xg4 10 hg ♗xg4 11 ♔g2 ♕d6 12 ♘e2 ♕g6 13 ♘xe5 ♕xe4+ 14 f3 ♕xe5 15 d4! favours White) 10 ♕e2 ♘d7 11 d4 f6 12 ♗e3 with somewhat better prospects for White.

B3

7 ♕e1 c5

Let us consider the following variations:

(a) **7 … ♘d7** 8 d4 ed 9 ♘xd4 ♘c5 (also possible is 9 … 0–0) 10 ♕e3 0–0 11 ♘c3 ♖e8 12 ♖d1 ♗d6 13 b4 ♘d7 14 ♘f5 ♘e5 15 ♘xd6 cd 16 ♕g3 (Short–Nunn, West Germany 1988). With 16 … ♕e7 Black is able to equalise.

(b) **7 … ♗e6** 8 b3 ♘d7 9 ♗b2 f6 10 d4 ♗d6 11 ♘bd2 ♕e7 with approximate equality (Schmid–Platz, Düsseldorf 1951).

8 ♘xe5

After 8 b3 ♗d6 9 ♗b2 ♕e7 10 ♘c3 0–0 11 h3 ♗e6 12 ♕e3 c4 Black has no particular problems (Nezhmetdinov–Krogius, Saratov 1953).

8 … ♕d4 *(164)*

And now:

(a) **9 ♘d3** c4 (also possible is 9 … ♕xe4 10 ♕xe4 ♘xe4 11 ♖e1 c4 12 ♘f4 ♘f6 13 b3 cb 14 ab ♔f8 with equal chances; Hecht–Szabó,

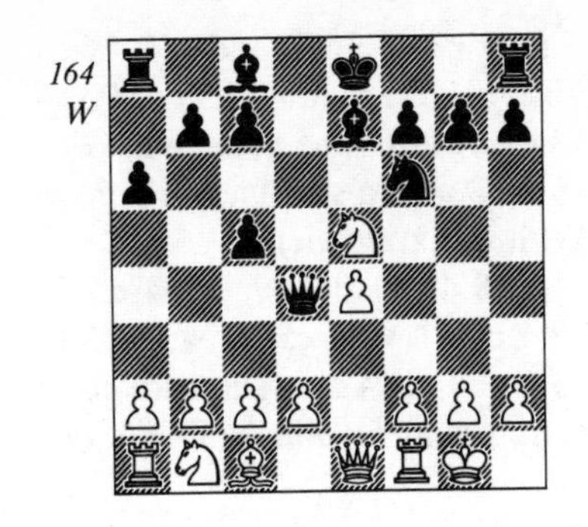
164
W

Kecskemét 1964) 10 ♘f4 g5! 11 ♘d5 ♘xd5 12 ed ♛xd5 and Black has at least equal chances.

(b) **9 ♘f3** ♛xe4 10 ♕xe4 ♘xe4 11 ♖e1 ♘d6 (11 ... ♘f6 12 b3! and then ♗a3 and d4!) 12 ♘c3 ♚d8 13 d4 c4 14 ♗f4 ♜e8 15 b3 cb 16 ab with a minimal advantage to White (Christiansen–Nunn, West Germany 1989).

C

6 ♖e1 b5

These moves are really an addition to the main line.

We shall, however, pause here to consider the move 6 ... d6. After 7 c3 ♗d7 8 d4 play has transposed to variations already considered above. We shall give some attention to the following continuations, which may be considered to be independent:

(a) **7 ♗xc6+** (7 d4 b5!) 7 ... bc 8 d4 ed or 8 ... ♘d7, also transposing to a known line.

(b) **7 c3** ♗g4!? (after 7 ... 0–0 8 d4 ed 9 cd d5 10 e5 ♘e4 11 ♘c3 ♘xc3 12 bc ♗f5 13 ♗xc6 bc 14 ♕a4; Fischer–Jimenez, Palma de Mallorca 1970; or 7 ... ♘d7 8 d4 0–0 9 ♗e3 ♗f6 10 ♘bd2 ♘e7 11 ♗b3 ♘g6 12 ♕e2 ♖e8 13 ♖ad1, Bronstein–Averbakh, Moscow 1961, Black is a long way from equality) 8 d3 (or 8 h3 ♗h5 9 ♗xc6 — 9 d3 ♛d7 10 ♘bd2 g5! — 9 ... bc 10 d4 ed 11 cd 0–0 12 ♘bd2 ♖e8 13 ♕c2 with better chances for White; Shamkovich–Spassky, Baku 1961) 8 ... 0–0 (interesting is 8 ... ♛d7!? 9 ♘bd2 g5 10 ♘f1 ♜g8, or 8 ... ♘d7 9 h3 ♗xf3 10 ♕xf3 ♘c5 11 ♗xc6+ bc 12 d4 ♘d7 13 ♘a3 ♗f6 14 ♘c4; Ljubojevic–Spassky, Bugojno 1986; in the first case play is unclear, while in the second White is somewhat better), and now:

(b1) **9 ♘bd2** ♜e8 10 ♘f1 (10 h3 ♗d7!? 11 ♘f1 — 11 d4 — 11 ... ♗f8 12 ♘g3 g6 13 d4 ♗g7 14 ♗c2 ♛e7 15 ♗e3 ♜ad8 16 d5 ♘b8 17 c4 with pressure for White; Psakhis–Romanishin, Dortmund 1981) 10 ... ♗f8 11 ♘g3 ♗d7 12 h3 g6 13 ♘h2 ♗g7 14 f4 d5 15 f5 ♘e7 16 ♗xd7 ♛xd7 17 ♕f3 gf 18 ef e4 19 de de 20 ♕f2 with a small advantage to White (Ehlvest–Spassky, Reykjavik 1988).

(b2) **9 h3** ♗d7 10 ♘bd2 ♜e8 11 ♘f1 ♗f8 12 ♘g3 g6 13 a3 h6 14 d4 ♗g7 with complicated play, closely echoing that in the previous variation. Let us continue our main variations.

7 ♗b3 ♗b7?! *(165)*

The main lines involve the moves 7 ... 0–0 and 7 ... d6, but these will be considered in later chapters. For the time being we give the variations associated with 7 ... ♗b7?!

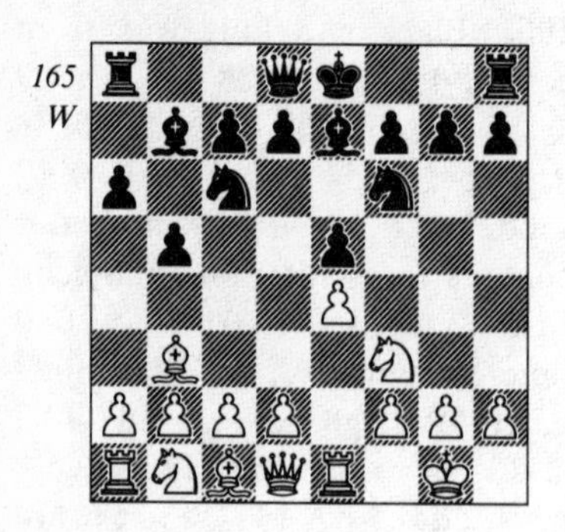
165
W

(a) **8 c3** d5 9 ed ♘xd5 10 ♘xe5 ♘xe5 11 ♖xe5 ♘f4 12 d4 ♘xg2 13 ♕e2 h6 14 ♕h5 g6 15 ♕h3 ♕c8 16 ♕g3 with a small advantage to White (Matanovic).

(b) **8 d4** ♘xd4!? 9 ♘xd4 ed 10 e5 ♘e4 11 ♕g4 c5 12 ♕xg7 ♖f8 13 ♕xh7 c4 14 ♖xe4 cb with good counterplay for Black (Trajkovic).

12 Marshall Attack and Anti-Marshall System

After the sequence 1 e4 e5 2 ♘f3 ♘c6 3 ♗b5 a6 4 ♗a4 ♘f6 5 0–0 ♗e7 6 ♖e1 b5 7 ♗b3 0–0 White is faced with a choice — to allow the Marshall Attack, involving the sacrifice of a pawn, or to take prophylactic measures to limit the tactical complications in the opening.

The main continuations are:

A 8 c3
B 8 a4

The sequence 8 d4 d6 9 c3 is discussed in the following chapter.

A

8 c3 d5!?

This bold positional pawn sacrifice, introduced into practice by Grandmaster Marshall in 1918, is one of the most fascinating chapters in the theory of the Spanish Opening.

Note that the more restrained 8 ... d6 leads to the complex of Closed Systems considered in the following chapters.

9 ed

This is a case where White is obliged to accept the challenge of an intense struggle. All the same, we shall give some consideration to the move 9 d4!?, which was rather popular in the 1950s and which is sometimes encountered today. After 9 d4 the following variations may arise:

(a) **9 ... ed** 10 e5 ♘e4 11 ♘xd4 (after 11 cd ♗g4 — also good is 11 ... ♘a5 12 ♗c2 f5! — 12 ♘c3 ♗xf3 13 gf ♘xc3 14 bc f5 or 14 ... ♕d7 Black has the better chances) 11 ... ♘xe5 13 f3 c5 13 fe (after 13 ♘c6 ♘xc6 14 ♗xd5 ♘xc3 15 ♘xc3 ♗b7, or 13 ♗f4!? ♗f6 14 ♗xe5 ♗xe5 15 ♘c6 ♗xh2+!? 16 ♔xh2 ♕h4+; Kruppa–Vladimirov, Frunze 1988, Black still has the better chances) 13 ... cd 14 cd (14 ♗xd5 dc!) 14 ... ♗g4 15 ♕d2 ♘c4 with excellent play for Black.

(b) **9 ... de** 10 ♘xe5 ♗b7 11 ♘xc6 (worse is 11 ♗g5 ♘xe5 12 de ♘xe5! 13 de ♘d7 with better chances for Black; Geller–Kavtorin, Odessa 1951; after 11 ♘d2 Black must evidently play 11 ...

♘a5; in the event of 11 ... ♗d6 — 11 ... ♘xe5 12 de ♘d7 13 ♘xe4 ♘xe5 14 ♕h5! favours White — 12 f4 ef 13 ♘dxf3 ♘xe5 14 de ♗c5+ 15 ♘d4 White's chances are slightly better) 11 ... ♗xc6 12 ♗g5 ♘d5 with approximate equality.

(c) **9 ... ♘xe4** 10 de ♗e6 leads to the Open Defence.

A passive continuation is 9 d3 de 10 de ♕xd1 11 ♗xd1 ♘d7 with equality.

After 9 ed Black has a choice of two lines:

A1 9 ... ♘xd5
A2 9 ... e4

A1

9 ... ♘xd5 *(166)*

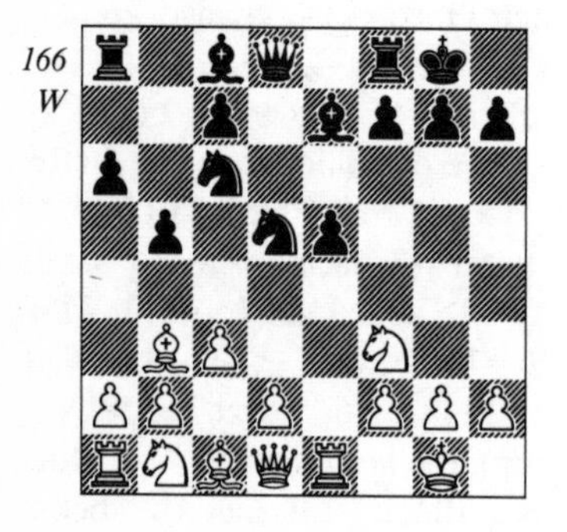

10 ♘xe5

Let us also consider the following variations:

(a) **10 a4** (10 d4 ed 11 cd ♘b6! is good for Black) 10 ... ♗b7 11 ab ab 12 ♖xa8 ♗xa8 13 ♘a3 ♘a5 14 ♗a2 e4 14 ♘e5 ♗xa3 (also good is 15 ... ♗d6) 16 ba ♕h4 with somewhat better chances for Black.

(b) **10 d3** ♗b7! (also not bad is 10 ... ♗g4 or 10 ... ♗f6) 11 ♘xe5 ♘xe5 12 ♖xe5 ♕d7 with compensation for the pawn.

10 ... ♘xe5
11 ♖xe5 *(167)*

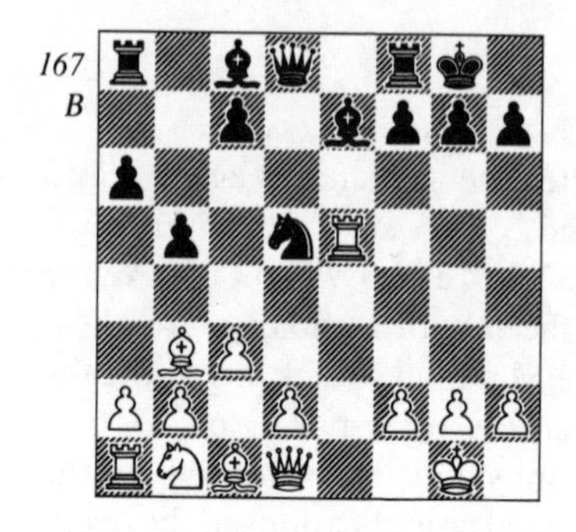

The basic position of this gambit system. For a long time the principal move was considered to be 11 ... ♘f6. There was a new wave of interest in the Marshall Attack when the variation with 11 ... c6 was established (in 1938), and this is now considered to be the main line.

The modern treatment of this variation is characterised by a variety of ways of seeking counterplay for Black. At the present time, together with the main plan — an attack on the kingside — endgame situations are also taken into account. The overall evaluation is that the Marshall Attack is viable and it is constantly being enriched with new ideas.

After 11 ♖xe5 Black has a choice:

A11 11 … c6
A12 11 … ♘f6

Before going on to analyse these lines, we shall consider the following variations:

(a) **11 … ♗b7**, and then:

(a1) **12 d4** ♕d7 13 ♘d2 (13 ♗xd5 ♗xd5 14 ♗f4 ♗b7 15 ♖e1 c6 16 dc ♕c6 17 ♕g4 ♗xc5 18 ♘d2 ♖ae8 with double-edged play; Dvoiris–Ermolinsky, USSR 1984) 13 … ♘f4 14 ♘e4 (14 ♘f3) 14 … ♘xg2 15 ♔xg2 ♗f6 16 f3 ♗xe5 17 de ♕f5 18 ♗e3 ♖ad8 19 ♕c2 ♕xe5 20 ♖e1 ♔h8 21 ♗d4 ♕f5 22 ♕f2 ♕g6+ 23 ♕g3! with better chances for White (Gufeld–Sarfati, Australia 1986).

(a2) **12 ♕f3!?** ♗d6 13 ♗xd5 c6 14 ♖e2 (or 14 ♖e1 cd 15 d4 ♕c7 16 g3 ♖ae8 with equal chances; Sokolov–Ermolinsky, USSR 1984) 14 … cd 15 d4 ♕c7 16 g3 ♖ae8 17 ♘d2 b4 18 cb ♕c2 19 ♖e3 ♗xb4 20 ♘f1 (Sokolov–Kharitonov, USSR 1984). After 20 … ♖e4 a complicated position arises, the consequences of which are unclear.

(b) **11 … ♘b6** 12 d4 ♗d6 13 ♗g5 (13 ♖e1; 13 ♖h5!?) 13 … ♕d7 14 ♖e1 ♗b7 15 ♘d2 ♖ae8 16 ♗h4 ♖xe1+ 17 ♕xe1 ♖e8 18 ♕d1 ♘d5 19 ♗g3 ♘f4 20 ♗xf4 ♗xf4 21 ♘f1 with a small advantage to White (Bertok–Stein, Stockholm 1962).

(c) **11 … ♘f4!?** 12 d4 ♘g6 13 ♖h5!? ♗b7 14 ♕g4! ♖e8 15 ♗e3 c5 16 ♘d2 ♗f6 17 ♘f3 with better play for White — Gutman).

A11

11 … c6

This continuation has been the main subject of investigation for more than fifty years. Black consolidates the position of his centralised knight and intends to combine threats on the kingside with play along positional lines. White has a wide choice:

A111 12 d4
A112 12 d3
A113 12 g3
A114 12 ♕f1
A115 12 ♗xd5

A111

12 d4 ♗d6

Here we have the next branch in the tree:

A1111 13 ♖e1
A1112 13 ♖e2

A1111

13 ♖e1

13 ♗g5?! ♕c7 14 ♖xd5 cd 15 ♗xd5 ♗xh2+ 16 ♔h1 ♖a7 17 g3 ♗xg3 18 fg ♕xg3 etc. favours Black.

13 … ♕h4
14 g3 ♕h3 *(168)*

Another critical position, where White has no shortage of choice.

15 ♗e3

This is the most common continuation. White aims to complete his development quickly. Besides

168
W

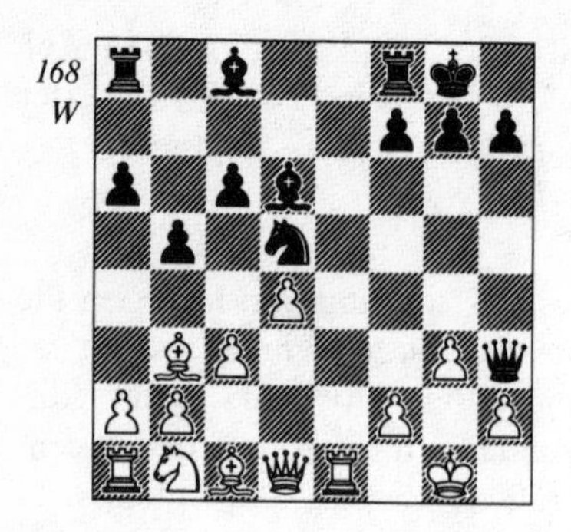

this move the following variations are possible:

(a) **15 ♖e4** g5! (15 ... ♗f5? 16 ♖h4!; 15 ... ♘f6 16 ♖h4 ♕f5 17 ♗f4!; 15 ... ♗d7 16 c4! bc 17 ♗xc4 ♖ae8 18 ♘d2 ♘f6 19 ♖h4! ♕f5 20 ♘f3 h6 21 ♗f4 ♗e7 22 ♘e5!; Sakharov–Peterson, Leningrad 1969; finally 15 ... ♕d7 16 ♘d2 ♘f6 17 ♖h4 ♗b7 18 ♘f3 c5 19 ♗f4! — Tal — in each case Black has difficulties) 16 ♕f3 (16 ♗xg5? ♕f5!; also in Black's favour is 16 ♘d2 f5 17 ♖e3 f4! 18 gf ♕h6 19 ♘e4 gf 20 ♖e1 ♗c7, or 16 ♕f1 ♕h5 17 f3 ♗f5! 18 ♗xd5 cd 19 ♖e1 ♖ae8 20 ♗e3 ♗h3 21 ♕f2 f5 etc.) 16 ... ♗f5 (16 ... f5? 17 ♖e5!) 17 ♗c2 (after 17 ♘d2 ♖ae8 18 ♗c2 ♘f6 19 ♖e5 ♗xc2, or 17 ♗xd5 cd 18 ♖e3 ♗e4! 19 ♖xe4 de 20 ♕f6 ♕g4!, Black's chances are clearly better) 17 ... ♗f4! (after 17 ... ♗xe4 18 ♗xe4 ♕e6 19 ♗xg5 f5 20 ♗d3 f4 21 ♕e4 ♕f7 22 ♘d2 ♖ae8 23 ♕f3 White's position is preferable) 18 ♗xf4 (or 18 ♘d2 ♘f6 19 ♖e1 ♗xc2 20 gf g4; Wang Zili–Ye Jiangchuan, China 1988) 18 ... gf (also good is 18 ... ♖ae8!?) 19 ♘d2 ♗xe4 20 ♗xe4 ♖ad8 and then ♖d6, and it is White who has the greater difficulties.

(b) **15 ♗xd5** cd 16 ♕f3. This continuation has not been studied very deeply. Playing the queen to f3 not only defends the king but also attacks the pawn on d5. But the complex of light squares in White's position is now in even greater need of defence.

16 ... ♗f5 17 ♕g2 (dangerous is 17 ♕xd5 ♖ae8 18 ♗d2 ♖e6 — not bad are 18 ... ♗g4, 18 ... ♗f4, or even 18 ... ♗d3!? — 19 ♘a3 ♗xa3 20 ba ♗c4 21 ♕f3; Chandler–P. Nikolic, Leningrad 1987) 17 ... ♕h5 18 f3! ♖ae8 19 ♗e3 ♖e6 20 ♘d2 ♖fe8 21 ♕f2 with complicated play and roughly equal chances (analysis by Keres, Nei and Suetin).

(c) **15 ♕d3** ♗f5 (15 ... f5? 16 ♕f3 ♖a7 17 ♗f4; 15 ... ♗g4 16 ♗e3 f5 17 f4!, and also 15 ... ♘f6?! 16 ♕f1 ♕f5 17 ♕g2! ♗b7 18 ♗d1! ♖ab8 19 ♗f3, all favour White — Boleslavsky) 16 ♕f1 ♕h5 (after 16 ... ♕g4 17 ♗e3 h5 18 ♘d2 h4 19 ♗d1 ♕g6 20 ♘f3 hg 21 fg ♗d3 22 ♕f2 ♖ae8 23 ♘h4 ♕h7 24 ♗f3 f5 25 ♗xd5+ cd 26 ♗f4 White has a marked advantage — Boleslavsky) 17 ♗e3 ♗h3 18 ♗d1 ♕f5 19 ♕e2 ♖ae8 20 ♘d2 c5 21 ♘f3 ♗f4! 22 ♘h4 ♕f6 23 ♕f3 cd 24 cd ♘xe3! 25 ♕xf4 ♕xf4 26 gf ♘d5 with equal chances (Bronstein).

15 ... ♗g4 *(169)*

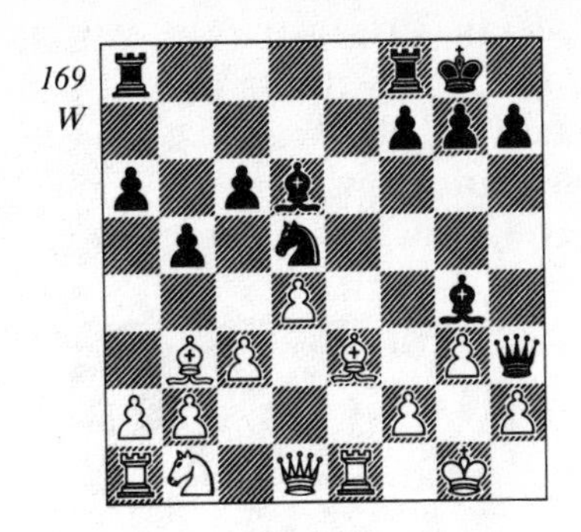
169
W

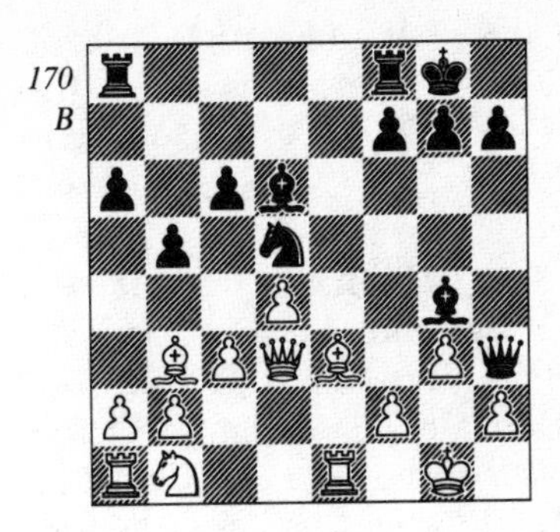
170
B

Black has to try to find the most active way to carry on the fight. We shall consider some other variations:

(a) **15 … ♖e8** 16 ♕f3 ♗g4 (16 … ♖a7 17 ♘d2 ♖ae7 18 ♗xd5 cd 19 ♘f1 h5 20 ♗d2 h4 21 ♖xe7 ♖xe7 22 ♘e3! favours White — Gutman) 17 ♕g2 ♕h5 18 ♘d2 ♗h3 19 ♗d1 ♕f5 20 ♕f3 ♕d3!? with complicated play where White has slightly better chances.

(b) **15 … ♗f5** 16 ♕f3 ♖ae8 17 ♘d2 ♗g4 18 ♕g2 ♕h5 19 a4! ♖e6 20 ab ab 21 ♗xd5 with advantage to White (Tal).

(c) **15 … h5?!** 16 ♕f3 h4 17 ♗xd5! cd 18 ♘d2 ♗e6 19 ♗f4 with advantage to White (Fischer–Wood, Havana 1965). Also in White's favour are: 15 … ♖a7 16 ♗xd5 cd 17 ♕f3 ♖e7 18 ♘d2 ♖fe8 19 a4; or 15 … ♘f6?! 16 ♕f3 ♗b7 17 ♗d2 ♔h8 18 ♗d1 ♖ae8 19 ♕g2 ♕f5 20 ♗f3 etc.

16 ♕d3 *(170)*

Black has a number of ways of getting counterplay in this position:

A11111 16 … ♖ae8
A11112 16 … f5
A11113 16 … ♘xe3

A11111

16 … ♖ae8

It is too early for Black to resort to tactical tricks: 16 … g5?! 17 ♗xg5! f5 18 ♘d2 f4 19 ♘e4! fg 20 fg ♖f3 21 ♕d2 ♖af8 22 ♗h4, or 16 … ♘f4? 17 ♕xf4 ♗xf4 18 ♕e4!

After 16 :.. ♖ae8 Black aims to double rooks on the e-file.

17 ♘d2 ♖e6

Comparatively rarely one sees 17 … f5. For example:

(a) **18 f4** ♔h8 19 ♗xd5 cd 20 ♕f1 ♕h5 21 a4 g5 (interesting is 21 … ba!? 22 ♖xa4 g5 23 ♖aa1 a5 24 fg f4 25 ♗f4 with equal chances; Ulmanis–van der Heijden, corr. 1986) 22 ab a5 23 f4 ♖e4!? 24 ♗f4! ♗xf4 25 gf h6 26 h3 ♗xh3 27 ♕f3 ♕h4 28 ♘xe4 fe 29 ♕f2 ♕g4+ 30 ♔h2 ♖f4 31 ♕g3 ♕f5 32 gh! with advantage to White (Varadi–Papai, corr. 1984).

(b) **18 ♕f1** ♕h5 19 f4 ♔h8 20

♗xd5 cd 21 a4 ba (or 21 ... g5 22 ab ab 23 fg ♖xe3 24 ♖xe3 f4 25 gf ♗xf4 26 ♖g3 ♕xg5 27 ♔h1 ♗d6 — 27 ... ♖g8 28 ♘f3 ♕f5 29 ♘e5! — 28 ♕g2 ♗xg3 29 ♕xg3 h5 30 ♖f1 ♖xf1 31 ♘xf1 ♕c1 32 ♔g1 with equality; Timman–Nunn, Brussels 1988) 22 ♕g2 (Dolmatov–E. Vladimirov, USSR 1989 went 22 ♖xa4 g5 23 ♖aa1 ♖e6!? 24 fg ♖fe8 25 gf h6 with sharp play) 22 ... ♖e4 23 ♘xe4!? fe 24 ♕f1! ♗f3! 25 ♕a6 ♕h3 26 ♖e2! ♗xe2 27 ♕xe2 g5 with double-edged play (Hindle–P. Littlewood, England 1987).

But let us return to the main line. White has a choice:

A111111 18 a4
A111112 18 c4

A111111

18 a4 *(171)*

Other variations:

(a) **18 ♗xd5** cd 19 a4 ba! 20 c4 (in Black's favour is 20 ♖xa4 f5 21 ♕f1 f4) 20 ... ♗b4! 21 cd ♗xd2 22 ♗xd2 ♖b6 with roughly equal play (Tal).

(b) **18 ♕f1** ♕h5 19 a4 (or 19 f4 ♔h8 20 ♗xd5 cd 21 a4 — 21 ♕g2 g5 22 ♕xd5 ♖d8 23 ♕c6 gf 24 ♗xf4 ♗xf4 25 gf ♗e2 26 ♔h1 ♖de8 27 ♖g1 ♕h4 with equal chances — Sokolov–Nunn, Rotterdam 1989 — 21 ... ba 22 ♖xa4 g5!?) 19 ... ♗h3 20 ♗d1 ♕f5 21 ♕e2 ♖fe8 (21 ... ♘f4 22 ♕f3 h5!) 22 ab ab 23 ♘f3 ♘xe3 24 fe ♖xe3 25 ♕xe3 ♖xe3 with sharp play (Suetin).

(c) **18 ♗d1** ♗xd1 19 ♖axd1 f5! 20 ♘f3! ♖g6 21 ♕f1 ♕h5 22 ♘e5 ♗xe5 23 de f4 ♗c1 ♖h6 with unclear consequences (Ljubojevic–Nunn, Amsterdam 1988).

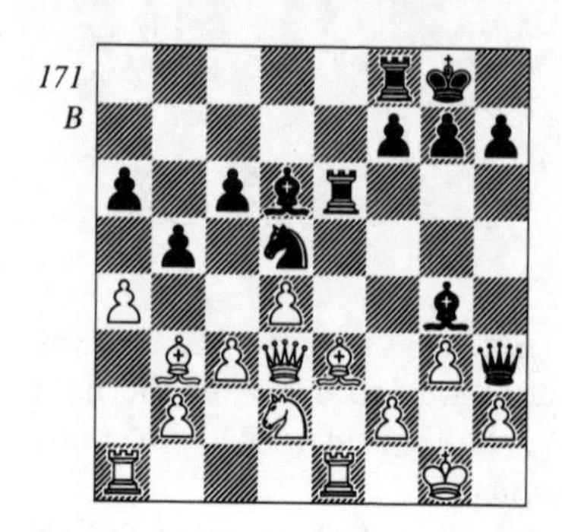
171
B

The tension is mounting sharply and the struggle is becoming one of strict calculation. Black has three main possibilities:

A1111111 18 ... f5
A1111112 18 ... ♕h5!?
A1111113 18 ... ba

A1111111

18 ... f5
19 ♕f1

Interesting is 19 f4!? ♖fe8 20 ab ♗xf4 (20 ... ab 21 ♗xd5 cd 22 ♕xb5) 21 ♗f2 (or 21 bc ♖xe3 22 ♗xd5+ ♔f8 23 ♖xe3 ♗xe3+ 24 ♔h1 ♗xd2 25 ♗g2 ♕h6 with unclear play) 21 ... ♗e2! (bad is 21 ... ♗xd2? 22 ♖xe6 ♖xe6 23 bc!) 22 ♖xe2 ♖xe2 23 bc ♖xf2 24 ♗xd5 ♔h8 25 ♔xf2 ♕xh2 26 ♗g2 ♗e3+ 27 ♕xe3 ♖xe3 28 ♔xe3 ♕xg2 29 ♖xa6 and Black has good drawing chances.

19 ... ♕h5

But not 19 ... f4? 20 ♗xf4 ♗xf4 21 ♕xh3 ♗xh3 22 ♖xc6!

20 f4 ba

Formerly the usual continuation in this position was 20 ... ♖fe8 (not 20 ... g5? 21 ab ab 22 fg! ♖xe3 23 ♖xe3 f4 24 ♖f3!) 21 ab (after 21 ♗xd5 cd 22 ♗f2 ♖e2 23 ♕g2 ♕f7 24 ab ab 25 ♘f1 h6 26 ♗h5 27 ♖xe2 ♖xe2 28 g4 ♖xb2! Black has good counterplay — Suetin) 21 ... ♖xe3 22 ♖xe3 ♖xe3 23 ba(?) ♗b8 (23 ... ♖e2 24 ♕xe2 ♗xe2 25 a7!, or 23 ... ♖e8 24 a7 ♖a8 25 ♗xd5+ cd 26 ♕g2, favours White — analysis by Boleslavsky and Suetin) 24 a7 ♗xa7 25 ♖xa7 ♖e2 26 ♖a8+ ♔f7 27 h4 ♖xd2 28 ♕a6 ♖e2 29 ♗xd5+! cd 30 ♕b7+ and White wins. Instead of 25 ... ♖e2 Black can play more forcefully with 25 ... h6 or 25 ... ♕e8! 26 ♖a1 ♖e2 27 ♘c4 ♔f8 28 ♘e5 ♘e3 29 ♗f7! ♕xe5! 30 de ♘xf1 31 ♗c5 ♖xh2 and Black has excellent play (Euwe).

Instead of 23 ba probably stronger is 23 bc! ♖e2 24 ♗xd5+ ♔f8 25 h3! ♗xh3 (or 25 ... ♖xd2 26 ♕xa6) 26 ♗f3 ♗xf1 27 ♗xh5 with a clear advantage to White (Gurevich–Grzeshowiak, corr. 1970).

21 ♖xa4

After 21 ♗xd5 cd 22 ♕g2 ♖fe8 (22 ... ♖e4 23 ♘xe4 fe 24 ♖xa4 is in White's favour) 23 ♕xd5 ♔h8 24 ♗f2 ♗e2 25 ♖xa4 (25 ♔g2 g5!? 26 ♕xf5 ♗g4 27 ♕xg5 ♗h3+ 28 ♔g1 ♖xe1+ 29 ♖xe1 ♖xe1+ 30 ♗xe1 ♖e2! with equality; and 25 ♘c4?! ♗c7! is in Black's favour) 25 ... ♗xf4 26 gf ♗c4 27 ♕xc4 ♕g4+ 28 ♔h1 ♖xe1+ 29 ♗xe1 ♖xe1+ 30 ♘f1 ♕f3+ 31 ♔g1 ♕e3+ with a draw (Tseshkovsky–Agapov, Kiev 1984).

21 ... ♖b8 *(172)*

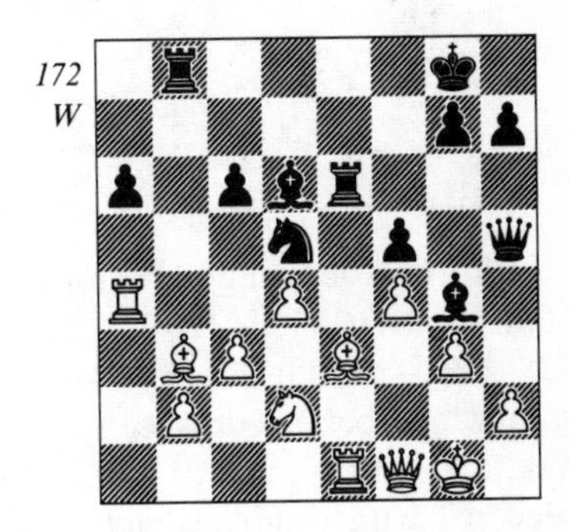

And now:

(a) **22 ♗xd5** cd 23 ♕g2 ♕e8 24 ♕xd5 ♔h8 25 ♔f2 ♖xb2 (in White's favour is 25 ... g5 26 ♖xa6 ♖xb2 27 ♕a8! ♖b8 28 ♕c6!) 26 ♖a2 ♖xa2 27 ♕xa2 g5 28 d5 (or 28 ♘c4 gf 29 ♘xd6 fe+ 30 ♖xe3 ♕h5) 28 ... ♖xe3 29 ♖xe3 ♗c5 30 ♘f1 ♗h3! 31 ♕xa6 ♗xf1 with equal chances (Fridstein).

(b) **22 ♖xa6** ♖be8 23 ♕f2 g5 24 ♗xd5 cd 25 ♖xd6 ♖xd6 26 fg ♖de6 with equal chances (Prandstetter–Blatny, Czechoslovakia 1985).

(c) **22 ♕xa6?** ♖xb3! 23 ♘xb3 ♘xe3 and Black wins.

(d) **22 ♕f2** ♖xb3 23 ♘xb3 ♗d1

and here White is in serious trouble.

A1111112

18	...	**♕h5!?**
19	**ab**	**ab** *(173)*

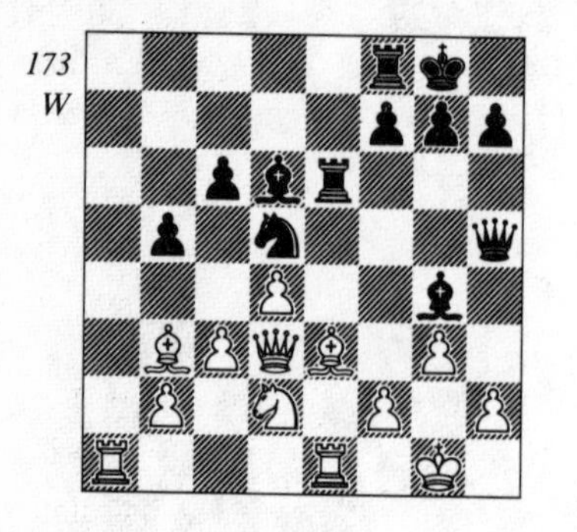

173
W

With the following variations:

(a) **20 ♕f1** ♗h3!? (20 ... ♖fe8 21 ♗xd5 ♕xd5 22 ♕g2 with somewhat better prospects for White — Tal) 21 ♗d1 ♕f5 22 ♕e2 c5! with double-edged play (Sax–I. Sokolov, Haninge 1989).

(b) **20 ♘f1** ♖fe8 (or 20 ... ♗f5 21 ♕d2 ♖fe8 22 ♗xd5 cd 23 ♗f4 ♖xe1 24 ♖xe1 ♖xe1 25 ♕xe1 ♗e4 with equality; Ivanchuk–I. Sokolov, Biel 1989) 21 ♗d1 ♗xd1 22 ♕xd1 ♕f5 23 ♗d2 ♖xe1 24 ♗xe1 h5 25 h4 c5! 26 b3! (Chandler–Nunn, Hastings 1987/8). By playing 26 ... g6! Black could have obtained full equality.

(c) **20 c4** ♘xe3 (or 20 ... bc 21 ♘xc4 ♗b4 22 ♖ec1 ♗e2 23 ♗d1 ♗xd3 24 ♗xh5 ♗xc4 25 ♖xc4 ♘xe5 26 fe ♗d2 with approximate equality; Parma–Geller, Yugoslavia vs USSR 1966) 21 ♖xe3 (21 fe? ♗xg3!) 21 ... ♗e2 22 ♕c2 ♖h6 23 h4 ♗f4 and Black has the better chances.

(d) **20 ♗xd5** ♕xd5! 21 c4 bc 22 ♕xc4 ♕h5 23 ♖a6 ♖fe8 24 ♖xc6 ♖h6 25 h4 ♖g6 26 d5 ♗d7 27 ♔g2 ♕f5! and White is in trouble.

(e) **20 ♗d1** ♗xd1 21 ♖axd1 f5 22 ♘f1 f4 and here Black has the better chances (Hellers–I. Sokolov, Haninge 1989).

A1111113

18	...	**ba**
19	**♖xa4**	

19 ♗xa4?! ♗f4 20 ♗xf4 ♘xf4 21 ♕f1 ♘e2+ 22 ♔h1 ♕h6 23 ♖ad1 ♖fe8 24 d5 ♕xd2! is in Black's favour (Tal).

19	...	**f5**
20	**♕f1**	**♕h5**

The alternative is 20 ... f4?! 21 ♕xh3 ♗xh3 22 ♖xa6 fe 23 ♖xe3 ♖xe3 (23 ... ♘xe3? 24 fe ♔f7 25 ♖xc6 ♔e7 26 ♗xe6 ♖xe6 27 ♖a6 is bad for Black) 24 fe ♗e7 25 e4! (after 25 ♖xc6 ♗g5 26 ♗xd5+ ♔h8 27 ♗g2 ♗xe3+ 28 ♔h1 ♗xg2+ 29 ♔xg2 ♗xd2 30 b4 g5 Black has maintained the equilibrium; Stein–Spassky, Moscow 1964) 25 ... ♗g5 26 ed ♗xd2 27 dc+ ♔h8 28 ♖a1 g6 29 ♗d5 ♗e3+ 30 ♔h1 ♖f2 31 c7 ♖xb2 (Parma–Spassky, Yugoslavia vs USSR 1965). By playing 32 c8(♕)+! ♗xc8 33 ♖a8!, White was able to win.

21	**f4** *(174)*

In the game Suetin–Geller, USSR Ch. 1963, there occurred: 21 c4!? f4 22 cd ♖xe3 23 fe fg 24 dc+ ♔h8 25 hg ♖xf1+ 26 ♖xf1 ♕g5 with great complications.

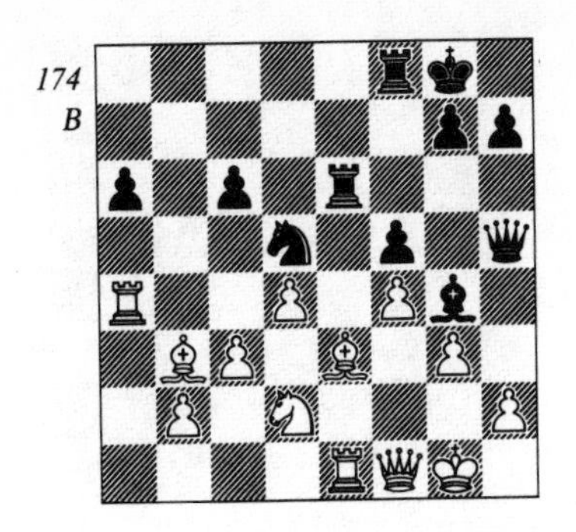
174
B

Now the following variations arise:

(a) **21 ... ♖b8** 22 ♗xd5 cd 23 ♖a6 (after 23 ♕g2 ♕e8 24 ♕xd5+ ♔h8 25 ♘c4 ♗f4 26 gf ♖g6 27 ♘d3 ♗h3!? 28 ♔f2 ♖b2 29 ♖e2 ♖g2 the chances are roughly equal) 23 ... ♕e8 (worse is 23 ... ♖be8 24 ♕b5! ♕f7 25 h3! with advantage to White) 24 ♗f2 ♕d7 25 ♖e6 ♕xe6 26 c4 with somewhat better play for White (Chandler–P. Littlewood, London 1987).

(b) **21 ... g5** 22 ♖xa6! gf 23 ♖xc6 fg 24 hg (24 ♕g2) 24 ... ♗xg3 25 ♕g2.

(c) **21 ... ♖fe8!** 22 ♖xa6! ♔h8 23 ♗xd5 cd 24 ♕f2 g5 25 fg f4 26 gf h6 27 c4! hg 28 ♖xd6 ♖xd6 29 fg ♗h3 30 cd ♕g4+ 31 ♕g3. In both cases White stands better (analysis by Suetin). White is also better after 21 ... ♔h8 22 ♘c4! ♘xe3 23 ♘xe3, or 21 ... a5 22 ♘c4 ♗c7 23 ♘e5.

A111112

18 c4!? *(175)*

There has still been very little study of this continuation. White aims to bring about rapid activity on the queenside. The following variations may arise:

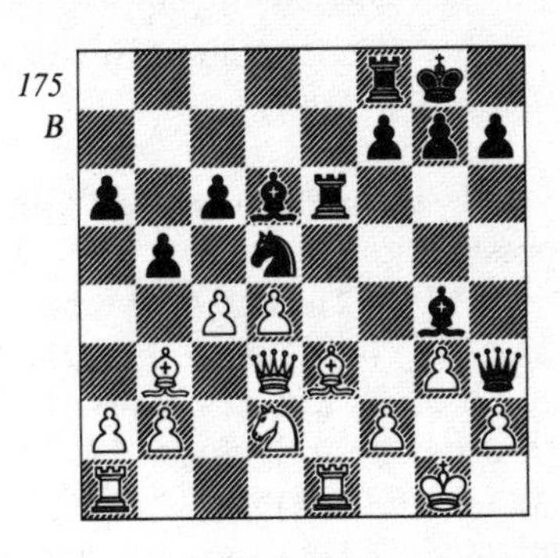
175
B

(a) **18 ... ♗f4!?** 19 ♕f1 (after 19 cd!? ♖h6 20 ♕e4 ♕xh2+ 21 ♔f1 ♗xe3 — or 21 ... f5 22 dc+ ♔h8 23 ♕d5 ♗xe3 24 ♖xe3 f4! — 22 ♖xe3 ♖f6 23 f3 ♗f5 24 ♕e5 ♕xd2!; Timman–Johansson, Reykjavik 1976, Black has excellent counterplay in either case; play becomes double-edged after 19 ♗xf4 ♘xf4 20 ♕f1 ♘e2+ 21 ♔h1 ♕h6) 19 ... ♘xe3 20 ♕xh3 ♗xh3 21 cb ♘c2! 22 ♗xe6 fe 23 gf ♘xa1 24 ♖xa1 ♖xf4 25 f3 cb 26 ♘e4! ♖xf3 27 ♘g5 ♖d3 28 ♖c1 with equal chances (Plachetka).

(b) **18 ... bc** 19 ♘xc4 ♗f4 20 ♕f1 ♕h6 21 ♗c1! ♗h3 22 ♖xe6 fe 23 ♕d1 ♗xc1 24 ♖xc1 ♕f6 25 f3 ♕xf3 26 ♕xf3 ♖xf3 27 ♘e5 ♖f8 28 ♘xc6 with a considerable advantage to White (R. Byrne–Geller, Las Palmas 1976).

A11112

16 ... f5

Black aims to launch a pawn attack on the kingside.

17 f4

Not without interest is 17 Qf1!? Qxf1+ 18 Kxf1 f4 19 gf Bxf4 20 Kg1 Be7! with approximate equality (Kindermann–I. Sokolov, Biel 1988).

17 ... g5?!

Let us briefly consider other possibilities:

(a) **17 ... Rae8** 18 Nd2 Kh8 19 Bxd4 cd 20 Qf1 Qh5 21 a4 g5 22 ab ab 23 fg Rxe3 24 Rxe3 f4 25 gf Bxf4 26 Rg3 Qxg5 27 Kh1 Rg8 28 Nf3 Qf5 29 Rxg4 with material advantage to White (Boleslavsky–Tal, Leningrad 1962).

(b) **17 ... Kh8!?** 18 Bxd5 cd 19 Nd2 g5 20 Qf1 Qh5 21 a4 ba 22 c4 Rab8 23 Rab1 Bh3 24 Qf2 Qg4 25 cd gf 26 Bxf4 Bxf4 27 Qxf4 Qxf4 28 gf Nb4 29 Kf2 Rxd4 30 Nf3 Rxd5 with roughly equal chances (Short–Ehlvest, Skelleftea 1989). The game Sokolov–Ehlvest, Rotterdam 1989, developed along similar lines, but instead of 21 a4 there occurred 21 fg f4 22 Bxf4 Rxf4 23 gf Rf8 24 Re5 Bxe5 25 de h6 26 Re1 hg 27 f5 with a small advantage to White.

18 Qf1 Qh5

19 Nd2 Rae8 *(176)*

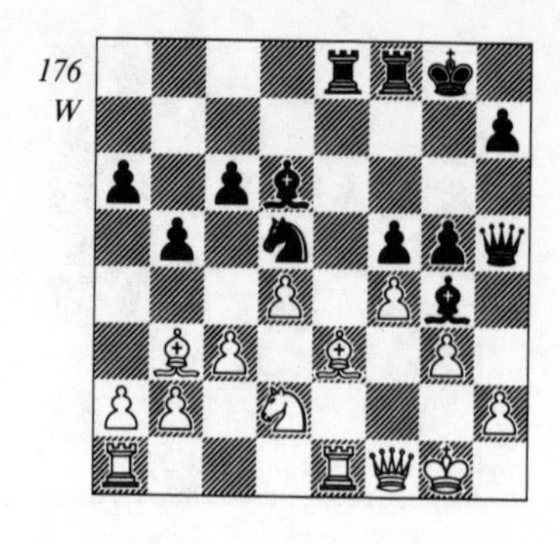

176 W

With the following variations:

(a) **20 Qg2!** gf 21 Bxd5+ Kh8 22 Bxf4 Bxf4 23 Bxc6! Be3+ 24 Kh1 Bh3 25 Qe2 Bg4 26 Bxe8 Rxe8 27 Qxe3! and White has a considerable advantage (Boleslavsky).

(b) **20 fg** Rxe3 21 Rxe3 f4 22 Rf3 Bxf3 23 Qxf3 Qxf3 with equal chances (Gutman).

(c) **20 Qf2** h6 21 a4 Kh8 22 Bxd5 cd 23 ab ab 24 b3 Re4 25 c4 gf 26 Bxf4 Bxf4 27 gf Rg8 28 Kh1 bc 29 bc dc and White will have quite a difficult time defending.

(d) **20 Bxd5+** cd 21 Qg2 Re4! 22 gf Kh8 23 a4 Bh3 24 Qf3 Rg4 25 ab a5! 26 Rxa5 f4 27 Bxf4 Bxf4 28 Re7 Qxg5 29 Raa7 Rh4 and the complications have turned out in Black's favour.

A11113

16 ... Nxe3?!

The popularity of this move was short-lived — it flashed past in the mid-1960s. Black tries to open up the centre, but objectively he has quite a few difficulties.

17 Rxe3 c5

And now:

(a) **18 Qf1!** Qh6 (in White's favour is 18 ... Qxf1+ 19 Kxf1 Rad8 20 Kg2!, or 18 ... Qh5 19 Nd2 Rad8 20 Bd1!) 19 Nd2 Rad8 20 Nf3 Bxf3 21 Rxf3 cd 22 cd Qd2 23 Rd3 and there is no doubting White's advantage.

(b) **18 ♗d5?!** ♖ad8 19 ♘d2 ♗c7! 20 ♗g2 ♕h6 21 ♘f3 ♗b6 22 ♘e5 ♗e6 with roughly equal chances (Barczay–Adorjan, Budapest 1970).

A1112

13 ♖e2 *(177)*

This continuation appeared only quite recently but it is now in fashion. We shall consider the following variations:

A11121 13 … ♕h4
A11122 13 … ♗c7

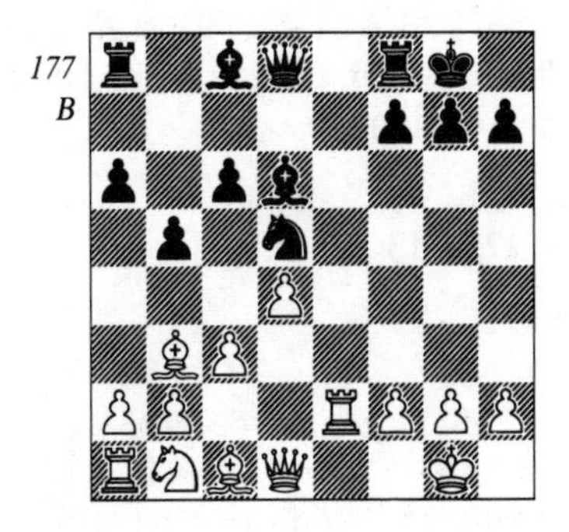

177
B

A11121

13 … ♕h4

Interesting is 13 … f5!?

14 g3

Now there is another branch in the analysis:

A111211 14 … ♕h3
A111212 14 … ♕h5

A111211

14 … ♕h3
15 ♘d2

Worthy of consideration is 15 ♕f1.

15 … ♗f5

After 15 … ♗g4 16 f3 ♗xf3 17 ♘xf3 ♕xf3 18 ♖f2 (18 ♕f1!?) 18 … ♕e4 19 ♕f3 ♖ae8 20 ♗d2 ♘f6 21 ♖e1 White has a small advantage (Sax–Nikolic, Plovdiv 1983).

After 15 … ♗f5 the following variations are possible:

(a) **16 ♗xd5** cd 17 f3 ♖ae8 18 ♘f1 h5 with equality (Y. Gruenfeld–Pinter, Zagreb 1987).

(b) **16 ♘e4** ♗g4 17 ♘g5 ♗xe2 18 ♕xe2 ♕d7 19 ♕d3 f5 with unclear play (Geller–Lukács, Coimbatore 1987).

(c) **16 ♗c2** ♗xc2 17 ♕xc2 f5 18 c4!? (18 f4 ♕g4 19 ♘f1 ♗f4 20 ♖f2 with unclear play) 18 … ♕g4 19 ♖e6 (Ljubojevic–Nunn, Szirak 1987). After 19 … f4! 20 ♕e4 ♘e3! 21 ♘f3! fg 22 ♕xg4 gf+ 23 ♔xf2 ♘g4+ 24 ♔g2 ♖f6 the game is roughly equal (Nunn).

(b) **16 ♕f1** ♕h5 17 ♗d1 (17 ♗xd5?! cd 18 ♕e1 ♗g4 19 ♖e3 f5 20 f4 g5 21 ♘f1 ♖ae8 22 ♖e5!? ♗h3! is to Black's advantage; Tischbierek–Blatny, Leipzig 1988) 17 … ♕g6 18 ♕g2 ♖ae8 19 ♘f3 ♖e2 20 ♗xe2 ♖e8 21 ♗e3! ♕e6! 22 ♘h4 ♘e3 23 fe ♕xe3+ 24 ♕f2 ♕xf2 25 ♔xf2 ♗e4! and Black's position is preferable.

A111212

14 … ♕h5
15 ♘d2 ♗h3
16 f3

Unclear play arises after 16 ♖e4 ♕g6, and after 16 ♖e1 then 16 … f5 is strong.

16 … ♗c7

After 16 ... f5!? 17 a4 or 17 c4, or 16 ... ♖ae8 17 ♖xe8 ♖xe8 18 ♘e4 ♗c7 19 ♗d2 ♕g6 20 ♗c2! (Garcia-Martinez–Pinter, Lucerne OL 1982), White has the better chances.

17 a4

Worthy of consideration is 17 ♘e4 ♖ae8 18 ♕d3 ♖e6 19 ♗d2 ♖g6 20 g4! ♗xg4 21 fg ♖xg4+ 22 ♘g3 f5 23 ♖g2 with advantage to White (Belyavsky–Malanyuk, USSR 1987).

17 ... b4
18 c4 ♘f6

The game Short–Nunn, Brussels 1986, continued: 19 ♘e4! (worse is 19 ♖e1 ♖ad8! 20 ♘e4 ♘xe4 21 ♖xe4 ♗f5 22 ♖e1 ♕h3! with full equality for Black; Kuporosov–Malanyuk, USSR 1985) 19 ... ♕g6 20 ♔f2! ♗f5 21 ♗c2 ♖fe8 22 ♗xf5 ♖xf5 23 ♖xe8 ♖xe8 24 ♔g2 and Black has quite a few difficulties.

A11122

13 ... ♗c7!?

Creating the threat 14 ... ♕d6, and if 15 g3 then 15 ... ♗g4. In this little-studied continuation the following variations may arise:

(a) **14 ♘d2** ♘f4 15 ♖e3 c5!? 16 ♘f3 ♗b7 17 dc?! ♕f6 with excellent play for Black (Oll–Tseshkovsky, USSR 1987).

(b) **14 ♗c2** ♗g4 15 f3 ♕d6 16 g3 ♗h5 17 ♖e5?! (correct is 17 ♘d2 f5 with approximate equality) 17 ... ♗g6 18 ♘d2 c5 19 ♗b3 c4 20 ♗c2 ♕xe5! 21 de ♘e3 and Black wins (Lensky–Al. Karpov, corr. 1988/9).

A112

12 d3

A modest move, interest in which has noticeably increased recently.

12 ... ♗d6
13 ♖e1

Now Black has a choice of two alternatives. Note also 13 ... ♖a7? 14 ♘d2!? ♘f4 15 ♘e4 ♘xd3 16 ♗g5! ♗e7 17 ♗xe7 ♖xe7 18 ♖e3! ♖d7 19 ♕h5 (Popovic–Velimirovic, Bor 1985). After 19 ... ♘f4 20 ♕g4 ♘g6 21 ♕g3, and then ♖ae1 and ♘g5, White has a secure initiative.

A1121 13 ... ♕h4
A1122 13 ... ♗f5

A1121

13 ... ♕h4
14 g3 ♕h3
15 ♖e4 ♕f5

After 15 ... ♘f6 16 ♖h4 ♕f5 17 ♗c2! ♖e8 18 ♘d2! g5 19 ♘e4 White dictates the "terms of trade" (Gutman).

16 ♘d2

After 16 ♖h4 (16 ♗c2? ♕g6 17 ♕f1 f5 18 ♖e1 f4!) 16 ... ♗b7 17 ♗c2 ♕e6! 18 c4 ♘b4 19 c5 ♘xc2 20 ♕xc2 f5! Black has the initiative (Tukmakov–Jansa, 1967).

16 ... ♕g6 *(178)*

With the following variations:

(a) **17 a4!** ♘f6 (after 17 ... ♗f5 18 ab ab 19 ♖xa8 ♖xa8 20 ♖e1 ♗d3 21 ♘f3, or 17 ... f5?! 18 ♖d4 f4 19 ♘e4; Zapata–Pavlovic, Belgrade 1988 the situation favours

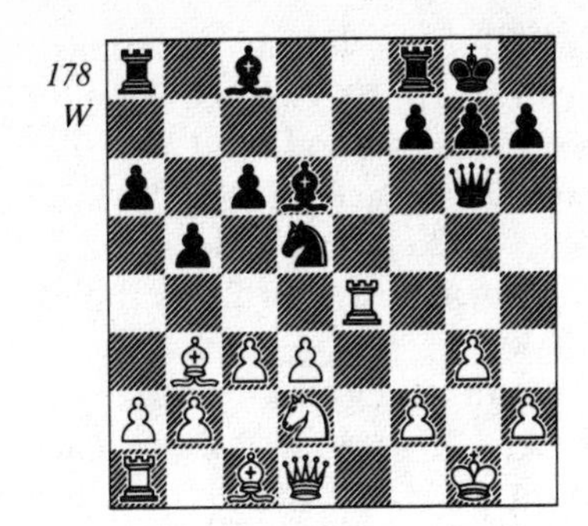

178
W

White) 18 ♖e1 ♗g4 19 f3 ♗f5 (or 19 … ♗h3 20 ♘f1 ♖ae8 21 ♗e3 h5 22 d4) 20 ♘e4 ♗xe4 21 fe ♗xg3 22 ♖e2 ♗f4 23 ♖g2 ♕h6 24 ♗f4 ♕xf4 25 ♕e2 — in both cases with somewhat better chances for White.

(b) **17 ♖e1** f5 (or 17 … ♗c7 18 ♘f3 ♗g4 19 ♘h4!) 18 c4 f4 19 ♘e4 fg 20 fg ♗g4 21 ♕c2 bc 22 dc ♖ae8!? 23 cd ♗f3 24 dc ♔h8 25 ♗d5 ♗g3 26 hg with roughly equal play (Andrijevic–Pavlovic, Yugoslavia 1988).

(c) **17 ♘f1** f5 (after 17 … ♘f6 18 ♖e1 ♗g4 19 f3 ♗f5 20 d4 ♖ae8 21 ♗e3 White has the better chances; Wedberg–Pinter, Haninge 1988; interesting is 17 … h5!? 18 a4 ♗g4 19 ♕e1 ♘f6 20 ♖e3 ♖ae8 21 ab ab 22 d4 h4 with chances for both sides; Kuzmin–Shulman, Minsk 1986) 18 ♖d4 f4 19 ♖xd5 cd 20 ♗xd5+ ♗e6 21 ♗xa8 ♖xa8 22 ♕f3 ♖f8 23 ♕e4 ♗f5 24 ♕d5+ ♔h8 25 a4 (Timman–Hübner, Tilburg 1985). After 25 … ♗xd3 26 ab ♗e4 27 ♕d4 fg 28 ♘xg3 ♗xg3 29 fg ab 30 ♗f4 h5 the game is level.

A1122

13 … ♗f5 *(179)*

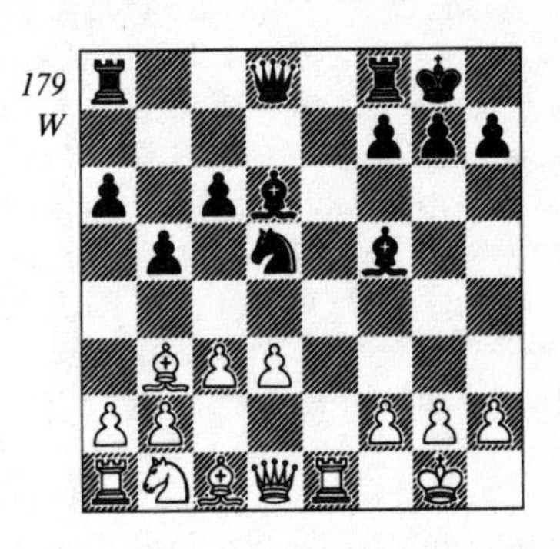

179
W

And now:

(a) **14 ♕f3** ♕d7 (14 … ♖e8) 15 ♗xd5 cd 16 ♗f4 ♗xf4 17 ♕xf4 ♗d3 18 ♘d2 ♖ae8 19 ♖e3 ♖xe3 20 ♕xe3 ♗g6 21 ♖e1 with somewhat better play for White (Smagin–Geller, USSR 1989).

(b) **14 ♘d2** ♘f4 15 ♘e4 ♘xd3 16 ♗g5 ♕d7 17 ♖e3!? ♗xe4 18 ♖xe4 ♖ae8 19 ♕g4 ♕xg4 20 ♖xg4 ♗e5 21 ♖b1 h5 with approximate equality (Kir. Georgiev–Nunn, Dubai OL 1986).

A113

12 g3

A favourite move of Fischer's. White strengthens the diagonal b8–h2 and prevents the manoeuvre ♕d8–h4. But these tactical considerations cannot change the strategic pattern of play.

12 … ♗d6

Worthy of consideration is 12 … ♗f6!? 13 ♖e1 c5 (13 … ♖a7!?) 14 d4 ♗b7!? 15 dc ♖e8 with good counterplay for Black (Braga–

Geller, Amsterdam 1986).

13 ♖e1 ♕d7!

After 13 ... ♘f6 14 d4 ♗g4 15 ♕d3 c5 16 ♗c2 (or 16 dc ♗xc5 17 ♕xd8 ♖axd8 18 ♗f4 h6 19 ♘a3 g5 20 ♗e3 ♗xe3 21 ♖xe3 ♖d2 with equal chances; Fischer–Spassky, Santa Monica 1966) 16 ... c4 17 ♕f1 ♕d7 18 f3 ♗h3 19 ♕f2 White has somewhat better play (Gutman).

14 d3 ♕h3

The important thing is not the route but the destination! Black's queen gets into position after 15 ♖e4 ♕f5 16 ♘d2 ♕g6, when there arises a position considered under variation A112.

A114

12 ♕f1?! *(180)*

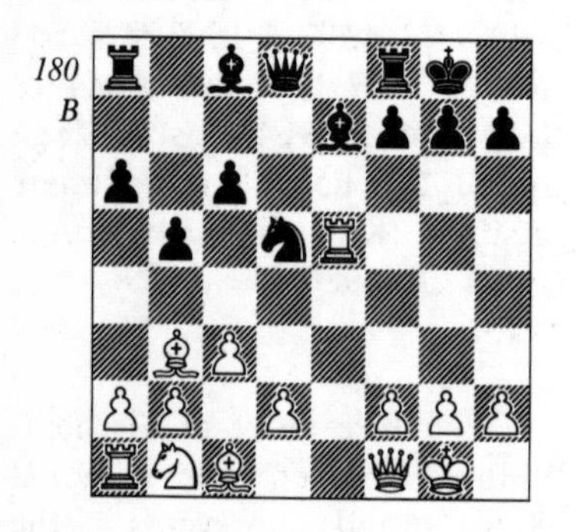

By such somewhat artificial means White wishes to strengthen his kingside. But in this line Black gets a very free game.

12 ... ♗d6
13 ♖e1 ♕h4
14 g3 ♕h5
15 d4

With the following variations:

(a) **15 ... ♗h3** 16 ♗d1 ♕f5 17 ♕e2 c5 (also good are 17 ... ♕d7 and 17 ... ♖ae8) 18 ♗e3 ♖ae8 19 ♘d2 cd 20 cd ♖e7 21 ♕f3 ♖fe8 with an initiative for Black (Boleslavsky).

(b) **15 ... ♗g4** 16 ♘d2 ♖ae8 17 f3 ♗h3 18 ♕f2 f5 19 ♖xe8 ♖xe8 20 c4 ♘f4!? and Black is definitely not worse (Kapengut–Malanyuk, USSR 1985).

A115

12 ♗xd5 cd
13 d4

White willingly exchanges his important bishop and strengthens Black's pawn skeleton in the centre, but avoids weakening the light squares. This noticeably restricts Black's counterplay, and in a number of variations Black's initiative fades away. On the other hand, White's possibilities are also limited. Thus, in a number of endgame positions Black's pawns on a6, d5 and b5 neutralise, as it were, White's 'quartet' of pawns on the queenside. Play ranges from active operations on the kingside to stubborn defence in the ending.

For many years this system was not fashionable, but it has been popular recently.

13 ... ♗d6
14 ♖e3

We shall consider the two main subvariations:

A1151 14 ... ♕h4
A1152 14 ... f5

A1151

14 ... ♕h4
15 h3 f5!? *(181)*

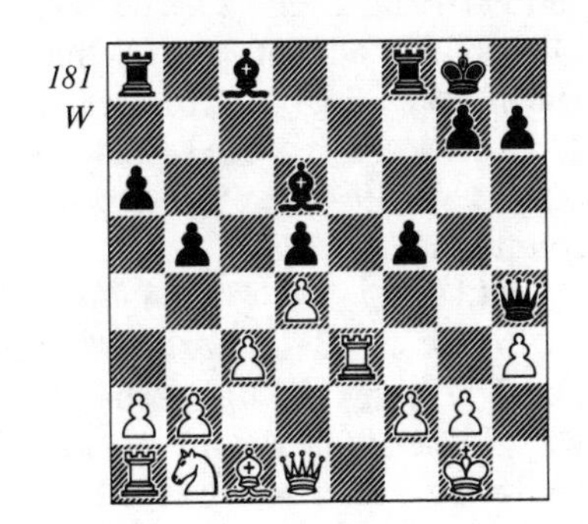
181
W

Other variations:

(a) **15 ... g5** (15 ... ♗f4? 16 g3 ♕g5 17 ♖e5!) 16 ♕f3 ♗e6 17 ♕f6, and now:

(a1) **17 ... ♕h5** 18 ♘d2 g4 19 ♖xe6 fe 20 ♕xe6+ ♕f7 21 ♕xd6 ♕xf2+ 22 ♔h2 ♖ae8! 23 ♕g3 with slightly better chances for White (Tal).

(a2) **17 ... ♖ae8** 18 ♘a3 ♕h5 19 ♗d2 h6 20 ♘c2 ♗f4 21 ♖d3 ♕e2 22 ♗xf4 gf 23 ♘e1 ♕b2 24 ♖ad1 ♔h7 (Hübner–Pinter, European Club Ch. 1989). By playing 25 ♖3d2 ♕c3 26 ♕f4 ♖g8 27 ♘d3 ♖g5 28 ♖c1 White could have obtained an advantage.

(a3) **17 ... ♖fe8!** 18 ♘a3 ♕h5 19 ♗d2 ♗e7! 20 ♕f3 ♕g6 21 ♖ae1 g4?! 22 ♕g3 hg 23 gh ♗d6 24 ♕xg6 hg with full equality for Black (Hübner–Nunn, Haifa 1989).

(b) **15 ... ♕f4** 16 ♖e5 ♕f6 17 ♖e1 ♕g6 18 ♕f3 ♗e6 19 ♗f4 ♗xf4 20 ♕xf4 ♗xh3 21 ♕g3 ♕c2 22 c4 (Kholmov–Tal, Kislovodsk 1966) 22 ... ♕xb2 23 ♘c3 ♗e6 24 ♗d7 with approximate equality.

Turning our attention to the mainline with 15 ... f5, we note the following variations:

(a) **16 ♕f3** ♗b7 17 ♘d2 g5 18 ♕e2!? (18 ♘f1 ♖f6 19 ♕e2 ♔f7 20 ♗d2 f4 21 ♖d3 ♖ae8 22 ♕g4 ♕xg4 23 hg ♗c8 24 ♔h2 h5! with better chances for Black; Bagirov–Vitomsky, USSR 1972) 18 ... f4 19 ♘f3 ♕h5? 20 ♘xg5 ♕g6 (20 ... ♕xg5 21 ♖g3!) 21 ♖e6 ♕xg5 22 ♖xd6 ♖ae8 23 ♖e6 ♔f7 24 ♖e5! is in White's favour (Hübner–Nunn, Skelleftea 1989).

(b) **16 ♕b3?** ♗b7 17 ♘d2 f4 18 ♘f3 ♕h5 19 ♖e1 g5 20 a4 ♔h8 and Black has dangerous threats (♖g8, g5–g4) (Suetin).

(c) **16 ♘d2** f4 17 ♖e1 ♗xh3 18 ♕f3 ♗xg2 19 ♕xg2 ♕h5 20 ♘f3 ♖f6 21 ♘g5 ♖f5 with sufficient counterplay for Black (de Firmian–I. Sokolov, Biel 1989).

A1152

14 ... f5

A natural reaction. But practice has shown that it is easier for White to cope with Black's offensive here than in the previous variation.

15 ♘d2

Unattractive is 15 ♕f3 ♖a7 16 ♘d2 g5! etc.

15 ... f4
16 ♖e1

And now:

(a) **16 ... ♖a7** 17 ♘f3 ♗g4 (17

... g5?! 18 ♘e5 ♖g7 19 a4!) 18 a4 ba 19 ♖xa4 g5 20 b3 ♖e8 21 ♕d3! with better chances for White.

(b) **16 ... ♕g5** 17 ♘f3 ♕h5 18 ♘e5! f3 19 gf ♗h3 20 f4 ♕h4 21 ♕f3 ♖ae8 22 ♕g3! and here Black has difficulties (Tal).

A12

11 ... ♘f6

This is nowadays encountered very rarely, although this was the move that laid the foundation for the study of the Marshall Attack. Black plans a piece attack on the kingside, which is where the battle takes place.

12 d4

Worse is 12 ♖e1 ♗d6 13 h3 ♘g4! 14 hg? ♕h4 15 ♕f3 ♗h2+ 16 ♔f1 ♗xg4 17 ♕e4 ♔h8 18 d4 ♕h5 and f7–f5!

12 ... ♗d6 *(182)*

182
W

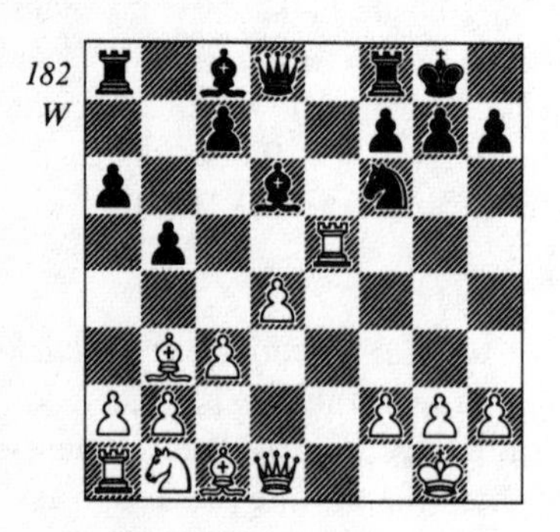

13 ♖e1

The alternative is 13 ♖e2, with the following variations: 13 ... ♘h5 (after 13 ... ♗b7 14 ♘d2 ♕d7 15 f3! ♖ae8 16 ♘f1 c5 17 dc ♗xc5+ 18 ♗e3 White's advantage is minimal; Hazai–Nikolac, Maribor 1985) 14 ♕d3 (worthy of consideration is 14 ♗e3! ♗b7 15 ♘d2 ♔h8 16 ♖e1 ♕h4 17 ♘f1 f5 18 f3 f4 19 ♗f2 ♘g3 20 ♕d3 ♕g5 21 ♗e6 with advantage to White; Hazai) 14 ... ♗g4 15 ♖e1 ♖e8 16 ♖xe8+ ♕xe8 17 ♗e3 ♘f4 18 ♗xf4 ♗xf4 19 ♘d2 c5 with good counterplay for Black.

13 ... ♘g4

No use is 13 ... ♗xh2+? 14 ♔xh2 ♘g4+ 15 ♔g1 ♕h4 16 ♕f3. Little-studied is 13 ... ♗b7 14 d5 ♕d7, after which it is hard for Black to show any compensation for the pawn.

14 h3

But not 14 g3? ♘xh2! 15 ♗d5 ♗xg3! etc.

14 ... ♕h4
15 ♕f3 ♘xf2

After 15 ... h5?! 16 ♗e3 ♘xe3! 17 ♖xe3 ♕f4 18 ♕xf4 ♗xf4 19 ♖e1 ♗f5 20 ♘a3 with advantage to White (Tal).

16 ♗d2! *(183)*

After 16 ♖e2 ♘g4 17 ♖e8 (17 ♕xa8? ♕g3 18 hg ♕h2+ 19 ♔f1 ♗g3 20 ♗e3 ♕h1+ 21 ♗g1 ♗h2 22 ♔e1 ♕xg1+ 23 ♔d2

183
B

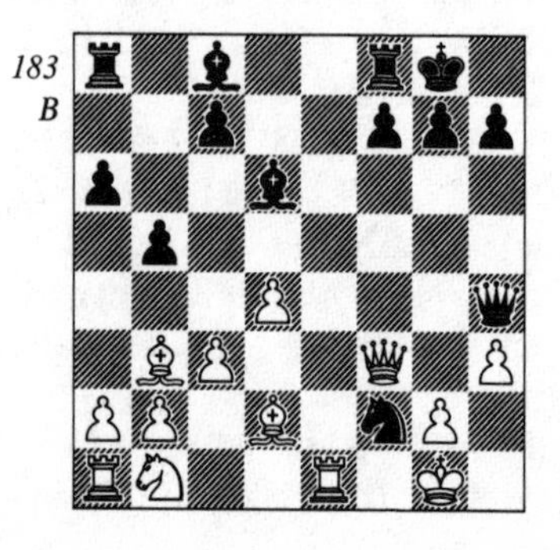

♕f4+ and Black wins) 17 ... ♘f6! 18 ♖xf8+ ♔xf8 19 ♘d2 ♖b8 20 ♘f1 ♗b7 with equal chances.

After 16 ♗d2! the following lines arise: 16 ... ♗b7 17 ♕xb7 (bad is 17 ♕xf2? ♗h2+ 18 ♔f1 ♗g3 19 ♕g1 ♖ae8 20 ♖e3 ♖e6! 21 d5 ♖f6+ 22 ♖f3 ♖xf3+ 23 gf ♖e8!) 17 ... ♘d3 18 ♖e2 ♖ae8 (or 18 ... ♕g3 19 ♔f1 ♕h2 20 g4! ♕xh3+ 21 ♕g2 ♕h4 22 ♗e3 ♖ae8 23 ♘d2 ♗f4 24 ♘f3 ♕h6 25 ♗c2!) 19 ♕xb7 ♖xe2 20 ♕xe2 ♕g3 21 ♕f3! ♕h2+ 22 ♔f1 ♕h1+ 23 ♔e2 ♘xb2 24 ♗e3 and in both cases White must win (Euwe).

A2

9 ... e4

This extravagant variation is not nowadays in fashion. Indeed, the 'waves' of interest in it over the years have not generally amounted to more than a storm in a teacup, although in practice it does contain some venom.

10 dc

After 10 ♘g5 ♗g4! 11 f3 (11 ♕c2 ♘e5 12 ♘xe4 ♘xe4 13 ♕xe4 ♗d6 14 f4 ♘g6 15 d4 ♕d7 16 ♖f1 ♖ae8 is in Black's favour) 11 ... ef 12 ♘xf3 ♘xd5 13 d4 ♗h4 14 ♖f1 ♕d7 15 ♗xd5 ♕xd5 16 ♗f4 chances are roughly equal (Tal and Gutman).

10 ... ef

Now White has a choice:

A21 **11 d4**
A22 **11 ♕xf3**

A21

11 d4 fg

Besides this capture the following variations are possible:

(a) **11 ... ♗g4** 12 gf! (12 h3 ♗h5 13 g4?! ♘xg4 14 ♕xf3 ♘f6 15 ♕g2 ♖e8 16 ♗g5 ♗g6 17 ♘d2 ♘h5 18 ♘f3 ♗xg5 19 ♕xg5 ♕xg5 20 ♘xg5 ♘f4 with equal play — Suetin) 12 ... ♗h5 13 ♗f4 ♗d6 14 ♗e5 with better chances for White.

(b) **11 ... ♗d6** 12 ♕xf3 (12 ♗g5!?) 12 ... ♖e8 13 ♗d2 ♗g4 14 ♕d3 ♖xe1 15 ♗xe1 ♕e8 16 ♘d2 ♕xc6 17 f3 ♗h5 18 ♗h4 with a clear advantage to White (Haller–Dalj, corr. 1970). In White's favour is 11 ... ♖e8 12 ♕xf3 ♗g4 13 ♕d3 ♕d6 14 ♗g5 (Suetin).

12 ♕f3

After 12 ♗f4 ♗g4! 13 ♕d3 ♘h5, or 12 ♗g5 ♘d5!? 13 ♗xe7 ♘xe7 14 ♕f3 ♕d6 15 d5 ♘g6, Black has a good game.

12 ... ♗e6 *(184)*

Not good is 12 ... ♘g4?! 13 ♗f4 ♔h8 14 ♘d2 g5 15 ♗g3 f5 16 h3 f4 17 hg fg 18 ♕xg3 ♗d6 19 ♕g2 ♖f4 20 e6! (Gutman).

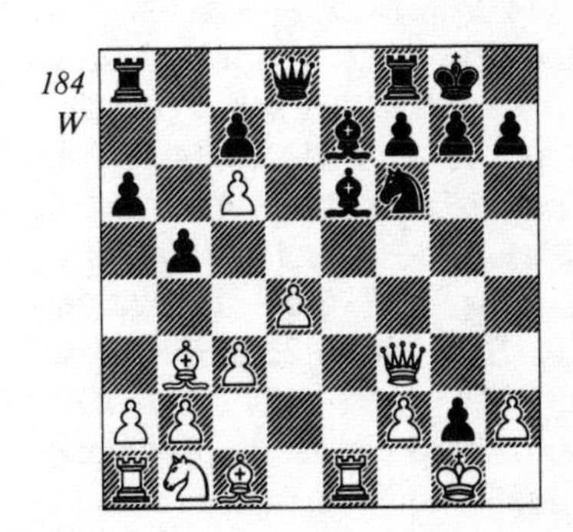

After 12 ... ♗e6 the following variations are possible:

(a) **13 ♗f4!** ♘d5!? 14 ♗g3 a5 15 ♘bd2! a4 16 ♗c2 with better prospects for White.

(b) **13 ♗g5** ♗d5 14 ♗xd5 ♘xd5 15 ♗xe7 ♘xe7 16 ♘d2 ♕d6 with sufficient counterplay for Black.

(c) **13 ♗xe6?!** fe 14 ♖xe6 ♘d5 15 ♕xg2 ♗h4! and Black has the better chances.

A22

11	**♕xf3**	**♗g4**
12	**♕g3** *(185)*	

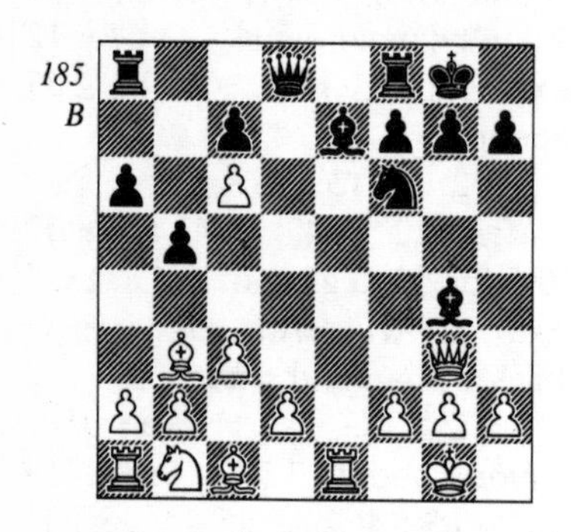

And now: 12 ... ♖e8 13 d4 (in Black's favour is 13 f3 ♕d3!, or 13 f4 ♗d6 14 ♖xe8+ ♕xe8 15 d4 ♕xc6 16 ♘d2 ♖e8 17 h3 ♖e2!) 13 ... ♗d6 14 ♖xe8+ (14 ♖e5? ♗xe5 15 de ♗d1!, or 14 f4 ♘h5, favours Black) 14 ... ♕xe8 15 ♕e3 ♕xc6 16 f3 ♖e8 17 ♕f2 ♖e7 18 ♗g5 ♕e8 19 ♘d2 ♖e2 20 ♕f1 ♗h3!? 21 gh h6 22 ♗xf7+ ♔xf7 23 ♘e4 ♗xh2+ 24 ♔h1 ♖xb2 with sharp play and approximate equality for Black (Tal).

B

The sharp nature of the counter-attack after 8 c3 d5!? is not to the taste of every player of the white pieces. This has given rise to various prophylactic measures, the most important of which is 8 a4, the 'anti-Marshall'. Although objectively this hardly offers any better prospects than 8 c3, the 'anti-Marshall' is regularly encountered, although the theory of it has not yet been perfected. It is a typically pragmatic system.

8	**a4**

Much less popular ways of avoiding the Marshall Attack are: 8 ♗d5?! ♘xd5 9 ed ♘b4; 8 h3 ♗b7 9 d3 d6; 8 ♘c3 d6 9 ♘d5 ♘a5; 8 d3 d6 etc.

Play develops along more forcing lines after 8 d4 ♘xd4!? (quieter is 8 ... d6), with the following variations:

(a) **9 ♗xf7+** ♖xf7! 10 ♘xe5 ♖f8 11 ♕xd4 c5 12 ♕d1 ♕c7 13 ♘g4 ♘xg4 14 ♕xg4 d5 15 ♕h5 de 16 ♘c3 ♖f5 17 ♕e8+ ♖f8 18 ♕h5 ♖f5 with a draw (Smejkal–Zaitsev, Polanica Zdroj 1970).

(b) **9 ♘xd4** ed 10 e5 ♘e8 11 ♕xd4 (or 11 c3 dc 12 ♘xc3 ♗b7 13 ♕g4 c5 with unclear play) 11 ... c5!? (11 ... ♗b7) 12 ♕e4 ♘c7 13 c4! bc?! 14 ♗c2 g6 15 ♘c3 ♖b8 16 ♗a4 ♖b6 with complicated play (van der Wiel–Kir. Georgiev, Wijk aan Zee 1988).

Here let me mention my own 'patent' move 8 a3. This often leads to the variation 8 ... d6 9 c3 etc. But besides 8 ... d6 other lines are possible. For example: 8 ... ♗b7 (interesting is 8 ... d5!? 9 ed ♘xd5 10 ♘xe5 ♘xe5 11 ♖xe5 c6 12 ♖e1 ♗d6 13 ♘c3) 9 d3 h6 10 ♘bd2 ♖e8 11 ♘f1 ♗f8 12 ♘g3 d5 13 ♗d2 ♕d7 14 ♕e2 with complicated play (Suetin–Plachetka, Dubna 1979).

After 8 a4 the main variations are:

B1 8 ... b4
B2 8 ... ♗b7

B1

8 ... b4

In White's favour is 8 ... ♖b8 9 ab ab 10 c3 d6 11 d4, and if 11 ... ed 12 cd ♗g4 then 13 h3 ♗h5 14 ♘c3 with advantage to White.

9 c3

Other continuations:

(a) **9 a5!?** d5!? (or the trivial 9 ... d6) 10 ed e4!? 11 dc ef 12 d4 fg 13 ♗g5 (13 c4!?) 13 ... ♘d5 14 ♗xe7 ♘xe7 15 d5 ♘g6 with good counterplay for Black (Suetin–Zaitsev, Moscow 1983).

(b) **9 d3** d6 10 ♘bd2 ♘a5 (also possible is 10 ... ♗e6 or 10 ... ♖b8) 11 ♗a2 ♗e6 12 ♘c4 ♘xc4 13 ♗xc4 ♗xc4 14 dc ♘d7 with full equality for Black.

(c) **9 d4** d6 10 de ♘xe5 (or 10 ... de 11 ♘bd2 ♗b7 12 ♕e2 ♘d4!? 13 ♕c4 ♗d6) 11 ♘xe5 de 12 ♕xd8 ♖xd8 13 ♘d2 a5 14 ♘c4 ♗d6 15 ♗g5 ♗e6 with approximate equality (Matulovic–Nemet, Yugoslavia 1972).

9 ... d6

Worthy of consideration is 9 ... d5!? 10 ed ♘xd5 (after 10 ... e4?! 11 dc ef 12 d4 fg 13 ♗g5 ♗g4 14 ♕d3 ♖e8 15 ♕g3 ♗h5 play is double-edged) 11 ♘xe5 ♘xe5 12 ♖xe5 ♘f6 13 d4 ♗d6.

10 a5

After 10 d4 ed (after 10 ... bc 11 de! ♘xe5 12 ♘xe5 de 13 ♘xc3 a5 14 ♘d5 White has the freer game; Keres–Smyslov, USSR Ch. 1955) 11 ♘xd4 (11 cd ♗g4 12 ♗e3 ♘a5 13 ♗c2 c5!) 11 ... ♗d7 12 cb ♘xb4 13 ♘c3 ♖b8 chances are equal (Keres).

10 ... ♖b8

In White's favour is 10 ... ♗g4 (10 ... ♗e6? 11 ♗a4 ♘xa5 12 cb favours White) 11 h3 ♗h5 12 ♗a4 ♘xa5 13 cb ♘b7 14 d4. After 10 ... bc 11 dc ♗e6 12 ♘bd2 ♗xb3 13 ♕xb3 ♕d7 White's chances are slightly better (Tal–Jansa, Sarajevo 1966).

11 ♗c4 *(186)*

White achieves nothing after 11 d4 bc! 12 bc ed 13 cd d5 14 e5 ♘e4!, or 11 d3 ♘d7 12 ♗a4 ♗b7 13 d4 bc 14 bc ed 15 cd ♗f6 etc.

186
B

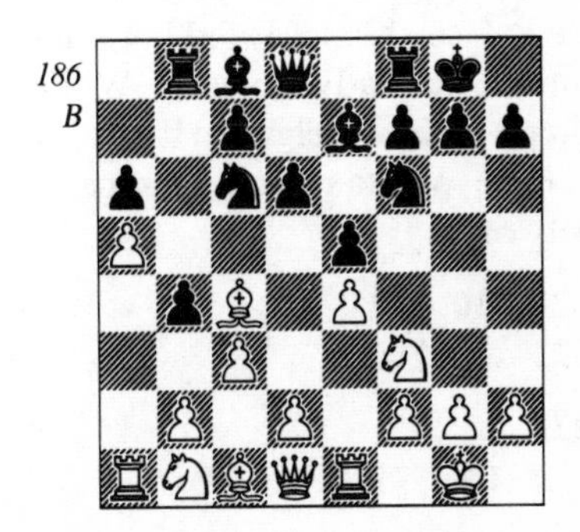

In this critical position the following variations are possible:

(a) **11 ... bc** (after 11 ... ♗b7 12 d3 d5 13 ed ♘xd5 14 ♕b3 White stands slightly better) 12 dc (12 ♘xc3 ♗g4) 12 ... ♗b7 13 ♘bd2 ♕c8 14 ♘f1 ♘d8 15 ♘g3 ♘e6 16 b4 ♖d8 with equal chances (Liberzon–Nikolaevsky, USSR 1966).

(b) **11 ... ♘a7!?** 12 ♕e2 ♗b7 13 d4 ♗xe4 14 de de 15 ♘bd2 ♗xf3 16 ♘xf3 c5 with full equality for Black (Ruderfer–Kirpichnikov, USSR 1967).

B2

8 ... ♗b7
9 d3

After 9 ♘c3 ♘d4!, or 9 c3 d5!, Black gets an excellent game.

9 ... d6 *(187)*

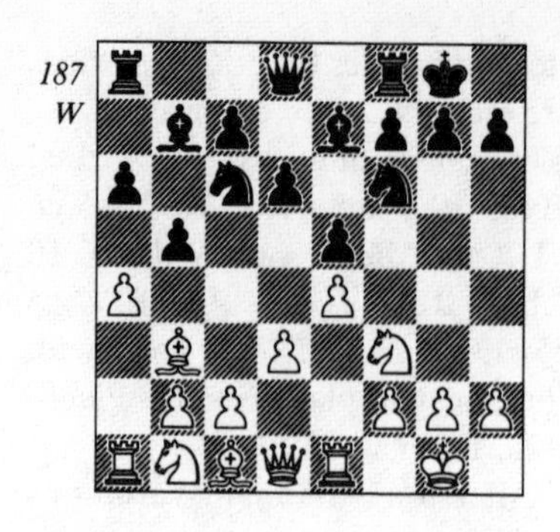

187
W

Let us consider the following variations:

(a) **9 ... ♖e8!?** 10 ♘c3 (or 10 c3 d6 11 ♘bd2 ♘a5 12 ♗a2 c5) 10 ... b4 11 ♘d5 ♘xd5 12 ♗xd5 ♗f6 13 ♗d2 ♖b8 14 c3!? bc 15 ♗xc3 ♕e7 with a strong position for Black (Suetin–Schmidt, Novi Sad 1989).

(b) **9 ... ♘a5** 10 ♗a2! d6 11 ♗d2 ♘c6 12 ♘c3 ♘d7 13 d4 with a clear advantage to White (Keres–Ivkov, Belgrade 1956).

Here White's main choice is between:

B21 10 ♘c3
B22 10 ♗d2

B21

10 ♘c3 ♘a5

White stands slightly better after 10 ... ♘d4 11 ♘xd4 ed 12 ♘e2 c5 13 ♘g3, or 10 ... b4? 11 ♘d5 ♘xd5 12 ♗xd5 ♘a5 13 ♗xb7 ♘xb7 14 c3 c5 15 cb cb 16 ♕b3 ♘c5 17 ♕d5 (Ljubojevic–Hübner, Tilburg 1985).

11 ♗a2 b4
12 ♘e2 c5 *(188)*

Let us briefly consider the following variations:

(a) **12 ... ♖b8** 13 ♘g3 b3 (after 13 ... ♗c8 14 d4 ♘c6 15 c3 bc 16 bc ♗g4 17 ♗e3 ed 18 cd ♘b4 19 ♗b1 ♖e8 20 h3 ♗c8 21 a5! White has some pressure; Yudasin–Agapov, USSR 1984) 14 cb (14 ♗d2!?) 14 ... c5 with roughly equal play (Psakhis–Geller, USSR 1982).

(b) **12 ... d5?!** 13 ed b3!? 14 ♗d2 (14 cb) 14 ... ♕xd5 15 ♘c3 ♕c6 16 cb ♖ad8 17 ♖xe5 ♗b4 18 ♕e2 ♕d6 19 ♖e1 ♕xd3 20 ♕xd3 ♖xd3 21 ♘e4! with better prospects for White (Gipslis–Ghitescu, Kecskemét 1968). Also in White's favour is 12 ... b3?! 13 cb c5 14 b4! cb 15 ♗d2 d5 16 ♘g3!

13 ♘g3

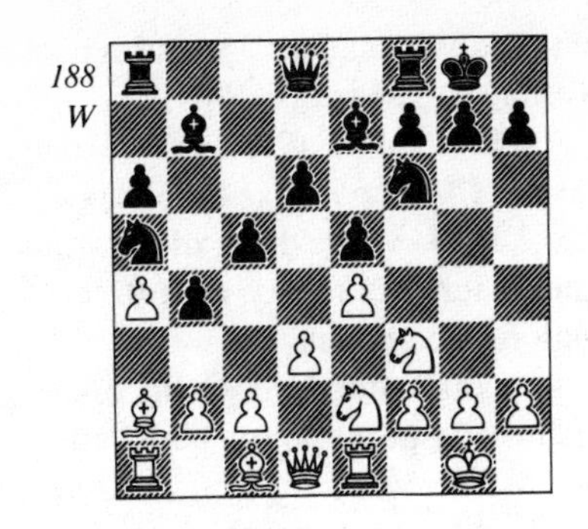
188
W

An alternative is **13 c3**, with the following variations:

(a) **13 ... bc** 14 bc c4 15 ♘g3 ♘d7!? (also possible is 15 ... ♖e8 16 dc ♘d7) 16 ♗a3 g6 17 d4 ♕c7! 18 ♖c1 ♖fe8 19 ♗b4 ♖ac8 20 ♘d2 d5! 21 ed ♗xd5 22 de ♗g5! with equal chances for Black (Kupreichik–Rodriguez, Minsk 1982).

(b) **13 ... c4!?** 14 ♘g3 (14 dc b3! with equality; Karpov–Nunn, London 1984) 14 ... cd 15 ♕xd3 b3 16 ♗b1 ♖e8 (also good is 16 ... ♘d7 or 16 ... g6) 17 ♘f5 ♗f8 18 ♗g5 h6 19 ♗xf6 ♕xf6 20 ♘e3 ♕d8 with equal chances (Psakhis–Hebden, Chicago 1983).

(c) **13 ... ♖b8** 14 cb cb 15 ♘g3 b3!? 16 ♗b1 d5 17 ♘xe5 de 18 d4 ♗b4! and here Black has no particular difficulties (Kupreichik–Psakhis, Yerevan 1982).

Let us return to the main line:

13 ... ♖b8

Also possible is 13 ... ♗c8 14 c3 bc 15 bc ♕c7, or 13 ... b3 14 ♗xb3! ♘xb3 15 cb ♘d7, with good chances of equality.

After 13 ... ♖b8 the following lines arise:

(a) **14 ♘d2** ♘e8 (after 14 ... ♗c8 15 h3 ♗e6 16 ♘c4 ♖e8 17 ♗d2 ♘c6 18 c3 d5 19 ed ♘xd5 20 a5! White stands somewhat better; Geller–P. Littlewood, Plovdiv 1983) 15 c3 bc 16 bc ♗c8 17 ♘f3 ♗f6 18 ♗e3 g6 with equal play (Gipslis–Ivkov, Zagreb 1965).

(b) **14 ♘f5** ♗c8 (also good is 14 ... b3 15 ♗xb3 ♘xb3! 16 cb ♗c8 17 ♘e3 ♗e6; Spassky–Karpov, London 1982) 15 ♘3h4 b3 16 ♗d2 (or 16 cb ♗e6 17 b4 c6 18 d4; Balashov–Razuvaev, USSR 1985) 16 ... bc 17 ♕xc2 ♖c8! with a lot of play for Black (Kupreichik–Malanyuk, Yerevan 1984).

B22

10 ♗d2 b4

A critical position. Let us consider some other possibilities for Black:

(a) **10 ... ♕d7** 11 ♘c3 ♘d4 12 ♘xd4 ed 13 ♘e2 c5 14 ♘g3 d5! 15 ed ♘xd5 16 h3 ♖fc8 17 ab ab 18 ♖xa8 ♗xa8 19 ♕g4 ♕xg4 20 hg e4! with excellent play for Black (Geller–Spassky, USSR 1963).

(b) **10 ... ♘d7** 11 ♘c3 ♘c5 12 ♗d5 b4 13 ♘e2 ♗f6 14 ♗e3 ♘e7 15 ♗c4 ♘e6 16 ♘g3 ♘g6 17 c3 bc 18 bc d5 with equality (Geller–Tal, Havana 1963).

In White's favour is 10 ... ♘d4?! 11 ♘xd4 ed 12 ab ab 13 ♖xa8 ♗xa8 14 c3 dc 15 ♘xc3 ♕d7 16 ♘e2 c5 17 ♘g3.

11 c3 *(189)*

After 11 a5!? d5 12 ♗g5 de 13 de ♘xe4 14 ♗xe7 ♘ex7 15 ♘xe5 ♘f5 (Kupreichik–P. Littlewood, Hastings 1982), or 11 ♗g5 ♘d7 12 ♗xe7 ♘xe7 13 ♘bd2 a5, chances are equal.

189
B

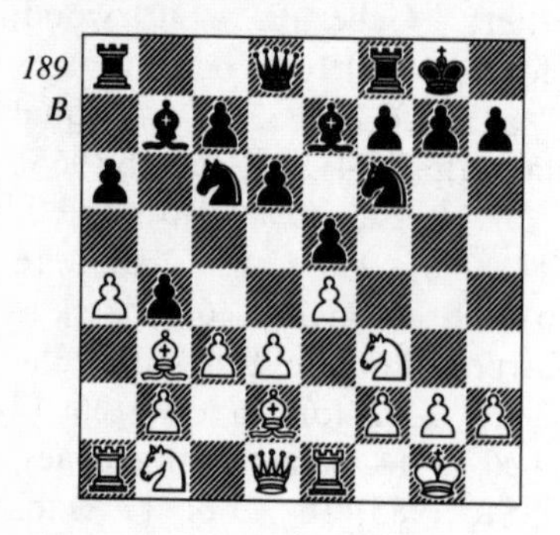

After 11 c3 the following variations are possible:

(a) **11 ... bc** 12 ♘xc3 ♘a5 13 d4 ♘xb3 14 ♕xb3 ♖b8 15 ♕c2 d5 with equal chances (Matulovic–Reshevsky, Maribor 1967).

(b) **11 ... d5!?** 12 cb de! 13 de ♘xb4 14 ♘xe5 ♘xe4 15 ♘xf7 ♖xf7 16 ♕f3 ♗d5 17 ♗xd5 ♘xd5 and Black has plenty of counterplay for the pawn.

In conclusion we shall once again compare points "for and against". It would appear that the solution to the principal problems is to be found in accepting the challenge and not avoiding the Marshall Attack. Incidentally, such is the logic of opening theory — no avoidance of the fight on White's part, even though such a decision may be reliable from a practical point of view, can rightfully be considered to have theoretical importance.

13 Unusual Closed Variations

We now come to the Closed Systems, which have enjoyed lasting popularity and can take many forms. Most commonly they arise from the move order 1 e4 e5 2 ♘f3 ♘c6 3 ♗b5 a6 4 ♗a4 ♘f6 5 0–0 ♗e7 6 ♖e1 b5 7 ♗b3 d6 *(190)*.

The systems which we are now going to study occupy a leading place in the theory of the Spanish Opening. Events in the centre in these cases are usually not forced, and the game may for a long time remain closed. All of this determines the complexity of the problems arising and this is why these systems remain permanently topical.

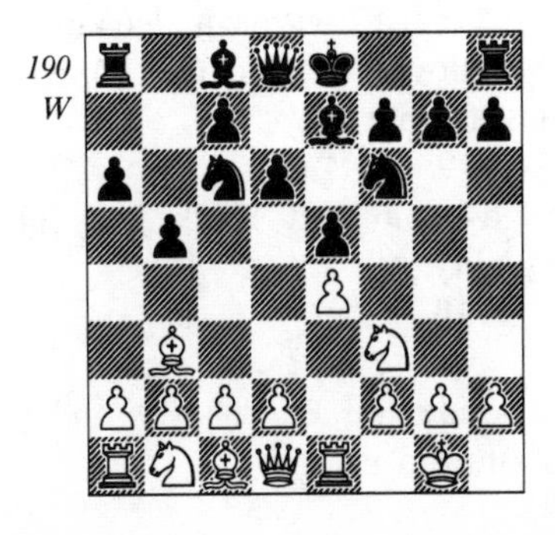

Before going on to consider the main lines, we shall take a look at some which are less popular:

A **8 a4** and **8 d4**
B **8 c3**

A

(a) **8 a4!?** This is a move rather neglected by theory and is rarely played. Black has a number of good lines. For example: 8 ... b4 9 d4!? ♗g4 10 de ♘xe5 (also not bad is 10 ... ♗xf3 11 ♕xf3 de 12 ♗c4 0–0 13 ♘d2 ♘d4!?; Balashov–Rivas, Minsk 1982) 11 ♘bd2 0–0 12 h3 ♗e6 13 ♘xe5 de 14 ♗xe6 fe 15 ♕e2 ♗c5 16 ♘b3 ♗d6! with double-edged play (Kupreichik–Zaitsev, Minsk 1983); 8 ... ♘a5 9 ab (interesting is 9 ♗a2 c5 10 d3) 9 ... ♘xb3 10 cb ♗b7 11 ba ♗xa6 12 d4 ♗b7 13 ♖xa8 ♕xa8 14 ♗g5 0–0 15 de de 16 ♘xe5 ♖d8 17 ♕e2 h6 18 ♕c4 hg 19 ♕xf7+ ♔h7 20 ♕xe7 ♗xe4 21 ♕e6 ♖e8! with approximate equality (Kupreichik–Kuzmin, Yerevan 1982).

Also not bad is 8 ... ♗g4, or 8 ... ♗d7 9 c3 ♘a5 10 ♗c2 c5 11 d4 ♕b8!? 12 ♗g5 h6 13 ♗h4

♗g4 14 ♘bd2 0–0 (Nunn–Romanishin, Wijk aan Zee 1985).

(b) **8 d4?!** ♘xd4 9 ♘xd4 ed 10 a4 ♗b7 11 c3 dc 12 ♘xc3 0–0 with excellent play for Black (Taubenhaus–Teichmann, Monte Carlo 1903).

White gets nothing after 8 h3?! ♘a5 9 ♘c3 0–0 10 d3 ♖e8 etc.

B

8 c3 0–0

Here we may single out the following alternatives:

(a) **8 ... ♘a5** 9 ♗c2 c5 10 d4 ♕c7 11 a4 (also good is 11 ♘bd2 ♘c6 12 dc dc 13 ♘f1 ♗e6 14 ♘e3) 11 ... b4 (passive is 11 ... ♖b8 12 ab ab 13 dc dc 14 ♘bd2 ♘c6 15 ♘f1 0–0 16 ♘e3 ♗e6 17 ♘g5 ♖bd8 18 ♕e2! with pressure for White; Levenfish–Lilienthal, Moscow 1939) 12 cb cb 13 h3 0–0 14 ♘bd2 ♗d7 15 ♘f1 ♖fe8 16 ♘e3 ♘c6 17 ♗b3! with pressure for White (Unzicker–Sanchez, Stockholm 1952).

(b) **8 ... ♗g4** 9 d3 ♘a5 10 ♗c2 c5 11 ♘bd2 0–0 12 h3! ♗h5 13 g4! ♗g6 14 ♘g3 (O'Kelly–van Scheltinga, Beverwijk 1963) and a typical position has arisen, which favours White.

The most common reply to 8 ... 0–0 is 9 h3, which is dealt with in the following chapters. Here we look at the alternatives:

B1 9 d3
B2 9 a4
B3 9 a3
B4 9 d4

B1

9 d3 *(191)*

191
B

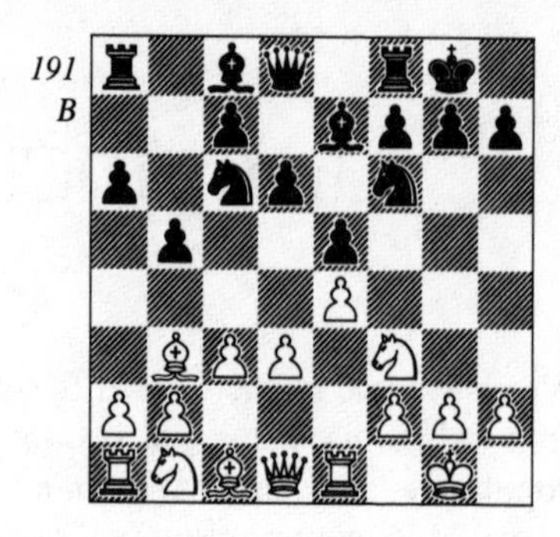

Avoiding skirmishes in the centre, White first intends to complete his development. But this can give him no more than a safe position — to a large extent his activity fades away. At the present time this continuation is hardly ever encountered.

9 ... ♘a5

Let us also consider some other lines:

(a) **9 ... ♗e6** 10 ♘bd2 (10 ♗c2 d5!; 10 ♗xe6 fe 11 ♘bd2 ♕d7) 10 ... ♗xb3 11 ♕xb3 (11 ab d5) 11 ... ♘d7 12 a4 ♘a5 13 ♕c2 c6 14 b4 ♘b7 15 c4 ♕c7 16 ♗b2 ba 17 ♖xa4 a5 with equal chances (Matulovic–Matanovic, Yugoslavia 1956).

(b) **9 ... ♘d7** 10 ♗c2 ♘b6 11 d4 ♗f6 and Black gets full equality.

10 ♗c2 c5
11 ♘bd2 ♘c6

Besides this, Black has a number of other plans:

(a) **11 … ♘d7** 12 ♘f1 ♗f6 13 ♘e3 ♘b6 14 d4 ♘ac4 15 ♘xc4 ♘xc4 16 b3 ♘a5 17 dc dc 18 ♕xd8 ♖xd8 19 ♗e3 ♘b7 with roughly equal chances (Ivkov–Matanovic, Zagreb 1955).

(b) **11 … ♖e8** 12 ♘f1 ♗f8 13 ♘e3 h6 14 a3 ♘c6 15 b4 a5 with double-edged play (Kostro–Nilsson, Poland 1969).

12 ♘f1 *(192)*

Black has no difficulties after 12 a4 ♗e6 (also not bad is 12 … ♗b7 13 ♘f1 ♖e8) 13 ♘f1 ♕c7 14 ♕e2 ♘h5 or 14 … ♘d7 15 ♘e3 ♘b6; or 12 ♕e2 ♖e8 13 ♘f1 d5 14 ed ♘xd5 15 ♗d2 ♗f8 16 ♘g3 (Ilyin-Zhenevsky–Botvinnik, USSR 1931).

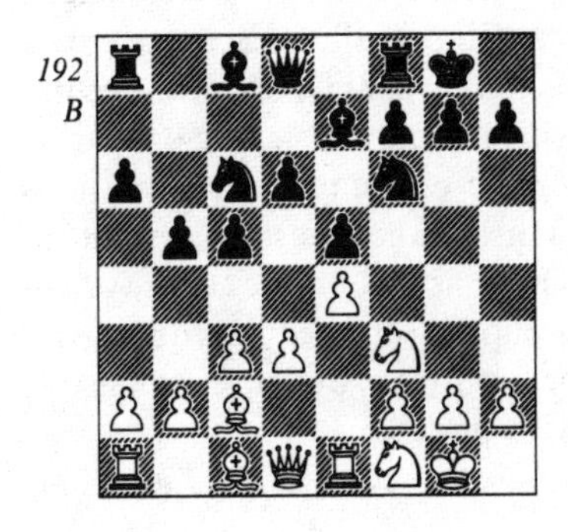
192
B

After 12 ♘f1 the following variations arise:

(a) **12 … ♖e8** 13 ♘e3 ♗f8 (dangerous is 13 … d5? 14 ed ♘xd5 15 ♘xd5 ♕xd5 16 d4! cd 17 ♗e4! with an attack for White; Alekhine–Eliskases, Podebrady 1936) 14 a4 ♗b7 (also good is 14 … ♗d7 15 ♗d2 g6) 15 h3 ♕c7 16 ♘f5 ♘e7 17 ♘3h4 ♘g6 18 ♗g5 ♘d7 19 ♘xg6 hg 20 ♘e3 ♘b6 with equal chances (Ivkov–Filip, Zagreb 1955).

(b) **12 … ♘d7** 13 ♘g3 ♘b6 14 h3 ♖e8 15 ♕e2 g6 and Black has a strong defence (Matulovic–Ivkov, Yugoslavia 1955).

(c) **12 … ♗e6** 13 ♘e3 h6 14 ♕e2 ♕c7 and then ♖ad8 with full equality for Black (Alekhine).

B2

9 a4

Not a very popular continuation. After 9 … b4! 10 d4 bc (also not bad is 10 … ♖b8 or 10 … ed 11 ♘xd4 ♗d7) 11 de (11 bc ♗g4 12 ♗e3 ed 13 cd d5 14 e5 ♘e4 is good for Black) 11 … ♘xe5 12 ♘xe5 de 13 ♘xc3 ♖b8 14 ♘d5 ♘xd5 15 ♗xd5 ♗b7 with equality (Polugayevsky).

B3

9 a3 *(193)*

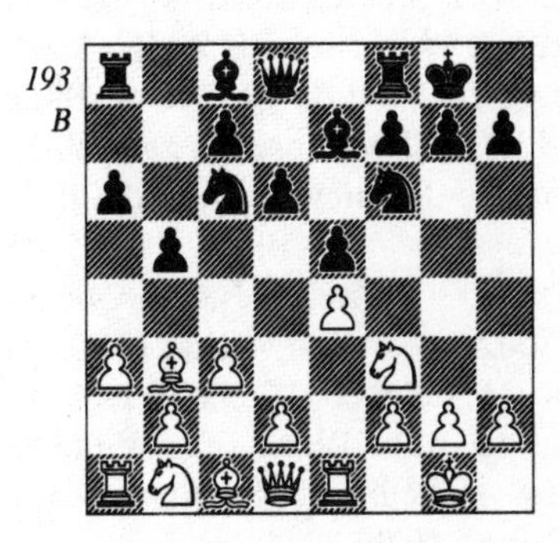
193
B

This move was first played in the game Suetin–Stein, USSR Ch. 1965. White does not wish to waste a tempo on the prophylactic move 9 h3 and so plays a different move, 9 a3, which is useful in a number of variations. (For example: 9 ... ♘b8 10 d4 ♘bd7 11 c4 c6 12 ♘c3 and Black does not have the move b5–b4.) I already have great experience with this move of my own invention. Objectively it cannot claim to lead to an advantage. Moreover it can hardly compete on equal terms with 9 h3! But the move has certain subtleties and for the unprepared opponent it is not easy to solve the practical problems which arise.

The following variations are possible:

(a **9 ... ♗e6** 10 d4 ♗xb3 (10 ... ♗g4!?) 11 ♕xb3 d5! 12 ed ♘a5 13 ♕c2 ed 14 cd ♘xd5 15 ♘c3 ♖e8 16 ♗g5 f6 17 ♗h4 ♘xc3 18 ♕xc3 ♘c4 with good chances of equality for Black (Suetin–Lukács, Leipzig 1986).

(b) **9 ... ♗g4** 10 h3 ♗h5 11 d3 ♘a5 12 ♗c2 c5 13 ♘bd2 ♕c7 14 ♘f1 ♖ad8 15 ♘g3 (15 g4!?) 15 ... ♗g6 16 ♘h4! d5 17 ♕e2 de 18 de c4 19 ♘hf5 with pressure for White (Suetin–Stoinev, Novi Sad 1989).

(c) **9 ... ♘d7** 10 d4 ♗f6 11 d5 ♘a5 (11 ... ♘e7) 12 ♗a2 ♘b6 13 ♘bd2 c6 14 b4! ♘ac4 15 ♗xc4 bc 16 dc ♗e6 17 ♗e3! ♖b8 18 ♘bd2 and Black has quite a few difficulties (Suetin–Lukács, Dubna 1979).

(d) **9 ... ♘a5** 10 ♗c2 c5 11 d4 ♕c7 12 ♘bd2 ♘c6 13 d5 (or 13 dc dc 14 ♘f1) transposing to the Chigorin System.

(e) **9 ... d5?!** 10 ed ♘xd5 (10 ... e4?! 11 dc ef 12 d4 fg 13 ♗g5 ♕d6 14 ♘d2! favours White; Suetin–Zaitsev, Sochi 1978) 11 ♘xe5 ♘xe5 12 ♖xe5 c6 13 d4 ♗d6 14 ♖e1 ♕h4 15 g3 ♕h3 16 ♗e3 ♗g4 17 ♕d3 ♖ae8 18 ♘bd2 and then c3–c4, with better chances for White (Suetin–Lilienthal, Kislovodsk 1967).

Possibly the best move after 9 a3 is 9 ... h6, and if 10 d4 then 10 ... ♗g4! with good counterplay for Black. Therefore White has to continue with 10 h3 and then d2–d4, transposing to the Smyslov System.

B4

9 d4

This natural desire to begin active operations immediately in the centre leads to double-edged play, since it allows Black to create pressure against White's centre with the move 9 ... ♗g4. Characteristic of a number of variations in this line is the strategic problem: which is the more effective — occupying the centre with pawns, or applying pressure against it with pieces?

9 ... ♗g4 *(194)*

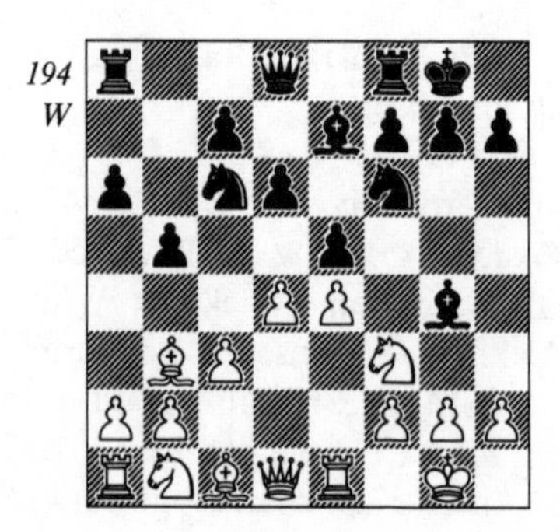
194
W

Worse is 9 ... ed 10 cd ♗g4 11 ♘c3! ♘a5 (or 11 ... ♗xf3 12 gf ♘a5 13 ♗c2 b4 14 ♘e2 c5 15 d5 ♘e8 16 ♘g3 g6 17 ♗h6 with an initiative for White) 12 ♗c2 c5 13 dc dc 14 e5 (Lasker–Bogoljubow, Moravská Ostrava 1923). After 9 ... ♗g4 White has two main plans:

B41 10 ♗e3
B42 10 d5

B41

10 ♗e3 *(195)*

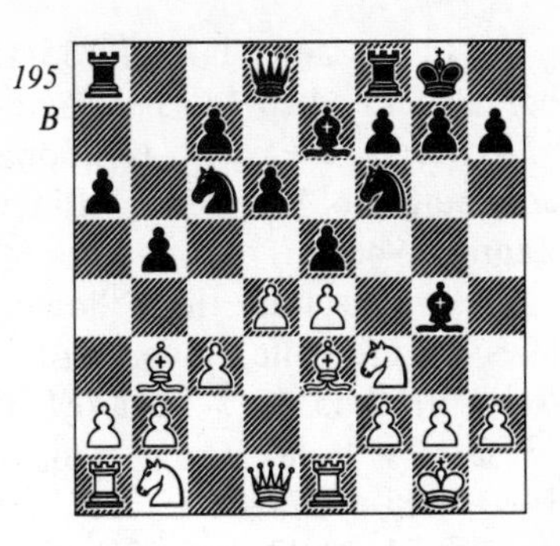
195
B

Let us also consider the following variations:

(a) **10 a4** ♕d7 11 d5 (11 ♕d3 ♗xf3 12 gf ed 13 cd ♘b4 14 ♕f1 c5! is good for Black) 11 ... ♘a5 12 ♗c2 c6 13 h3 ♗h5 14 dc ♕xc6 (also not bad is 14 ... ♘xc6) 15 ♘bd2 ♘b7 16 ♘f1 ♘c5 17 ♘g3 ♗g6 18 ♘h4 ♖fe8 19 ♘hf5 ♗f8 20 ♕f3 ba 21 h4 h5! and already White has to fight for equality.

(b) **10 ♕d3** ♗xf3 11 gf ♘a5 12 f4 ♘xb3 13 ab ♘d7 14 ♘a3 ed 15 cd c5 16 d5 ♗f6 17 ♔c2 ♖e8 and here White has difficulties (Tolush–Bronstein, USSR Ch. 1958).

(c) **10 h3** ♗xf3 11 ♕xf3!? ed 12 ♕d1 dc 13 ♘xc3 ♘a5 14 ♗c2 ♖e8 (also good is 14 ... c5 15 ♘e2 ♘c6 16 ♘g3 ♘d4) 15 f4 b4 16 ♘d5 ♘xd5 17 ♕xd5 c6 18 ♕d3 g6 19 ♔h1 ♗f8 20 ♖f1 d5! with better chances for Black.

10 ... ed

The classical continuation, which has been the centre of attention for a long time. We shall also consider the following variations:

(a) **10 ... d5!?** 11 ed ed 12 ♗xd4!? (12 ♗g5 ♘xd5!? 13 ♗xd5 ♕xd5 14 ♗xe7 ♗xf3 15 ♕xf3 ♕xf3 16 gf ♖fe8 17 cd ♘xe7 with excellent play for Black; Toth–Perenyi, Italy 1977) 12 ... ♘xd4 13 cd ♖e8 (also not bad is 13 ... ♗b4 14 ♘c3 a5 15 a3 ♗xc3 16 bc a4 17 ♗a2 ♕d6 18 h3; Gulko–Geller, Lvov 1978; with 18 ... ♗h5! Black can maintain equal chances) 14 h3 ♗h5 15 ♘c3 ♗d6 16 ♕d3 ♗g6 17 ♕f1 b4 18 ♖xe8 ♘xe8 19 ♘a4 ♗e4 and Black has no difficulties (van Riemsdijk–Wang Zili, Thessaloniki OL 1988).

(b) **10 ... ♗h5!?** 11 ♘bd2 (or 11 h3 ♖e8 12 ♘bd2 ♗f8 13 d5 ♘a5 14 ♗c2 ♖c8 15 b4 ♘b7 16 a4 c6 17 ab ab 18 ♖a7 ♕c7 19 dc ♕xc6; Gulko–Romanishin, Lvov 1978) 11 ... d5!? 12 ed ♘xd5 13 de ♘xe5 14 ♗g5 ♘d3 15 ♗d5 ♗g5 16 ♗xa8 ♘xe1 17 ♕xe1 ♗d2 (Chandler–Romanishin, Leningrad 1987), with equal play in both cases.

(c) **10 … ♖e8** 11 ♘bd2 d5 12 h3! ♗h5 13 g4 ed 14 ♘xd4 ♘xd4 15 cd ♗g6 16 e5 with positional advantage to White (Puc–Bidev, Zagreb 1946).

Note also that the following lines are in White's favour: 10 … ♘xe4 11 ♗d5 ♕d7 12 ♗xe4 d5 13 ♗xh7+ ♔xh7 14 de ♕e6 (or 14 … ♕f5 15 ♘d4!) 15 ♗d4!; 10 … ♕c8 11 ♘bd2 ♘a5 12 ♗c2 c5 13 d5 ♘e8 14 h3!; 10 … ♕d7 11 ♘bd2 ♖ad8 12 a4 ♕c8 13 ab ab 14 ♕e2; and finally 10 … ♘a5 11 de ♗xf3 12 ♕xf3 de 13 ♗c2 ♘c4 14 ♗c1 c5 15 ♖d1 ♕c7 16 ♘bd2.

11 cd ♘a5

Interesting is 11 … d5!? 12 e5 ♘e4 13 h3 (13 ♘c3 ♘xc3 14 bc ♘a5 — 14 … ♕d7!? — 15 ♗c2 ♘c4 16 ♗c1 ♕d7 or 16 … f5 leads to equality; also interesting is 13 ♘bd2!? ♘xd2 — 13 … ♘a5 — 14 ♕xd2 ♗xf3 15 gf ♗b4 16 ♕c2 ♘a5! and then ♘c4 with approximate equality — Suetin) 13 … ♗h5 14 g4 (14 ♘c3 ♘xc3 15 bc ♘a5 16 ♗c2 ♘c4 17 g4 ♗g6 18 ♗f5!; Sznapik–van der Wiel, Copenhagen 1984) 14 … ♗g6 15 ♘h2 a5 (15 … ♗b4!?) 16 a4 ba 17 ♗xa4 ♘b4 with roughly equal chances (Khalifman–Aseev, USSR 1983).

12 ♗c2 *(196)*

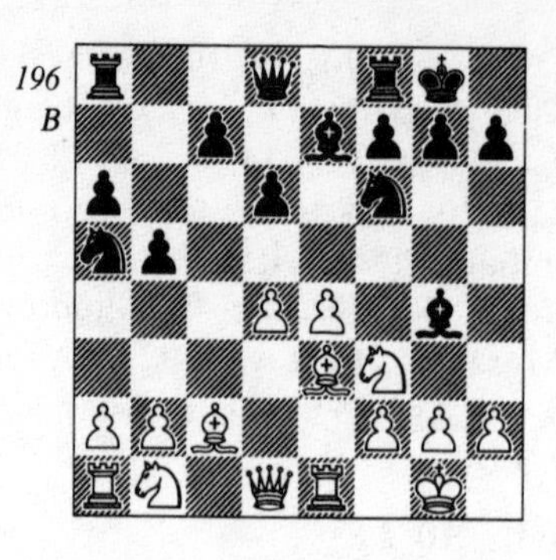

196
B

A critical position, where Black has the following possibilities:

(a) **12 … ♘c4** 13 ♗c1 c5 14 b3 ♘b6 (14 … ♘a5 15 d5! ♘d7 16 ♘bd2 ♗f6 17 ♖b1 ♘e5 — 17 … c4!? — 18 h3 ♘xf3+ 19 ♘xf3 ♗xf3 20 ♕xf3 ♖e8 21 ♗f4! with somewhat better chances for White; Tal–Gligoric, match 1968) 15 ♘bd2, and now:

(a1) **15 … ♖c8** 16 ♗b2 ♘fd7 17 h3 ♗h5 18 dc ♘xc5 19 g4 ♗g6 20 ♘d4 ♗f6 21 ♘2f3 ♖e8 with plenty of counterplay for Black (Lukin–Geller, USSR 1978).

(a2) **15 … ♘fd7** 16 h3 ♗h5 17 d5!? ♗f6 18 ♖b1 ♗c3 19 ♖e3 b4 20 g4 ♗g6 21 ♘f1 with a small advantage to White (Yudasin–Timoshchenko, USSR 1982).

Worthy of consideration is 15 dc!? (instead of 15 ♘bd2) 15 … dc 16 ♘bd2 ♘fd7 17 ♗b2 ♖e8 18 e5 ♘f8 19 ♕e2 ♗h5 20 a4! with some pressure for White.

(b) **12 … c5** 13 dc!? dc 14 ♘bd2 ♘d7 15 h3 (or 15 ♕b1 ♖e8 16 e5 ♘f8 17 ♗f5 ♗xf5 18 ♕xf5 ♕d5 19 b3 c4 20 ♖ed1 ♕b7 21 bc ♘xc4 22 ♘xc4 bc 23 ♕c2 ♕c7; Barle–Nikolic, Yugoslavia 1985; or 15 ♗f4 ♕b6 16 e5 ♖ad8; Gulko–Geller, USSR 1985) 15 … ♗h5 16 ♖c1 (or 16 g4!? ♗g6 17 ♘h2 ♘c6 18 f4 f6 19 ♘df3 ♕c7 20 ♘h4 ♗f7 with equal play; Kurajica–

Jelen, Yugoslavia 1977) 16 … ♖e8 17 b3 ♖c8 18 ♗b1 ♗f6 19 ♕e2 ♗b2 20 ♖cd1 ♗c3 21 e5! with a certain initiative for White (Tseshkovsky–Dorfman, Moscow 1985).

B42

10 d5

Perhaps it is precisely this straightforward move, closing the centre, which at the present time sets Black the most problems in the variation with 9 d4. The struggle revolves mainly around the centre, where Black has the possibility of undermining it with c7–c6 and, after White exchanges pawns, of bringing about an effective opening-up of the game by means of d6–d5.

In evaluating the situations which arise, one should not lose sight of the fact that, after the game is opened up, White's pieces will come alive, especially his light-squared bishop. As a rule, a dynamic game develops.

10 … ♘a5
11 ♗c2 c6

A natural and apparently correct reaction.

Let us also consider the following variations:

(a) **11 … ♕c8!** 12 h3 (12 a4 c6!) 12 … ♗d7 13 ♘bd2 c6 14 dc (or 14 b4 ♘b7 15 dc ♕xc6 16 ♗b2 ♘d8 17 ♗d3 ♘e6 18 c4 ♕b7 19 a3 ♘f4 20 ♗f1 ♖ac8 21 ♖ac1 ♗c6 with full equality for Black; Tseshkovsky–Romanishin, USSR 1979) 14 … ♗xc6 (14 … ♕xc6 15 ♘f1 ♘c4 16 a4 ♖ac8 17 ♘g3 with a minimal advantage to White; Khalifman–Balashov, USSR 1987) 15 b4!? ♘b7 16 ♘f1 ♘d8 17 ♘g3 ♘e6 18 ♗b3 with unclear play (Khalifman–Belyavsky, USSR 1988).

(b) **11 … ♕d7!?** 12 ♘bd2 c6 13 h3 ♗h5 14 b4! ♘b7 15 ♘f1 and the unfortunate position of the knight on b7 clearly gives White the better game (Spielmann–Marshall, Carlsbad 1911).

In White's favour is 11 … ♘c4 12 h3 ♗d7 13 a4 ♘b6 14 a5 ♘c8 15 b3 c5 16 b4 (Sax–Gligoric, Osijek 1978), or 11 … c5 12 h3 ♗d7 13 ♘bd2.

12 h3 *(197)*

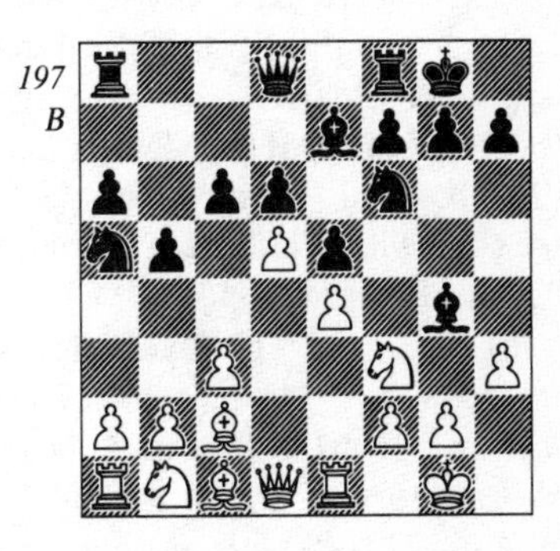

197
B

A topical continuation, which still contains a few mysteries. Until recently the most frequent continuation was 12 dc ♕c7 13 ♘bd2, with the following variations:

(a) **13 … ♕xc6** 14 ♘f1 (14 h3 ♗e6!) 14 … ♘c4 (also possible is 14 … ♖fe8!? 15 h3 ♗e6) 15 ♕e2 ♖fc8 16 ♘e3 ♘xe3 17 ♗xe3 h6 18 ♗d2 ♗d8 19 ♗b3 ♗h5 with a comfortable game for Black

(Karestoichev–Kolarov, Bulgaria 1960).

(b) **13 … ♘xc6** 14 h3 (14 ♘f1 b4!) 14 … ♗e6 15 ♘g5 ♗d7 16 ♘f1 ♖ac8 17 ♘e3 g6 18 ♗d2 ♘d8 19 ♗b3 ♔g7 and Black's defence is strong (Stein–Tukmakov, Sochi 1970).

12 … ♗xf3

Let us also consider other variations:

(a) **12 … ♗c8** 13 dc ♕c7 14 ♘bd2 (or 14 a4 b4 15 cb ♘c6; Malanyuk–Smyslov, USSR 1988); by playing 16 b5!? ab 17 ♘c3 ba 18 ♖xa4 White was able to maintain the pressure) 14 … ♕xc6 15 ♘f1 (or 15 ♖e3!? g6 16 b4 ♘c4 17 ♗xc4 bc 18 ♖e1 ♕c7 19 ♘h2 d5 with equality; Soltis–Reshevsky, USA 1957) 15 … h6 16 ♘g3 ♖e8 17 ♘h4 ♗f8 18 ♘hf5 ♗b7 19 ♘h5 and White's prospects are somewhat better (Khalifman–Petran, Rotterdam 1988).

(b) **12 … ♗d7** 13 ♘xe5! de 14 d6 ♗xd6 (or 14 … ♗e6 15 de ♕e7 16 ♕f3 ♖fd8 17 ♕g3 ♘d7 18 b3 ♘c6 19 ♘d2 a5 20 ♘f3 f6 21 ♘h4 a4 22 ♘f5 with pressure for White; Khalifman–Nenashev, USSR 1987).

(c) **12 … ♗h5** 13 dc ♘xc6 14 ♗g5! ♕b6 15 ♘bd2 ♖ad8 16 ♗b3 ♘d7 17 ♗e3 ♕c7 18 ♘f1 ♘a5 19 ♘g3 ♗g6 20 a4 ♘c5 21 ♗xc5! dc 22 ♗d5 with clearly better prospects for White (Belyavsky–Kuzmin, Lvov 1977).

13 ♕xf3 cd
14 ed ♘c4 *(198)*

198
W

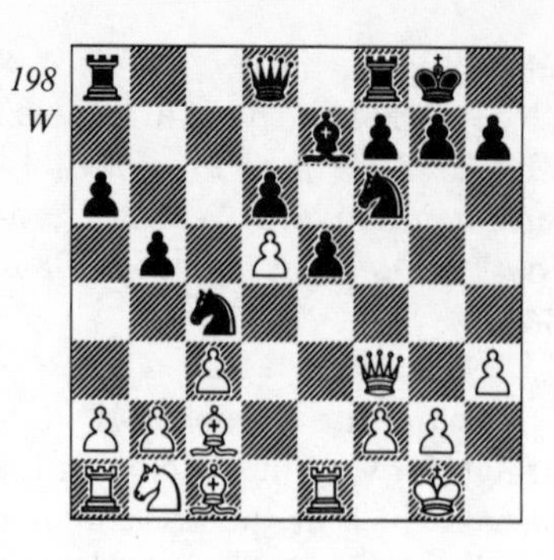

Other possibilities are evidently worse:

(a) **14 … ♖c8** 15 b3 g6 (15 … ♘b7 16 b4!) 16 ♗h6 ♖e8 17 ♘d2 ♕c7 18 ♖e3 ♘h5 19 g4 ♘g7 20 h4 ♖f8 21 h5 b4 22 c4 with strong pressure for White (Vasyukov–Vogt, Cienfuegos 1975).

(b) **14 … ♕c7** 15 ♘d2 g6 16 b4 and here Black has difficulties (Vogt–Lukács, Kecskemét 1977).

15 ♘bd2

After 15 a4?! ♘b6 16 ♖d1 ♕c7 17 ab ab 18 ♘a3 b4!? Black has good counterplay (Bronstein–Geller, USSR 1975).

15 … ♘b6

After 15 … ♖c8 16 ♘xc4 ♖xc4 17 a4 White has some initiative.

16 ♘f1 *(199)*

199
B

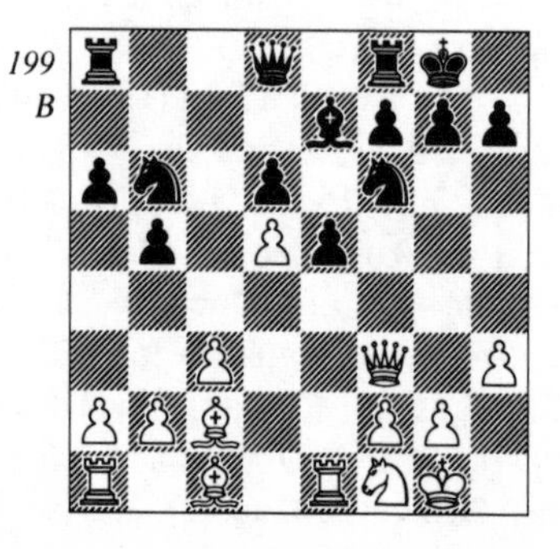

And now:

B421 **16 ... ♘bxd5**
B422 **16 ... ♘e8**

B421

16 ... ♘bxd5
17 ♘g3 ♘c7

Interesting is 17 ... g6 18 ♗h6 ♖e8 19 ♘f5 ♗f8 (Nikitin).

18 a4

Also possible is 18 ♘f5 ♘e6 19 a4 ba 20 ♖xa4 g6 21 ♘xe7+ ♕xe7 22 ♗h6 and then ♖xa1, with an initiative for White (Gufeld–Gaprindashvili, Tbilisi 1977).

18 ... ba

And now:

(a) **19 ♗xa4** ♖b8 20 b4 ♘e8 21 ♗e3 ♘b5 22 ♗c2 ♖c8 23 ♖xa6 ♖xc3 24 ♖a8 ♕c7 25 ♕d5 (Romanishin–Geller, USSR Ch. 1975). By playing 25 ... ♘d4! Black was able to equalise.

(b) **19 ♘e4!?** ♘xe4 20 ♖xe4 a3 21 ♖xa3 ♗g5 22 ♗xg5 ♕xg5 23 ♖ea4 ♕c1+ with chances for both sides (Tseshkovsky–Zakharov, USSR 1976).

B422

16 ... ♘e8

Other variations:

(a) **16 ... ♘fd7** 17 ♘g3 g6 18 ♗h6 ♖e8 19 ♘f5!? ♘c5 20 ♘xe7+ ♕xe7 21 ♖ad1 ♖ac8 22 ♕g3 and White stands better (Lemachko–Akhmilovskaya, match 1977).

(b) **16 ... ♕c7** 17 ♘g3 g6 18 ♗h6 ♖fc8! 19 ♖ad1 ♘fd7 20 ♘f5 ♗f8 21 ♖e4?! ♕d8 22 ♖g4 ♖c4! and White's attack has choked.

14 a4

And now:

(a) **17 ... ba!** 18 ♗xa4 ♘xa4 19 ♖xa4 f5 20 c4 ♕c8 21 ♗d2 ♘f6 22 ♘g3 g6 23 ♖ea1 ♘d7 24 ♕e2 ♘b6 25 ♖b4 ♗d8 26 b3 with a small advantage to White (Gufeld–Tseitlin, USSR 1976).

(b) **17 ... g6** 18 ab ab 19 ♗h6 ♘g7 20 ♗d3 b4 21 cb ♖xa1 22 ♖xa1 ♗g5 23 ♗xg5 ♕xg5 24 ♖a7 ♕f4 25 ♕xf4 ef 26 b5 with a clear advantage for White in the ending (Adorjan–Gligoric, Osijek 1978).

In White's favour is 17 ... ♘xa4 18 ♗xa4 ba 19 ♖e4! ♗g5 20 ♗xg5 ♕xg5 21 ♖exa4 etc.

14 Chigorin Defence

In the remaining chapters we shall deal with the Closed Systems which arise after the sequence 1 e4 e5 2 ♘f3 ♘c6 3 ♗b5 a6 4 ♗a4 ♘f6 5 0–0 ♗e7 6 ♖e1 b5 7 ♗b3 d6.

8 c3 0–0
9 h3 *(200)*

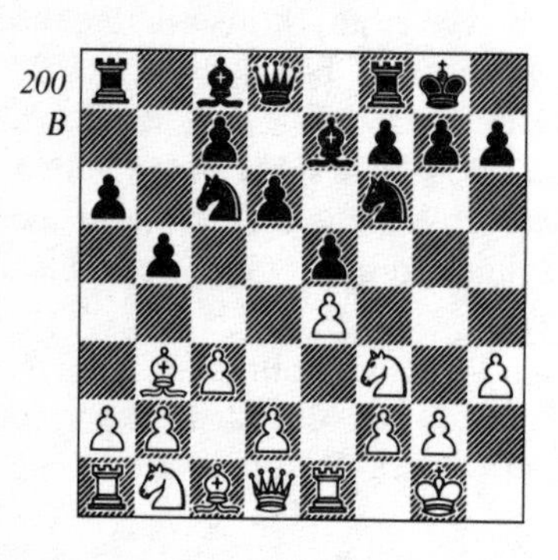

200
B

Only familiarity with the material in the previous chapter will help the reader to understand how this modest move can be such an important link in White's plans. This is the position that forms the starting-point for our remaining analysis. Black has a wide choice in this position: Chigorin's Defence — 9 ... ♘a5; Chigorin's Classical System — 9 ... ♘d7; the system with 9 ... ♗e6; Smyslov's System with 9 ... h6; the Modern System — 9 ... ♗b7 10 d4 ♖e8; the system with 9 ... a5; and finally the Breyer System — 9 ... ♘b8. We shall start with the most 'orthodox'.

9 ... ♘a5
10 ♗c2 *(201)*

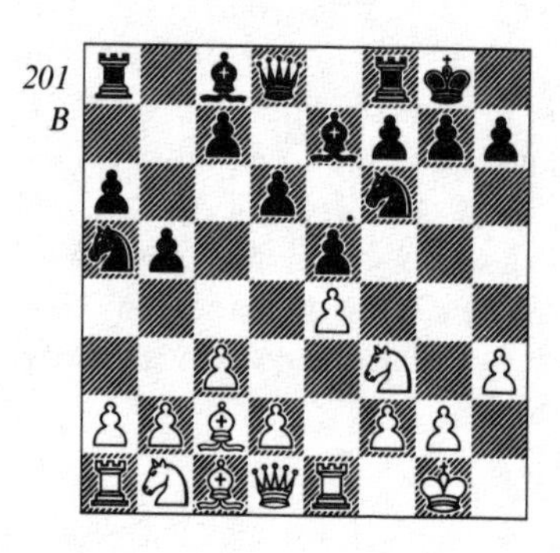

201
B

10 ... c5

Black begins active counterplay on the queenside. Not in the spirit of this system is 10 ... c6 11 d4 (also good is 11 a4) 11 ... ♕c7 12 ♘bd2 (a line that has not been tested is 12 ♘h2!? c5 13 de de 14 ♘d2) 12 ... ♘d7 (worthy of consideration is 12 ... ♖e8 13 ♘f1 ♘c4 14 a4 ♘b6 15 ab cb 16

♕e2 ♗f8 with a solid defensive position for Black; Olafsson–Lombardy, Reykjavik 1957) 13 ♘f1 ♗f6 14 ♘e3 ♘b6 15 ♘g4 ♗xg4 16 hg c5 17 d5! with advantage to White (Konstantinov–Simagin, USSR 1948).

White also has the better prospects after 10 … ♘d7 11 a4 b4 12 d4 c5 13 cb cb 14 b3 ♗f6 15 ♗b2 (Zakharov–Budarin, USSR 1962).

Hardly ever played are 10 … ♘c4?! 11 d4 ♗b7, and 10 … ♗b7 11 d4 d5.

11 d4

11 a4?! ♗d7 12 d4 ♕c7 13 ♘bd2(?) cd 14 cd ♖fc8 favours Black (Fine–Reshevsky, AVRO 1938).

After 11 d4 Black has a choice between 11 … ♕c7, 11 … ♘c6 and 11 … ♘d7. Each of these moves gives rise to a large number of sub-variations.

We shall first consider the following possibilities, which are of a rather tactical nature:

(a) **11 … cd** 12 cd ♗b7 13 ♘bd2 (interesting is 13 ♘c3 ♕c7 14 ♕e2 ♖ac8 15 ♗d3 ♖fe8 16 ♗g5 h6 17 ♗d2 ♘c4, or 13 d5 ♖c8 14 ♘d2 ♘h5 15 ♗d3 ♘f4 16 ♗f1; Ioseliani–Chiburdanidze, match 1988) 13 … ♖c8 (more circumspect is 13 … ♘c6 14 d5 ♘b4 15 ♗b1 a5 16 ♘f1 ♘a6 17 ♘g3 ♗c8 18 ♗d3 ♗d7 19 ♗e3 and Black is only slightly worse — Fischer–Unzicker, Leipzig OL 1960) 14 ♘f1 (also good is 14 d5! ♕c7 15 ♗d3 ♘d7 16 ♘f1 ♘c5 17 b3) 14 … d5?! 15 de ♘xe4 16 ♘1d2! (this is more accurate than 16 ♘g3 f5 17 ef ♗xf6 18 ♗xe4 de 19 ♘xe4 ♗xe4 20 ♕xd8 ♖fxd8 21 ♖xe4 ♖c2! with excellent play for Black) 16 … ♘c4 17 ♘xc4 ♖xc4 18 ♗b3 ♖c8 19 ♘d4 ♔h8 20 ♕g4 ♗c5 21 ♗e3 with better chances for White (Aronin–Saigin, Moscow 1960).

(b) **11 … ♗b7** 12 de de 13 ♘bd2 (13 ♘xe5? ♕xd1 14 ♗xd1 ♘xe4 15 ♗f3 ♖ad8 and Black stands better — Geller) 13 … ♕d6!? (better is 13 … ♕c7) 14 ♕e2 ♘h5 15 g3 g6 16 ♘f1 ♘c4 17 a4 ♕e6 18 b3 ♘d6 19 g4 ♘g7 20 ♘g3 with slightly better play for White (Boleslavsky–Mnatsakanyan, USSR 1963).

(c) **11 … d5?!** 12 ♘xe5 de 13 ♗g5 ♗b7 (or 13 … cd 14 cd ♗b7 15 ♘c3 ♖c8 — 15 … b4 16 ♘xe4 ♘xd4 17 ♗xe7 ♕xe7 18 ♗xe4 ♗xe4 19 ♖xe4 f6 20 ♕a4! — 16 ♗xf6 ♗xf6 17 ♗xe4 ♗xe4 18 ♖xe4 ♗xe5 19 de ♕xd1+ 20 ♖xd1 ♘c4 21 ♘d5 ♘xb2 22 ♖b1 ♖c2 23 ♘b4! with a clear advantage to White; Suetin–Dashkevich, Minsk 1959) 14 dc! ♗xc5 15 ♕xd8 ♖fxd8 16 b4 ♗d6 17 ♘g4! and there is no doubt about White's advantage (analysis by Boleslavsky and Suetin).

But let us return to the main variations:

A 11 … ♕c7 (Classical)

B 11 … ♘c6 (Borisenko)

C 11 … ♘d7 (Keres)

A

11 ... ♕c7

The most important continuation. The main line is invariably associated with 12 ♘bd2. But first we shall consider the nowadays rare possibilities on White's 12th move:

(a) **12 b4!?** cb 13 cb ♘c6 (or 13 ... ♘c4 14 ♘d2 ♗b7 — 14 ... d5!? 15 ed ed 16 ♘xc4 bc 17 ♕xd4 ♗xb4 with double-edged play; Tal–Geller, USSR Ch. 1958 — 15 ♘xc4 bc 16 d5! a5 17 b5 a4! 18 ♖b1 ♘d7 19 g4 — 19 ♗e3 — 19 ... ♘b6 20 ♗e3 ♗c8 21 ♕e2 ♗d7 22 ♖ec1 ♖fc8 23 ♘d2 with complicated play, where White's chances are to be preferred — analysis by Boleslavsky and Suetin) 14 ♗b2 (14 a3 ed! 15 ♗b2 ♗e6 16 ♘xd4 ♘xd4 17 ♗xd4 ♗d7 18 ♘c3 ♗f6 with good play for Black — Suetin) 14 ... ♘xb4 15 ♗b3 ♘c6 16 ♘c3 (16 ♕c2!?) 16 ... ♗b7! (16 ... ed 17 ♘xd4 ♘xd4 18 ♕xd4 ♕a7 19 ♘d5! ♗d8 20 ♕d3 ♘c8 21 e5! with a strong attack for White; Suetin–Mikenas, Moscow 1958) 17 ♖c1 ♕d8 18 ♘d5 ♘a5 19 ♘xe7+ ♕xe7 20 ♗a3 ♘xb3 21 ab ♘xe4 22 de ♖fd8 23 ed ♕f6 24 d7 a5 25 ♕c2 ♕f5 with sufficient compensation for Black (Vasyukov–Kholmov, USSR Ch. 1967).

(b) **12 ♗g5** ♘c4 13 b3 ♘b6 14 ♘bd2 h6! 15 ♗e3 ♖fe8 16 ♖c1 ♗f8 17 ♘h2 ♗b7 18 ♕f3 ♘bd7 and chances are equal (Westerinen–Ivkov, Palma de Mallorca 1968). Note that after 12 b3 ♖e8 13 d5 ♘b7 14 c4 ♗d7 15 ♗d3 ♖eb8 (Bronstein–Gligoric, Belgrade 1954), or 12 d5 ♗d7 13 ♘bd2 c4 14 ♘f1 ♘b7 (Keres), Black has sufficient defensive resources when the game is closed. Black gets good counterplay after 12 a4 ♗d7 13 ♘bd2 cd 14 cd ♖fc8!

12 ♘bd2 *(202)*

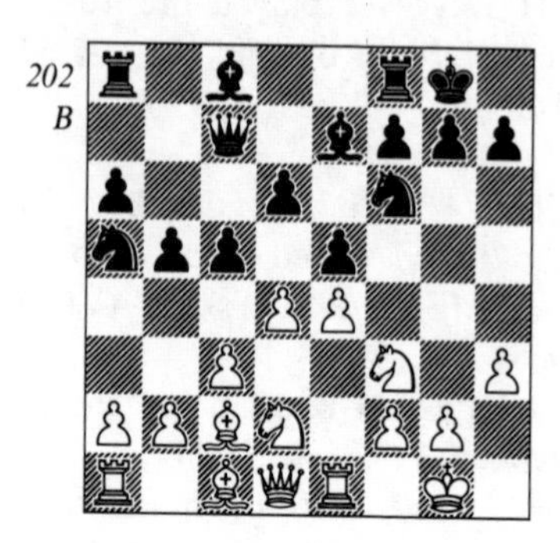

Black now has a rather wide choice:

A1	**12 ... ♘c6**	(Classical)
A2	**12 ... ♗d7**	(Smyslov)
A3	**12 ... ♗b7**	
A4	**12 ... ♖d8?!**	
A5	**12 ... cd**	

A1

12 ... ♘c6

This is the Classical approach. Briefly the rarer variations:

(a) **12 ... ♖e8** 13 b4! cb 14 cb ♘c6 15 a3 ♗f8 16 ♗b2 ♗d7 17 ♖c1 ♖ac8 18 ♘f1 with better chances for White (the manoeuvre ♘e3–d5!).

(b) **12 ... ♗e6?!** 13 de de 14

♘g5 ♖ad8 15 ♕e2 ♗f8 16 ♘f1 ♘c4 17 a4 with pressure for White (Boleslavsky–Cherepkov, USSR Ch. 1961).

(c) **12 … ♔h8?!** (Chigorin) 13 b4! cb 14 cb ♘c6 15 a3 ed 16 ♗b2 and here Black has difficulties.

(d) **12 … g6** 13 ♘f1 (13 b4!?) 13 … ♖e8 14 ♘e3 ♔g7 15 b4 cb 16 cb ♘c4 (16 … ♘c6 17 ♗b2!) 17 ♘xc4 bc 18 ♕d2! and Black has a difficult position (Boleslavsky and Suetin).

I should like to draw the reader's attention to the effectiveness of the flank thrust b2–b4, directed like a 'ricochet' at Black's central foundations.

After 12 … ♘c6 White's main choice is between:

A11 **13 dc** (Rauzer)
A12 **13 d5** (Closed)

But here too we cannot dispense with the examination of other possibilities for White:

(a) **13 ♘f1?!** cd 14 cd ♘xd4 15 ♘xd4 ed 16 ♘g3 ♘d7 17 ♘f5 ♗f6 18 ♗b3 (after 18 ♖e2 ♕b6 19 ♖d2 ♘e5 20 ♘xd4 ♘c4 21 ♖d3 ♗b7 22 b3 ♘e5 23 ♖d2 d5 24 f4 de! Black has excellent counterplay — Suetin) 18 … ♕b6 19 ♗d5 ♗b7 with equal chances (Klovan–Gipslis, USSR 1964).

(b) **13 ♗b1!?** (Simagin) 13 … ♗d8!? 14 de de 15 ♘f1 ♘e7 16 a4 ♗b7 and Black has no difficulties (Simagin–Bronstein, Moscow 1947).

(c) **13 a3!?** ♗d7 (after 13 … ♘d7 14 de — 14 d5 — 14 … de 15 a4 ♘b6 16 ab ab 17 ♖xa8 ♘xa8 18 ♘f1; Tal–Cherepkov, USSR 1969; or 13 … cd 14 cd ed 15 ♘b3 ♘d7 16 ♘bxd4 ♘xd4 17 ♘xd4; Suetin–Jansa, Budapest 1970, White's position is preferable) 14 b4 cd 15 cd ♖fc8 16 ♗b3 a5 17 ♗b2 ab (not bad is 17 … ed 18 ♘xd4 ♘xd4 19 ♗xd4 ab 20 ab ♖xa1 21 ♕xa1 ♗e6 (Gufeld–Smyslov, Moscow 1969) 18 ab ♖xa1 19 ♗xa1 ed 20 ♘xd4 ♘xd4 21 ♗xd4 ♗e6 with sufficient counterplay for Black (Gufeld–Karpov, USSR 1971).

A11

13 dc dc

By fixing the pawn structure, White intends to combine active operations on the flanks with manoeuvres in the centre, in the hope of establishing pieces on d5 and f5.

14 ♘f1

In passing we shall examine some alternative continuations:

(a) **14 a4** ♗e6 (also possible is 14 … ♖b8 15 ab ab 16 ♘f1 ♖d8 or 16 … ♗d6) 15 ♘g5 ♗d7 (interesting is 15 … ♖ad8!? 16 ♘xe6 fe 17 ♕e2 c4 18 ab ab 19 b3 ♗c5 20 bc ♘h5! with plenty of counterplay for Black; van den Berg–Nei, Beverwijk 1966) 16 ♘f1 h6 17 ♘f3 ♗e6 18 ♘h4 ♖ad8 19 ♕f3 ♘h7 20 ♘f5 ♗g5 with full equality for Black (Zaitsev–Smyslov, USSR Ch. 1969).

(b) **14 ♘h2** ♗e6 (also possible is 14 … c4 15 ♘df1 ♗c5, or 14

... ♖d8 15 ♕f3 ♗e6 16 ♘df1 ♖d7) 15 ♘f1 ♖ad8 16 ♕f3 c4 (sufficient for equality is 16 ... ♖fe8 17 ♘e3 ♘d4! 18 cd cd 19 ♗b3!, or 16 ... ♘a5 17 ♘e3 ♘c4) 17 ♘e3 ♕a5!? 18 ♖ef1 b4 19 ♘f5 ♗xf5 20 ef e4 21 ♗xe4 ♘e5 22 ♕e2 bc 23 bc ♖fe8 24 ♗c2 ♘d3 with good play for Black (Bagirov–Kolpakov, Leningrad 1969).

14 ... ♗e6

Other variations briefly:

(a) **14 ... ♗d6** 15 ♘h4! ♘e7 16 ♕f3 ♖d8 17 ♘e3 ♕b7 18 ♘g4! ♘xg4 19 hg ♘g6 20 ♘f5 ♗e6 21 g5 ♗c7 22 ♗e3 c4 23 ♖ed1 ♖xd1+ 24 ♖xd1 ♖d8 25 g3 ♖xd1+ 26 ♕xd1 ♕c6 27 a4! and in the ending which has arisen Black has quite a few difficulties (Fischer–Filip, Curaçao 1962).

(b) **14 ... ♖d8?!** 15 ♕e2 ♖b8 16 ♘e3 g6 17 ♘g5 ♗b7 18 ♗b3 ♖f8 (18 ... c4? 19 ♘xc4!) 19 ♘d5 ♘xd5 20 ♗xd5 ♗f6 21 ♕f3 with strong pressure for White (Suetin–Averbakh, USSR Ch. 1965).

15 ♘e3

After 15 ♘h4!? g6 16 ♕f3 ♔h8 17 ♗g5 ♘g8 18 ♕g3 f5?! 19 f4!? there arises a sharp position with somewhat better chances for White (Balashov–Mecking, Hastings 1966/7).

15 ... ♖ad8

16 ♕e2 c4!? *(203)*

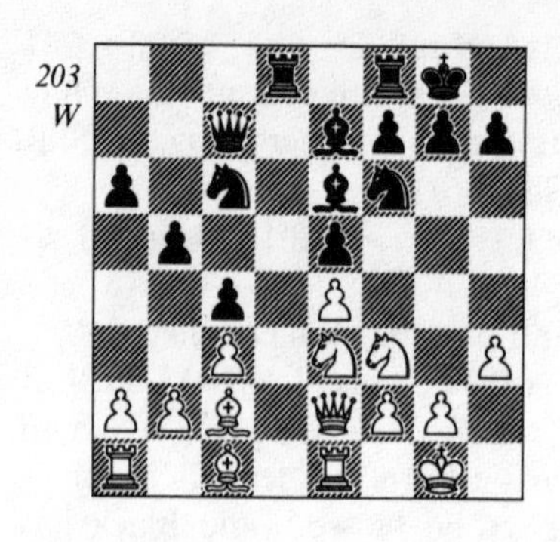

203
W

This is a modern dynamic continuation. For a long time the centre of attention was 16 ... g6 17 ♘g5 ♗c8 (17 ... ♘h5 18 ♘d5! ♗xd5 19 ed ♗xg5 20 ♗xg5 ♖xd5 21 ♗e4 ♖d6 22 ♗e3 gives White a strong initiative) 18 a4 (18 ♘d5 ♘xd5 19 ed ♖xd5 20 ♘xh7 ♔xh7 21 ♕h5+ with a draw) 18 ... ♕b7 (in White's favour is 18 ... c4 19 ab ab 20 b3 ♘a5 21 bc bc 22 ♗a3! ♖fe8 23 ♗xe7 ♖xe7 24 ♖ed1 ♖ed7 25 ♖xd7 ♖xd7 26 ♖a4!; Suetin–Kamyshev, Tbilisi 1951) 19 ab ab 20 h4 (20 ♘d5!?) 20 ... ♗d6 21 ♘d5 ♘h5 22 ♘f3 f6 23 ♗h6 ♖f7 24 ♖ed1 with a small advantage to White (Smyslov–Botvinnik, match 1957).

17 ♘g5

The alternative is 17 ♘f5 ♖fe8 (after 17 ... ♗xf5 18 ef ♖fe8 — or 18 ... h6 19 ♘d2 — 19 ♗g5 White has a clear positional advantage) 18 ♗g5 (18 ♘3h4!? ♘d7!) 18 ... ♘d7 19 ♗xe7 (19 ♘xe7+ ♘xe7 20 a4 f6 with equality) 19 ... ♘xe7 20 ♘g5 ♘f8 21 a4 f6 22 ♘xe6 ♘xe6 and Black has a secure defence (Jansa–Lanc, Czechoslovakia 1970).

17 ... h6!?

Worthy of consideration is 17 ... ♗c5!? Premature is 17 ...

♘d4(?) 18 cd ed 19 e5! with advantage to White.

18 ♘xe6 fe *(204)*

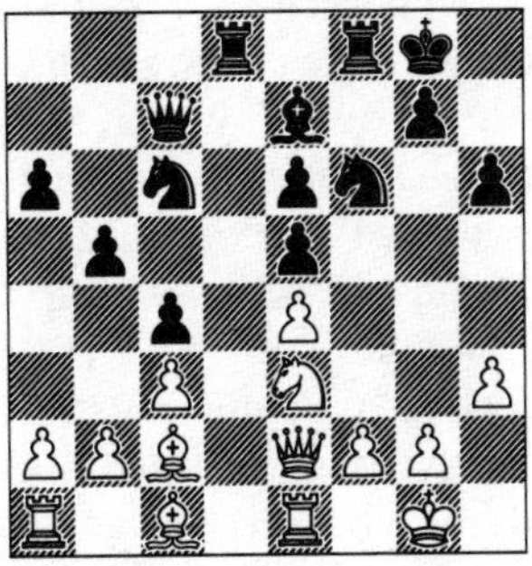

19 a4!?

19 b3 ♗c5 20 ♖d1 ♘d4!, and still more so 19 b4? ♘d4! 20 cd ed 21 a3 d3 22 ♗xd3 ♖xd3 (Fischer–Kholmov, Havana 1965), are not very attractive for White. The move 19 g3 is a curious alternative.

19 ... ♗c5
20 ab ab
21 ♖ef1 ♕b6

In a game between the readers of the newspapers *Zarya Vostok* and *Pravda Ukraina* (1969) there occurred 22 ♔h1 ♘e7 23 g3 ♕c6 24 ♘g2 ♖f7 25 ♔h2 ♖df8 26 f3 ♘g6 with a complicated and roughly equal game.

A12

13 d5

This plan, closing the centre while gaining a tempo, has long been known and was rather popular in the 1920s. Nowadays interest in it has risen considerably. Black has two continuations:

A121 13 ... ♘a5

A122 13 ... ♘d8

A121

13 ... ♘a5
14 b3 ♗d7
15 ♘f1 ♘b7
16 c4

After 16 ♘g3 ♖fb8 17 ♘f5 ♗f8 18 ♘h2 ♘d8 19 ♘g4 ♘xg4 20 hg f6 21 ♕e2 ♘f7 Black's defence is strong (Kostro–Usachy, corr. 1973).

16 ... ♖fb8
17 ♘e3 bc

After 18 ♘xc4 ♗f8 19 a4 ♘a5 20 ♘fd2 g6 chances are equal (Alexander–Keres, Hastings 1937/8).

A122

13 ... ♘d8 *(205)*

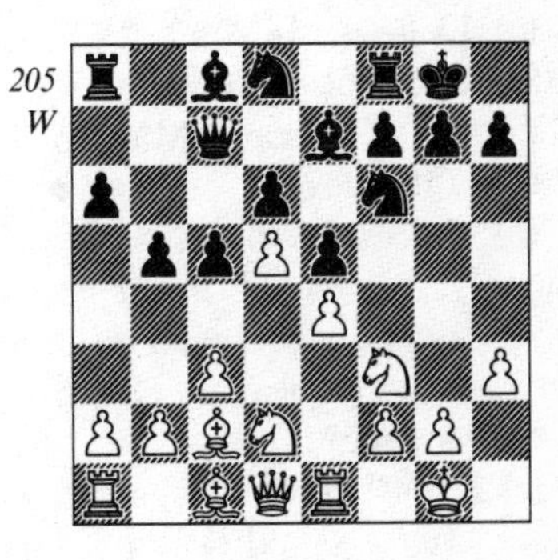

In this position the following variations are possible: 14 a4 ♖b8 (14 ... b4? 15 ♘c4 a5 16 ♘fxe5! ♗a6 17 ♗d3 de 18 d6! is clearly in White's favour (Capablanca–Vidmar, New York 1927) 15 ab (worthy of consideration is 15 b4 or 15 c4) 15 ... ab 16 b4 c4 17 ♘f1 ♘e8 18 ♘3h2 f6 (18 ... ♗f6!?) 19

f4 ♘f7 20 ♘f3 g6 21 f5 ♘g7 22 g4 with complicated play, where White has slightly better chances (Karpov–Spassky, USSR 1973).

A2

12 ... ♗d7

This flexible system was first played by Smyslov in the 1950s, but nowadays it has virtually disappeared from practice. The reason is that it is somewhat passive. Black intends to complete his development quickly and consolidate his kingside (♖e8, ♗f8, g6 and ♗g7), but in solving his defensive tasks he ignores the creation of active counterplay.

13 ♘f1

Let us consider the following variations:

(a) **13 de** de 14 ♘h2 ♖ad8 15 ♕f3 ♗e6 16 ♘df1 with equal chances (Evans–Matanovic, Varna OL 1962).

(b) **13 d5** ♖fc8 (or 13 ... c4 and then ♘b7–c5) 14 ♘f1 ♗f8 15 g4 c4 16 ♘g3 g6 with a solid position for Black (Ciocaltea–Domnitu, Netanya 1965).

(c) **13 b4?!** cb 14 cb ♘c6 15 a3 ♖ac8 16 ♗b3 ed 17 ♗b2 d3 18 ♘f1 a5! and it is White who already has difficulties (analysis by Boleslavsky and Suetin).

13 ... ♖fe8 *(206)*

An alternative is 13 ... ♘c4 14 b3 (not bad is 14 ♘e3 ♘xe3 15 ♗xe3 ♗c6 16 ♘d2 ♘d7 17 f4 with definite pressure for White — Suetin) 14 ... ♘b6 15 ♘e3 c4 (after 15 ... ♗e6 16 ♕e2 ♖ad8 17 c4 White takes control of the d5-square) 16 bc ♘xc4 17 ♘xc4 bc 18 ♗a3! ♖fe8 19 ♖b1 ♖ab8 20 ♕e2 with pressure for White on the queenside (Suetin–Lilienthal, Moscow 1955). White also has somewhat better chances after 13 ... cd 14 cd ♖ac8 15 ♘e3 ♘c6 16 d5!? ♘b4 17 ♗b1 a5 18 a3 ♘a6 19 b4! ♖a8 20 ♗d2 (Mokry–Smejkal, Calcutta 1986). Unattractive is 13 ... ♖ad8? 14 ♘e3 g6 15 b4! cb 16 cb ♘c6 17 a3 ♖fe8 18 ♗b2 ♗f8 19 ♘d5! with a clear advantage for White (Suetin–Ljuboshits, Tallinn 1956).

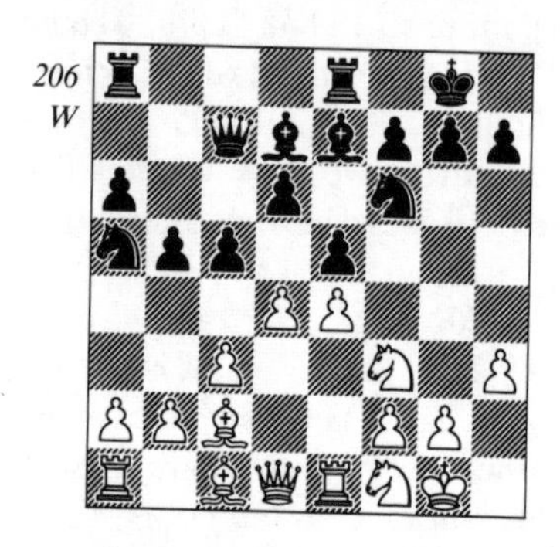

14 b3!

An idea of Geller's. White has a number of other possibilities, of which we may single out the following:

(a) **14 a4** cd 15 cd ♘c6 16 ♘e3 ♘b4 17 ♗b3 ba 18 ♗xa4 ♗xa4 19 ♖xa4 a5 20 ♘f5 ♗f8 21 ♗g5 ♘d7 with equal play (Keres–Gligoric, Bled 1959).

(b) **14 ♘e3** g6 15 b4!? (15 de de 16 ♘h2 ♖ad8 17 ♕f3 ♗e6 18 ♘g4 ♘xg4 19 hg ♘c4 20 ♘d5

♗xd5 21 ed ♘b6 22 ♖d1 ♖d7 with equal chances; Geller–Gligoric, Bled 1961) 15 … cb 16 cb ♘c4 17 ♘xc4 bc 18 ♖e3 ed 19 ♘xd4 d5 20 e5 ♘e4 with good counterplay for Black (analysis by Suetin).

14 … g6

15 ♗g5

With the following variations:

(a) **15 … ♗c6** 16 ♘g3 ♔h8 17 d5 ♗b7 18 a4 ♘g8 19 ab ab 20 ♗xe7 ♘xe7 21 ♖a2 f6 22 ♘d2 ♖ec8 23 c4 b4 24 ♕g4 with a minimal advantage to White (Khasin–Liberzon, Kislovodsk 1964).

(b) **15 … ♗e6** 16 ♘e3 ♖ad8 17 ♖c1 ♘h5 18 b4! ♘c4 19 ♗xe7 ♖xe7 20 ♘xa4 ♗xa4 21 bc dc 22 d5 with better chances for White (Geller–Euwe, Havana 1963).

(c) **15 … ♘h5** 16 ♗xe7 ♖xe7 17 ♘e3 ♘f6 18 ♖c1 ♘b7 19 b4 c4 20 a4 ♖ae8 21 ab ab 22 ♖a1 ♗c6 23 ♖a6 ♕c8 24 d5 with pressure for White (Stein–Matanovic, Tel Aviv 1964).

A3

12 … ♗b7

This manoeuvre leads to lively tactical play. Black's plans are principally based on the counter-thrust d6–d5. This plan is frequently adopted after the preliminary exchange 12 … cd 13 cd.

13 ♘f1

Worthy of consideration is 13 d5. For example: 13 … ♗c8 14 b3 ♘b7 (14 … c4) 15 ♘f1 ♘b7 16 c4 ♖fb8 17 ♘e3 ♗f8 18 ♘f5 ♘d8 19 ♘h2 ♘e8 20 h4 f6 21 h5 with pressure for White (Karpov–Andersson, Stockholm 1969). After the quiet 13 de de 14 ♘h4 g6 15 ♘f1 ♖ad8 16 ♕f3 ♘c4 17 ♗h6 ♖fe8 18 ♘f5 ♗f8 19 ♗g5 ♖e6 Black has a secure position. On the other hand, after 13 a4!? cd 14 cd ♖ac8 15 ♗b1 ♘h5!? 16 ♘xe5 de 17 ♕xh5 ♗b4! play is double-edged (Suetin).

13 … cd

An alternative is 13 … ♖e8 14 ♘g3 g6 15 d5 ♗f8 16 ♘h2 ♗g7 17 ♘g4 ♘xg4 18 hg ♘c4 19 b3 ♘b6 20 ♗e3 c4 21 ♕e2 ♖eb8 22 ♖ec1 a5 23 ♗d1 ♖a7 24 ♖ab1 ♖c8 25 g5 with slight pressure for White (Sellos–Ivkov, Buenos Aires OL 1978).

14 cd ♖ac8 *(207)*

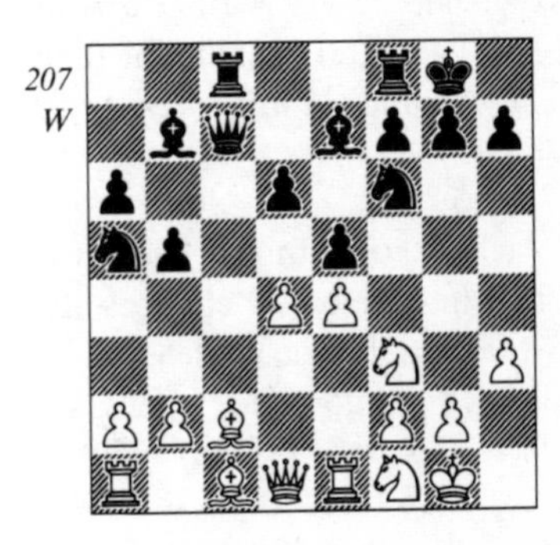

207
W

15 ♗d3

Besides this move White has two other important continuations:

(a) **15 ♖e2** ♘d7!? (15 … d5 leads to the main line, and 15 … ♘h5 16 d5 ♘f4 17 ♗xf4 ef 18 b3 promises White an advantage) 16 d5! ♘c5 17 b3! with a spatial advantage for White (Gligoric–Letelier, Asuncion 1960).

(b) **15 ♗b1**, with the following variations:

(b1) **15 … d5** 16 ed!? ed 17 ♗g5! h6 (17 … ♗xd5 18 ♘xd4 ♖fd8 19 ♘f5) 18 ♗xh6! gh 19 ♕d2 ♗xd5 20 ♕xh6 ♗xf3 21 ♘g3 e4 22 ♗xe4 ♘xe4 23 ♘h5 ♗f6 24 ♖xe4 with a strong attack for White (Thelen).

(b2) **15 … ♘h5!?** 16 d5 ♘f4 17 ♘g3 ♗d8! 18 ♗xf4 ef 19 ♘h5 ♘c4 20 ♖e2 ♘e5 with good prospects for Black (Ljubojevic–Pomar, Vienna 1984).

(b3) **15 … ed!?** 16 ♘xd4 ♖fe8 17 ♘g3 d5 18 ed ♘xd5 19 ♗e4 ♗b4 20 ♗d2 ♗xd2 21 ♕xd2 ♘c4 22 ♕c1 ♘f4 23 b3 ♗xe4 24 ♘xe4 ♘d3 25 ♕g5 ♕d8 26 ♕xd8 ♖exd8! with full equality for Black (Kindermann–Honfi, Budapest 1986).

15 … d5

An idea of Panov's. Note that White has the better chances after 15 … ♘c6 16 ♘e3 ♖fe8 17 ♘f5 ♗f8 18 ♗g5 ♘d7 19 ♖c1 (Fischer–Keres, Zürich 1959), or 15 … ♘d7 16 d5 f5 17 ♘e3 f4 18 ♘f5 ♗d8 19 ♗d2 etc.

16 de

16 ed e4!

16 … ♘xe4

17 ♘g3 f5

After 17 … ♗b4 18 ♖e2 f5 19 ef ♘xg3 20 fg ♕xg3 21 ♗f5! (Petrosian–Trifunovic, Leningrad 1957), or 17 … ♖fd8 18 ♕e2 ♗b4 19 ♖f1 ♕c6 20 ♘g5! (Bronstein–Panov, Moscow 1946), White stands clearly better.

18 ef ♗xf6

19 ♗xe4

Worse is 19 ♘xe4 de 20 ♗xe4 ♖fd8! 21 ♕e2 ♖e8 22 ♘d2 ♕d7 23 ♕f1 ♘c6 with full equality for Black.

19 … de

20 ♘xe4 ♗xe4

In White's favour is 20 … ♘c4 21 ♖b1 ♖cd8 22 ♕e2 ♗xe4 23 ♕xe4, or 20 … ♕c2 21 ♕e2! ♗xe4 22 ♕xe4 ♗xb2 23 ♗xb2 ♕xb2 24 ♕e6+ ♔h8 25 ♕xa6 etc.

21 ♖xe4 ♕c2 *(208)*

After 21 … ♘c4 22 ♖b1 ♕f7 23 ♖e2 ♖fd8 24 ♕f1 ♕g6 25 ♗e3 Black has no compensation for the pawn (Zagorovsky–Razinnin, USSR 1956).

208
W

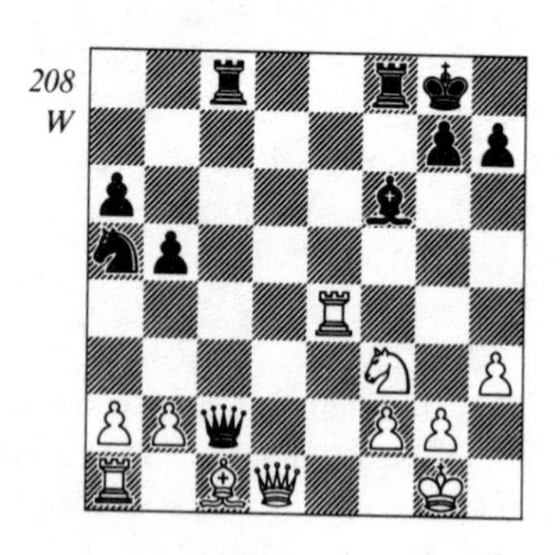

22 ♕d5+ ♔h8

23 ♘e1

And now:

(a) **23 … ♕c6** 24 ♕xc6 ♘xc6 25 ♖b1 ♘d4 26 ♗d2 with an extra pawn for White (Suetin–Blatny, Lyon 1955).

(b) **23 … ♕c7** 24 ♗f4 ♕a7 25 ♖b1 ♘c4 26 b3 ♖cd8 27 ♕e6 ♘d2 28 ♗xd2 ♖xd2 29 ♖e2 and here too White has a pawn more.

A4

12 … ♖d8?!

This was introduced into practice by Keres in 1953. But its success turned out to be a flash in the pan, as deeper investigation detected the defects of this extravagant system. Nowadays it is virtually never played.

13 ♘f1

Closing the centre does not promise White any real advantage: 13 d5 ♗e7 14 ♘f1 ♖ab8 15 g4 h5 etc.

13 … cd

After 13 … d5? 14 de de 15 ♘1d2! ef 16 ef ♗xf6 17 ♕xf3 ♗e6 18 ♘e4 ♗e7 19 ♕h5! with a strong attack for White, or 13 … ed 14 cd d5? 15 ed ♘xd5 16 ♘g5! etc., Black has serious difficulties.

11 cd d5?! *(209)*

In White's favour is 14 … ♘c6 15 ♘e3 ♘xd4 16 ♘xd4 ed 17 ♕xd4 d5?! 18 ♘xd5 ♘xd5 19 ed ♕xc2 20 ♖xe7.

209
W

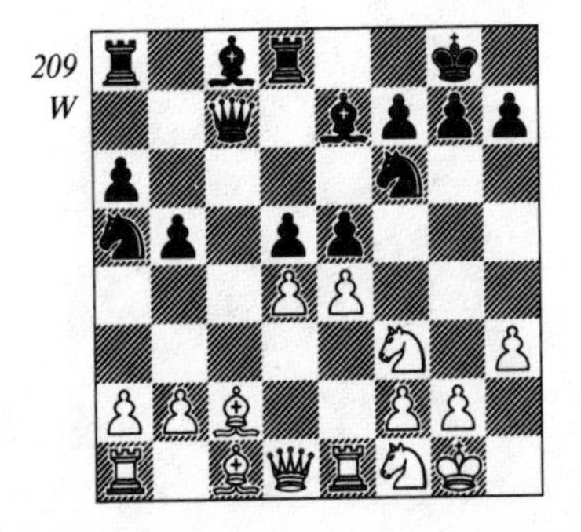

Now the following variations may arise:

(a) **15 ♘xe5** de (15 … ♘xe4 16 ♘e3!) 16 ♘g3! ♘c6 (after 16 … ♗d6 17 ♗f4!, or 16 … ♗b7 17 ♘f5 ♗d6 18 ♘g4!, Black has severe problems) 17 ♘xc6 ♕xc6 18 ♘xe4 ♗b7 19 ♗g5 ♕b6 20 ♘xf6+ ♗xf6 21 ♕d3 g6 22 ♗xf6 ♕xf6 23 ♖ad1 with an extra pawn for White (Boleslavsky–Vistanetskis, Minsk 1957).

(b) **15 ed** ed 16 ♗g5 h6 (after 16 … ♗b7 17 ♖c1 ♕d7 18 ♘g3 h6 19 ♖xe7 ♕xe7 20 ♘f5, or 16 … ♘xd5 17 ♖c1 ♕d6 18 ♗e4!, White stands clearly better) 17 ♖c1 ♕d6 18 ♗h4 ♘xd5 19 ♗g3 with an initiative for White.

A5

12 … cd
13 cd

We shall consider the following continuations:

A51 13 … ♘c6
A52 13 … ♗b7

After 13 … ♘d8?!, besides the move 14 ♘f1 just considered, also possible is 14 b3!? For example: 14 … ed (14 … d5) 15 ♗b2 ♘c6 16 ♘xd4 ♘xd4 17 ♗xd4 ♗b7!? (or 17 … ♗e6 18 ♖c1 ♕a5 19 ♗b1 d5 20 ♗c3 ♕a3!? with unclear play) 18 ♖c1 ♕a5 19 ♗b1 ♖ac8 20 ♖xc8 ♖xc8 21 ♘f1 ♖e8 22 ♖e3! with somewhat better play for White. In the game Karpov–van der Sterren, Wijk aan Zee 1988, there was played: 13 … ♗d7 14 ♘f1 ♖ac8 15 ♖e2 ♖fe8

16 d5 ♘h5 17 ♗d3 g6 18 ♘e3 ♘f4 19 ♖c2 ♕b6 20 ♗f1 f5 21 ef gf 22 b4 ♘b7 23 ♗b2 ♖xc2 24 ♕xc2 ♖e8 25 ♕b1 ♖f8 26 a3. Here, after 26 ... ♘h5!? 27 ♕c2 ♖c8 28 ♕d2 ♘g7, Black was able to maintain the equilibrium.

A51

13 ... ♘c6

After a long crisis-period, this continuation, where the fight takes place on the queenside, is again topical.

White has two alternatives:

A511 14 ♘b3
A512 14 a3

A511

13 ♘b3

The most common continuation. Let us also briefly consider the following variations:

(a) **14 d5** ♘b4 15 ♗b1 a5 16 a3 ♘a6 17 b4 ♗d7 (after 17 ... ab 18 ab ♕c3 19 ♘b3 ♕xb4 20 ♗d3 White stands better) 18 ba!? ♕xa5 19 ♘b3 ♕b6 and now 20 ♗e3 with a small advantage to White (Mazzoni–Safvat, Tel Aviv OL 1964).

(b) **14 ♗b1!?** (Simagin) 14 ... ♗d7 15 ♘f1 ♖fe8 16 d5 ♘a5 17 b3 ♘b7 18 ♗b2 ♘c5 with roughly equal play (Simagin–Hunter, corr. 1967).

14 ... a5

After 14 ... ♗b7 15 d5 (also good is 15 ♗g6 h6 16 ♗h4 ♘b4 17 ♗b1 ♖ac8 18 ♖e2 ♘h5 19 a3 ♘c6 20 d5; Unzicker–Keres, Moscow 1956) 15 ... ♘a5 16 ♘xa5 ♕xa5 17 a4 ♖fc8 18 ♗d3 (Larsen–Keres, Zürich 1959), or 14 ... ♖d8 15 ♗d2! ♕b8 16 d5! (Smyslov–Keres, Moscow 1941), White stands clearly better.

15 ♗e3 a4
16 ♘bd2 *(210)*

210
B

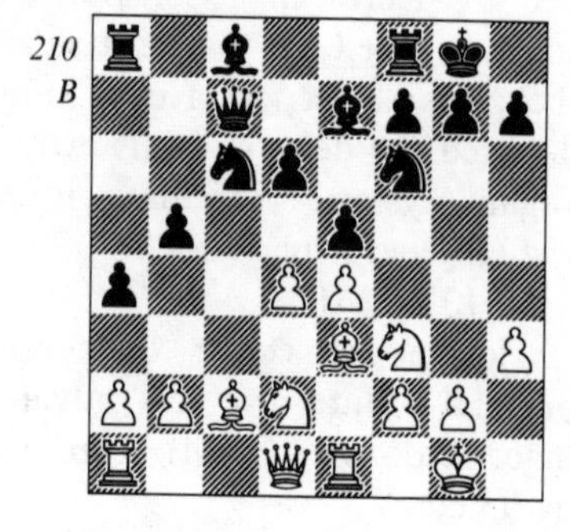

In this critical position Black has a choice of:

A5111 16 ... ♘b4
A5112 16 ... ♗e6
A5113 16 ... ♗d7

A5111

16 ... ♘b4
17 ♗b1 ♗d7

But not 17 ... a3?! 18 ♕b3 ♕a5 19 de de 20 ♕xa3 with advantage to White.

18 a3 ♘c6 *(211)*

211
W

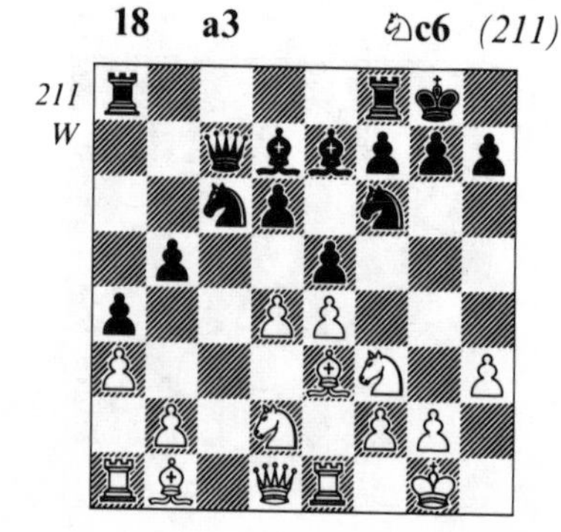

In this critical position the following continuations are possible:

(a) **19 ♗d3** ♘a5 (19 ... ♕b8!? was played in Gufeld–Kasashvili, Biel 1989, which continued 20 ♕e2 ♘a5 21 ♖ac1 ♖e8 22 ♖c2 ♗d8 23 de de 24 ♘b1! ♘d3 25 ♘c3 b4 26 ab ♕xb4 27 ♗c4! with advantage to White) 20 ♖c1 ♕b8 21 ♕e2 ♖e8 22 de de 23 ♗c5 ♗d8 24 ♕e3 ♖a6 25 ♗f1 ♘b7 26 b4! with pressure for White (Sokolov–Torre, London 1984).

(b) **19 ♕e2** ♕b7 20 ♗d3 ♖fe8 21 ♖ac1 ♖ab8 22 de de 23 ♘b1 ♗d8 24 ♖c5! b4 25 ♖b5 ♕a8 26 ♖c1 and here too Black has difficulties (Karpov–Hort, Lucerne OL 1982).

A5112

16 ... ♗e6

After 16 ... ♗a6 17 ♖c1 ♕b7 18 ♗b1 (18 a3 ♗d8 19 b4!?) 18 ... ♗d8 19 b4 (Keres), or 16 ... a3 17 ba ♖xa3 18 ♕c1! ♕a5 19 ♗b3, Black has difficulties. Little studied is 16 ... ♗b7!? 17 ♖c1 ♖ac8 18 ♗b1!? ♕b8 19 ♘f1 ♘a5 20 ♖xc8 ♖xc8 21 ♗g5 with pressure for White.

17 a3

Possible is 17 d5 ♘b4 18 ♗b1 ♗d7 19 ♘f1 ♖fc8 20 ♕d2 ♘a6 21 ♘g3 and White's position is preferable (Garcia–Ivkov, Havana 1965).

17 ... ♘a5 *(212)*

And now:

(a) **18 ♗d3** ♕b3 19 ♕e2 ♗d7 (or 19 ... b4 20 ab! ♕xb4 21 ♖b1 ed 22 ♗xd4 ♘c6 23 ♗c3! —

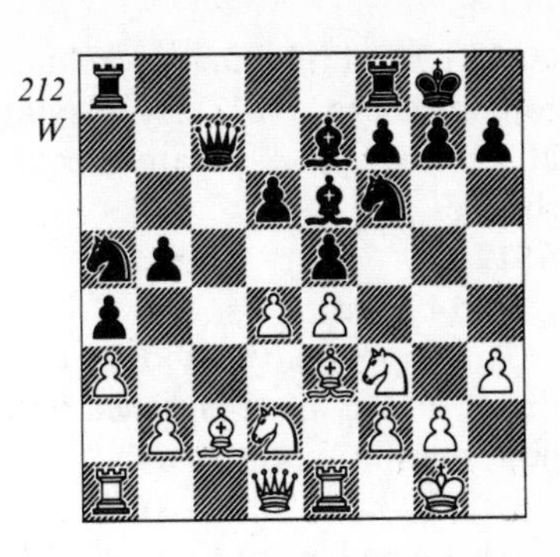
212
W

Matanovic) 20 ♖ec1 ♖e8 (20 ... ♗d8 21 ♖ab1; 20 ... ♖a6 21 d5!) 21 ♖ab1! ♗d8 22 b4! ab 23 ♘xb3 ♘xb3 24 ♖xb3 ♕b7 25 ♘d2 (Hazai–Barle, Maribor 1985). In both cases White stands better.

(b) **18 ♘g5** ♕c8 19 ♗d3 ♗d7 20 f4 with advantage to White (Wood).

(c) **18 ♖c1** ♕b8 19 ♗d3 b4 20 d5 ♗d7 21 ♘c4 ♘xc4 22 ♖xc4 ba 23 ba ♕b3 with good counterplay for Black (Gligoric–Keres, Hastings 1964/5).

A5113

16 ... ♗d7

With the following variations:

(a) **17 ♖c1** ♕b8!? (or 17 ... ♕b7 18 ♘f1 ♖c8 19 ♘g3 ♗d8! with roughly equal play) 18 ♕e2 ♖e8 19 ♗d3 ♘b4 20 ♗b1 ♗d8 21 de de 22 ♘g3 with a minimal advantage to White (Lobron–Torre, Hannover 1983).

(b) **17 a3** ♖fe8 (after 17 ... ♖ac8 18 ♗d3 ♕b8 19 ♕e2 ♘a5 20 ♖eb1 ♖fe8 21 b3! with a somewhat better game for Black; Sokolov–Smagin, Moscow 1983) 18 ♗d3 ♕b7 19 ♕e2 ♕d8 20 d5

♘a5 21 ♖eb1 (Hübner–Korchnoi, Johannesburg 1981). By playing 21 … ♗b6! Black obtained equal chances.

A512

14 a3

This apparently modest continuation has been enriched with new ideas in recent years.

14 … ♗d7

Also possible is 14 … ♗d8!? 15 b4 ♕a7 16 ♘b3 ♗b6 17 ♗e3 ♖e8 18 de de (Zaitsev–Kholmov, USSR 1967), or 14 … ♕a7!? 15 d5 ♘d4 16 ♘xd4 ♕xd4 17 ♕e2 ♗d7 18 ♗d3 ♕e7 19 ♘f1 g6 20 ♘g3 ♘e8. In each case Black has a secure position.

15 d5

An alternative is 15 ♘b3 a5 16 ♗e3 (or 16 d5 ♘b8 17 ♗d2 a4 18 ♘c1 ♖c8 19 ♗c3 ♘a6 20 ♘d3 ♗d8 21 ♖c1 ♕a7; Timman–Torre, Tilburg 1982) 16 … a4 17 ♘bd2 ♖fc8 18 ♖c1 with equal chances (Torre–Petrosian, Rio de Janeiro 1979).

15 … ♘a5
16 ♘f1 ♖fc8

A line which has not been deeply studied is 16 … ♘h5 17 ♗d3 g6 18 ♗h6 ♖fc8 19 ♘e3 ♕d8 with complicated play (Smyslov–Botvinnik, USSR 1940).

17 ♗d3 ♗d8!?

After 18 ♘g3 ♕e7 19 ♖f1! ♗b6 20 ♘h4 g6 21 ♔h1 ♘e8 22 f4 ♖xc1 23 ♖xc1 ef 24 ♘e2 ♗f2 25 ♘f3 ♗e3 26 ♕e1 ♗xc1 27 ♘xc1 White has better prospects (Tseshkovsky–Dorfman, Lvov 1977).

A52

13 … ♗b7
14 d5 ♖ac8

After 14 … ♗c8 15 ♘f1 (also good is 15 b3 ♗d7 16 ♘f1 ♘b7 17 ♗d2 a5 18 a3 ♕b8 19 b4!, as in Kir. Georgiev–Pinter, Haifa 1989) 15 … ♘e8 16 b3 g6 17 ♘e3 ♘g7 18 ♗d2 ♘b7 19 ♖c1 ♗d7 20 b4! White has strong pressure (Boleslavsky–Bondarevsky, Tbilisi 1951).

15 ♗d3

An interesting line is 15 ♗b1 ♘d7 16 ♘f1.

15 … ♘d7
16 ♘f1 ♘c4

16 … ♘c5 17 ♗c2!

17 ♘g3

In the game Suetin–Krogius, USSR Ch. 1960, there followed: 17 … ♘c5 18 ♗c2 g6 19 b3 ♘b6 20 ♗h6 ♖fe8 21 ♖c1 ♗f8 22 ♗d2! ♕e7 23 ♗a5 with pressure for White.

B

11 … ♘c6

The idea of this variation, introduced into practice by Borisenko, is in many respects similar to that in the variations considered above. In some lines the black queen goes to b6. On the other hand, White may immediately close the centre with d4–d5, giving himself greater space. We shall consider the two main continuations:

B1 12 ♘bd2
B2 12 d5

B1

12 ♘bd2

Worthy of consideration is 12 a4, but White gets nothing after 12 ♗e3 ed! 13 cd ♘b4.

12 ... ♕b6!?

After 12 ... cd 13 cd ed 14 ♘b3 d3?! 15 ♗xd3 ♗b7 16 ♗d2 ♖e8 17 a4 White has the initiative (Geller–Romanishin, Lvov 1977).

13 dc dc

14 ♘f1

After 14 ... ♗e6 15 ♘e3 ♖ad8 16 ♕e2 c4 17 ♘g5 (17 ♘f5 ♗xf5 18 ef ♖fe8) 17 ... g6 18 a4 ♔g7 19 ab ab 20 ♖b1 ♘a5 21 ♘f3 ♕c7 22 ♘d5 ♘xd5 23 ed ♗xd5 24 ♘xe5 White has the initiative (Tal–Bronstein, USSR Ch. 1959).

B2

12 d5 ♘a5 *(213)*

The alternative is 12 ... ♘a7 13 ♘bd2 ♗d7 14 ♘f1 ♘c8 15 b3 (15 g4 h5!) 15 ... ♘b6 16 ♘xe5! de 17 d6 ♗c6 18 de ♕xe7 19 ♕f3 ♕e6 20 ♘e3 c4 21 ♗a3 with strong pressure for White (Boleslavsky–Zakharyan, USSR 1966).

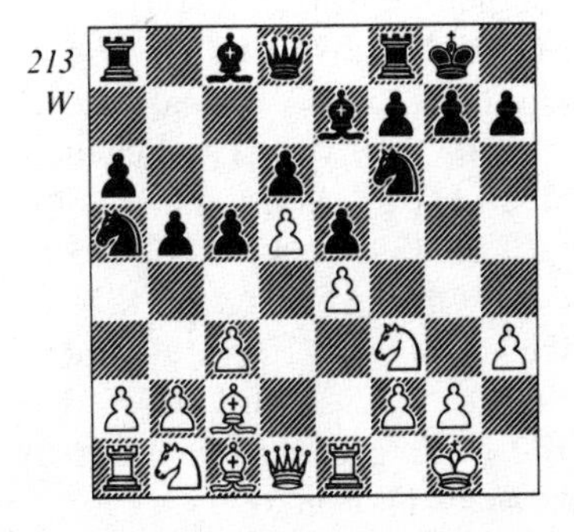
213
W

After 12 ... ♘a5 the following variations arise:

(a) **13 b3** ♘e8 (Cabrilo–Romanishin, Vrsac 1989 went 13 ... g6 14 ♗h6 ♖e8 15 ♘bd2 ♗f8 16 ♗g5 h6 17 ♗e3 ♗g7 18 b4 ♘b7 19 a4 ♗d7 20 ♘f1 ♕c7 21 ♕d2 ♔h7 22 ♘g3; by 22 ... a5! Black could now have obtained equality) 14 a4 ♗d7 15 ab ab 16 ♗e3 g6 17 ♘bd2 ♘g7 18 b4 cb 19 cb ♘c4 20 ♘xc4 bc 21 ♕d2 f5 with roughly equal play (Psakhis–Romanishin, Moscow 1986).

(b) **13 ♘bd2** g6!? (13 ... ♗d7 14 b4!, or 13 ... c4 14 ♘f1 ♘b7 15 g4!, favours White) 14 b4 ♘b7 15 a4 ♗d7 16 ♘f1 ♕c7 17 a5 ♖ac8 18 ♗d3 ♘h5 19 ♗h6 ♖fe8 20 ♖c1 ♗f8 with double-edged play (Psakhis–Romanishin, Sochi 1984).

C

11 ... ♘d7

This is one of the numerous ‘discoveries’ by Keres in the Spanish Opening and was first played in 1962. The Keres System is one of the most valuable and endurable. The idea of the knight manoeuvre consists in exerting pressure with pieces on White’s central foundations. Black prepares for forced events in the centre, exchanging on d4 and creating piece pressure along the long diagonals. White may either prevent this by continuing with 12 dc or comply with his opponent’s plans by playing 12 ♘bd2.

C1 12 dc
C2 12 ♘bd2

C1

12 dc dc
13 ♘bd2

Analogous to the strategy in the Rauzer System, White intends to carry out a plan connected with invasion on the squares d5 and f5. But with correct defence Black gets a comfortable game.

13 … f6! *(214)*

The most accurate path to equality. We shall also consider the following variations:

(a) **13 … ♕c7** 14 ♘f1 ♘b6 15 ♘e3 ♖d8 16 ♕e2 ♗e6 17 ♘d5! ♘xd5 18 ed ♗xd5 19 ♘xe5 ♖a7 20 ♗f4! with a dangerous initiative for White (Fischer–Keres, Curaçao 1962).

(b) **13 … ♗b7** 14 ♕e2 (14 ♘f1 ♘c4! 15 ♘g3 g6 16 b3 ♘d6 with equal play; Tal–Romanishin, Jurmala 1983) 14 … ♕c7 15 ♘f1 ♘c4 16 b3 ♘b6 17 c4! ♖fe8 18 ♗b2 ♗f8 19 ♖ad1 ♗c6 (Short–Portisch, Tilburg 1988). By playing 20 ♘3d2 and then ♘e3, White was able to maintain his pressure.

214
W

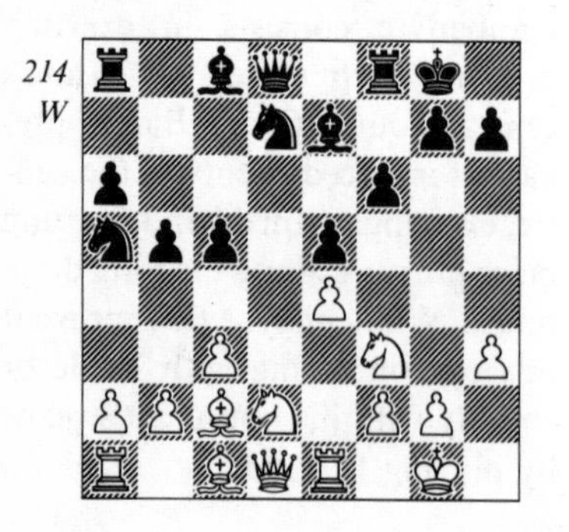

After 13 … f6 the following variations arise:

(a) **14 ♘f1** ♘b6 15 ♕e2 ♗e6 (more accurate is 15 … ♖a7 16 ♘e3 ♗e6) 16 ♘e3 (and better here is 16 ♖d1 ♕c7 17 ♘e3 and then ♘d5) 16 … ♖a7 17 ♘f5 (or 17 ♖d1 ♖d7!) 17 … ♖fe8 18 ♘xe7+ ♖xe7 19 b3 ♖d7 20 ♘h4 ♕c7 21 ♘f5 ♖fe8 22 ♖cd1 ♖ed8 with equal play (Ivkov–Quinones, Amsterdam 1964).

(b) **14 ♘h2** ♘b6 15 ♕f3 ♘ac4 16 ♘df1 ♖a7 17 ♘g3 ♖f7 with a solid position for Black (Tal–Grushevsky, Moscow 1963).

(c) **14 ♘h4** ♘b6 15 ♕f3 (or 15 ♕e2 ♗e6 16 ♘f1 ♖a7 17 ♘g3 ♖f7 18 f4!? with double-edged play; Sokolov–Rodriguez, Biel 1985) 15 … ♖e8 16 ♖f1 ♖a7 17 ♕g3 ♔h8 18 f4 (Zaitsev–Dragunov, corr. 1963). With 18 … ef 19 ♗xf4 ♘bc4 Black was able to obtain a comfortable game.

(d) **14 ♘c4?** bc 15 ♕d5+ ♔h8 16 ♕xa8 ♘b6 17 ♕a7 ♘c6! leads to the loss of White's queen.

C2

12 ♘bd2

Other variations:

(a) **12 b3** ed 13 cd ♘c6 14 ♘c3 ♗f6 15 ♗e3 cd 16 ♘xd4 ♘xd4 17 ♗xd4 ♗b7 with equal chances (Stein–Darga, Amsterdam 1964).

(b) **12 d5** ♘b6 13 ♘bd2 (13 g4 h5! 14 ♘h2 hg 15 hg ♗g5! favours Black; Fischer–Keres, Curaçao 1962) 13 … f5 14 ef ♗xf5 15 ♘e4 ♕d7 with excellent counterplay for Black (Voronkov).

12 ... cd

12 ... ed 13 cd ♘c6 14 d5 ♘ce5 15 a4 b4 16 ♘xe5 ♘xe5 17 f4 ♘g6 18 ♘c4 (18 ♘f3) 18 ... a5 19 b3 ♗a6 20 ♗d3 ♗f6 21 ♖a2 ♗xc4 22 ♗xc4 ♗d4 23 ♔h2 ♖a7 24 g3 is in White's favour (Yurtaev–Nenashev, USSR 1988).

13 cd ♘c6 *(215)*

Other possibilities for Black are worse:

(a) **13 ... ♗f6** 14 ♘f1 ♘c6 15 ♗e3 ed 16 ♘xd4 ♘de5 17 ♗b3 ♗d7 18 ♘g3 g6 19 f4 ♘c4 20 ♗xc4 bc 21 ♖c1 d5 22 e5 (Suetin–Ciocaltea, Tbilisi 1969).

(b) **13 ... ed** 14 ♘b3 (or 14 ♘xd4 ♗f6 15 ♘f1 ♘e5 16 ♘e3 g6 17 ♘d5 ♗g7 18 a4 ba 19 ♗xa4 ♗b7 20 ♗d2 ♘ac4 21 ♗c3) 14 ... ♗f6 15 ♘xa5 ♕xa5 16 ♗g5 ♕d8 17 ♗xf6 ♕xf6 18 ♘xd4 ♘e5 19 ♗b3 ♗d7 20 ♖c1 ♖fd8 21 ♕d7 ♘g6 22 ♖cd1 ♘e5 23 f4! (Spassky–Averbakh, Kharkov 1963).

In all cases White has the better game.

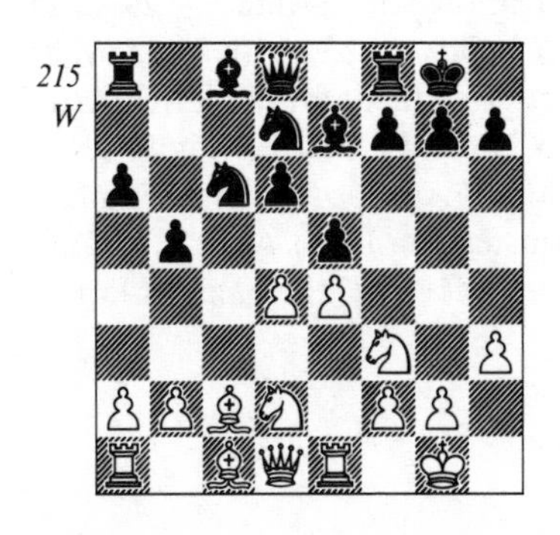
215
W

14 ♘b3

The most common continuation. We shall briefly consider other lines for White:

(a) **14 d5** ♘b4 15 ♗b1 a5 16 a3 (or 16 ♕e2 ♖b8 17 ♘b3 ♘a6!) 16 ... ♘a6 17 b4 ♘b6! 18 ♕d3 ♗d7 19 ♗d3 ♘c7 20 ♗b2 f5! 21 ef a4 22 ♕a2 ♗xf5 23 ♗xf5 ♖xf5 and Black has the better chances (Suetin–Tal, USSR Ch. 1965).

(b) **14 a3** ed 15 ♘b3 ♘de5! 16 ♘fxd4 ♗f6 17 ♗d2 (17 ♗e3 ♘xd4 18 ♗xd4 ♘c4 19 ♖b1 ♗e5) 17 ... ♘xd4 18 ♘xd4 ♘d3! with excellent play for Black (Tal–Keres, Curaçao 1962).

(c) **14 ♘f1** ♗f6 (or 14 ... ed 15 ♘xd4 ♘xd4 16 ♕xd4 ♘e5 17 ♖d1! ♕c7 — 17 ... ♗b7 18 ♘g3 ♗f6; Timman–Romanishin, Wijk aan Zee 1985 — 18 ♘e3 ♗xh3 19 ♘d5 ♕d8 20 ♘xe7+ ♕xe7 21 ♕xd6 with an extra pawn for White) 15 ♗e3 ed 16 ♘xd4 ♘de5 17 ♗b3 ♗b7! 18 ♘g3 ♘g6 19 ♕d2 ♘xd4 20 ♗xd4 ♗e5 with roughly equal play (Suetin).

14 ... a5 *(216)*

Interesting is 14 ... ♘b6 15 d5 ♘a7 16 ♘a5 ♗d7 17 ♗d2 ♕b8 18 ♗b4 ♗d8! 19 ♕d2 (19 b3!) 19 ... ♘c4 20 ♘xc4 bc 21 a4 a5 22 ♗c3 ♘c8 23 ♘h2 ♗b6 with quite good counterplay for Black (Geller–Dorfman, USSR Ch. 1977).

After 14 ... a5 White has a choice of two lines:

C21 15 ♗e3
C22 15 ♗d3

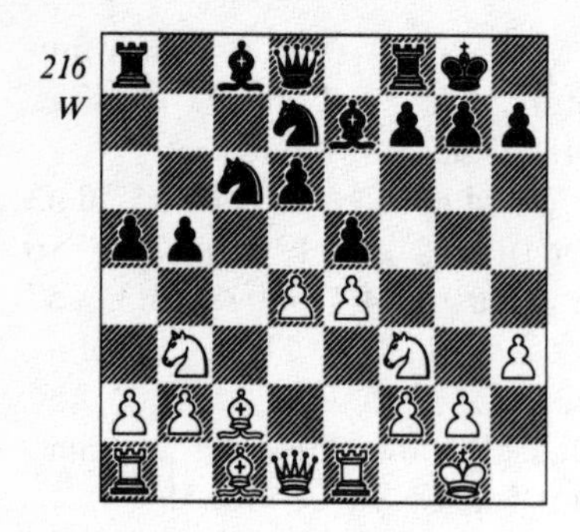
216
W

C21

15 ♗e3 a4

And now: 16 ♘bd2 ♗f6 17 ♘f1 ed 18 ♘xd4 ♘xd4 19 ♗xd4 ♘e5 20 ♘e3 ♗b7 21 ♕d2 a3 22 b4! ♗g5 23 ♖ad1 with somewhat better chances for White (Gligoric–Tal, Amsterdam 1964).

C22

15 ♗d3

This manoeuvre was played for the first time in the game Suetin–Stein, Moscow 1964. Its tactical basis can be seen in the following variation: 15 ... a4? 16 ♗xb5 ab 17 ♗xc6 ♖xa2 18 ♖xa2 ba 19 ♕a4! Also in White's favour is 15 ... b4, or 15 ... ♕b6 16 ♗e3 ♕b7 17 a3 a4 18 d5 ♘cb8 19 ♘c1 ♘a6 (Gufeld–Kats, Moscow 1964). Here White underlined his advantage with the move 20 b4!

15 ... ♗a6

After 15 ... ♖b8 16 ♕e2 ♗a6 17 ♗d2 ed 18 ♘bxd4 ♘xd4 19 ♘xd4 ♘e5 20 ♖ad1 ♕b6 21 ♗e3 ♕b7 22 ♘f5 White has unpleasant pressure (Tal–Reshevsky, Amsterdam 1964).

16 d5

After 16 ♗e3 a4 17 ♘c1 ed 18 ♘xd4 ♘xd4 19 ♗xd4 ♘e5 20 ♗f1 ♘c6 21 ♗e3 ♗f6 22 ♘d3 ♖e8 23 ♖c1 (23 ♖b1) 23 ... ♗b7 23 f3 a3 25 b3 b4 chances are roughly equal (Smyslov–Lengyel, Amsterdam 1964).

16 ... ♘b4

And now:

(a) **17 ♗b1** a4 18 ♘d4!? ed 19 a3 ♘xd5 20 ed ♗f6 21 ♘xd4 ♗xd4 22 ♕xd4 ♘c5 23 ♗c2 and White's position is preferable (Suetin).

(b) **17 ♗f1** a4 18 a3 ♘xd5 19 ♕xd5 ♘b6 (or 19 ... ab 20 ♗xb5 ♘f6 21 ♕d3 ♗xb5 22 ♕xb5 ♕b8 23 ♕xb8 ♖axb8 24 ♗g5 ♖fc8 25 ♖ac1 h6 26 ♖xc8 ♖xc8 27 ♗xf6 ♗xf6 28 ♖e3 ♖c1 — 28 ... ♖c2 29 ♖b3 d5 30 ♘e1 ♖e2 31 ♔f1 ♖e4 32 ♖d3! ♖c4 33 ♖d5 with advantage to White — 29 ♔h2 ♖c2 30 ♖xb3 with somewhat better chances for White) 20 ♕d1 ab 21 ♕xd3 ♕d7 22 ♗g5!? ♗xg5 23 ♘xg5 (Hellers–Timman, Amsterdam 1986). After 23 ... ♘a4 24 ♖ad1 ♕e7! the game is level.

15 Classical Chigorin and Smyslov Variations

In this chapter we discuss some of the important Closed Systems which arise after 1 e4 e5 2 ♘f3 ♘c6 3 ♗b5 a6 4 ♗a4 ♘f6 5 0–0 ♗e7 6 ♖e1 b5 7 ♗b3 d6 8 c3 0–0 9 h3, including the Classical Chigorin (9 … ♘d7), the fashionable 9 … ♗e6, and Smyslov's variations, 9 … ♕d7 and 9 … h6. In the next chapter we shall analyse 9 … ♗b7 and 9 … a5, and in the final chapter the Breyer Variation, 9 … ♘b8.

A 9 … ♘d7
B 9 … ♗e6
C 9 … ♕d7
D 9 … h6

A

9 … ♘d7

This plan, consolidating the square e5, was also introduced into practice by Chigorin. Nowadays it is played quite frequently.

10 d4

Nowadays 10 d3 is rarely played. Black has quite a few replies, each of which has its merits: 10 … ♘a5, 10 … ♖e8, 10 … ♗b7, 10 … ♗f6. For example: 10 … ♗f6 11 ♘bd2 ♘b6 12 ♘f1 ♗e6 13 ♘e3 ♕d7 and Black has no difficulties (Boleslavsky–Botvinnik, Groningen 1946).

Also rarely encountered is 10 a4. After 10 … ♗b7 play transposes to one of the main lines. But there are some original variations:

(a) **10 … ♘c5** 11 ab ♘xb3 12 ♕xb3 ♖b8 13 ♕c4!? ♗e6 14 ♕xc6! ♖b6 15 ♕xb6 cb 16 ab ♕c7 17 d4 ♖a8 18 ♗e3 ♗c8 19 de de 20 a7! with advantage to White (Suetin).

(b) **10 … b4** 11 ♗d5 ♗b7 12 cb ♖b8 13 b5 ab 14 ab ♘b4 15 ♗xb7 ♖xb7 16 ♘c3 and White's position is preferable (Schmid–Keres, Tel Aviv OL 1964).

After 10 d4 Black has a choice between:

A1 10 … ♗f6
A2 10 … ♘b6

A1

10 … ♗f6 *(217)*
11 a4

217
W

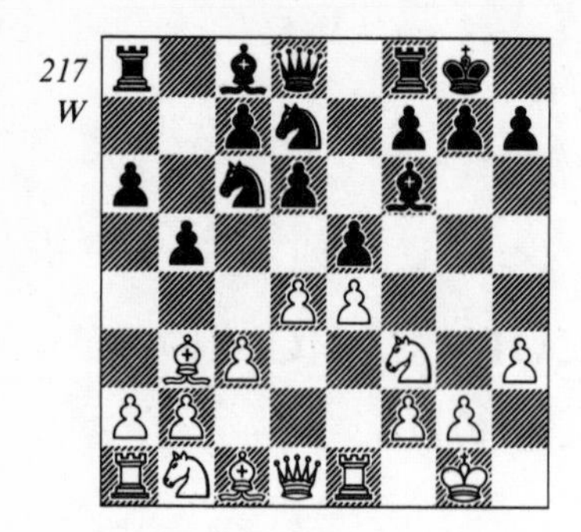

Other possibilities for White:

(a) **11 ♗d5** ♗b7 12 de de 13 ♗e3 ♘a5 14 ♗xb7 ♘xb7 15 ♕c2 ♕e7 (also possible is 15 ... ♘dc5! 16 ♖d1 ♕e7 17 ♘bd2 ♖fd8 18 ♘f1 h5! with equal chances; van der Wiel–Short, Tilburg 1988) 16 ♘bd2 ♖fd8 17 ♖ed1 ♕e6 18 ♘f1 ♗e7 19 a4 f6 20 b4 c6 21 ♘3d2 ♘d6 22 f3 ♖fc8 23 ♗f2 ♘b7 with definite pressure for White (Sax–Karpov, Rotterdam 1989).

(b) **11 a3!?** ♗b7 12 ♗a2 ♘e7 13 d5 ♘b6! and then c7–c6, with counterplay for Black.

(c) **11 d5** ♘a5 12 ♗c2 ♘b6 (12 ... c5) 13 ♘bd2 c6 14 dc ♕c7 15 ♘f1 ♕xc6 16 ♕d3 ♕c7 17 ♖d1 ♖d8 with equality (Stein–Lengyel, Kecskemét 1968).

(d) **11 ♗e3** ♘a5 (11 ... ♗b7 12 ♘bd2 ♘e7 13 ♗c2 c5 14 d5 ♘b6 15 b4 cb 16 cb ♗c8 17 a4; Dolmatov–Malanyuk, USSR 1989) 12 ♗c2 ♘c4 13 ♗c1 ♗b7 (after 13 ... c5 14 b3 ♘cb6 15 ♗e3 c4 16 d5 ♗b7 17 b4 a5 18 a4! Black has difficulties; Karpov–Torre, Hannover 1983) 14 b3 ♘cb6 15 ♗e3 ed (15 ... ♖e8 16 d5! ♖c8 17 ♘bd2 c6 18 c4! favours White; Spassky–Petrosian, World Ch. 1969) 16 cd c5 17 ♘bd2 cd 18 ♗xd4 ♖e8 19 ♘f1 ♘e5 with full equality for Black (O'Kelly).

(e) **11 ♘bd2** ♗b7 12 ♘f1 ♘e7 13 ♘g3 c5 14 ♘h5 ♘g6 15 ♗c2 ♖e8 16 d5 ♘gf8 17 ♗e3 ♗e7 18 ♘g3 g6 19 b3 with a small advantage to White (Dolmatov–Balashov, USSR 1989).

After 11 a4 Black's main choice is between:

A11 11 ... ♘a5
A12 11 ... ♗b7

Fairly often one encounters 11 ... ♖b8. For example: 12 ab ab 13 ♗e3 (after 13 d5 ♘e7 14 ♘a3 ♘c5 — or 14 ... b4 15 cb ♖xb4 16 ♗d2 ♖b8 17 ♗c3 g6 with a solid defence for Black; Suetin–Sokolsky, Minsk 1953 — 15 ♗c2 c6 16 b4 ♘a6 17 dc ♘c6 18 ♕e2 ♘c7 19 ♖d1 ♗e6 20 ♖b1 ♕d7 21 ♘g5 ♗xg5 22 ♗xg5 f6 23 ♗e3 ♖fd8 24 ♗d3 ♘e7 with approximate equality; Popovic–Agdestein, Belgrade 1989) 13 ... ♘e7 14 d5 (14 ♘g5!? h6 15 ♗xf7+ ♖xf7 16 ♘e6 leads to a draw; Sax–Karpov, Skelleftea 1989; as does 14 ♘bd2 c5 15 ♘f1 cd 16 cd ed 17 ♗xd4 ♘c6; Spassky–Smyslov, Bugojno 1989) 14 ... ♘c5 (or 14 ... g6 15 ♘a3 ♗g7 with a solid defence for Black; Ljubojevic–Smyslov, Bugojno 1984) 15 ♗c2 c6 16 b4 ♘a6 17 dc ♘xc6 18 ♘a3 ♘c7 19 ♕e2 ♕e8 20 ♖ed1 ♗e7 21 ♗d3 ♘f8 and

White has the better chances (Nunn–Karpov, Rotterdam 1989).

A11

11 ... ♘a5
12 ♗c2 ♘b6 *(218)*

In White's favour is 12 ... ♗b7 13 ♘a3! ed 14 ♘xd4 ♘c6 15 ab ♘xd4 16 cd ab 17 ♕d3! (Spassky–Portisch, match 1977), and still more so 12 ... b4? 13 d5! bc 14 b4! ♘b7 15 a5!

218
W

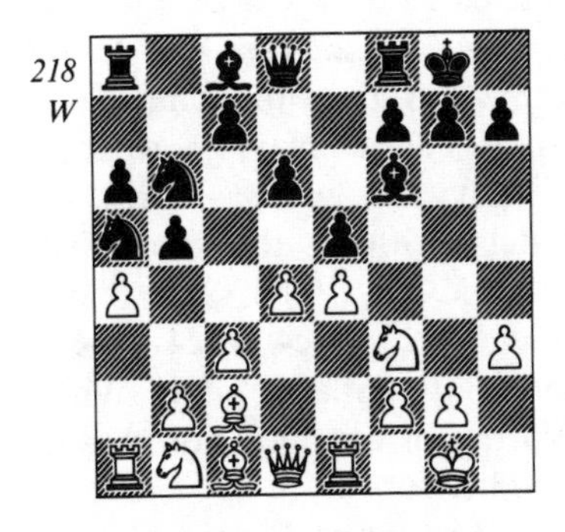

After 12 ... ♘b6 the following variations may arise:

(a) **13 ab** ab 14 ♘bd2 (White gets nothing after 14 de de 15 ♗e3 ♘b7, or 14 ♘h2 c5, but an interesting line is 14 d5!? c6 15 dc ♕c7 16 ♘a3 ♗e6 — 16 ... ♕xc6 17 ♕d3 ♗a6 18 ♘d4! ♕d7 19 ♘dxb5!; Suetin–Stein, USSR Ch. 1965 — 17 ♘xb5 ♕xc6 18 ♘a3 ♘ac4 and Black has plenty of counterplay — Suetin) 14 ... c5 15 ♘f1 cd 16 cd ed 17 ♕d3 ♗e5 (also possible is 17 ... g6 18 ♗h6 ♖e8 19 ♘xd4 ♗d7 20 ♘xb5 d5! with counterplay for Black; Stein–Keres, Tallinn 1965) 18 ♕xb5 ♗a6 19 ♕b4 ♘c6 20 ♕d2 ♘c4 with roughly equal chances (Suetin).

(b) **13 b4** ♘ac4 14 a5 ♘d7 15 ♗b3 ed 16 cd c5 17 ♗f4 (an equal game arises after 17 bc ♘xc5 18 ♗xc4 bc 19 e4 de 20 dc e4! — Fischer) 17 ... cb 18 ♘bd2 d5 19 ed ♘xa5 20 ♗d6 ♘xb3 21 ♕xb3 ♖e8 22 ♗c7 ♖xe1+ 23 ♖xe1 ♕f8! 24 ♘e4 a5 25 ♘d6 a4 26 ♕xb4 ♗e7 27 ♘xe5 ♘xe5 28 de ♗d7 with equal chances (Fischer).

A12

11 ... ♗b7
12 ab

The continuation 12 ♘a3 has been comparatively unexplored. For example: 12 ... ed!? (in the game de Firmian–Benjamin, USA 1988, there occurred 12 ... ♕b8?! 13 ♗g5! ed 14 ♗xf6 ♘xf6 15 cd with better play for White) 13 cd ♘a5 (worthy of consideration is 13 ... ♖e8!? After 13 ... ♘b6 14 ♗f4 ba 15 ♗xa4 ♘xa4 16 ♕xa4 a5 17 ♗d2 ♖e8 18 d5! ♘b4 19 ♗xb4 cb 20 ♕xb4 ♖b8 21 ♕c4! White has a clear advantage; Kasparov–Karpov, 18th game, World Ch. match 1990) 14 ♗a2 (nothing is to be gained by 14 ab ab 15 ♘xb5? ♘xb3 16 ♖xa8 ♕xa8 17 ♕xb3 ♗xe4 18 ♘xc7? ♕c6! etc.) 14 ... b4 15 ♘c4 ♘xc4 16 ♗xc4 ♖e8 17 ♕b3 ♖xe4 18 ♗xf7+ ♔h8 19 ♗e3 ♖e7 20 ♗d5 (Kasparov–Karpov, 12th game, World Ch. match 1990), and here Black should apparently have played 20 ... ♗xd5 21 ♕xd5 ♘b6 22 ♕c6 ♕e8, maintaining a sufficiently solid defence.

Also interesting is 12 ♗e3. In an important test, Kasparov–Karpov, 8th game, World Ch. match 1990, there followed 12 … ♘a5 13 ♗c2 ♘c4 14 ♗c1 d5!? 15 de ♘dxe5 16 ♘xe5 ♘xe5 17 ab ab 18 ♖xa8 ♕xa8?! (more prudent is 18 … ♗xa8 19 ed ♕xd5 20 ♕xd5 ♗xd5 21 ♗f4 ♘c4 22 b3 ♘d6 23 ♗xd6 cd with a probable draw — a recommendation of Tal's) 19 f4 ♘g6 20 e5 ♗h4 21 ♖f1 (21 f5!?) 21 … ♗e7 22 ♘d2 ♗c5+ 23 ♔h2 d4 24 ♕e2! with an initiative for White.

12 … ab

13 ♖xa8 ♕xa8 *(219)*

After 13 … ♗xa8 14 d5 ♘e7 15 ♘a3 ♘c5 16 ♗c2 c6 17 b4 ♘a6 18 dc ♘xc6 19 ♕d3 ♘c7 20 ♖d1 ♕a8 21 ♕xd6 ♘e6 22 ♕d3 ♘g6 23 ♖e1 ♕b7 24 g3 White stands better (Hübner–Short, Skelleftea 1989).

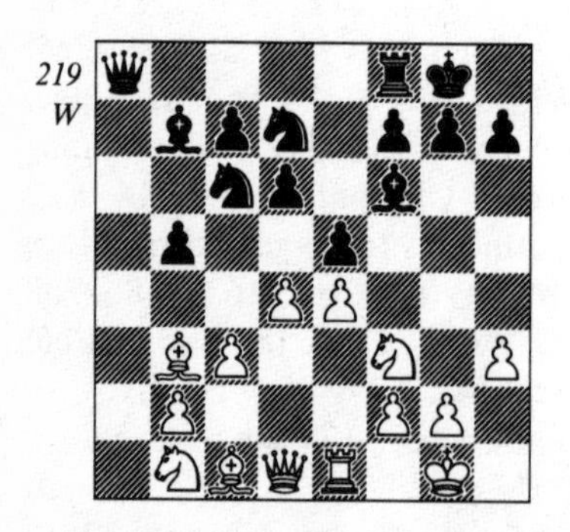
219
W

After 13 … ♕xa8 the following variations are possible:

(a) **14 d5** ♘a5 (after 14 … ♘e7 15 ♘a3 ♗a6 16 ♘c2 ♘c5 17 ♘b4 ♘xb3 18 ♕xb3 ♗b7 19 ♗e3 ♖b8 20 ♘d2 White's chances are to be preferred; Suetin–Borisenko, Kharkov 1956) 15 ♗c2 ♘c4! (in the game Tal–Stein, USSR 1965, there followed 15 … ♗e7 16 ♘a3 c6 17 dc ♗xc6 18 ♕e2 ♕a6 19 ♘d2 ♖b8 20 b4! with somewhat better play for White) 16 b3 ♘cb6 17 ♘a3 (on 17 ♘bd2 there would follow 17 … c6) 17 … ♗a6 18 ♘h2 c6 19 dc ♕xc6 20 ♗d2 ♗e7 21 ♘g4 ♖a8 22 ♘e3 ♘f6 23 ♘f5 ♗f8 24 ♗g5 with complicated, double-edged play; Kasparov–Karpov, 6th game, World Ch. match 1990). In the game there followed 24 … ♘bd7 25 c4! bc 26 bc ♗xc4 27 ♘xc4 ♕xc4 28 ♗b3 with an initiative for White. Worthy of consideration was 24 … d5!?

(b) **14 ♘a3** b4 15 ♘c4 bc 16 bc ♘a5 17 ♘xa5 ♕xa5 18 ♕c2 ed 19 cd ♗xd4 20 ♗d2 ♕c5 21 ♘xd4 ♕xd4 22 ♗c3 ♕c5 23 ♕d2 ♔h8 24 ♗d4 ♕h5 25 ♗g4! with a dangerous initiative for White (Tal–Karpov, Skelleftea 1989).

A2

10 … ♘b6!?

The nature of play here is noticeably different from that in the previous variation. Black aims to develop rapid counterplay in the centre.

11 ♘bd2

After 11 ♗e3 ed 12 cd ♘a5 13 ♗c2 c5 14 ♘c3 ♘ac4 15 ♗c1 cd 16 ♘xd4 ♗f6 (Gligoric–Olafsson, Bled 1959), or 11 de ♘xe5 12 ♘xe5 de 13 ♕h5 ♗f6 (or 13 ... ♕d6) 14 ♘d2 ♕e7 15 ♘f1 ♗e6 16 ♘e3 g6 (Fischer–Keres, Zürich 1959), Black has full equality.

11 ... ♗f6 *(220)*

After 11 ... ed 12 cd d5 (12 ... ♘b4 13 d5!) 13 ♗c2 (after 13 e5 ♗f5 14 ♘f1 ♘b4 15 ♘g3 ♗g6 Black has a solid defence; but White has the better chances after 13 ed! ♘xd5 14 ♘e4 ♘f6 15 ♗c2 ♘b4 16 ♘xf6+ ♗xf6 17 ♗e4 ♘d5 18 ♕c2; Stein–Tarasov, Moscow 1961) 13 ... ♗e6 14 e5 ♕d7 15 ♘b3 ♗f5 16 ♗g5 ♖fe8 17 ♗xe7 ♖xe7 18 ♖c1! ♘b4 19 ♘c5 ♗xc2 20 ♕d2! with advantage to White (Fischer–Reshevsky, Santa Monica 1966).

220
W

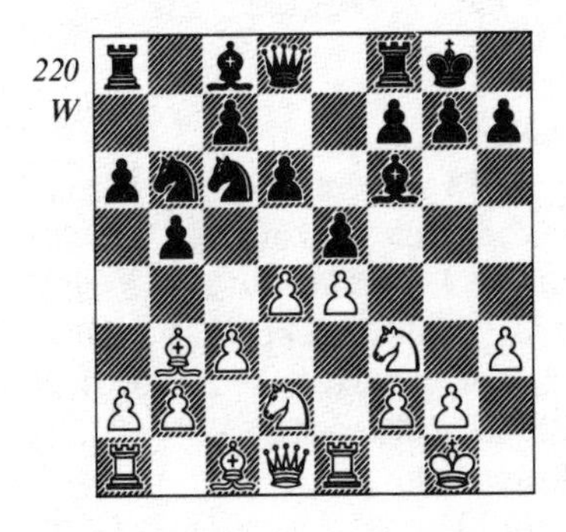

Here the following variations are possible:

(a) **12 d5** ♘a5 13 ♗c2 c6 (13 ... g6 14 ♘f1 ♗g7 15 ♗g5 f6 16 ♗e3; Belyavsky–Spassky, Barcelona 1989) 14 dc ♕c7 15 ♘f1 ♕xc6 16 ♘e3 ♘ac4 17 ♘g4 ♗e7 18 b3 ♘a5 19 ♗a3 with pressure for White in the centre (Vasyukov–Smyslov, USSR Ch. 1967).

(b) **12 ♘f1** ♖e8, and now:

(b1) **13 ♘1h2** ed 14 cd ♘a5 15 ♗c2 c5 16 ♘g4 ♗xg4 17 hg cd (17 ... g6 18 e5!, or 17 ... ♘c6 18 e5!, is dangerous for Black — recommendation of Petrosian and Suetin) 18 g5 ♗e5! 19 ♘d4 g6 20 f4 ♗g7 21 f5?! (21 b3!) 21 ... ♖c8 22 f6 ♗f8 23 b3 d5 with excellent play for Black (Smirin–Balashov, USSR 1989).

(b2) **13 ♘g3** g6 14 ♗h6 a5 15 ♗c2 ♗d7 16 d5 ♘e7 17 ♕e2 ♗g7 18 ♗xg7 ♔xg7 19 ♗d3 f5 20 ef ♘exd5 21 fg ♘f4 with chances for both sides (Sax–Tal, Skelleftea 1989).

(b3) **13 ♗c2** ed (or 13 ... g6 14 ♘e3 ♗g7 15 d5 ♘e7 16 b3 ♖f8; Fedorowicz–Razuvaev, New York 1989) 14 cd ♘b4 15 ♗b1 c5 16 a3 ♘c6 17 e5 de 18 dc ♕xd1 19 ♖xd1 ♘a4 20 ♗e4 ♗b7 with equality (Ljubojevic–Spassky, Barcelona 1989).

B

9 ... ♗e6

A solid continuation. The exchange of light-squared bishops reduces White's chances of a king-side attack. As a rule White changes plan here and organizes an offensive on the queenside. Black in turn strives to open up the game in the centre.

10 d4

White gets nowhere after 10 ♗xe6 fe 11 d4 ♕d7 12 de de 13 ♕xd7 ♘xd7.

10 ... ♗xb3

Now White has a choice:

B1 11 ♕xb3
B2 11 ab

B1

11 ♕xb3

We shall single out the two currently popular main variations:

B11 11 ... ♕b8
B12 11 ... d5

But first we shall consider the following variations:

(a) **11 ... ♕d7** (11 ... ed?! 12 cd ♘a5 13 ♕c2 c5 14 dc dc 15 ♘c3 ♘c6 16 ♗g5! ♘b4 17 ♕e2 ♕d3 18 a3 ♕xe2 19 ♖xe2 ♘c6 20 e5 ♘d7 21 ♖d1 ♘b6 22 e6! with an initiative for White — Boleslavsky) 12 ♗g5 h6 13 ♗xf6 ♗xf6 14 d5 ♘e7 (or 14 ... ♘a5 15 ♕c2 c6 16 dc ♕xc6 17 ♘bd2 ♖ac8 18 ♖ac1 ♖fd8 19 ♘f1 with a small advantage to White; Smyslov–Botvinnik, Moscow 1951) 15 ♘bd2 g6 16 a4 (16 c4!?) 16 ... ♗g7 17 c4 bc 18 ♘xc4 ♖ab8 19 ♕d3 f5 20 ♘fd2 ♔h7 21 f3 c6 with roughly equal play (Unzicker–Pfleger, West Germany 1963).

(b) **11 ... ♖e8** 12 ♘bd2 (12 d5 ♘a5 13 ♕c2!) 12 ... ed 13 cd ♘a5 14 ♕d1 (or 14 ♕c2 c5!) 14 ... c5 15 ♘f1 (15 b3!?) 15 ... ♗f8 16 ♘g3 cd 17 ♘xd4 g6 18 ♗f4 ♕b6 19 ♖c1 ♗g7 with equal chances (Ioseliani–Chiburdanidze, match 1988).

B11

11 ... ♕b8

12 ♗g5

After 12 ♘bd2 ♕b6 (or 12 ... ♘a5 13 ♕c2 c5!) 13 d5 ♘a5 14 ♕c2 c6 15 b4 ♘b7 16 dc ♕xc6 17 ♗b2 ♖fc8 Black has full equality (Ioseliani–Chiburdanidze, match 1988).

12 ... h6
13 ♗h4 *(221)*

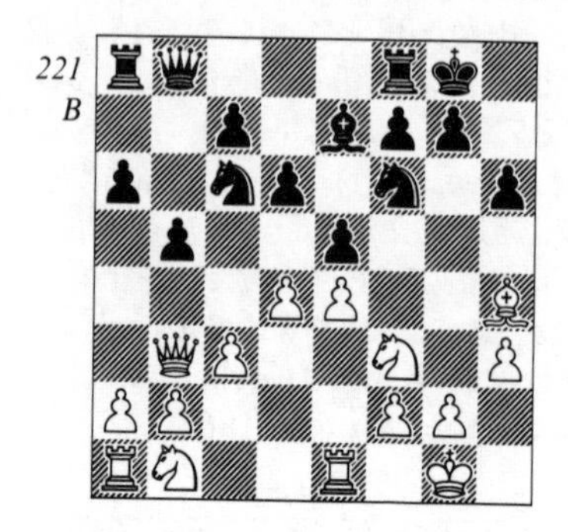

221
B

And now:

(a) **13 ... ♘d7** 14 ♗xe7 ♘xe7 15 ♘bd2 c5 16 ♖ad1 ♕c7 17 ♘f1 ♘f6 18 ♘g3 ♖fd8 19 ♖d2 ♖d7 20 ♖ed1 ♖ad8 21 a4 ed 22 cd d5! 23 e5 ♘e4 24 ♘xe4 de 25 e6 c4 26 ♕e3 fe 27 ♕xe4 ♖d6 with equality (Romanishin).

(b) **13 ... ♕b6** 14 de (14 ♘bd2!?) 14 ... de 15 ♘bd2 ♗c5 16 ♘f1 ♘h5 and here Black is not worse (Rodriguez–Smagin, Sochi 1988).

(c) **13 ... ♘a5** 14 ♕d1 c6 15 ♘bd2 ♖e8 16 b4 ♘b7 17 ♘f1 g6 18 ♗xf6 ♗xf6 19 d5 c5 with full equality for Black (Gipslis–Nei, USSR Ch. 1963).

B12

11 ... d5!?

A fashionable continuation. Practice has shown that opening the centre is entirely appropriate.

12 ed ♘a5
13 ♕c2

After 13 ♕d1 ed (13 ... e4!?) 14 ♘xd4 ♖e8 15 b4 ♘c4 16 a4 ba 17 ♘d2 ♕xd5 18 ♖xa4 ♘xd2 19 ♗xd2 ♘e4 20 ♖a5 c5 Black is not worse (Belyavsky–Tal, Montpellier 1985).

13 ... ed *(222)*

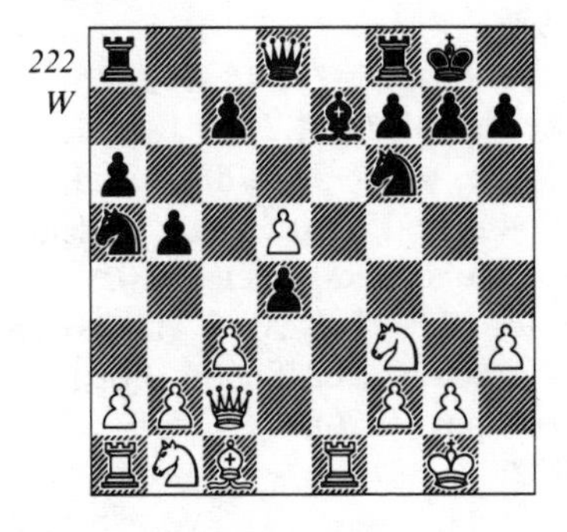

222
W

And now:

(a) **14 cd** ♘xd5 15 ♘c3 ♘xc3 (15 ... c6 16 b3 — 16 ♘e4 ♖c8 17 b3 ♘b7 18 ♗d2 c5 with equality — 16 ... ♗b4 17 ♗d2 ♗xc3 18 ♗xc3 ♘b7 19 ♗d2 with a minimal advantage to White; Short–Nikolic, Tilburg 1988) 16 ♕xc3 ♘c4 17 ♗f4 ♗d6 18 ♗xd6 ♕xd6 19 ♖ac1 ♖ac8 with approximate equality (Short–van der Sterren, Wijk aan Zee 1986).

(b) **14 ♘xd4** ♖e8 (or 14 ... ♘xd4 15 ♘d2 ♖e8 16 ♘e4 ♕d7 17 ♗g5 ♗xg5 18 ♘xg5 ♘f6 19 ♘f5 with some pressure for White; F. Olafsson–Forintos, Athens 1969) 15 a4 ♕xd5 (after 15 ... ♘xd5 16 ♗xe7 ♘xe7 17 ♘d2 c5 18 ♘4f3 White's position is preferable; Short–Sharif, Lucerne 1985) 16 ab ab 17 ♗d2 ♔f8 18 ♗f4 ♗d6 19 ♗xd6 ♕xd6 20 ♘d2 ♖xe1+ 21 ♖xe1 ♕d5 22 ♖a1 and White's chances are slightly better (Sokolov–P. Nikolic, Brussels 1988).

B2

11 ab

This continuation perhaps sets Black the most problems. White takes aim against the pawn on a6 and forms a cluster of queenside pawns. As main variations we shall single out:

B21 11 ... ♖e8
B22 11 ... ed

Other possibilities for Black:

(a) **11 ... ♕d7** (or 11 ... ♕c8 12 ♗g5 h6 13 ♗h4 ♖e8 14 d5!) 12 d5 ♘d8 13 c4 c6 (13 ... b4 14 c5 c6 15 ♗g5!) 14 ♘c3 cd (14 ... b4 15 dc! ♕xc6 16 ♘d5!, or 14 ... ♕b7 15 ♗g5 bc 16 bc ♕xb2 17 ♕d3 ♕b7 18 ♖fb1 ♕c7 19 dc ♘xc6 20 ♗xf6 ♗xf6 21 ♘d5!, favours White — Suetin) 15 ♘xd5 ♘xd5 16 ♕xd5! with a positional advantage to White (Aronin–Kholmov, Moscow 1967).

(b) **11 ... ♕b8** 12 d5 (12 ♗g5) 12 ... ♘d8 13 ♕d3 (13 c4) 13 ... c6 14 c4 bc 15 bc cd 16 cd a5 17 ♘c3 ♘d7 18 ♗e3 g6 19 g4! ♘b7 20 ♘a4 f5 21 gf gf 22 ef ♕e8 23 ♔h2 ♕h5 24 ♖g1+ ♔h8 25 ♘g5 with an initiative for White

(Suetin–Bykhovsky, Moscow 1968).

B21

11 ... ♖e8
12 d5

An alternative is 12 ♗g5! h6 (in White's favour is 12 ... ♘d7 13 ♗e3 ed?! — 13 ... ♗f6 — 14 cd d5 15 ed ♘b4 16 ♘c3 ♘b6 17 ♘e5 ♘6xd5 18 ♕h5!; Tal–Averbakh, USSR 1974) 13 ♗xf6 (13 d5?!) 13 ... ♗xf6 14 d5 with slight pressure for White (Studenetsky).

12 ... ♘b8
13 c4

The following variations may arise:

(a) **13 ♘bd2** c6 14 dc ♕c7 15 b4 ♕xc6 16 ♘b3 ♘bd7 17 ♘a5 ♕c7 with equal play (Unzicker–Pfleger, Hastings 1971/2).

(b) **13 ♘a3** ♘bd7 14 ♘d2 ♕c8 15 ♘c2 c6 16 dc ♕xc6 17 c4 ♗f8 with complicated play, where White's chances are slightly better (Ciocaltea–Vogt, Bucharest 1974).

(c) **13 ♗g5** ♘bd7 14 ♘a3 ♘d5 15 ♕xd5 ♗g5 16 ♕c6! ♘c5 17 ♘xb5 ab 18 ♘g5 ♖b8 19 b4 with equal chances (Adorjan–Portisch, Budapest 1971).

13 ... ♘bd7 *(223)*

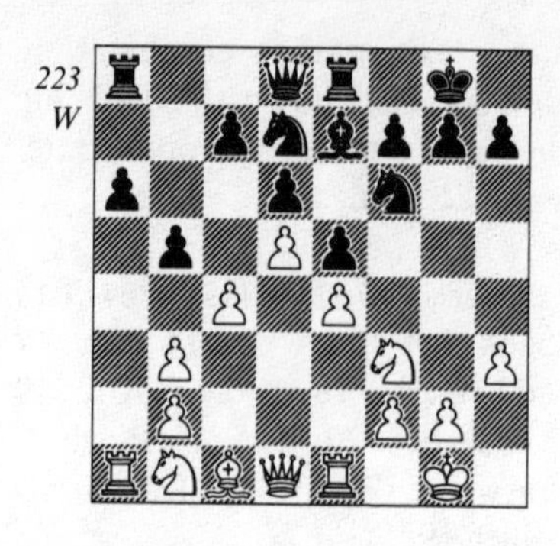

223
W

After 13 ... c6 14 dc b4 15 ♗g5 ♘h5 16 ♗xe7 ♖xe7 17 ♘bd2 ♕c7 18 ♘f1 ♕xc6 19 ♘g3 ♘f6 20 ♘f5! White's pressure is very effective (Suetin–Forintos, Sarajevo 1965).

Now the following variations are possible:

(a) **14 ♕d3** b4 15 ♗d2 c5 16 ♗e3 ♘bd7 17 ♘bd2 h6 18 ♘f1 ♘h7 19 ♘g3 ♗g5 20 ♘f5 ♕f6 21 ♘h2 (Psakhis–Smagin, Protvino 1988).

(b) **14 ♘c3** ♕b8 15 ♕c2 ♕b7 16 ♗e3 ♖eb8 17 ♖a2 h6 18 ♖d1 c6 19 dc ♕xc6 20 ♕d3 bc 21 bc ♖b4 22 ♘d5 ♘xd5 23 cd (Gufeld–Forintos, Kecskemét 1968).

(c) **14 ♕c2** ♕c8 15 ♘c3 c6 16 dc ♕xc6 17 ♕e2 (Suetin–Portisch, Budapest 1970).

B22

11 ... ed
12 cd

12 ♘xd4 ♕d7 13 ♘d2 ♖fe8 presents no difficulties for Black.

12 ... d5

After 12 ... ♘b4 good for White are both 13 d5 c5 (13 ... ♘d7 14 ♘a3 c5 15 dc ♘xc6 16 ♘c2 ♘c5 17 ♘fd4 is in White's favour) 14 dc d5 15 e5 ♘e4 16 ♘c3 ♘xc3 17 bc ♘xc6 18 ♕d3 ♖e8 19 e6!? (Suetin–Nei, USSR 1974), and 13 ♘c3 c5 14 ♗e3.

13 e5 ♘e4

Interesting is 13 ... ♘d7 14 ♗e3 ♘b4 15 ♕d2 ♖e8 16 ♘c3 c5 with unclear play (van der Wiel–Motwani, Thessaloniki OL 1988).

14 ♘c3 f5
15 ef ♗xf6

After 15 ... ♘xf6 16 ♘e5 (16 ♕e2 ♗d6!; 16 ♗g5) 16 ... ♘b4 17 ♘a2 ♕e8 18 ♘xb4 ♗xb4 19 ♖e3 ♗d6 20 ♘c4 ♕d7 21 ♘xd6 ♕xd6 with equal chances (Geller–Smagin, Riga 1985).

16 ♘xe4 de
17 ♖xe4 ♕d5
18 ♖g4 ♖ad8

The following variations have also been played:

(a) **18 ... ♘d8** 19 ♕c2 ♘e6 20 ♗e3 ♖fe8 21 b4 c6 22 ♖e4 ♖e7 23 ♘e5 ♘d8 24 f4 with advantage to White (Suetin–Kholmov, Minsk 1952).

(b) **18 ... ♘e7** 19 ♕c2 (19 ♗h6?! ♘f5 20 ♗g5 h5 21 ♖f4 ♗xg5 22 ♘xg5 ♘d4! with equal chances; Psakhis–Arnason, Sochi 1988) 19 ... ♘f5 20 ♕e4 ♕xe4 21 ♖xe4 ♖ae8 22 ♖xe8 ♖xe8 23 ♔f1 ♘xd4 24 ♘xd4 ♗xd4 25 ♖xa6 ♖f8 26 f3 with a small advantage to White (Velimirovic–Kurajica, Kavalla 1985).

19 ♗e3 h5

19 ... ♘b4 20 ♕d2 h5 21 ♖f4!

20 ♖f4! ♘b4

20 ... g5? 21 ♖xf6 ♖xf6 22 ♘xg5!

21 ♕d2

Also good is 21 ♕b1 ♕xb3 22 ♖f5!

21 ... c5

21 ... ♕xb3? 22 ♖a3 ♕xc4 23 b3!

22 ♖ac1

After 22 ... ♕xb3 23 ♖xc5 ♖c8 24 ♖ff5! ♘d3 25 ♖xc8 ♖xc8 26 ♗g5! Black is in trouble (Suetin–Zinn, Havana 1968).

C

9 ... ♕d7

This somewhat pretentious manoeuvre was introduced into practice by Smyslov at the end of the 1950s. Its popularity (if one may use such a word) turned out to be extremely short. Even here, of course, there are some strategic 'tricks', but on the whole Black has quite a few difficulties to overcome.

10 d4 ♖e8 *(224)*

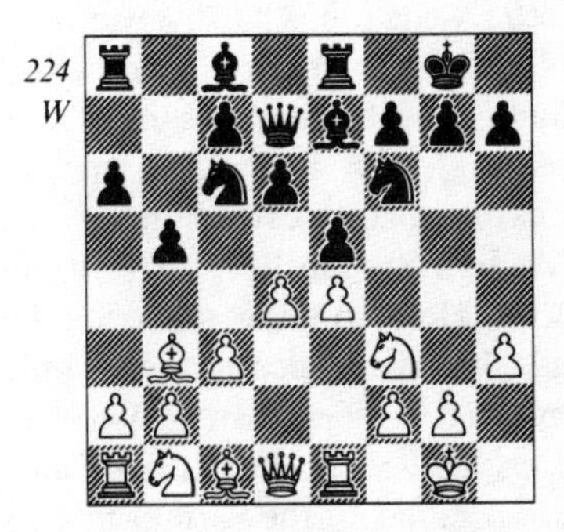
224
W

A critical position, in which the following variations may arise:

(a) **11 ♘bd2** ♗f8 12 d5 (after 12 ♘f1 ed — also possible is 12 ... g6 13 de de 14 ♗g5 ♗g7 15 ♘e3 ♘a5 — 13 ♘xd4 ♗b7 14 f3 g6 15 ♗g5 ♗g7; or 12 ♗c2 ♗b7 13 d5 ♘e7 14 c4 c6 Black has full equality) 12 ... ♘e7 (12 ... ♘a5) 13 ♘f1 g6 14 c4 ♗g7 15 c5! ♘h5 16 a4 dc 17 ab ♗b7 18 ba ♗xa6 19 ♗e3 with strong pressure for White (Fischer–Wade, Buenos Aires 1960).

(b) **11 Bg5** h6 12 Bh4 Bb7 13 Nbd2 Bd8 14 a3 Nh5 15 Nf1 Nf4 16 Bg3 Ng6 17 h4 Bf6 18 h5 Nf8 19 d5 with a spatial advantage to White.

(c) **11 Ng5** Nd8 12 f4 Bb7 13 d5 c6 14 c4 bc 15 Bxc4 cd 16 Bxd5 Nxd5 17 ed ef 18 Bxf4 Bxg5 19 Rxe8+ Qxe8 20 Bxg5 Qe5 with a lot of play for Black (Polugayevsky).

D

9 ... h6

This system too was introduced into practice by Smyslov in 1959 and was widely taken up. But in latter years it has hardly ever been played in its original form. It has had an extremely peculiar fate, serving, as it were, as a springboard in the evolution of the Modern System: 9 ... Bb7 10 d4 Re8. Here too the move h7–h6 has found application, but only by virtue of necessity. We shall consider here the variations which are peculiar to the variation in its original form.

10 d4 Re8

Now White has a choice:

D1 11 Nbd2
D2 11 Be3

Before considering these, we note that White achieves nothing after 11 d5 Na5 12 Bc2 c6, or 11 c4 Nxd4 12 Nxd4 ed 13 Qxd4 Be6 etc. The following variations deserve greater attention:

(a) **11 a4** Bd7 (11 ... Bb7 will be examined in the next chapter) 12 ab ab 13 Rxa8 Qxa8 14 Na3 Qb8 15 Ba2 Bf8 16 Qb3 Nd8 17 Bb1 c5 with equal play (Gligoric–Porath, Tel Aviv OL 1964).

(b) **11 Bc2** Bf8 12 d5 Ne7 13 a4 Bd7 14 ab ab 15 Rxa8 Qxa8 16 Na3 Rb8 17 b4 c6 with active counterplay for Black (Jansa–Filip, Mariánské Lázne 1965).

(c) **11 a3!?** (Suetin) 11 ... Bf8 12 Bc2 (12 Nbd2) 12 ... Bb7 13 d5 (13 b4?! a5! 14 Bb2 ab 15 cb Nxd4 16 Nxd4 ed 17 Qxd4 Be6) 13 ... Na7 (also not bad is 13 ... Na5 14 Nbd2 c6!) 14 a4 bc 15 Bxc4 c6 16 Nc3 Nb5! with full equality for Black (Suetin–Gligoric, Budva 1967).

D1

11 Nbd2 Bf8 *(225)*

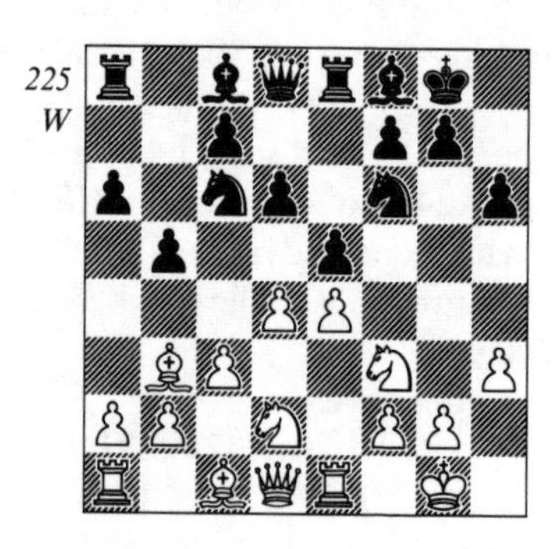

12 Nf1

The most common reply. Let us also consider the following continuations:

(a) **12 a3**, and now:

(a1) **12 ... Bb7** 13 Bc2 d5!? (13 ... Nb8 leads to the Breyer System) 14 de Nxe5 15 Nxe5 Rxe5 16 f4 Bc5+ 17 Kh1 Nxe4 18

♘xe4 ♖xe4 19 ♗xe4 de 20 ♕e2!; or 13 ... ♕d7 14 b4 d5 (14 ... a5 15 d5!) 15 ♘xe5 ♘xe5 16 de ♖xe5 17 f4 ♖ee8 18 e5 is good for White.

(a2) **12 ... ♗d7** 13 ♗c2 a5!? (in White's favour is 13 ... ♕b8 14 b4 a5 15 ♘b3, or 13 ... g6 14 d5! ♘e7 15 b4) 14 d5 (also not bad is 14 a4) 14 ... ♘e7 15 a4 c6 16 dc ♗xc6 17 ab ♗xb5 18 ♗a4! with definite pressure for White (Sanakoev–Chebetchek, corr. 1971).

(b) **12 ♗c2** ♗b7 (or 12 ... ♗d7 13 ♗d3 ♕b8 14 b3 g6 15 ♗b2 ♗g7 16 d5 ♘e7 17 c4 ♘h5 18 ♗f1 ♘f4 19 c5 c6! — Teleshev–Korolev, corr. 1985) 13 d5 ♘b8 14 ♘f1 ♘bd7 15 ♘g3 g6 with equal chances (Studenetsky). Note also that White achieves nothing after 12 de ♘xe5 13 ♘xe5 de 14 ♕f3 ♗e6, or 12 d5 ♘b8 (also possible is 12 ... ♘e7 13 a4 ♗d7) 13 ♘f1 ♗b7 etc. After 12 ♘f1 Black's two most important lines are:

D11 12 ... ♗d7
D12 12 ... ♗b7

D11

12 ... ♗d7

In White's favour is 12 ... ed 13 cd d5 14 e5, or 12 ... g6 13 ♘g3 ♗g7 14 de de 15 ♕e2 ♘a5 16 ♗c2 c5 17 a4.

13 ♘g3

White achieves nothing after 13 ♗c2 g6 14 ♗d2 ♗g7, or 13 d5 ♘a5 14 ♗c2 c6!, or 13 de ♘xe5 14 ♘xe5 de.

13 ... ♘a5

14 ♗c2 *(226)*

226
B

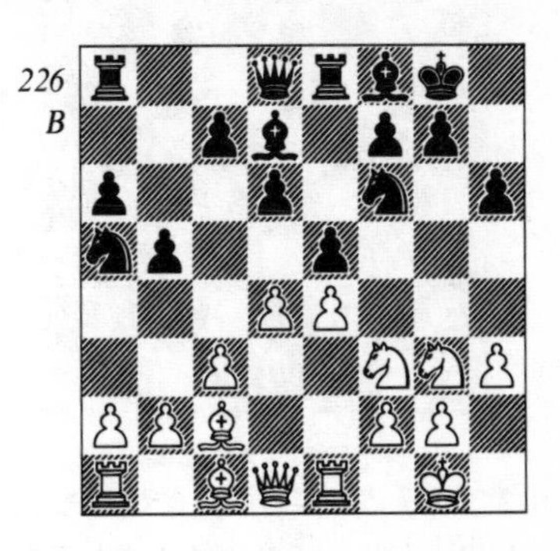

In this position the following variations are possible:

D111 14 ... c5
D112 14 ... ♘c4

D111

14 ... c5
15 b3 ♘c6

Worse is 15 ... g6 16 ♗e3 ♗g7 17 d5 ♘h7 18 ♕d2 h5 19 ♘h2, or 15 ... cd 16 cd ♘c6 17 ♗b2 ♖c8 18 ♕d2 ♕b6 19 ♖ad1, when in either case White has a lasting initiative.

16 d5

White achieves nothing after 16 ♗e3 cd 17 cd ed 18 ♘xd4 d5! 19 ed ♘b4!; or 16 a3 a5 17 d5 ♘e7 18 a4 ba 19 ba g6; or 16 ♗b2 b4! etc.

16 ... ♘e7
17 ♗e3 *(227)*

After 17 c4 ♘g6 18 ♘f5 ♘f4, or 17 a4 ♕c7 18 ♗e3 ♘g6 19 ♕d2 ♖ec8, Black has equal chances.

After 17 ♗e3 the following variations arise:

(a) **17 ... g6** 18 ♕d2 ♔h7 19

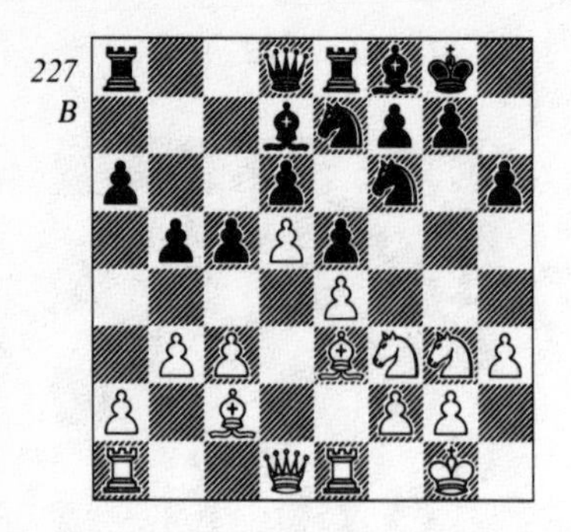
227
B

♘h2! ♗g7 20 f4 ef 21 ♗xf4 c4 22 ♘f3 with better chances for White (Sigurjonsson–Smejkal, Raahe 1969).

(b) **17 ... ♘g6** 18 ♕d2 a5 19 a4! ba 20 ba ♕c7 21 ♖eb1 ♖eb8 22 ♕c1 ♘e7 23 ♘d2 and then ♘c4, with pressure for White (Adorjan–Scholl, Amsterdam 1971).

(c) **17 ... d5** 18 a4! also favours White.

D112

14	**...**	**♘c4**
15	**b3**	**♘b6**

And now: 16 ♘h2 c5 17 f4! cd 18 cd ♕c8!? (18 ... ♖c8 19 ♘f3 ♕c7 20 ♗d3 ed 21 ♗b2! favours White) 19 ♖e2 ♕c3 20 ♗e3 ed (20 ... ef 21 ♗xf4 g5 22 ♗e3 ♘fd5 23 ♘f1 ♘b4 24 ♗f2!) 21 ♗f2 ♖ac8 22 ♗d3! ♕c7 23 ♘f3 g6 24 ♗xd4 with better chances for White (Tal).

D12

12	**...**	**♗b7**
13	**♘g3**	**♘a5**
14	**♗c2**	**♘c4**

Let us consider some other variations:

(a) **14 ... c5** 15 b3 cd 16 cd ♘c6 17 d5 ♘e7 18 ♗e3 g6 19 ♕d2! with pressure for White (Boleslavsky).

(b) **14 ... d5?!** 15 ♘xe5 de 16 ♘h5! (Gligoric).

(c) **14 ... g6** 15 b3 ♗g7 16 ♗d2 ♘c6 17 d5 ♘e7 18 c4 bc 19 bc c5 20 ♕c1! (Studenetsky). In both cases Black has difficulties.

After 14 ... ♘c4 White has a choice between:

D121 15 b3
D122 15 ♗d3
D123 15 a4

D121

15	**b3**	**♘b6**
16	**a4** *(228)*	

Neither 16 ♗d2 c5 nor 16 ♗b2 c5 17 dc dc 18 c4 ♘bd7 19 ♕e2 b4 20 ♖ad1 ♕a5 21 ♗b1 ♖e6! (Geller–Gligoric, Belgrade 1970) promise anything for White. Also after 16 ♖b1!? c5 17 ♖b2 ♕c7 Black has a solid position (Gligoric).

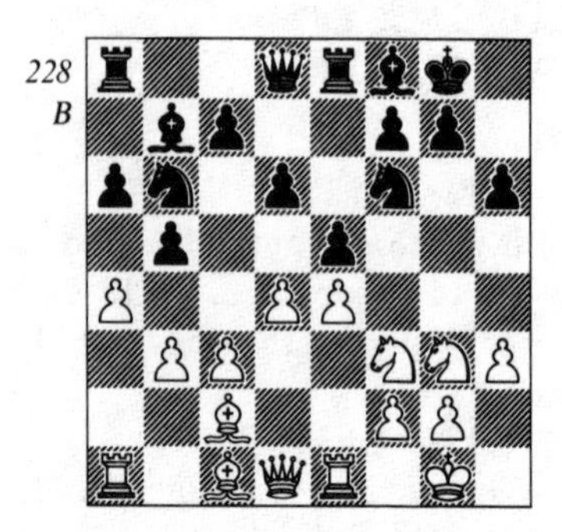
228
B

In this position Black has the following variations to choose from:

(a) **16 … ba** 17 ba a5 18 ♗d3 d5 19 ed ed 20 c4 ♖xe1+ 21 ♕xe1 c6 22 dc ♗xc6 23 ♗d2 ♘xa4 24 ♘e5 ♕e8 25 ♘xa6 ♕xc6 26 ♘e4 ♘b2 27 ♗b1 d3! with good counterplay for Black (Shulman–Krivonosov, USSR 1978).

(b) **16 … d5!?** 17 ♘xe5 de 18 ♘xe4!? (an equal game results after 18 ♗b2 c5, or 18 ♘g4 ♘bd7 19 ♘xf6+ ♘xf6 20 c4 ♗b4; Ivkov–Gligoric, Yugoslavia 1972).

(c) **16 … c5** 17 d5 a4 18 b4 ♗c8 19 ♗e3 ♗d7 20 a5 ♘c8 21 ♕d2 with lasting pressure for White (Fischer–Gligoric, Zagreb 1970).

D122

15 ♗d3 ♘b6
16 ♗d2 c5

After 16 … g6 17 ♕c1! ♔h7 18 c4 (18 ♘h2!?) 18 … bc 19 ♗xc4 d5 20 ♗xd5! ♘bxd5 21 de ♘d7 22 ed (Dely–Polgar, Hungary 1968/9), or 16 … ♘bd7 17 a4 c6 18 ♘h2 and then f2–f4, White has the better chances.

17 d5 ♗c8!

After 17 … g6 18 b3 ♕c7 19 c4 b4 20 ♘h2 ♗g7 21 ♘g4 (Kostro–Balinas, Lugano OL 1968), or 17 … c4 18 ♗c2 ♘fd7 19 ♘h2 g6 20 f4! (Matulovic–Minic, Vinkovci 1968), the positive aspects of White's game are clearly illustrated.

18 ♘h2 *(229)*

Now the following lines may arise:

(a) **18 … ♘h7** 19 ♖f1 ♗e7 20 f4 ef 21 ♗xf4 ♗g5 22 ♕f3 ♖a7! 23 ♘g4 ♗xf4 24 ♕xf4 ♗xg4 25

229
B

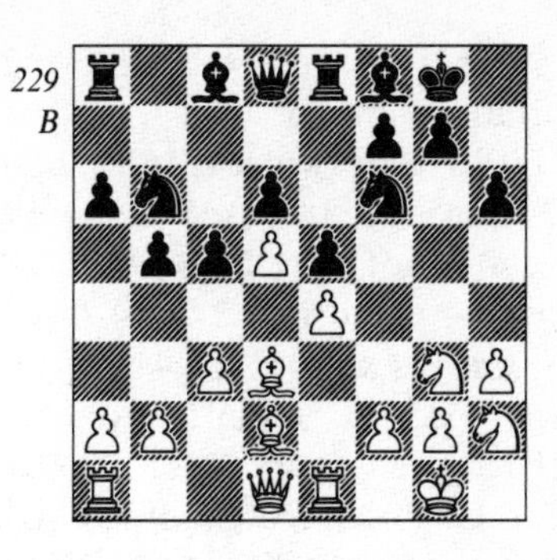

♕xg4 ♕g5 with equal chances (Hecht–Gligoric, Büsum 1969).

(b) **18 … g6** 19 f4 ef 20 ♗xf4 ♔h7 21 ♖f1 ♕e7 22 ♕d2 ♗g7 23 ♖ae1 (Suetin–Cobo, Havana 1969).

(c) **18 … c4** 19 ♗f1 ♘fd7?! 20 b3 ♕c7 21 ♘g4! (Medina–Matulovic, Palma de Mallorca 1968). Here, and also after 18 … ♖a7 19 b3 g6 20 c4, or 18 … ♘a4 19 ♖b1 ♗d7 20 b3 ♘b6 21 c4, Black experiences difficulties.

D123

15 a4 d5! *(230)*

Worse is 15 … c5 16 b3 ♘b6 17 d5! c4 18 b4 ♗c8 19 ♗e3 ♗d7 with lasting pressure for White (Fischer–Gligoric, Zagreb 1965).

230
W

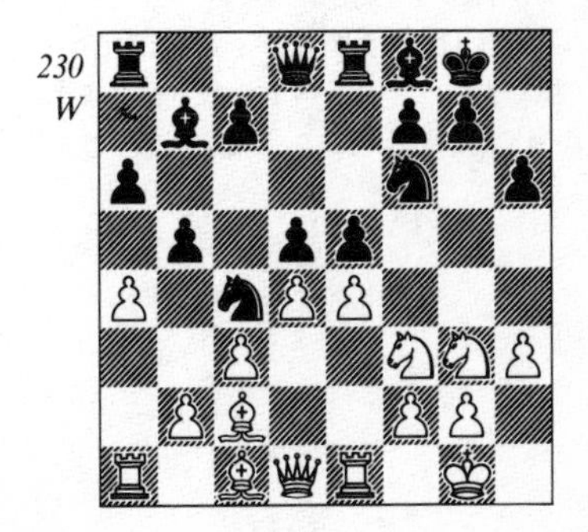

After 15 … d5! the following variations are possible:

(a) **16 b3** de (worse is 16 … ♘b6 17 ♘xe5 de 18 ♘xe4 ♘xe4 19 ♗xe4 ♗xe4 20 ♖xe4 ♕f6 21 ♘c6! — Gligoric) 17 ♘xe4 ♘xe4 18 ♗xe4 ♗xe4 19 ♖xe4 ♕d5 20 ♖g4 ♘a5 21 ♗xh6!? ♘xb3 22 ♖b1! ba 23 ♘xe5 ♕e6! 24 ♕f3 (Tal–Gligoric, match 1968). By playing 24 … f5 Black was able to obtain an equal game.

(b) **16 ♘xe5** ♘xe4 (after 16 … ♘xe5 17 de ♘xe4 18 ♘xe4 de 19 ♕xd8 ♖exd8 20 ab ab 21 ♖xa8 ♗xa8 22 ♔f1 White has a somewhat better game; Matulovic–Ostojic, Skopje 1969) 17 ab ab 18 ♖xa8 ♗xa8 19 ♘xc4 bc 20 ♗xe4 de 21 ♕a4 ♗d5 with full equality (Matulovic–Gligoric, Sarajevo 1969).

(c) Note that after **16 ed** ed 17 ♖xe8 ♕xe8 18 ♕xd4 ♗xd5 19 ♘h5 ♘xh5 20 ♕xd5 ♘f6, or 16 ab ab 17 ♖xa8 ♗xa8 18 b3 de 19 ♘xe4 ♗xe4! 20 ♗xe4 ed, Black has not the slightest difficulty.

D2

11 ♗e3 ♗f8

12 ♘bd2 *(231)*

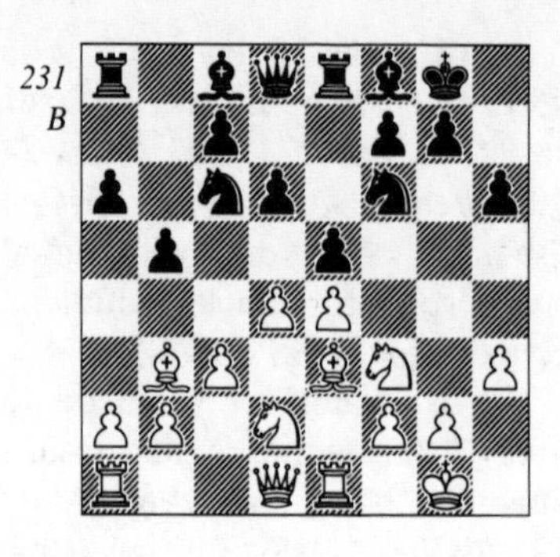

231
B

With the following variations:

(a) **12 … ♗d7** 13 ♕b1!? ♖b8 14 a3 a5 (or 14 … ♕c8 15 ♗a2 ♘d8 16 b4 ♘h5 17 ♕d3 c6 18 ♖ad1 ♘e6 19 de ♘ef4 20 ♗xf4 ♘xf4 21 ♕e3 de 22 ♗xf7+ ♔xf7 23 ♘xe5 ♖xe5 24 ♕xf4+ ♔e6 25 ♘f3 with double-edged play) 15 ♗a2 a4 16 b4 ab 17 ♕xb3 ♗e6 18 ♕c2 ♗xa2 19 ♖xa2 ♕d7 20 a4 ed 21 ♗xd4 ♘xd4 22 cd ba 23 ♖xa4 c5 with equal chances (Savon–Geller, Petropolis 1973).

(b) **12 … ♗b7** 13 d5 (interesting is 13 ♕b1 ♘d8 14 a4 ♘bd7 15 ♕d3 with pressure for White) 13 … ♘e7 (13 … ♘a5!? 14 ♗c2 c6) 14 ♘h2 ♘g6 15 a4 c6 16 dc ♗xc6 17 ♘g4 and White's position is preferable (Ivkov–Portisch, Sarajevo 1963).

(c) **12 … ♘a5** 13 ♗c2 c5 14 a3 c4 15 a4 ♗d7 16 ♕e2 ♕c7 17 ♖a2! and White stands better (Stein–Gligoric, Yugoslavia 1965).

16 Zaitsev Variation and 9 ... a5

In this chapter we deal with two very fashionable Closed Systems, Zaitsev's 9 ... ♗b7 and the previously rarely seen 9 ... a5.

1 e4 e5 2 ♘f3 ♘c6 3 ♗b5 a6 4 ♗a4 ♘f6 5 0–0 ♗e7 6 ♖e1 b5 7 ♗b3 d6 8 c3 0–0 9 h3:

A 9 ... ♗b7
B 9 ... a5

A

9 ... ♗b7

This continuation, introduced into practice by Flohr and Lilienthal as long ago as the 1940s, is today experiencing a revival. The reason is to be found in the increased popularity of the variation 10 d4 ♖e8, where Black attempts, in a way, to improve upon the Smyslov System.

10 d4

Rarely encountered is 10 d3. The following variations are not without interest: 10 ... ♘a5 11 ♗c2 c5 12 ♘bd2 ♖e8 (or 12 ... ♕c7 13 ♘f1 ♖fe8 14 ♘g3 ♗f8 15 ♗g5 ♘d7 16 b4!; Kuzmin–Psakhis, USSR 1982) 13 ♘f1 ♖c8 14 ♘g3 g6 15 a3 ♗f8 16 b4 ♘c6 17 ♗b3 ♘b8 18 ♕e2 with an initiative for White (Kuzmin–Balashov, USSR 1982).

Let us consider the main lines, in the order in which they first appeared:

A1 10 ... ed
A2 10 ... ♘a5
A3 10 ... ♖e8

A1

10 ... ed
11 cd d5
12 e5 ♘e4

This is the variation worked out by Flohr and Lilienthal.

13 ♘c3

But not 13 ♘bd2 ♘a5 14 ♗xd5 ♘xf2!

13 ... ♘a5
14 ♗c2 f5

14 ... ♗b4? 15 ♘xe4 de (15 ... ♗xe1? 16 ♘f6+!) 16 ♖xe4 f5 17 ef ♕xf6 18 ♗g5 ♕f7 19 ♖h4! is bad for Black (Ivkov–Puc, Bled 1950). Also in White's favour is 14 ... ♘xc3 15 bc.

15 ef ♗xf6
16 ♘xe4 de
17 ♗xe4 ♗xe4
18 ♖xe4 c5 *(232)*

Or 18 ... ♕d5 19 ♖e2 ♖ad8 20 ♗f4 ♘c6 21 ♗xc7 ♖d7 22 ♗b6 with an extra pawn for White.

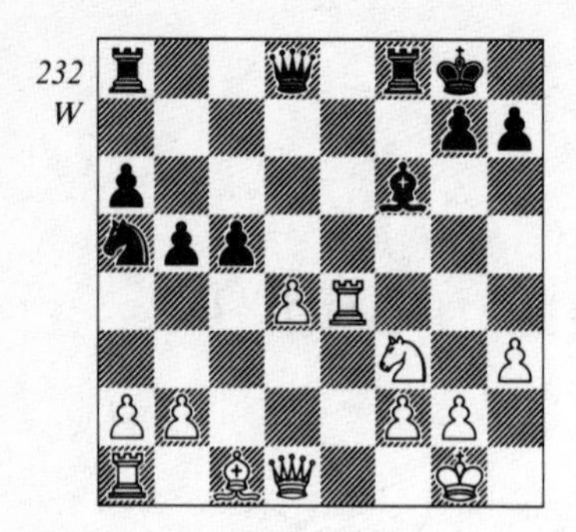

232
W

Now the following variations may arise:

(a) **19 Be3** Qd5 20 Qc2 cd 21 Bxd4 Rac8 22 Bc3 Rc5 23 Qe2 with better chances for White (Schmid–van Scheltinga, Lenzerheide 1956).

(b) **19 Rg4** cd 20 Bg5 d3 21 Bxf6 Qxf6 22 Qxd3 Qxb2 23 Qd5+ Kh8 24 Re1 Rad8 25 Rf4! with a dangerous initiative for White (Tal–Lehmann, Hamburg 1960).

A2

10 ... Na5
11 Bc2 Nc4

In White's favour is 11 ... d5? 12 Nxe5! Nxe4 13 Nd2 f6 14 Nd3 Bd6 15 Nc5!

12 b3

After 12 a4 Re8 13 b3 (13 Bd3 d5!) 13 ... Nb6 14 de de 15 Qe2, or 12 Nbd2 Nxd2 13 Bxd2 d5!?, or 12 Qe2 Re8 13 a4 d5! 14 ab ab 15 Rxa8 Qxa8 16 Nxe5 Nxe5 17 de Nxe4 18 Qxb5 Bh4! (Zhelendinov–Lutikov, USSR 1968), Black's counterplay gives him equality.

12 ... Nb6

13 Nbd2 *(233)*

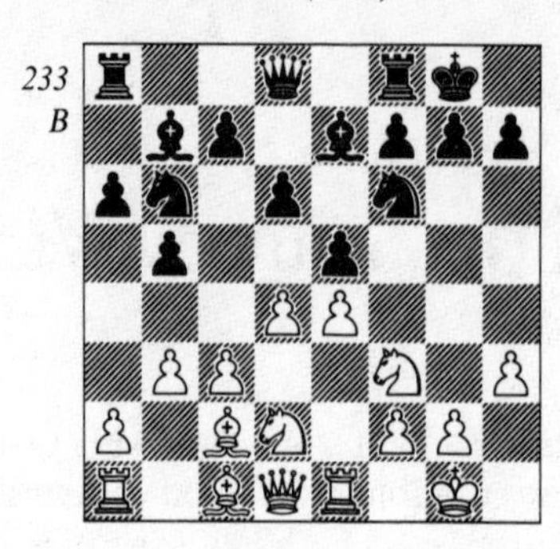

233
B

Black has a choice between:

A21 13 ... Nbd7
A22 13 ... Re8

Worse is 13 ... Nfd7? 14 Nf1 Bf6 15 N1h2 g6 16 Ng4! Bg7 17 de Nxe5 18 Ngxe5 de 19 Qe2 Qh4 20 Ba3! with a clear positional advantage to White (Tseshkovsky–Zakharov, Sochi 1976).

A21

13 ... Nbd7
14 b4

A plan of Fischer's. Play has transposed to a variation of the Breyer System with an extra tempo for White, which gives him an advantage.

14 ... ed

14 ... a5(?) 15 Nb3 ab 16 cb is in White's favour.

15 cd a5
16 ba c5

Or 16 ... Rxa5 17 d5! c5 18 dc Bxc6 19 Nd4 with advantage to White (Fischer).

17 e5

White's initiative is very dangerous (Fischer–Stein, Sousse 1967).

A22

13 … ♖e8

Here too Black has great difficulties. The following variations are typical: 14 ♘f1 (also good is 14 de de 15 ♘xe5 ♗c5 16 ♘g4! and if 16 … ♘xe4 then 17 ♗xe4 ♗xe4 18 ♘xe4 ♕xd1 19 ♘ef6+ etc.) 14 … c5 15 ♘g3 ♗f8 16 a4 c4 17 a5! ed! 18 cd cb 19 ♗xb3 ♘c4 20 ♗xc4 bc 21 d5 ♖c8 22 ♗e3 ♘d7 23 ♕b1 ♗a8 24 ♖c1 g6 25 ♖a4 ♘c5 26 ♗xc5 ♖xc5 27 ♖cxc4 ♖xc4 28 ♖xc4 ♕a5 29 ♕c4 and it is hard for Black to equalise (Belyavsky–Klovan, USSR 1977).

A3

10 … ♖e8

This move was first played by Zaitsev in 1976 and at the present time is extremely popular. Its tactical basis can be seen in the following variation: 11 ♘g5 ♖f8 12 f4!? ef 13 ♗xf4 ♘a5 14 ♗c2 ♘d5! For example: 15 ed ♗xg5 16 ♕h5 h6 17 ♗g3 g6 18 ♕f3 ♘c4 19 ♘a3 ♘b6 20 ♗b3 h5 21 ♘c2 ♕f6 22 ♕e4 a5 23 a3 ♘c4 with excellent play for Black.

Let us consider other continuations on Black's 10th move:

(a) **10 … ♕d7!?** 11 ♘bd2 ♖ad8!? (after 11 … ♖ae8 12 ♘f1 — or 12 ♗c2 — 12 … ♗d8 13 ♘g3 h6 14 ♗c2 ♔h8 15 b3 ♘g8 16 d5 ♘ce7 17 c4 White stands clearly better; Karpov–Zaitsev, USSR 1969) 12 d5 ♘b8 13 ♘f1 (13 ♗c2 or 13 c4 — Suetin) 13 … c6 14 ♗g5 with pressure for White (Suetin).

(b) **10 … ♘d7?!** 11 ♘bd2 ♗f6 (11 … ed 12 cd ♘b4 13 ♘f1 c5 14 a3 ♘c6 15 d5 ♘ce5 16 ♘xe5 de 17 d6 ♗f6 18 ♗d5 ♗xd5 19 ♕xd5 ♘b6! with equality; Ehlvest–Karpov, USSR 1988) 12 ♘f1 ♖e8 13 ♘g3 g6 14 ♗h6 ♘a5 15 ♗c2 c5 16 d5 with pressure for White (Ljubojevic–Karpov, Turin 1982).

(c) **10 … ♖c8?!** 11 ♘bd2 ed 12 cd b4 13 ♕e2 c5 14 a3! ♘c6 15 dc dc 16 e5 ♘d5 17 ♘e4 c4 18 ♗c2 and it is hard for Black to equalise.

(d) **10 … ♘a5?!** 11 ♗c2 (11 de de 12 ♘xe5) 11 … ♘c4 12 b3 ♘b6 13 ♘bd2 ♖e8 14 de de 15 ♘xe5 ♗d6 16 ♘f3 ♗xe4 with slightly better chances for White (van der Wiel–Karpov, Rotterdam 1989).

Here the main variations are:

A31 11 ♘bd2
A32 11 a4

Let us also consider the following variations:

(a) **11 de!?** ♘xe5 (11 … de? 12 ♗xf7+! ♔xf7 13 ♕b3+) 12 ♘xe5 de 13 ♕f3! c5 14 ♘d2 c4 15 ♗c2 ♕c7 16 ♘f1 ♖ad8 17 ♘g3 ♘d7 18 b4 ♘b6 19 ♘f5 with some pressure for White on the kingside (Tseitlin–Vasyukov, USSR 1979).

(b) **11 ♗g5** h6 12 ♗h4 ♘h7 (interesting is 12 … ♘xe4!) 13 ♗g3 ♗f6 14 ♕d3 ♘a5 15 ♗c2 c5 16 d5 ♘c4 17 b3 ♘b6 18 ♘bd2 ♘f8 19 a4 ba 20 ba a5 21 ♕f1 c4! with equality (Psakhis–Balashov, USSR 1983).

A31

11 ♘bd2

In practice, when the players only want a draw they sometimes play 11 ♘g5 ♖f8 12 ♘f3 ♖e8 13 ♘g5 ♖f8 etc. But this has no real significance for theory.

11 … ♗f8

In this section we shall principally consider the moves:

A311 12 ♗c2
A312 12 a3

But first we shall consider the following variations:

(a) **12 d5!?** ♘e7 (also possible is 12 … ♘a5) 13 c4 c6 14 ♗c2 bc 15 dc ♘xc6 16 ♘xc4 h6 17 ♗d2! ♖c8 18 ♖c1 ♘d4 19 ♗a4! with slight pressure for White (Ermenkov–Lukács, Albena 1985).

(b) **12 ♘g5?!** ♖e7 13 d5 ♘a5 14 ♗c2 c6 15 b4 ♘c4 16 ♘xc4 bc 17 dc ♗xc6 18 a4 ♗b7 19 ♘f3 h6 20 ♘d2 ♕c7 21 ♕e2 ♖c8 22 ♗a3 d5 23 b5 d4! with excellent counterplay for Black (Timman–Karpov, Bugojno 1982).

A311

12 ♗c2 g6 *(234)*

Frequently 12 … ♘b8 is played here, after which 13 a4 or 13 b4 ♘bd7 transposes to the Breyer System, considered in the next chapter. However, after 13 b3 the following variations may arise:

(a) **13 … ♘bd7** 14 d5 (14 ♗b2 g6 15 a4 ♖b8 16 ♗d3 c6 17 ♕c2 ♘h5 18 ♘h2 ♘f4 19 ♗f1 ♘e6 20 ♘g4 ♗g7 with equality; Ljubojevic–Karpov, Tilburg 1986) 14 … c6 15 c4 ♕c7 (after 15 … a5 16 ♕e2 b4 17 dc ♗xc6 18 a4 ♘c5 19 ♘h2 g6 20 ♘g4 ♘fd7 21 ♘f3 ♘e6 22 ♗b2 ♘ec5 23 ♖ed1 with somewhat better play for White; Suetin–Psakhis, Sverdlovsk 1978) 16 ♘f1 ♖ec8 17 ♘e3 g6 (after 17 … cd?! 18 cd a5 19 ♗d2 b4 20 a3! ♘c5 21 ab ab 22 ♖xa8 ♖xa8 23 ♕b1 ♕b6 24 ♘c4 ♕b5 25 ♗e3; Geller–Belyavsky, Sochi 1986, or 17 … a5 18 ♗d2 bc?! 19 bc ♘c5 20 ♘f5; Geller–Lukács, Sochi 1984, White has a considerable advantage. However, an interesting line is 17 … ♘c5 18 ♘d2 a5 19 a4 ba 20 ba cd 21 cd ♗a6 22 ♖a3 g6 with roughly equal play; Petrienko–Klovan, USSR 1984) 18 ♗d2 ♘c5 19 ♘g4 ♘xg4 20 hg cd 21 cd ♘a4! and Black has at least equal chances (Psakhis–Smejkal, Szirak 1986).

(b) **13 … c6** 14 ♘f1 ♘bd7 15 ♘g3 g6 16 ♗g5 ♗g7 17 ♕d2 ♕e7 18 a4 ♕f8 19 ♗d3 ♖ad8 20 ab ab 21 ♖a7 with some initiative for White (Ljubojevic–Torre, Biel 1985).

In White's favour is 12 … h6?! 13 d5 ♘b8 14 b3 c6 15 c4 ♘bd7 16 a4 bc 17 bc a5 18 ♘b3 ♘b6 19 ♗d3 ♕d7 20 ♗d2 ♘xa4 21 ♗f1 cd 22 ed ♖a7 23 ♖a3 with pressure for White on the queenside (Geller–Zaitsev, Yerevan 1982).

In this position White again has two main lines:

A3111 13 b3
A3112 13 d5

A3111

13 b3

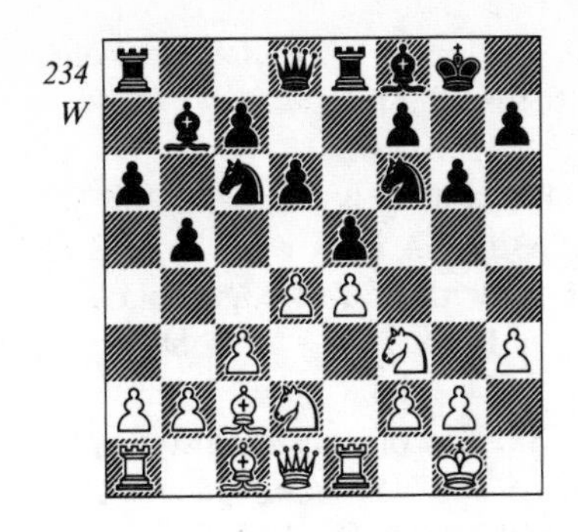
234
W

Other possibilities for White briefly:

(a) **13 a4** ♗g7 14 d5 ♘b8 15 ♗d3 ba 16 ♕xa4 c6 17 c4 ♕c7 18 ♘b3 ♘bd7 19 ♗d2 ♖eb8 20 ♕a3 with pressure for White (Spassky–Geller, Bugojno 1982).

(b) **13 ♘b3(?)** ed 14 cd ♘b4 15 d5 c6 16 dc ♗xc6 17 ♘bd4 ♗xe4 (17 ... ♗b7!) 18 ♗xe4 ♖xe4 19 ♖xe4 ♘xe4 and Black has no difficulties (Geller–Belyavsky, USSR Ch. 1978).

13 ... ♘b8

Besides this move, which is played most frequently, Black also has the following possibilities:

(a) **13 ... d5!?** 14 de ♘xe5 15 ♘xe5 ♖xe5 16 f4 ♗c5+ with double-edged play (Hübner–Belyavsky, Tilburg 1986).

(b) **13 ... b4?!** 14 d5 bc 15 ♘c4 ♘b4 16 ♘a5 ♗c8 17 a3 ♘xc2 18 ♘c6 ♘xe1 19 ♘xd8 ♘xg2 20 ♔xg2 ♖xd8 21 ♗g5 ♗g7 22 ♖c1 ♗d7 23 ♗xf6 ♗xf6 24 ♖xc3 ♖dc8 25 ♕e1 ♖a7 26 ♘e1 ♔g7 27 ♘d3 a5 28 b4 with a small advantage to White (Hübner–Hort, Biel 1986).

14 d5 c6
15 c4 *(235)*

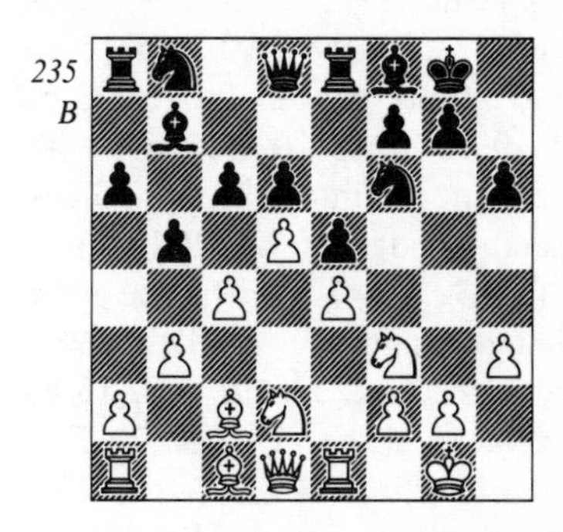
235
B

In this critical position the following variations may arise:

(a) **15 ... ♗h6** 16 a4 (or 16 b4 bc 17 dc ♘xc6 18 ♘xc4 ♗xc1 19 ♖xc1 ♘xb4 20 ♗b3 ♕e7! 21 ♕xd6 ♗xe4 22 ♕xe7 ♖xe7 23 ♘fxe5 a5! with sufficient counterplay for Black; Geller–Gligoric, Yugoslavia 1979) 16 ... b4 17 ♘f1 (or 17 ♗b2 ♘bd7 18 a5 ♘c5 19 ♘f1 cd 20 cd ♗c8 21 ♗c1 ♗xc1 22 ♕xc1 ♗d7 with excellent play for Black; Kir. Georgiev–Hazai, Warsaw 1987) 17 ... ♗xc1 18 ♕xc1 a5! with approximate equality (Pitisaar–Korolev, corr. 1988).

(b) **15 ... ♘bd7** 16 a4 ♕c7 17 ♗a3 ♖ec8 18 ♗d3 cd 19 cd ♕b6 20 b4 ♖c3 (Smyslov–Gligoric, Bugojno 1984).

(c) **15 ... a5** 16 ♘f1 ♘bd7 17 ♗g5 ♗e7 18 ♗e3 ♕c7 19 ♖c1 ♖ec8 20 ♗d3 bc 21 bc ♗a6 22 ♖e2 ♖ab8 23 ♖ec2 ♕b7 24 ♖c3 ♕a8 25 ♘g3 ♗d8 (Karpov–Belyavsky, USSR 1983). In both cases Black is close to equality.

A3112

13 d5

And now:

(a) **13 ... ♘b8** 14 b3 c6 15 c4 ♘bd7 16 a4 ♕c7 17 ♘f1 bc 18 bc cd 19 cd ♖ec8 20 ♖a2 a5! with sufficient counterplay for Black (Levin–Podgaets, USSR 1978).

(b) **13 ... ♘e7** 14 b3 (in the game Geller–Eingorn, USSR 1985, there occurred 14 ♘f1 ♗g7 15 b3 ♘xe4! 16 ♗xe4 f5 17 ♗c2 e5 18 ♘d4 ♘xd5 19 ♘e2 ♘xc3! with advantage to Black; Black also stands better after 19 ♗d2 c5! 20 ♘e2 ♘b6!) 14 ... c6 15 c4 ♗g7 16 ♘f1 ♘h5?! 17 ♗d2 ♖c8 18 ♘e3 ♕d7 19 a4 cd 20 cd ♘f4 21 ♗b4 f5 22 ab ab 23 ♖a7! with better chances for White (Suetin–I. Zaitsev, Sochi 1977).

A312

12 a3

A flexible but somewhat passive continuation. Most often Black reacts in the spirit of the Breyer System: ♘c6–b8–d7.

12 ... h6

Other possibilities:

(a) **12 ... g6** 13 ♗a2 (after 13 ♗c2 ♘b8 14 b4 ♘bd7 15 ♗b2 ♗g7 16 ♕b1 d5 the game is roughly level; Smagin–Psakhis, Moscow 1982) 13 ... ♗g7 14 d5 (14 b4 d5!?) 14 ... ♘e7 15 b4 a5 16 ba ♖xa5 17 c4 c6 18 dc with better chances for White (Gufeld–Timoshchenko, USSR 1981).

(b) **12 ... ♕d7** 13 ♗a2 a5 14 a4 ba 15 d5 ♘b8 16 c4 ♘a6 17 ♗b1 c6 18 ♗c2 ♘c5 with good chances of equality (Gufeld–Nikolic, Athens 1985).

13 ♗c2

Interesting is 13 ♗a2 ♘b8 (13 ... ♕d7) 14 ♕b3 ♕d7 15 ♕c2 c5 16 b4 with double-edged play.

13 ... ♘b8

14 b4

Worthy of consideration is 14 b3!? ♘bd7 15 ♗b2 g6 16 ♖b1 ♗g7 17 de de 18 c4 (Romanishin–Balashov, USSR 1983).

14 ... ♘bd7

15 ♗b2 *(236)*

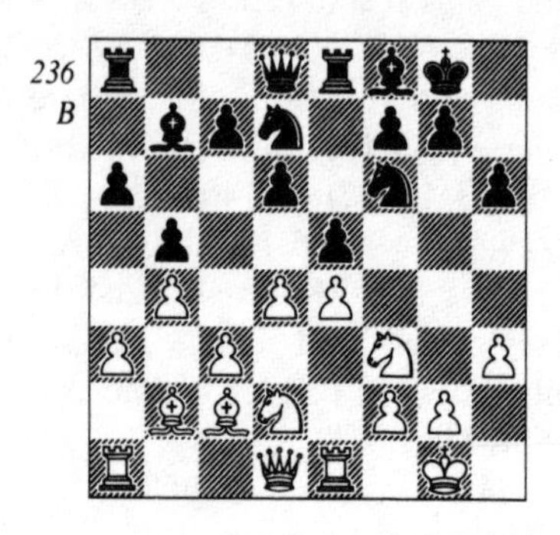
236
B

And now:

(a) **15 ... g6**, with the following variations:

(a1) **16 ♕b1** ♗g7 17 ♘b3 ♖b8 (on 17 ... d5 there follows 18 ♘a5, but 17 ... ♖c8 18 ♘a5 ♗a8 19 d5 ♘b6 leads to approximate equality) 18 ♘a5 ♗a8 19 d5 ♘b6 20 ♕a2 (also good is 20 ♗b3) 20 ... ♕d7 21 ♖ad1 ♘h5 22 ♘d2 c6 23 dc ♗xc6 24 c4 with a minimal advantage to White (Ehlvest–Razuvayev, St. John 1988).

(a2) **16 c4** ed 17 cb ab 18 ♘xd4 c6 19 a4 ba 20 ♗xa4 ♕b6 21 ♘c2

♕c7 22 ♗b3 ♗g6 23 ♖a5! with pressure for White (Rusanov–Korolev, corr. 1987).

(a3) **16 ♖b1** c6! 17 ♘b3 ♖c8 18 de de 19 c4 c5 with equality (Hjartarson–Karpov, Linares 1989).

(b) **15 ... c5**, and now:

(b1) **16 ♖b1** c4 17 d5 g6 18 ♘f1 ♗g7 19 ♘g3 ♘b6 20 ♗c1 ♕c7 21 ♘h2 with better chances for White (Romanishin–Geller, USSR 1982).

(b2) **16 bc** dc (or 16 ... ed 17 cd dc3 — 17 ... dc5 18 ♖c1!? ♖c8 19 ♗b1 ♘h5 20 e5 ♘f4 21 ♘e4 favours White; Nunn–Greenfeld, Groningen 1988 — 18 ♗xc3 ♗d6 19 e5 ♘d5 20 ♗b2 ♗c7 21 ♖c1 ♘f4 22 ♗b1 ♗a5! with good play for Black) 17 ♘e5! ♘xe5 18 de ♘h5 19 c4 ♘f4 20 ♖e3 ♘g6 21 a4 with strong pressure for White (Am. Rodriguez–Frey, Medina del Campio 1986).

(b3) **15 ... a5!?** 16 ♗d3 (16 ba!?) 16 ... c6 17 ♘b3 ab 18 cb ed 19 ♘fxd4 c5 20 bc dc 21 ♘xd5 ♘xe4 with excellent play for Black (Hjartarson–Karpov, match 1989).

A32

11 a4

This at first glance somewhat trivial move was for a long time unfashionable, but in recent years there has been an 'explosion' of interest in it. The tense positions which arise have today become the centre of attention, and the theory of this line is developing at an extremely fast pace.

11 ... h6

Black is essentially forced to transpose to the Smyslov System. For example: 11 ... ♗f8 (11 ... ♘a5 12 ♗c2 ♗f8 13 de de 14 ♕xd8 ♖exd8 15 ♘bd2 ♘d7 16 b4 ♘c4 17 ♘xc4 bc favours White) 12 d5 (also good is 12 ♗g5 h6 13 ♗xf6 ♕xf6 14 ♗d5 ♖eb8 15 ab ab 16 ♖xa8 ♗xa8 17 ♘a3! with pressure for White; Murey–Kudrin, New York 1982) 12 ... ♘a5 (or 12 ... ♘b8 13 ab ab 14 ♖xa8 ♗xa8 15 ♘a3 c6 16 dc ♗xc6 17 ♗g5 ♘bd7 18 ♘c2 with advantage to White) 13 ♗a2 c6 14 ♘a3 cd 15 ed ba 16 ♕xa4 ♘xd5 17 ♘g5! ♖e7 18 b4 ♘xc3 19 ♕c2! g6 20 ♕xc3 ♖c8 21 ♕g3 ♘c6 22 ♕h4 h5 23 ♕e4! and White wins (Karpov–Miles, London 1984).

12 ♘bd2

The most important continuation. After 12 d5 ♘a5 13 ♗a2 c6 14 ♘a3 ♕c7 15 ♘h4 cd 16 ed ♘c4 17 ♘f5 ♗xd5 18 ab ab 19 ♘xb5 ♕d7 20 ♘xe7+ ♖xe7 21 b3 ♖xa2! 22 ♖xa2 ♕xb5 23 bc ♕xc4 Black gets good play (Ljubojevic–Karpov, Lucerne OL 1982).

12 ... ♗f8

Let us consider the following substantial variations:

(a) **12 ... ed** 13 cd ♘b4, with the following variations:

(a1) **14 ab** ab 15 ♖xa8 ♗xa8 (15 ... ♕xa8?! 16 e5 de 17 de ♘fd5 18 ♘e4 c5 19 e6!; de Firmian–Nikolic, Tunis 1985) 16 e5 (16 ♕e2!?) 16 ... de 17 de ♘fd5 18 e6 fe 19 ♘e5 and Black has difficulties in either case.

(a2) **14 d5** c5 15 dc ♘xc6 16 ♘f1 ♗f8 17 ♘g3 ♘a5 18 ♘d4 d5 19 f4 ♘c4 20 e5 ♘e4 21 ♘xe4 de 22 ♗xc4 bc 23 ♗e3 (Tseshkovsky–Ivanov, USSR 1984). With 23 ... f6 Black was able to maintain the equilibrium.

(a3) **14 ♕e2** ♗f8 15 e5 de!? (after 15 ... ♗c6 16 ab — 16 ♕d1 de 17 de — 16 ... ♗xb5 17 ♕d1 ♘fd5 18 ♘e4 c6 19 ♘c3 ♖b8 20 ♘xb5 ab 21 ed ♗xd6 22 ♗d2 ♕c7 23 ♕b1 White has a slight positional advantage; Kasparov–Karpov, 44th game, World Ch. match 1984) 16 de ♕d3! 17 ♕xd3 ♘xd3 18 ♖e3 ♘xc1 19 ♖xc1 ♘d5 20 ♗xd5 ♗xd5 21 ab ab 22 ♖xc7 ♖a1+ 23 ♔h2 ♖a2 24 ♖c2 b4 with roughly equal play (Aseev–Ivanov, Kostroma 1985).

(b) **12 ... ♕d7** 13 ab (13 d5 ♘e7 14 c4 ♘g6 15 ♗c2 c6 16 b3 b4 17 ♘h2 ♕c7 18 ♘g4 with a small 'plus' to White; Hübner–Portisch, Brussels 1986) 13 ♗c2 ed 14 cd ♘b4 15 ♗b1 g6 16 d5 c6 17 ♕b3 a5 18 dc ♕xc6! 19 ♕c2 ♗g7 with counterplay for Black; Ivanovic–Nikolic, Niksic 1983) 13 ... ab 14 ♖xa8 ♗xa8 15 d5 ♘a5 (after 15 ... ♘d8 16 ♘f1 h6 17 ♘3h2 ♘b7 18 ♗c2 ♘c5 19 b4 ♘a6 20 ♘g4; Kasparov–Karpov, 46th game, World Ch. match 1984, or 15 ... ♘b8 16 ♘f1 ♘a6 17 ♗g5 ♗e7 18 ♘g3 g6 19 ♕d2 ♗b7 20 ♖a1 ♖a8 21 ♗c2 c6 22 dc ♗xc6 23 ♖d1 ♖d8 24 ♕e3 ♕b7 25 ♗h6 ♘c7 26 ♘f5!; Kasparov–Smejkal, Dubai OL 1986, White has the better chances) 16 ♗a2 c6 17 b4 ♘b7 18 c4 ♖c8 19 dc ♕xc6 20 c5!? ♘d8 21 ♗b2 bc with good counterplay for Black (Kasparov–Karpov, World Ch. match 1985).

13 ♗c2 *(237)*

Or 13 d5 ♘b8 (worse is 13 ... ♘e7 14 c4 ♕d7 15 ♗c2! c6 16 b3 ♕c7 17 ♘f1 ♘d7 18 ♘e3; Jansa–Nikolic, Esbjerg 1982, or 13 ... ♘a7 14 ♘f1 c6 15 ♘3h2 cd 16 ed ♘c8 17 ♘g4 ♘xg4 18 hg ♘b6 19 ♘g3 ba 20 ♗xa4; Nunn–Smejkal, Dubai OL 1986) 14 c4 c6 15 ab ab 16 ♖xa8 ♗xa8 17 dc bc 18 ♗a4 ♕c7 19 ♘xc4 ♗xc6 with equality (Kasparov–Dorfman, USSR 1978).

237
B

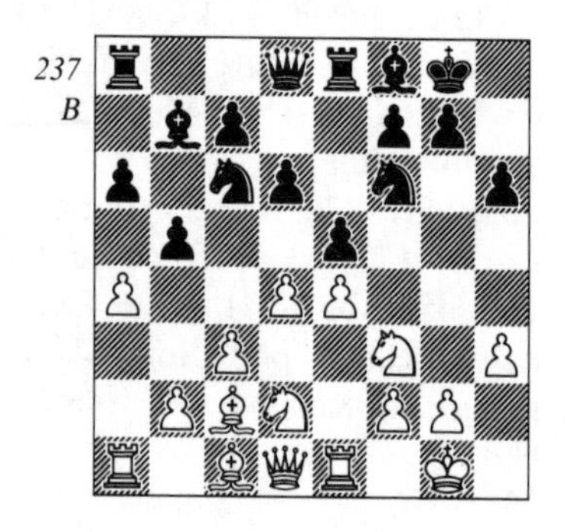

13 ... ed

This move is the introduction to lively piece play. We shall also look at the following variations:

(a) **13 ... ♘b8** 14 ♗d3 c6 15 ♘f1 ♘bd7 16 ♘g3 ♕c7 17 ♗d2 g6 18 ♕c1 ♔h7 19 b3 ♗g7 20 ♕c2 with slight but lasting pressure for White (Kasparov–Karpov, 9th game, World Ch. 1985).

(b) **13 … ♖b8**, with the following possibilities:

(b1) **14 ab** ab 15 ♗d3 ♗c8 16 ♘f1 (16 ♘b3 ♗d7 17 ♗d2 ♕c8 18 ♕c2 ♘d8 with equality; Tal–Gligoric, Bugojno 1984) 16 … ♗d7 (16 … b4 17 ♘g3 bc 18 bc ed 19 cd ♘b4 20 ♗b1 c5 21 ♗f4! ♖b5 22 ♕d2 ♖a5 23 ♖xa5 ♕xa5; Timman–Karpov, Tilburg 1986; after 24 ♕b2! White would have had the better chances) 17 ♘g3 ♕c8! 18 ♗e3 (18 ♗d2!?) 18 … ♕b7 (Hjartarson–Karpov, Dubai OL 1986). After 19 ♕e2! ed 20 cd ♘b4 21 ♗b1 c5 22 dc dc 23 e5 White has some initiative. Also interesting is 19 d5.

(b2) **14 d5** ♘e7 15 b3 c5 16 b4 c4 17 ♘f1 g6 18 ♘g3 ♗g7 19 ♘h2 ♔h8 20 ♗e3 ♘xe4 21 ♗xe4 f5 22 ♕d2 fe 23 ♗xh6 and here White stands better (Kir. Georgiev–van der Sterren, Wijk aan Zee 1988).

(b3) **14 ♗d3** ♗c8 15 ♘f1 ♗d7 16 ♘g3 ♕c8 17 ♗f1 ♕b7 18 a5 ♕c8 19 ♘h2 ♘a7 20 f4 ef 21 ♗xf4 ♘g6 22 ♗d2 c5 23 ♘f3 b4!? 24 cd d5 25 e5 ♘e4 with equal chances (Belyavsky–Gligoric, Sochi 1986).

(b4) **14 ♗b1!?** ♗c8 15 ♘f1 b4 16 ♘g3 bc 17 bc g6 with equal chances (Ehlvest–Podgaets, USSR 1985).

(c) **13 … ♕d7** 14 d5 ♘e7 15 b3 and c3–c4, with pressure for White (Spassky–Balashov, Toluca 1982).

14 cd

After 14 ♘xd4 ♘xd4 15 cd g6 16 b3 ♗g7 17 ♗b2 ♖e7 18 ♕b1 ♕e8 19 b4 h5 20 f3 ♔d7 Black has quite a good game (Lanka).

14 … ♘b4

15 ♗b1 *(238)*

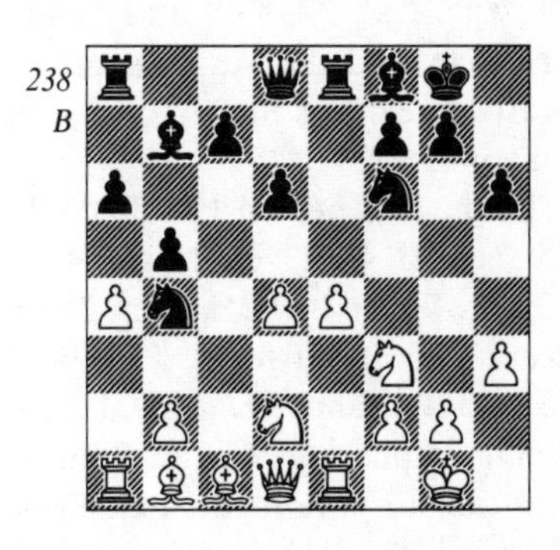

15 … c5

This forceful undermining of the centre is the focus of attention, but there are quite a few other continuations:

(a) **15 … ba** 16 ♖xa4 a5 17 ♖a3 (or 17 b3 ♖a6 18 ♗b2 d5 19 e5 ♘d7 20 ♘f1 c5 with chances for both sides; Gufeld–Dydyshko, USSR 1982), and now:

(a1) **17 … ♖a6**, with the following subvariations:

(a1i) **18 d5** c6 19 dc ♗xc6 20 ♘d4 ♗b7 with approximate equality.

(a1ii) **18 ♘h2** g6 19 f3! (after 19 f4 d5! 20 e5 ♘e4 21 ♘g4 c5 22 ♘xe4 de 23 dc ♗xc5+ 24 ♗e3 ♗f8 25 ♘f6+ ♖xf6 26 ♕xd8 ♖xd8 27 ef ♘d3 Black is not worse — Ivanchuk–Karpov, Linares 1989; Black also has no difficulties after 19 ♘g4 ♘xg4 20

♕xg4 c5 21 dc dc 22 e5 ♕d4!) 19 ... ♕d7 20 ♘c4 ♕b5 21 ♖c3 ♗c8 22 ♗e3 ♔h7 23 ♕c1 c6 24 ♘g4 ♘g8 25 ♗xh6! ♗xh6 26 ♘xh6 ♘xh6 27 ♘xd6 ♕b6 28 ♘xe8 ♕xd4 29 ♔h1 ♕d8 30 ♖d1 ♕xe8 31 ♕g5 ♖a7 32 ♖d8 and White has a clear advantage (Kasparov–Karpov, 2nd game, World Ch. match 1990).

(a1iii) **18 ♖ae3** a4 19 ♘f1 d5 20 e5 ♘e4 21 ♘1d2 c5 22 ♘xe4 de 23 ♗xe4 ♗xe4 24 ♖xe4 c5 25 e6 ♖exe6 26 ♖xe6 fe 27 ♘e5 ♕c7 28 ♕f3 (Balashov–Karpov, USSR 1983). By playing 28 ... ♘c2 Black was able to obtain equal chances.

(a1iv) **18 ♘h4?** ♘xe4! 19 ♘xe4 ♗xe4 20 ♗xe4 d5! 21 ♖ae3 ♖ae6 22 ♗g6?! (somewhat better is 22 ♗xd5 ♕xd5 23 ♘f3) 22 ... ♕xh4 and Black emerges with an extra pawn (Timman–Karpov, match 1990).

(a2) **17 ... g6** 18 ♖ae3 (18 e5!? de 19 de ♘h5 20 ♕b3!; Kasparov–Belyavsky, Moscow 1982) 18 ... ♗g7 19 ♘f1 c4 20 ♘g3 cd (20 ... ♕b6!?) 21 ♘xd4 d5 22 e5 ♘e4 23 ♘xe4 de 24 ♗xe4 ♗xe4 25 ♖xe4 (Sax–Belyavsky, Moscow 1982). By playing 25 ... ♖c8! Black could have maintained the equilibrium.

(a3) **17 ... c5** 18 d5 ♗a6 19 ♘h2 g6 20 ♘g4 ♗g7 21 ♘e3 ♗b5 22 ♘ec4 a4 23 ♖ae3 ♕b8 with double-edged play (Vasyukov–Dydyshko, USSR 1982).

(a4) **17 ... ♕d7** 18 ♘h4! ♕b5 19 ♖f3 ♘h7 20 ♖g3 ♘g5 21 ♘hf3 ♘xf3+ 22 ♘xf3 ♕h5 23 ♗d2 ♖e7 24 ♕c1 ♔h8 25 d5 c5 26 ♖g4 with strong pressure for White (Ehlvest–Belyavsky, USSR 1984).

(b) **15 ... ♕d7** 16 ♖a3 ba 17 ♖xa4 a5 18 ♖a3 ♕b5 19 d5!? c6 20 ♘d4 ♕b6 21 ♘c4 ♕d8 and Black has a solid defence (Rodriguez–Geller, Moscow 1984).

(c) **15 ... g6** 16 ♖a3 (interesting is 16 e5! de 17 de ♘h5 18 ab ab 19 ♖xa8 ♕xa8 20 ♘e4 with an initiative for White; Matulovic–Lukács, Vrnjacka Banja 1985) 16 ... ♗g7 17 ♖ae3 ba 18 ♕xa4 a5 19 ♘f1 (19 ♘c4!?) 19 ... d5?! 20 e5 ♘e4 21 ♘1d2 c5! 22 ♘xe4 de 23 ♗xe4 cd 24 ♗xb7 de 25 ♗xe3 with better prospects for White.

(d) **15 ... ♘d7!?** 16 ♘f1 (16 ♘b3 c5) 16 ... c5 17 ♘g3 g6 18 ♗f4 ♘c6 19 dc ♘xc5 20 ab ab 21 ♖xa8 ♗xa8 22 ♕d2 h5 23 ♗a2 ♕a5 with equal chances (Tseshkovsky–Butnoris, USSR 1982).

16 d5

Only with this move is White able to fight for the initiative. Other variations are worse:

(a) **16 dc** dc 17 e5 ♘d7 18 ab ab 19 ♖xa8 ♗xa8 20 e6 ♖xe6 21 ♖xe6 fe 22 ♘e4 ♘d5 (also possible is 22 ... ♕e7) 23 ♕e2 ♕b6 24 ♘g3 c4! with advantage to Black (Gudzhev–Korolev, corr. 1988).

(b) **16 b3** cd 17 ♘xd4 ba 18 ♖xa4 a5 19 ♗b2 g6 20 ♗c3 ♖c8! with equal chances (Kasparov–Balashov, USSR 1982).

16 ... ♘d7

An alternative is 16 ... g6 17 ♘f1 ♗g7 18 ab (18 ♘g3 ♘d7 19

♖a3) 18 ... ab 19 ♖xa8 ♕xa8 20 ♗f4 ♘d7 21 ♕d2 ♕a1 22 e5 with double-edged play (Y. Gruenfeld–Greenfeld, Israel 1984).

17 ♖a3

After 17 ♘f1 f5!? 18 ef ♘f6! Black is doing fine.

17 ... c4 *(239)*

Let us also consider the following variations:

(a) **17 ... f5!?** 18 ef (after 18 ♖ae3 f4 19 ♖3e2 — or 19 ♖a3 ♕f6 20 ♘b3 ♘b6 21 ♘a5 ♖ab8; de Firmian–A. Ivanov, Chicago 1988 — 19 ... ♘e5 20 ♘f1 ♘xf3 21 gf ♕h4 22 ♘h2 ♖e5 23 ♕d2 ♕xh3 24 ♕xf4 ba; Timman–Karpov, match 1990, Black has good counterplay; instead of 18 ... f4, the critical Kasparov–Karpov, 20th game, World Ch. match 1990, went 18 ... ♘f6? and after 19 ♘h2 ♔h8 20 b3! ba 21 ba c4 22 ♗b2 fe 23 ♘xe4 ♘fxd5 24 ♖g3 ♖e6 — 24 ... ♖c8 may be better — 25 ♘g4 ♕e8 26 ♘xh6 c3 — 26 ... ♖xh6 27 ♘xd6! ♕d7 28 ♘f5 ♖h7 29 ♘xg7! — 27 ♘f5 cb 28 ♕g4 White had a very strong attack) 18 ... ♘f6 (Worse are 18 ... ♖xe1+ 19 ♕xe1 ♗xd5 20 ♘e4 ♗f7 21 f6! with an attack for White; Ivanchuk–Lukács, Debrecen 1988, and 18 ... ♗xd5 19 ♘e4 ♗f7 20 axb5; Kasparov–Karpov, 22nd game, World Ch. match 1990) 19 ♘e4, and now:

(a1) **19 ... ♗xd5** 20 ♘xf6+ (after 20 ♖ae3 ♗xe4 21 ♗xe4 d5 22 ♗b1 ♖xe3 23 ♖xe3 d4 play is double-edged; S. Horvath–Zoebisch, Hungary 1988) 20 ... ♕xf6 21 ♗d2 ♕xb2 22 ♗xb4 (22 ♖ae3 merits consideration) 22 ... ♗f7! 23 ♖e6?! ♕xb4 24 ♖b3 ♕xa4 25 ♗c2 ♖ad8! and it is hard for White to demonstrate compensation for the loss of material (Kasparov–Karpov, 4th game, World Ch. match 1990).

(a2) **19 ... ♘bxd5** 20 ♘h2 (after 20 ♘h4 — 20 ♘fd2 ♗c6 — 20 ... ♘c7 21 ♘xf6+ ♕xf6 22 ♘g6 ♖xe1+ 23 ♕xe1 ♖e8 24 ♖e3 ♖xe3 25 ♕xe3 ba 26 ♗a2+ ♗d5 Black has a good game; de Firmian–A. Ivanov, San Mateo 1989) 20 ... ♘xe4 21 ♗xe4 ♖xe4 22 ♖xe4 ♘c3 23 ♖xc3 ♗xe4 24 ♖g3 ♔h8 25 ♕g4 ♗d5 with roughly equal chances (de Firmian–A. Ivanov, Las Vegas 1989).

(b) **17 ... ba?!** 18 ♘h2 f5 19 ♖g3 ♘f6 20 e5 de 21 ♗xf5 ♕xd5 22 ♘g4 ♘xg4 23 ♕xg4 and White has good chances of an attack against the black king (Zhelendinov).

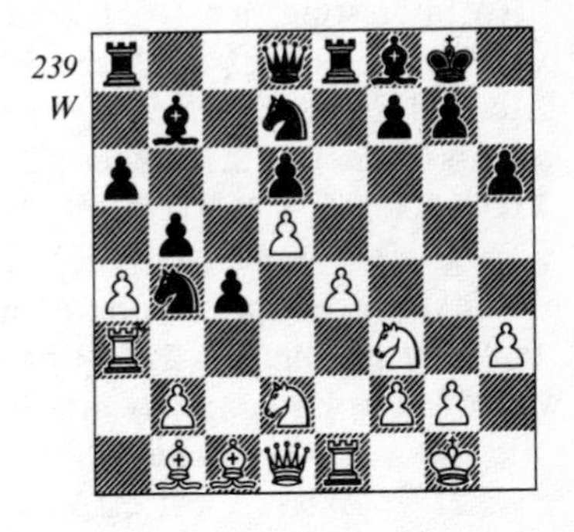
239
W

Here White has a choice of two main continuations:

A321 18 ♘d4
A322 18 ab

A321

18 ♘d4 ♕f6

An alternative is 18 … ♘e5 19 ab ♕b6 20 ♘xc4!? (or 20 ♘2f3 ♘bd3 21 ♗e3 ♘xe1 22 ♘xe1 ♕c7 23 ♘ef3 ab 24 ♘xb5 ♕d7 with double-edged play; Sokolov–Psakhis, Volgograd 1985) 20 … ♘xc4 21 ♖g3! ♗c8 22 b3! (22 ♗xh6 ab 23 ♘f3 ♖a1 24 b3 ♘e5 25 ♕d2 ♘g6 26 ♗e3 ♕a5 27 ♗d4 with roughly equal chances) 22 … ♘e5 23 ♗e3 (23 ♗xh6 ♘bd3!) 23 … ♘g6 24 f4 ♕d8 25 f5 ♘e5 26 ♕d2! a5 27 ♗xh6 with a dangerous attack for White.

In the event of 18 … ♕b6?! 19 ♘f5 ♘e5 20 ♖g3 ♔h7 21 ♘f3 ♗c8 22 ♘xg7 White wins (I. Sokolov–P. Nikolic, Lugano 1987).

19 ♘2f3 ♘c5

After 19 … ♘d3 20 ♗xd3 b4 21 ♗xc4 ba 22 b3 ♘c5 23 ♕c2 ♕g6 play is unclear.

20 ab

An interesting line is 20 ♖ee3 ba (20 … ♘bd3 21 ab ♘xe4 22 ♗xd3 cd 23 ♕xd3 ♘c5 24 ♕e2 favours White) 21 ♖ac3 ♘bd3 22 ♖xc4 ♘xc1 23 ♕xc1 ♖ac8 24 ♗c2 g6 25 ♘c6 ♗xc6 26 dc h5 (Sokolov–Karpov, Rotterdam 1989). By playing 27 ♖a3 White was able to obtain an advantage.

20 … ab

21 ♘xb5 ♖xa3

22 ♘xa3 ♗a6

After 22 … ♘bd3 23 ♗xd3 ♘xd3 24 ♖e3! ♗a6 25 ♕a4 White's position is preferable.

23 ♖e3 ♖b8

24 e5! de

25 ♘xe5 ♘cd3!

25 … ♘bd3? 26 ♕c2! leads to loss of material for Black. (This possibility was overlooked in Kasparov–Karpov, 16th game, World Ch. match 1986 — Ed.)

26 ♘g4 ♕d4

Or 26 … ♕h4 27 ♖g3 ♔h8 28 ♗d2 ♗d6 29 ♖f3 ♘xb2 30 ♕e2 ♕e7 with equality (Nunn–Psakhis, Hastings 1987).

27 ♘c2 ♘xc2

28 ♗xc2 ♗d6

Worse is 28 … ♗c5 29 ♕f3!

29 b3

After 29 … ♕a1 30 bc ♗xc4 31 ♗xd3 ♗xd3 32 ♖e1 ♗g6 33 ♗d2 ♖b1 34 ♕e2 ♖xe1+ 35 ♕xe1 ♕xe1+ 36 ♗xe1 ♗e4 37 ♘e3 the game is drawn (Dvoiris–Timoshchenko, USSR 1988).

A322

18 ab ab

19 ♘d4 ♖xa3

After 19 … ♕b6!? 20 ♘f5 g6 21 ♘f1 ♔h7(?) (21 … ♖xa3 22 ba ♘xd5 23 ed ♖xe1 24 ♕xe1 gf with unclear play) 22 ♕d2! White was clearly better in O. Efimov–Feigelson, USSR 1988.

20 ba ♘d3

21 ♗xd3 cd *(240)*

And now:

(a) **22 ♗b2** ♕a5 23 ♘f5 (Kasparov–Karpov, 14th game, World Ch. match 1986). Here, 23 … g6 24 ♘b3 ♕a4 25 ♕xd3 ♘e5 26 ♗xe6 ♖xe5 27 f4 ♖e8 28 ♘g3 with roughly equal chances.

240
W

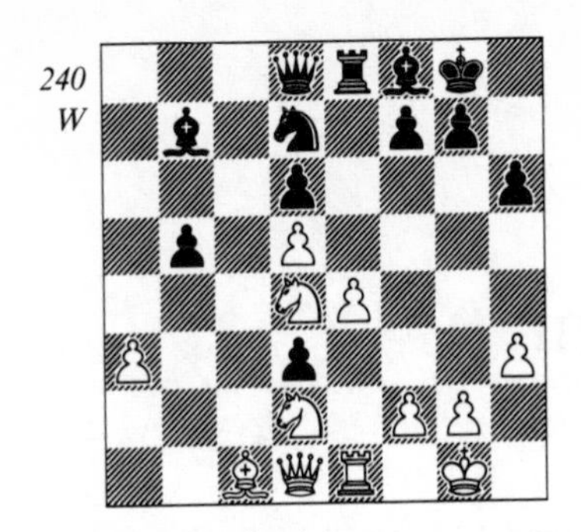

(b) **22 ♖e3!?** ♘e5 (interesting is 22 ... ♘c5!?) 23 ♘4f3 f5!? 24 ♘xe5 ♖xe5 25 ♗b2 ♖e7 26 ef!? (after 26 ♕b3 fe 27 ♖xe4 ♖xe4 28 ♘xe4 ♕a8 29 ♕xd3 ♗xd5 30 ♘g3!? ♗xg2 31 ♕g6 ♗f3! Black has a good game; Glek–Kuzmin, USSR 1988) 26 ... ♖xe3 27 fe ♗xd5 28 ♕g4 ♕c8 29 ♕d4 ♗c4 30 ♘xc4!? bc 31 f6 ♕c7 32 a4 gf 33 ♗c3 with advantage to White (Glek–Kharlamov, corr. 1988/9).

B

9 ... a5!?

This system was introduced into practice by Keres and Bondarevsky but until recently was seldom played. Now some interest in it has been awakened. Frequently in this variation the fight takes place on the queenside.

10 d4 *(241)*

Let us consider the following variations:

(a) **10 d3** a4 11 ♗c2 ♗e6 (after 11 ... ♖e8?! a strong reply is 12 c4!; after 11 ... ♗d7 12 ♘bd2 ♕b8(?) — 12 ... ♖e8!? — 13 d4 ♕b7 14 ♘f1 ed?! 15 cd ♘b4 16 ♗b1 ♖ad8 17 ♘g3 ♖fe8 18 ♗d2 ♘a6 19 e5! White has the advantage; Ehlvest–P. Nikolic, Reykjavik 1988) 12 ♘bd2 d5 13 ed ♕xd5 14 ♕e2 ♖fe8 with equality (Borsony–Bernstein, corr. 1963).

(b) **10 a4** b4 11 d4 (or 11 d3 ♗a6 12 ♕c2 ♖b8 13 ♘bd2 d5! 14 ed ♘xd5 15 ♘xe5 ♘xe5 16 ♖xe5 ♘f4 17 ♗c4 ♗d6 with chances for both sides — Euwe) 11 ... bc 12 bc ed (12 ... ♗b7!? — Keres) 13 ♘xd4 (13 cd d5 14 e5 ♘e4 (favours Black) 13 ... ♘xd4 14 cd d5 15 e5 ♘e4 16 ♗a3 (or 16 ♘d2 ♘xd2 17 ♗xd2 c5) 16 ... ♗b4 17 ♗xb4 ab 18 f3 ♘g5 19 f4 ♘e4 with double-edged play (Hübner–Agdestein, Wijk aan Zee 1988).

After 10 d4 the following variations may arise:

(a) **10 ... a4** 11 ♗c2 (11 ♗d5!) 11 ... ♗d7 (11 ... ♖e8) 12 ♗e3 ed 13 cd ♘b4 14 ♘c3 ♘xc2 15 ♕xc2 b4 16 ♘e2 c5 17 d5 ♖e8 18 ♘g3 ♗f8 19 ♘ad1 with advantage to White (Psakhis–Smagin, Sochi 1988).

(b) **10 ... ed** 11 cd (after 11 ♘xd4 ♘xd4 12 cd ♗b7 13 ♘d2 c5 14 ♗c2 cd 15 ♘f3 d5 16 e5 ♘e4 17 ♘xd4 f6! with good play for Black; Averbakh–Bondarevsky, Moscow 1948) 11 ... a4 12 ♗c2 ♘b4 13 d5! ♘d7 (after 13 ... ♘xc2 14 ♕xc2 ♘d7 15 ♘d4 White stands better) 14 ♘a3 ♗f6 15 ♘xb5 ♘c5 16 ♘bd4 ♗a6 17 ♖e3 ♘xc2 18 ♕xc2 ♖e8 19 ♘c6 ♕d7 20 e5 with a marked advantage to White (Spassky–Keres, USSR Ch. 1961).

17 Breyer System

Finally, we shall discuss the Breyer System, one of the most highly regarded and resilient variations of the Spanish. It most commonly arises after the move order 1 e4 e5 2 ♘f3 ♘c6 3 ♗b5 a6 4 ♗a4 ♘f6 5 0–0 ♗e7 6 ♖e1 b5 7 ♗b3 d6 8 c3 0–0 9 h3.

9 … ♘b8

Essentially this system was worked out in the 1950s by the Soviet players Borisenko and Furman (but according to a rather unclear 'legend' this move was played in 1911 by Breyer). Black intends to regroup his forces to more flexible positions: ♘bd7, ♖e8, ♗f8 and ♗g7, which entails a loss of time, but practice has shown that this system is sufficiently dynamic. Play becomes lively, with plenty of possibilities for both sides.

White has two main continuations:

A 10 d4
B 10 d3

Also encountered is 10 a4. For example: 10 … ♗b7 11 d3 ♘bd7 12 ab ab 13 ♖xa8 ♗xa8 (13 … ♕xa8? 14 ♘h4!) 14 ♘a3 ♗c6 (also good is 14 … ♕b8 15 ♘c2 ♘c5) 15 ♘c2 ♘c5 16 ♘b4 ♗b7 17 ♗a2 ♘cd7 18 ♗b1 ♖e8 19 d4 c5 20 de ♘xe5 with equal chances (Ivkov–Padevsky, Zagreb 1965).

A

10 d4 ♘bd7 *(241)*

This is more accurate than 10 … ♗b7, after which there may follow 11 de! de (11 … ♘xe4 12 e6! fe — 12 … f5 13 ♘bd2 d5 14 ♘f1 ♕d6 15 ♘e3 c6 16 ♘xf5! ♖xf5 17 ♖xe4! de 18 ♕xd6 ♗xd6 19 e7+ and White wins – 13 ♗xe6+ ♔h8 14 ♗d5 ♘c5 15 ♗xb7 ♘xb7 16 a4! favours White; Gligoric–Benkö, Bled 1959) 12 ♕xd8 ♗xd8 13 ♘xe5 ♘xe4 14 ♗e3! ♗e7 (or 14 … ♗f6 15 ♘g4 ♘d7 16 ♘d2 ♘xd2 17 ♗xd2 ♖fe8 18 ♗f4; Keres–Benkö, Bled 1959) 15 ♘d2 ♘xd2 16 ♗xd2 ♗d6 17 ♗f4 (also good is 17 a4 ♘c6 18 ♘xf7! ♖xf7 19 ab ♘e7 20 ♗f4; Jansa–Illecko, USSR 1959) 17 … ♘c6 18 ♘xf7 ♖xf7 19 ♗xd6 cd 20 ♖ad1 ♖f8 21 ♖xd6 g6 22 ♖d7 ♔g7 23 ♗xf7 ♖xf7 24 ♖ed1 with a clear advantage to White (analysis by Suetin).

241
W

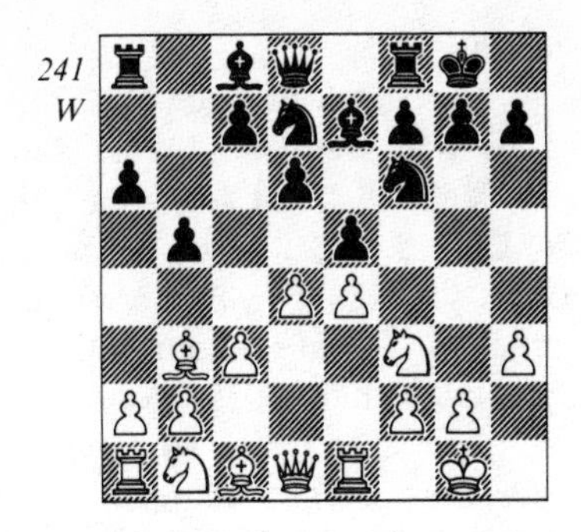

Now White has a choice:

A1 11 ♘bd2
A2 11 ♗g5
A3 11 c4
A4 11 ♘h4!?

A1

11 ♘bd2 ♗b7
12 ♗c2 ♖e8 *(242)*

For a long time a frequently-played continuation was 12 ... c5, with the following variations:

(a) **13 d5** g6 14 ♘f1 ♘h5! 15 ♗h6 ♖e8! 16 b3 ♗f6 17 a4 ♗g7 18 ♗g5 ♕c7 19 g3 ♘hf6 20 ♕d2 ♘b6 21 ♘e3 h5 with equal play (Hartston–Gligoric, Bath 1973).

(b) **13 ♘f1** ♖e8 14 ♘g3 (or 14 d5 g6 15 b3 ♘b6 16 ♕e2 ♘h5 17 ♗h6 ♗f8 with equality; Schmid–Gligoric, Nice OL 1974) 14 ... ♗f8 15 d5 g6 16 ♗g5! h6 17 ♗h4 ♗g7 18 ♕d2 h5! and Black has a strong defensive position (Suetin–Matanovic, Belgrade 1974).

(c) **13 b3** ♖e8 14 d5 g6 15 a4 ♖b8 (15 ... ♘h5!?) 16 b4! c4 17 ♘f1 ♗f8 18 ♗g5 ♗g7 19 ♕d2 ♘b6 with a freer game for White (Kavalek–Gligoric, Nice OL 1974).

In White's favour is 12 ... d5?! 13 de ♘xe4 14 ♘xe4 de 15 ♗xe4 ♗xe4 16 ♖xe4 ♘xe5 17 ♖d4 ♘xf3+ 18 ♕xf3 ♕c8 (Hjartarson–Reshevsky, Reykjavik 1984). By playing 19 ♗f4 c5 20 ♖e4 ♗f6 21 ♗d6 ♖d8 22 ♗e7 ♗xe7 23 ♖xe7 ♖f8 24 ♖f1 White could have obtained a clear advantage (Romanishin).

242
W

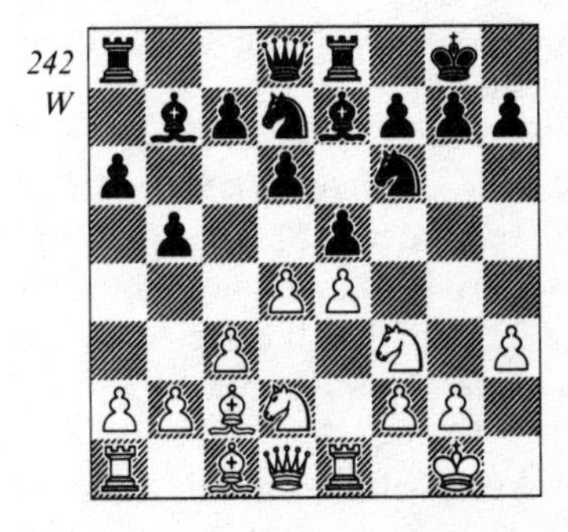

From the many continuations for White here we shall single out:

A11 13 ♘f1
A12 13 b4
A13 13 b3
A14 13 a4

Not very promising for White is 13 c4?! ♗f8 14 b3 ed 15 ♘xd4 bc 16 bc ♘c5 with a good game for Black.

A11

13 ♘f1 ♗f8

Recently in this position a counter in the centre, 13 ... d5!?, has been tried. The following variations are possible: 14 ♘xe5

(White also gets an advantage after 14 de ♘xe4 15 ♗f4 ♘f8 16 ♘e3 ♘e6 17 ♗h2 ♗c5 18 ♘d4) 14 ... ♘xe5 (14 ... ♘xe4? 15 ♖xe4! or 15 ♘xf7!) 15 de ♘xe4 16 f3, and now:

(a) **16 ... ♘g5** 17 ♘g3 f6 18 ♗xg5! fg 19 ♕b1! ♗c5+ 20 ♔h2 h6 21 ♕d1 ♖e6 22 ♘f5 ♕f8 23 ♕d3 g6 24 ♘d4 (Chandler–Sax, West Germany 1985).

(b) **16 ... ♘c5** 17 b4 ♘d7 18 f4 c5 19 ♕d3 ♘f8 20 bc ♗xc5+ 21 ♗e3 (Greenfeld–Shvidler, Israel 1984).

(c) **16 ... ♗c5+?!** 17 ♗e3 ♗xe3+ 18 ♘xe3 ♘c5 19 f4!? d4 20 cd ♘e6 (Plaskett–Tringov, Plovdiv 1984). And now: 21 ♕h5! g6 22 ♕h6. In all cases Black has considerable difficulties.

14 ♘g3

White achieves nothing after 14 de de 15 ♘3h2 ♘c5 16 ♕f3 ♘e6. But worthy of consideration is 14 ♗g5 h6 15 ♗h4, with the following variations:

(a) **15 ... g6** (worse is 15 ... g5? 16 de ♘xe5 17 ♗g3 ♘ed7 — 17 ... ♘g6 — 18 ♘3d2 ♗g7 19 ♗h2 d5 20 e5! with advantage to White; Romanishin–Kraidman, Hastings 1976/7) 16 ♘3d2 ♗g7 17 d5 c6 18 c4 ♕c7 19 ♘e3 ♘b6 20 dc ♗xc6 21 cb ab 22 ♕f3 ♘fd7 with roughly equal chances (Sokolov–Belyavsky, Belfort 1988).

(b) **15 ... c5** 16 de de 17 ♘3h2 ♕c7 18 ♕f3 ♗e7 19 ♘e3 g6 20 ♖ad1 with slight pressure for White (Timman–Garcia, Las Palmas 1981).

(c) **15 ... ♕c8** 16 de de 17 ♘3h2 c5 18 ♕f3 ♕c6?! (18 ... a5 and then ♖a6) 19 ♖ad1 c4 20 ♘e3 g6 21 ♖d2 ♗e7 22 ♖ed1 ♕e6 23 ♘hg4 ♔g7 24 b3 with a better game for White (Romanishin–Spassky, Tilburg 1979).

14 ... g6

Or 14 ... c5!? 15 d5 g6 16 ♗g5 h6 17 ♗e3 ♘b6 18 b3 with an insignificant advantage to White (Gufeld–Psakhis, USSR 1982).

15 a4

The most common continuation. In the event of 15 b3 ♗g7 16 d5 ♘b6 17 ♗e3 ♖c8 18 ♕d2 c6 (Martinez–Spassky, San Juan 1969), or 15 ♗d2 ♗g7 16 ♕c1 d5!? 17 ♗g5 ♕c8! 18 ♘xe5 ♘xe5 19 de ♘xe4 20 ♗xe4 de 21 ♗f6 ♗xf6 22 ef ♕f6 (Balashov–Spassky, Sochi 1973), or 15 ♗g5 h6 16 ♗d2 c5! 17 de ♘xe5 (Karpov–Portisch, Milan 1975), Black has full equality.

In the game Smirin–Belyavsky, USSR 1989, there occurred 15 ♗g5 h6 16 ♗d2 ♗g7 17 ♕c1 ♔h7 (after 17 ... h5 18 ♗h6 ♘h7 19 ♕d2 ♗xh6 20 ♕xh6 ♕f6 21 a4 ♘df8 22 d5 White stands slightly better: Smirin–G. Georgadze, USSR 1989) 18 h4 d5 19 ed ed. After 20 h5!? dc 21 ♗xc3 ♗d5 chances are equal.

15 ... c5

Untried is a recommendation of Boleslavsky's: 15 ... ed 16 cd d5!? After 15 ... ♗g7 16 d5 (16 ♗d3!?) 16 ... ♘c5 17 b4 ♘xa4 18 ♗xa4 ba 19 ♕xa4 ♕d7 20 c4 White has slight but firm pressure (Jansa–Milicevic, Kragujevac 1974).

16 d5 *(243)*

Without doubt the most solid continuation. In the event of 16 ♗e3 ♕c7 17 ♕d2 cd 18 cd ♘b6 19 ♗g5 ♗g7, or 16 b4?! cd 17 cd d5 18 de de 19 ♘xd4 ♘xe4 20 ♗xe4 ♗xe4 21 ♖xe4 ♘xe5 (Karpov–Tukmakov, USSR Ch. 1970), and also after 16 b3 ♗g7 17 de ♘xe5 18 ♘xe5 de 19 ♗e3 ♕xd1 20 ♖exd1 ♗f8 (Keres–Reshevsky, Petropolis 1973), Black has no difficulties.

After 16 d5 Black has a choice between:

A111 16 … ♘b6
A112 16 … c4

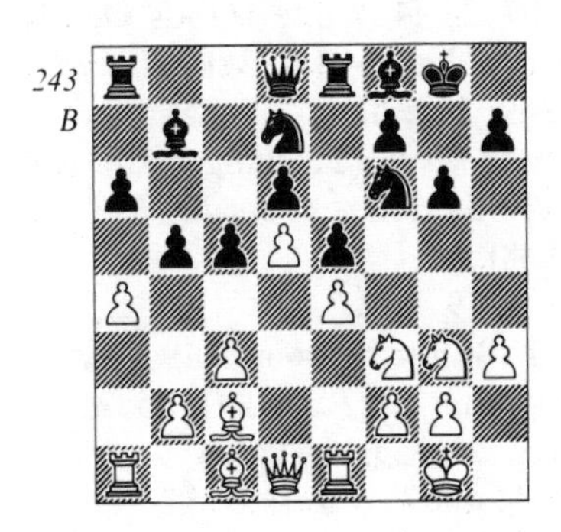

243 *B*

In the game Dvoiris–G. Georgadze, USSR 1989, Black achieved equality with 16 … ♗g7 17 c4 ♘b6 18 ♘d2 ba 19 ♗xa4 ♘xa4 20 ♕xa4 ♘d7!

A111

16 … ♘b6
17 ♕e2!

After 17 a5!? ♘c4 18 b4 cb 19 cb ♖c8 (Karpov–Portisch, Madrid 1973), or 17 ♘d2 c4 18 a5 ♘bd7 19 b3 cb 20 ♗xb3 ♘c5 (Karpov–Gligoric, Portoroz 1975), Black has good counterplay.

17 … ♘xa4
18 ♗xa4 ba
19 ♖xa4 *(244)*

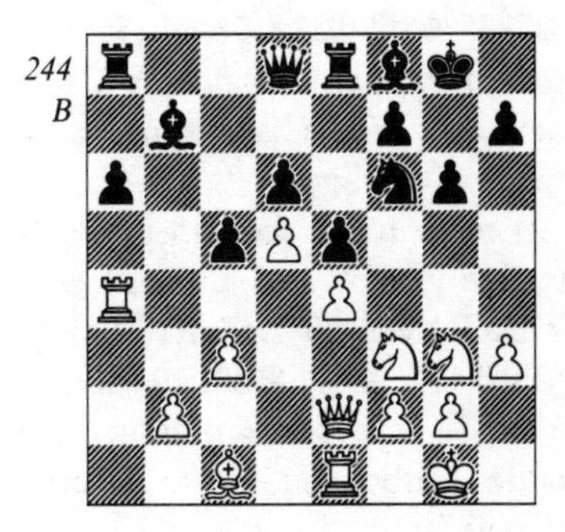

244 *B*

And now:

(a) **19 … ♗c8** 20 ♗g5 (worthy of consideration is 20 ♗d2 a5 — 20 … ♖b8 — 21 b4! cb 22 cb ♗a6 23 b5!; Tal–Vogt, Leningrad 1977, or 20 b3 ♖b8 21 ♖a3 ♖e7 22 c4 ♖eb7 23 ♕c2 ♘e8 24 ♗d2 ♘g7 25 ♘h2 f5; Karpov–Smejkal, Moscow 1977) 20 … h6 21 ♗e3 (21 ♗xf6!? ♗xf6 22 b4) 21 … ♖b8 22 ♖ea1 ♘h7 (22 … ♘d7) 23 ♕c2 h5 24 ♘d2 ♗e7 25 ♘c4 (Geller–Romanishin, USSR 1978). White has strong pressure on the queenside.

A112

16 … c4

Nowadays this is the most popular continuation.

17 ♗g5

The alternative is 17 ♗e3 ♘c5, with the following variations:

(a) **18 ♘h2** ♕d7 19 ♗g5 ♗e7 20 f4 ef 21 ♗xf4 h5 22 ♘f3 ♘h7 23 ♗e3 ♘xa4 24 ♗xa4 ba 25 ♖xa4 ♖ac8 26 ♘f1 f5 27 ♘1d2 (Damjanovic–Vogt, Lublin 1974).

(b) **18 ♕e2** ♕c7 (18 … ♘fd7) 19 ♘d2 ♖ab8 20 ♖ec1 ♗c8 21 ab ab 22 b3 cb 23 ♘xb3 ♘a4 24 ♗d3 ♗d7 25 ♕d2 ♖ec8 26 c4 (Jansa–Smejkal, Czechoslovakia 1972). In both cases White has a small positional advantage.

In reply to 17 ♗e3 an interesting line is 17 … g6 18 ♕d2 ♕e7 19 ♖a3 ♖ec8 20 ♖e1 ♕f8 (20 … ♕d8!?) 21 ♕c1 ♕d8 22 ab ab 23 ♗a7! with some pressure for White (Ljubojevic–Hort, Lucerne OL 1982).

17 … h6

The main response. Other possibilities briefly:

(a) **17 … ♗g7** 18 ♕d2 ♘c5 19 ♘h2 (19 ♗h6!?) 19 … h5 20 ♔h1 (20 ♘f3 ♕c7 21 ♖a3) 20 … ♕c7 21 ♗h6 ♗h8 22 f4 (Balashov–Baikov, USSR 1974).

(b) **17 … ♖b8** 18 ♕d2 ♘c5 19 ab (19 ♖f1!?) 19 … ab 20 ♘h2 ♗c8 21 ♖f1 ♗g7 22 ♔h1 ♖f8 23 f3 ♕e7 24 f4 (Tal–Portisch, Varese 1976).

(c) **17 … ♘c5** 18 ♕d2 ♗e7 19 ♗h6 ♘fd7 20 ♘h2 ♖b8 21 ♖f1 (Kavalek–Spassky, Montreal 1979).

In all cases White has the better chances.

18 ♗e3 ♘c5

After 18 … ♖b8 19 ♕d2 h5 20 ♘g5 ♘h7 21 ♘xh7 ♔xh7 22 ♖f1 ♔g8 23 f4! White stands better (Tal). Not without interest is 18 … ♕c7 19 ♕d2 ♔h7 20 ♘h2 ♗g7 (Balashov–Vogt, Leipzig 1973).

19 ♕d2

Worthy of consideration is 19 ♕c1! h5 (19 … ♔h7 20 ♘h2 and then ♖f1) 20 ♘g5 ♖c8!? (20 … ♗h6? 21 ♗xc5 ♖xc5 22 ♘xf7!) 21 ♔h1 ♖c7 22 ab ab 23 ♖a5 ♕d7 24 f4 with pressure for White (Popovic–Belyavsky, USSR 1988). Also not bad is 19 ♖f1 ♗g7 20 ♕d2 ♔h7 21 ♘h2 and then f2–f4 (Timman–Portisch, Reggio Emilia 1984/5); or 19 ♔h1!? ♖b8 (after 19 … ♕e7?! 20 ♕d2 h5 21 ♗g5 ♗g7 22 ♘h4 ♕f8 23 ♖f1 ♘h7 24 f4 White stands clearly better; Nunn–Belyavsky, Lucerne 1989) 20 ♕d2 h5 21 ♘g5 ♗h6 22 ab ab 23 f4 (Ye Jiangchuan–van der Sterren, Thessaloniki OL 1988).

19 … h5

In White's favour is 19 … ♔h7 20 ♘h2! ♗g7 21 ♖f1 h5 22 f3 ♕e7 23 ♗g5! ♕f8 24 f4! ef 25 ♖xf4 ♘fd7 26 ♖af1 ♘e5 27 ♘xh5! gh 28 ♕e2 ♕h8 29 ♖h4 with a powerful attack for White (Spassky–Portisch, match 1977).

20 ♗g5

An alternative is 20 ♘g5 ♗h6 (20 … ♗g7 21 ab ab 22 ♖xa8 ♗xa8 23 f4 ef 24 ♗xf4 ♕e7 25 ♘f3 ♗b7 26 ♗g5 ♕c7 27 ♘d4 with better chances for White;

Short–Spassky, Montpellier 1985) 21 ♖e2 ♕e7 22 ♖ae1 h4 23 ♘f1 ♘h5 24 g3 hg 25 fg f6 26 g4 (Nunn–Belyavsky, Szirak 1987). By playing 26 ... ♘f4 27 ♗xf4 ♗xg5 28 ♗xg5 fg Black would have had excellent play.

20 ... ♗e7

21 ♗h6 *(245)*

Interesting is 21 ♖a3!?

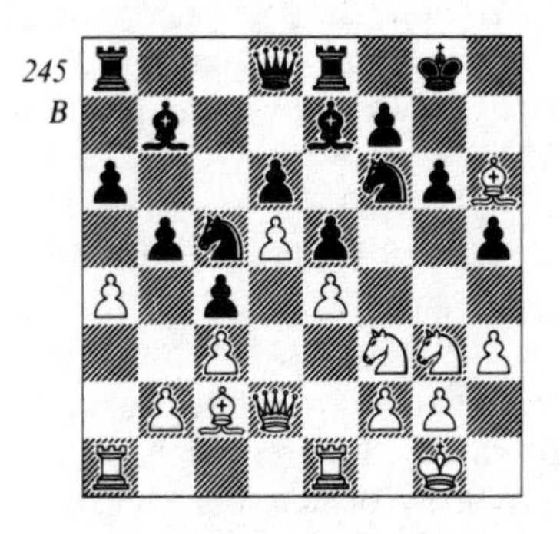

From the diagrammed position the following lines are possible:

(a) **21 ... ♘h7** 22 ♖a3 ♖b8 23 ♖ea1 (or 23 ♗e3 ♗f6 24 ab ab 25 ♖ea1 ♗c8 26 ♘e2 ♗d7 with equal chances; van der Wiel–Timman, Amsterdam 1988) 23 ... ♗c8 24 ab ab 25 ♗e3 ♗f6 26 ♘e2!? ♗d7 (Timman–Portisch, Brussels 1988). After 27 ♘c1 White would have had a minimal advantage.

(b) **21 ... ♘fd7** 22 ♕e3 (22 ♖f1!?) 22 ... ♖b8 23 ♖f1 ♗f8 24 ♗xf8 ♖xf8 25 ♘d2 ♗c8 26 f4 ef 27 ♕xf4 ♘e5 28 ♘f3 ♕e7 with equal play (Ljubojevic–Belyavsky, Belgrade 1987).

(c) **21 ... ♗f8** 22 ♗xf8 ♖xf8 23 ♕h6 ♘h7 24 h4?! ♕f6 25 ♘g5 ♕g7 with equality (Raaste–Valkesalmi, Espoo 1989).

A12

13 b4!? ♗f8

In White's favour are 13 ... a5?! 14 ♘b3 ab 15 cb ♕b8 16 ♘a5 (Suetin–Tringov, Titovo-Uzice 1968), and also 13 ... d5?! 14 ♘xe5 ♘xe5 15 de ♘xe4 16 ♘xe4 de 17 ♕g4 c5 18 ♗xe4 ♗xe4 19 ♕xe4 (Kavalek–Robatsch, Sarajevo 1968).

14 a4 *(246)*

After 14 ♗b2 ♘b6 (also played are 14 ... g6 and 14 ... a5) 15 a3 ♘fd7 (15 ... a5!?) 16 c4 bc 17 de ♘xe5 18 ♘xe5 de 19 ♕e2 c5 20 bc ♗xc5 21 ♘xc4 ♘xc4 22 ♕xc4 ♕b6 Black has sufficient counterplay (Hartston–Spassky, Bath 1973).

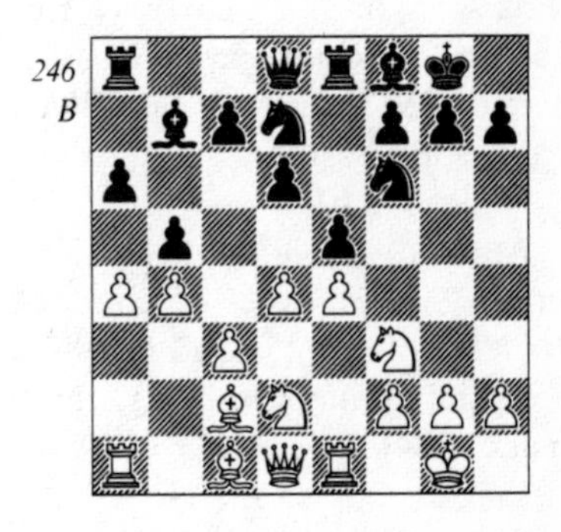

In this position the following variations arise:

(a) **14 ... ♘b6** 15 a5 (nothing is to be gained from 15 ab ab 16 ♖xa8 ♕xa8) 15 ... ♘bd7 16 ♗b2 ♖b8 (after 16 ... ♕b8 17 c4! bc 18 ♗a4 c6 — 18 ... ♖d8!? — 19 ♘xc4 ed 20 ♕xd4 d5 21 ed ♖xe1+

22 ♘xe1 White is clearly better; Kavalek–Reshevsky, USA 1973) 17 ♖b1 (also possible is 17 ♘c4!? ed 18 cb ab 19 ♘xd4 g6 20 f4 ♗g7 21 ♖b1 ♖c8 22 ♗b3 ♘f8 23 ♗a1 ♖e7 24 ♕f3; Sakharov–Mukhin, USSR 1976) 17 … ♗a8 18 ♗a1!? (18 c4) 18 … g6 19 ♗d3 (19 de!? ♘xe5 20 ♘xe5 de 21 c4 with a minimal advantage to White — Y. Gruenfeld–Ehlvest, Zagreb 1987) 19 … ♗g7 20 c4 bc 21 ♗xc4 ed 22 ♗xd4 ♘xe4 23 ♘xe4 ♖xe4 24 ♗xa6 ♗xd4 25 ♘xd4 c5 26 ♘c2! cb 27 ♕xd6 b3 28 ♘e3 ♖e6 29 ♕d4! with somewhat better chances for White (Vukcevic–Kraidman, Hastings 1976/7).

A13

13 b3 ♗f8

Also possible is 13 … g6 14 ♗b2 ♘h5, or 13 … c6 14 a4 ♗f8 15 ♗b2 g6 (Ljubojevic–Spassky, Tilburg 1983). In each case Black has a solid position.

14 ♗b2

Alternatively: 14 a4 g6 15 d5 c6; or 14 ♘f1 c5!; or 14 d5 c6 15 c4 ♕c7 16 ♘f1 g6 17 ♗d2 bc 18 bc a5 (Ljubojevic–Reshevsky, New York 1984).

14 … g6

Also possible is 14 … c5 15 d5 ♗c8 16 ♗d3 ♖b8 17 ♕e2 ♘b6 18 ♔h2 ♘h5 19 g3 g6 20 c4 b4 21 ♕e3 ♗g7 with full equality for Black (Kovacs–Portisch, Hungary 1965).

15 a4 ♗g7

Also not bad is 15 … ♘h5 16 c4 c6 17 ♘f1 ed! 18 ♗xd4 c5 with counterplay for Black.

16 ab

After 16 ♗d3 c6 17 ♕c2 ♕c7 18 b4 ♘b6 19 a5 ♘a4 Black's game is satisfactory (Haag–Forintos, Hungary 1965).

16 … ab

After 17 ♗d3 c6 18 ♕c2 ♖xa1 19 ♖xa1 d5!? (also possible is 19 … ♕c7 20 de ♘xe5!) 20 de ♘xe4 21 ♘xe4 de 22 ♗xe4 ♘xe5, or 20 ♘xe5 ♘xe5 21 de ♘xe4, or 20 ed ♘xd5, Black enjoys a free position.

A14

13 a4 ♗f8

13 … c5 14 d5 c4 15 b4 cb 16 ♘xb3 ♕c7 17 ♗d2 ♘b6 18 ♘a5 ♘a4 19 ♗xa4 ♕xa4 20 c4 with an initiative for White (Sokolov–Belyavsky, Linares 1989).

Worthy of consideration is 13 … ♖b8!? 14 ♘f1 ♗f8 15 ♘g3 c5 16 ♗d3 ♕b6 17 b3 cd 18 ab ab 19 ♗b2 ♘e5 20 ♘xd4 ♘xd3 21 ♕xd3 d5 with roughly equal play (Timman–Belyavsky, Linares 1989).

14 ♗d3

14 ♘f1 ed 15 ♘xd4 c5!, or 14 b3 c5!? 15 ♗b2 ♕c7 16 ♗d3 ed 17 cd ba 18 ♖xa4 cd 19 ♗xd4 ♘c5 with equality (Mikhalchishin–Belyavsky, USSR 1988).

14 … c6 *(247)*

Interesting is 14 … d5!? 15 ab de 16 ♘xe4 ♘xe4 17 ♗xe4 ♗xe4 18 ♖xe4 ab 19 ♗g5 f6 20 ♗h4 ♖xa1 21 ♕xa1 ♗d6 22 ♕a2 ♔h8 23 de ♘xe5 with chances for both sides (Ljubojevic–Portisch, 1986).

In White's favour is 14 … ed(?)

15 cd c5 16 ab ab 17 ♖xa8 ♗xa8 18 d5! (Short–Hjartarson, Amsterdam 1989).

247
W

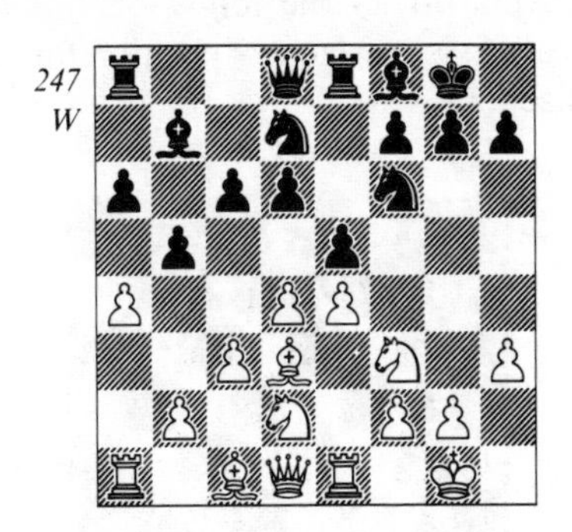

In the position after 14 ... c6 the following variations arise:

(a) **15 b3** ♖b8 (or 15 ... g6!? 16 ♗a3 ♕c7 17 ♕c2 ♗g7 — 17 ... ♖ad8 18 ♖ad1! — 18 ♗f1 d5 19 ed ♘xd5 20 c4 b4!? 21 cd ba 22 d6 ♕xd6 23 ♘c4 ♕b4 with equality; A. Sokolov–Belyavsky, USSR 1989) 16 ♗a3 ♘h5 17 ♗f1 (17 g3) 17 ... ♘f4 18 ♕c2 ♗c8 19 ♖ad1 ♕b6 20 b4 ♕d8! 21 a5 ♕f6 22 g3 ♘e6 23 ♗g2 ed 24 cd ♘xd4 25 ♘xd4 ♕xd4 26 ♕c6 ♕f6 with equality (A. Sokolov–Belyavsky, USSR 1988).

(b) **15 ♕c2** g6 16 b3 ♖c8 (16 ... ed 17 cd d5?! 18 e5 ♘h5 19 ♘f1 — 19 e6! — 19 ... ♘g7 20 ♗h6 is to White's advantage; Short–Spassky, Belfort 1988) 17 ♗b2 ♘h2 18 ♗f1 ♘f4 19 g3 ♘e6 20 h4 (20 b4) 20 ... ♕b6 21 ♗h3 ♖cd8 22 ♖ad1 ♗g7 23 ♘f1 with a small advantage to White (Hübner–Smejkal, West Germany 1989).

(c) **15 ♘f1** g6 (after 15 ... d5 16 ♗g5 dc 17 ♖xe4 ♗e7 18 ♖e1 ed 19 ♘xd4 ♗f8 20 ♘f5 White has definite pressure; Balashov–Belyavsky, USSR 1989) 16 ♘g3 ♗g7 17 ♗d2 ♕c7 18 ♕c1 d5 with roughly equal chances (Smagin–Klovan, Minsk 1986).

A2

11	**♗g5**	**♗b7**
12	**♘bd2**	**h6**

This is the most frequent continuation in the nowadays rare variation with 11 ♗g5. Other possibilities:

(a) **12 ... ♖e8** 13 a4 c5 14 de de 15 ♗xf6 ♘xf6 16 ab ab 17 ♖xa8 ♗xa8 18 ♘xe5 c4 19 ♗c2 ♗c5 20 ♘ef3 ♕b6 21 ♕e2 ♘h5 22 ♘f1 ♘f4 and Black has good counterplay for the pawn (Ivkov–Robatsch, Sarajevo 1968).

(b) **12 ... ♘e8** 13 ♗xe7 ♕xe7 14 ♘f1 g6 15 ♕d2 ♗g7 16 ♖ad1 ♘ef6 17 ♘g3 with better play for White (Schwarzbach–Karlstötter, Austria 1965).

13 ♗h4

After 13 ♗xf6 ♗xf6 14 d5 ♘b6 and 15 ... c6, or 14 ♘f1 ed 15 ♘xd4 ♘c5, Black has no difficulties.

The most important continuations after 13 ♗h4 are:

A21 13 ... c5
A22 13 ... ♖e8

A21

13 ... c5 *(248)*

After 13 ... ♘h7 14 ♗g3! ♗f6 15 ♕e2 ♘g5 16 ♖ad1 ♖e8 17 de ♘xf3+ 18 ♘xf3 de 19 ♘h4! ♗xh4

20 ♕g4 White has a strong initiative (Tal–Krogius, USSR 1965).

248
W

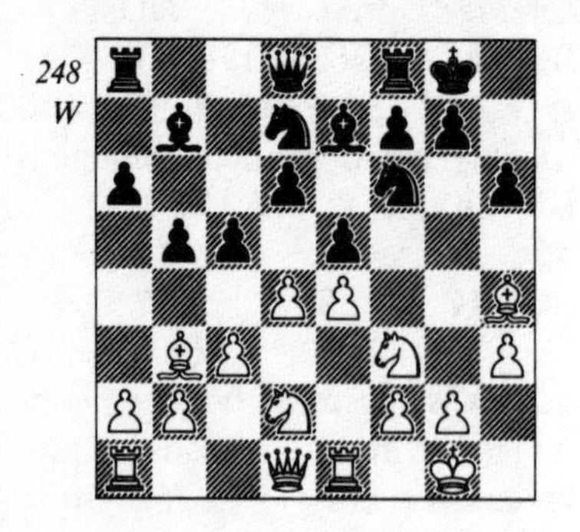

In this position the following variations are possible:

(a) **14 a4** ♕c7 15 ♕e2 c4 16 ♗c2 ♖fe8 17 b4 ♘f8! 18 de de with equality (Kostro–Matanovic, Vrnjacka Banja 1967).

(b) **14 ♗g3** ♕c7 15 ♘h4 ♖fe8 16 a4 ♗f8 17 ♘g6 ed 18 cd cd 19 ♖c1 ♕b6 and Black is no worse (Matulovic–Matanovic, Vinkovci 1968).

(c) **14 ♗c2** ♖e8 15 a4 ♕b6 16 ♘f1 ♗f8 17 ab ab 18 ♖xa8 ♗xa8 19 de de (Sakharov–Tringov, Kiev 1964). White gets nothing after 14 ♕e2 ♘h5! 15 ♗xe7 ♕xe7.

A22

13	**...**	**♖e8**
14	**a4** *(249)*	

White achieves very little after 14 ♗g3 ♗f8 15 ♘h4 c5 16 de de 17 ♕f3 c4 18 ♗c2 g6 (Browne–Smejkal, Wijk aan Zee 1971); or 14 ♕e2 c5 15 ♖ad1 ♕c7 16 de de 17 c4 ♘f8 18 ♗g3 ♗d6 (Gipslis–Matanovic, Zagreb 1965); or 14 ♗c2 ♗f8 15 a4 g6 16 de de 17 ♕e2 c6 18 b4 ♕c7 (Tringov–Lengyel, Sarajevo 1965). In each case the chances are equal.

After 14 a4 the following line leads to a satisfactory position for Black.

249
B

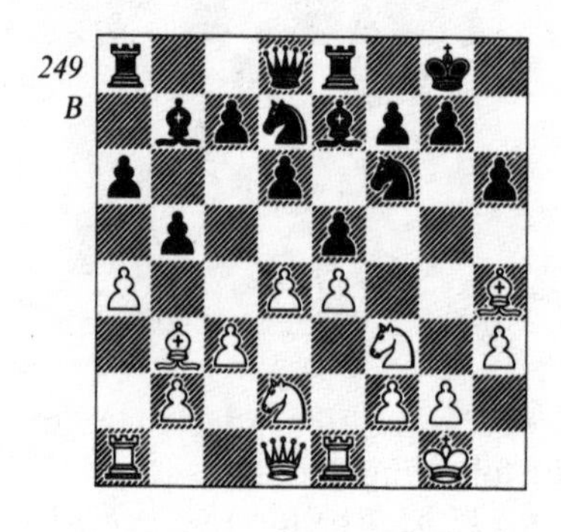

14 ... ed! 15 ♘xd4 ♘xe4 (also possible is 15 ... c5 16 ♘f5 ♗f8) 16 ♗xe7 ♖xe7 17 ab ab 18 ♖xa8 ♗xa8 19 ♘xb5 with full equality.

A3

11	**c4!?**	

This active plan was most popular in the 1950s and has consequently been studied thoroughly. But nowadays interest in it has fallen sharply.

11	**...**	**c6**

Other continuations:

(a) **11 ... c5!?** 12 de ♘xe5! 13 ♘xe5 de 14 ♘c3 ♗d7 (also possible is 14 ... ♕xd1 15 ♖xd1 ♖b8 16 a4 ♗e6) 15 a4 bc 16 ♗xc4 ♗e6 17 ♗e2 ♗xc4 18 ♕xc4 ♕d4 19 ♕e2 h6 20 ♖d1 ♕b4 and Black has sufficient defensive resources (Suetin–Forintos, Titovo Uzice 1966).

(b) **11 ... b4** 12 c5! ♗b7 13 ♕c2 ed 14 c6! d3 15 ♕c4 ♘b6 16 cb ♘xc4 17 ba(♕) ♕xa8 18 ♗xc4 ♘xe4 19 ♗d3 d5 20 a3 ♘c5 21 ♖xe7! ♘b3 (or 21 ... ♘xd3 22 ♗d2 b3 23 ♖xc7) 22 ♖xc7 ♘xa1 23 ab ♕b8 24 ♗f4 ♕xb4 25 ♗e5 ♘b3 26 ♘c3 and White has a strong positional advantage (analysis by Boleslavsky and Suetin).

(c) **11 ... ♗b7** 12 c5! (in the event of 12 ♘c3 c6 13 a3 h6 14 ♗e3 ed!? 15 ♘xd4 ♖e8 play becomes double-edged; Suetin–Smagin, Sibenik 1988) 12 ... ed (12 ... dc 13 de) 13 cd ♗xd6 14 ♘xd4 with better chances for White (Suetin).

12 c5

The main continuation, which leads to a collection of forced variations. Let us also consider the other possibilities:

(a) **12 ♕c2** ♗b7 13 ♘c3 b4 14 ♘e2 ed 15 ♘exd4 g6 16 ♘e2 ♘c5 17 ♘g3 a5 18 ♕e2 ♘fd7 19 ♗f4 ♘e6 20 ♗h6 ♖e8 21 ♖ad1 ♕c7 22 ♘h2 ♗f6 with full equality for Black (Tal–Timman, Sochi 1973).

(b) **12 ♘bd2** ♗b7 13 ♗c2 c5 14 d5 ♘b6 15 b3 ♗c8 and the blocked nature of the position will give rise to a lengthy positional struggle.

(c) **12 ♘c3** b4 13 ♘a4 c5 14 dc dc presents no difficulties for Black. This also applies, to varying extents, to the following variations: 12 cb ab 13 ♘c3 ♗a6!; 12 a3 bc 13 ♗xc4 ♘xe4; 12 a4 bc 13 ♗xc4 ♘xe4! etc.; 12 ♗g5 h6 13 ♗h4 ♘h5! (Tukmakov–Karpov, Leningrad 1973).

12 ... ♕c7

After 12 ... ♗b7 13 ♘c3 ♕c7 14 cd ♗xd6 15 ♗g5 ed 16 ♘xd4!, or 12 ... dc 13 de ♘e8 14 e6!, White stands clearly better.

13 cd ♗xd6

14 ♗g5 *(250)*

After 14 ♘c3 ed 15 ♘xd4 ♘c5 16 ♕f3 ♗e5 17 ♘f5 ♘xb3 18 ab ♗e6 Black has no difficulties.

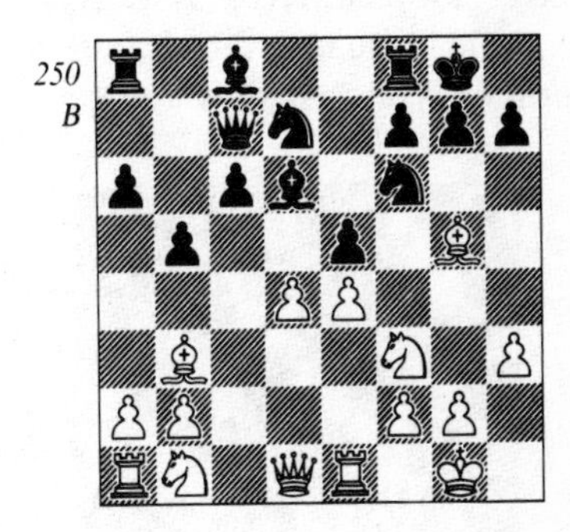

After 14 ♗g5 the following variations may arise:

(a) **14 ... ed!** 15 ♗xf6 (15 ♕xd4 c5 — 15 ... ♘e5 — 16 ♕e3 c4 17 ♗c2 ♖e8 18 ♗xf6 ♘xf6 19 e5 ♗c5 with equal play) 15 ... gf! 16 ♘xd4 (16 ♕xd4 ♘e5 17 ♘bd2 ♖ad8 18 ♕e3 ♘d3!) 16 ... ♘c5 17 ♘f5 ♗xf5 18 ef ♖ad8 19 ♕h5 ♘d3 and Black is certainly no worse (Gligoric–Petrosian, Los Angeles 1963).

(b) **14 ... h6** 15 ♗h4 ♘h7 16 ♗g3 ed 17 e5! with excellent play for White. Also in White's favour is 14 ... c5 15 dc ♗xc5 16 ♘c3

♗b7 17 ♖c1 ♕b6 18 ♖e2 ♖fe8 19 ♘d5; or 14 ... ♗b7 15 ♘c3 ed 16 ♕xd4 c5 17 ♕d2 c4 18 ♗c2 ♖fe8 19 ♖ad1.

A4

11 ♘h4!? *(251)*

This sharp continuation, which is frequently associated with the sacrifice of a pawn, was introduced into practice by Simagin in 1961 and was immediately subjected to serious analysis. But fashion passes quickly and now it is no longer adopted. Here, as with 11 c4, the inadequate strategic foundation of White's plan is apparent.

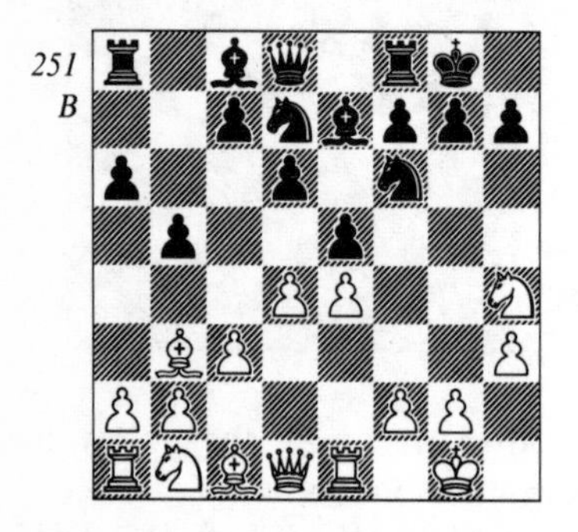

251
B

The following variations arise:

(a) **11 ... ♖e8** 12 ♘f5 ♗f8 13 ♘d2 (13 f4!) 13 ... c5 14 ♘f3 ed 15 cd ♗b7 16 ♘g3 cd 17 ♕xd4 ♘c5 with roughly equal chances.

(b) **11 ... ♘xe4!?** 12 ♘f5 ♘df6 (or 12 ... ♘ef6 13 ♗g5 ♘b6 14 ♘xe7+ ♕xe7 15 ♘d2 ♗b7 16 f4! e4 17 d5 ♘bxd5 18 ♘xe4 with double-edged play) 13 ♕f3 ♗b7 (in White's favour is 13 ... ♗xf5 14 ♕xf5 ed 15 ♖xe4 ♘xe4 16 ♕xe4 ♗g5 17 ♗d2 ♗xd2 18 ♘xd2 dc 19 bc ♕g5 20 ♘f3 ♕c5 21 ♖e1) 14 ♗c2 ♘c5 15 ♕g3 ♘e6 16 de de 17 ♗b3 ♘e4! 18 ♕g4 ♘f6 19 ♘xe7+ ♕xe7 20 ♕h4 ♘d5 21 ♕xe7 ♘xe7 22 ♗xe6 fe 23 ♖xe5 ♖ad8 with sufficient counterplay for Black.

(c) **11 ... ed** 12 cd ♘b6 13 ♘f3 c5 14 ♗f4 ♗b7 15 dc dc 16 ♕xd8 ♗xd8 17 ♗d6 ♖e8 18 ♗xc5 ♘bd7 19 ♗d4 ♘xe4 20 ♘c3 ♗f6 21 ♗d5! and White's chances are clearly better (Fischer–Robatsch, Vinkovci 1968).

(d) **11 ... g6** 12 ♗h6 ♖e8 13 f4 (13 ♘f3) 13 ... c5! with good counterplay for Black.

(e) **11 ... ♘b6** 12 dc (also possible is 12 ♘d2 c5 13 de de 14 ♘f5 ♗xf5 15 ef and then g2–g4; Fischer–Benkö, USA 1965/6) 12 ... de 13 ♘d2 ♘xe4 14 ♖xe4 ♗xh4 15 ♖xe5 with an initiative for White (Schmid–Tatai, Venice 1966).

(f) **11 ... ♗b7** 12 ♘f5 ♖e8 13 ♘xe7+ ♖xe7 14 f3 h6 15 ♗e3 or 15 d5 with a small but lasting positional advantage.

B

10 d3

This modest continuation was popular in the 1950s and 1960s, before this system had been thoroughly investigated. But fashion has changed rather quickly and now this move is extremely rare. Practice has shown that, with correct play, Black has no difficulties.

10 ... ♘bd7

An alternative is 10 ... c5. For

example: 11 ♘bd2 ♕c7 (11 ... ♘c6 leads to similar variations) 12 ♘f1 ♘c6 13 ♘g3 ♗d7 transposing to a variation with 9 d3, examined earlier in this book, which is rather harmless for Black.

11 ♘bd2 ♗b7
12 ♘f1 ♘c5

Also possible is 12 ... ♖e8 13 ♘g3 ♗f8 14 ♘g5 d5!? 15 ed ♘c5 16 c4 c6! (Lehmann–Durao, Malaga 1970); or 12 ... c5 13 ♘g3 g6 14 ♗h6 ♖e8 15 ♕d2 ♗f8 16 ♖ad1 ♗xh6 17 ♕xh6 ♖e7! and then ♕f8 (Blackstock).

13 ♗c2 ♖e8

A critical position, in which the following variations may arise:

(a) **14 ♘g3** ♗f8 15 b4 (or 15 ♘f5 d5 16 ed ♕xd5 17 ♗g5 e4 18 de ♘fxe4 19 ♕xd5 ♗xd5 with double-edged play (Tal–Robatsch, Havana 1963) 15 ... ♘cd7 16 d4 (16 ♗b3 d5!) 16 ... a5 (not bad is 16 ... g6 17 ♗d2 ♗g7 18 a4 d5; Geller–Reshevsky, Petropolis 1973) 17 ♗d2 ab 18 cb ed 19 ♘xd4 d5! 20 ed ♖xe1 21 ♗xe1 ♗d5 22 a3 ♕b8 23 ♘gf5 c5 with full equality for Black (Tal–Timman, Niksic 1983).

(b) **14 ♘e3** ♗f8 15 b4 ♘cd7 16 ♗b3 h6 (also playable is 16 ... ♘b6 or 16 ... c5) 17 c4 c5 18 a3 cb 19 ab bc 20 ♗xc4 d5 with equality (Matanovic–Hennings, Helsinki 1972).

(c) **14 ♘3h2** d5 (also possible is 14 ... ♘e6) 15 ♕f3 ♘e6 16 ♘g3 g6 17 ♗h6 ♗f8 18 ♗xf8 ♖xf8 19 ♗b3 de 20 ♘xe4 ♘xe4 21 de ♕e7 with a solid defence for Black (Ivkov–Lengyel, Venice 1966).

Over the last few years, the author has had to occupy himself with the theory and methodology of the Spanish Opening perhaps more than anyone before (I am speaking here of my literary work). I can only confirm that the fate of any opening system is as changeable as that of people, social organisations, or even states. As a rule, profound elaboration of specific systems has a tendency to bring about long pauses, and then other systems, which had been overshadowed, begin to catch up. In this way, opening theory progresses in fits and starts, and the Spanish Opening is a good illustration. Nevertheless, no system is likely to succeed unless it has a sound strategic foundation, which many variations of the Spanish clearly have.

A. Suetin

Index of Variations